Contents

■ ■ ■ ■

Acknowledgments

■ ■ ■ ■

Many of the essays in this anthology developed out of a working conference on Latin American cinema sponsored by the UCLA Film and Television Archive on 16–19 February 1995. The conference, which followed upon the archive's Mexican Cinema Project, brought together leading scholars and Ph.D. students in the United States who were working on Latin American cinema. I want to thank the following people at the archive for their critical foresight and generous support: Robert Rosen, Geoffrey Gilmore, Steven Ricci, and Andrea Alsberg. The conference was made possible through grants from the MacArthur and Rockefeller foundations.

I am grateful to the participants for their many contributions both during and after the conference: Ernesto Acevedo-Muñoz, Luisela Alvaray, Charles Ramírez Berg, Maylei Blackwell, Gilberto Blasini, Julianne Burton-Carvajal, María Elena de las Carreras, Sergio de la Mora, Susan Dever, Elena Feder, Claire Fox, Ilene Goldman, Monica Hulsbus, Randall Johnson, Ana M. López, Kathleen Newman, Vinicius Novarro, Christopher Ortiz, Laura Podalsky, Cathy Rivera, Roberto Rodriguez-Moya, Jorge Ruffinelli, Karen Schwartzman, Cristina Venegas, and Jim Wiltgen. I owe a special debt of gratitude to Ana M. López for graciously sharing her extensive knowledge and appreciation of Latin American cinema. Without her guidance I would not have been able to undertake this project.

Micah Kleit and Jennifer Moore at the University of Minnesota Press provided encouragement and thoughtful advice throughout the process of editing this anthology. I want to thank Ann Marie Stock and the anonymous reader for their assiduous evaluation of the manuscript. Their comments aided immensely in revising the anthology. Lastly, I am grateful to Kathleen McHugh for her insightful comments and support in helping me to make the final revisions to my introduction.

Film and Video Distributors

■ ■ ■ ■

Almost all the films and videos considered in this anthology can be obtained through the Latin American Video Archives (LAVA), which provides an on-line searchable database and ordering service for thousands of Latin American titles. Many are subtitled in English. The service acts as an intermediary for hundreds of U.S. and foreign distributors and individual filmmakers and videomakers.

LAVA may be contacted as follows:

International Media Resource Exchange
124 Washington Place
New York, NY 10014
212-463-0108
http://www.lavavideo.org/lava/

Sergio Toledo's *Vera* is available from Kino International:

Kino International
333 West 39th Street
New York, NY 10018
800-562-3330
http://www.kino.com

Introduction
Chon A. Noriega

■ ■ ▥ ▦

This project begins with an ironic observation: in the current "global" moment, the study of Latin American cinema has become insistently *national*,
struggling in the space between the residual and emergent metanarratives
that have set the terms through which the entire region is understood and
studied. I use "residual" and "emergent" to signal the concurrent presence
and influence of two modes of understanding Latin American history as
well as to suggest that one mode is becoming dominant as the other loses
ideological force. With respect to cinema studies, each mode has circumscribed not only a set of critical approaches but also the very object of study
itself. In the former, pan-Americanism vis-à-vis the United States correlated
to a focus on the New Latin American Cinema of the 1960s. In the latter,
a critical insistence on the place and function of the nation-state within an
emerging globalism correlated, first, to telecommunication studies and,
more recently, to historiographic models for studying the national film industries in Latin America. A closer look at each of these modes will provide
a brief history of the field as it relates to the nation-state, internationalism,
and globalism—that is, the contested terrain in which this anthology locates its critical project.

In the residual metanarrative, scholars are encountering the historiographic limitations of the particular transnational paradigm articulated by
the New Latin American Cinema and its critics. Here, Bolívar and Martí's
political dream of pan-American unity, articulated as a hemispheric nationalism (the *gran patria* of *nuestra América*), underscored the film movement's
rejection of both Hollywood and the national industries in Latin America.
This rejection was not without profound contradictions. As Patricia Aufderheide notes: "What had been a diverse film movement led by middle-

class young men, many of them influenced by Italian neo-realism, came to have a name and enough coherence to muster debates over its direction during the political polarization throughout Latin America in the 1960s."[1] Thus, while New Latin American Cinema became a "staging ground" for political struggle, it did so within a region without a strong tradition of civil society, while the filmmakers themselves were quickly assimilated into the auteur-as-nation-as-genre sensibilities of the international art cinema.

Nevertheless, New Latin American Cinema provided not just a unique instance of a transnational film and social movement, or, conversely, the most recent addition to an international bourgeois culture located in film festivals, but also a theoretical paradigm that in many ways restricted critical interest to the radical cinema of the 1960s and 1970s. The impact in the United States has been twofold. In the 1970s, English-language translations of the major manifestos in *Cineaste,* together with related publications in *Framework* and *Jump Cut,* provided a common reference point for U.S. filmmakers and scholars associated with the New Left and various civil rights and identity-based movements. It is within this milieu that Chicano and other body-based cinemas named themselves. As a consequence, however, "Chicano cinema" continues to be seen—both within critical writings and international exhibitions—through the filter of New Latin American Cinema, while it is rarely accounted for within U.S. film and television history. In the 1980s, New Latin American Cinema became the axis upon which such film scholars as Julianne Burton-Carvajal, Robert Stam, and Ana M. López, among others, introduced the region's cinema into the theoretical debates then taking place in the field.[2] Although this scholarship remained a sidebar to the implicitly "white" Anglophone and Eurocentric concerns of film studies in the United States, it did set the terms for a meeting ground between minority and postcolonial discourses. Interestingly, and belatedly, it also ensured that New Latin American Cinema figured as the most prominent example within the all-too-brief accounts of Latin America in the major textbooks for the field.[3]

In the emergent metanarrative, telecommunications and not the "movies" exemplifies the processes of globalization in Latin America (as elsewhere), while it also constitutes a cultural arena within which local and regional production still remains a dominant and determining force.[4] Unlike the cinema, wherein international markets have been dominated by Hollywood throughout most of the twentieth century, telecommunications has been both a state infrastructure and a national cultural formation around the world, so that its globalization has followed a more multicentric and regional path. Herein lies the imperative—voiced most insistently outside the United States—to read the "local," "popular," and "national" into the discussion of the rise of U.S.-dominated global media.[5] There is more at stake than in the United States, where the death of the nation has been greatly exaggerated within critical discourse.

In the United States, universalism masks the underlying nationalism of critical discourse, while the nation and state are treated as interchangeable constructs, thereby allowing some critics to assume that the state itself is irrelevant in the face of global capital. Although there are problems with any investment in a national identity, the above stance effectively removes both national community and state policy from the discussion altogether. Along these lines, then, the rise of global media threatens to reduce cinema studies to a quaint aesthetic project far removed from an active engagement in today's vexing concerns over the future of democracy, the public sphere, civil society, public interest policy, and human rights. This situation is as much a consequence of the dominance of telecommunications as it is of the failure of cinema studies to realize that the state—and not just the unconscious and commodity culture—plays a role in our dreams.

To sum up, these two metanarratives—one producing a systemic analysis of national telecommunications infrastructures that have become increasingly regional and global; the other articulating a radical cultural politics haunted by class, gender, and race as it mediates between the national and the transnational—mark a fairly typical divide between an emphasis on political power with cultural consequences and one on cultural formations expressive of a political ideology. Such is the nature of the beast that walks across the current "global" moment. Our question here has to do with the place of theatrical cinema and narrowcast video as a cultural formation imbricated within national-cum-global power relations and as an object of study requiring both disciplinary and methodological considerations.

Visible Nations brings together new work that attempts to advance scholarship beyond the particular transnational and antinarrative critical framework inspired by the New Latin American Cinema without at the same time losing sight of its political, formal, and supranational concerns. Such an attempt is by no means new, perhaps being first articulated by Kathleen Newman as editor of a special issue of *Iris: A Journal of Theory on Image and Sound* in 1991 and amplified by Ana M. López in several key essays and papers that marked a renewed critical interest in the question of the national industrial cinemas in Latin America.[6] Likewise, Ann Marie Stock's anthology, *Framing Latin American Cinema: Contemporary Critical Perspectives,* attempts to step outside the "geopolitical specificity" for Latin American cinema as either national or regional expression.[7] Although Stock's formulation confuses geopolitical specificity with an analytic grounded in self-evident national and regional categories, she nevertheless calls attention to this issue, bringing together work that examines the specific *trans*actions and *inter*connections that are part and parcel of the history of Latin American cinemas.

Meanwhile, New Latin American Cinema continues to be the critical framework for other recent publications that deal with something more akin to "contemporary cinema" in Latin America: Zuzana M. Pick's *The New Latin American Cinema: A Continental Project* and Michael T. Martin's anthology *New Latin American Cinema,* vol. 2, *Studies of National Cinemas.*[8] But rather than either praise or bury the New Latin American Cinema as *the* or even *a* theoretical paradigm with which to approach the region, it is perhaps wiser to follow the path of Ana M. López, whose work has served more than any other to *historicize* that movement and its critical literature, film production, and exhibition history.[9] In this manner, New Latin American Cinema can be seen within its own historical moment and geopolitical specificity. It is not uncommon, however, for scholars to backdate and postdate a movement's time frame—its gravitational (or explanatory) forces are as diachronic as they are synchronic. But movements, like nations, are not only sovereign but also limited.[10] However difficult it may be to draw definitive boundaries, a simple fact remains: all movements start at some point, then come to an end or become something else, and it is only in that particularity that they can begin to have a more general significance, both within and across historical periods.[11]

Perhaps the problem is that the study of social movements and the study of nations constitute antithetical approaches, especially insofar as each approach finds not so much a historical object as a theoretical raison d'être. In this manner, critical approach and historical object become isomorphic to such an extent that they also seem autochthonous, finding their origins nowhere else. But it is in the historical and historiographic limitations of both social movements and nations that we find an alternative to this conundrum. In turning to the nation, we do not want to repeat the same mistake. Instead, *Visible Nations* takes up three areas in which scholars of Latin American cinema have "returned with a difference" to the question of the nation. These areas, which correspond with the book's three sections, include (1) retheorizing national cinema through revisionist accounts of the classical period, (2) exploring the representation of desire and the nation in contemporary cinema, and (3) examining the global politics of community-based and independent media. In some respects, these areas work around the question of New Latin American Cinema per se, but they do so by placing the "nation" itself under the lens of a transnational gaze. An increasing number of studies explore individual national cinemas in Latin America, especially those of Argentina, Brazil, Cuba, and Mexico.[12] But Ann Marie Stock is correct in identifying these works as the flip side of the regional emphasis on New Latin American Cinema itself.[13] Both tend to proclaim their object of study to be sui generis. The difference proposed by this book is none other than the troubling fact of difference. Nations must necessarily posit their uniqueness vis-à-vis other nations, nationalism being a matter of both discourse and geography, with bodies caught in the middle. Thus, as Néstor García Canclini concludes, "identity, as a narrative we constantly reconstruct with others, is also a coproduction."[14] Looking at national cinema, then, provides an opportunity to make visible the contours of that coproduction. Rather than proclaim that the nation does or does not exist as the proper object of critical "obsessions," this book considers the style through and the ends toward which the nation has been represented, desired, and contested in various Latin American cinemas. The goal is to move toward a historiography that studies national cinemas, not as sui generis and self-evident categories but as objects of knowledge that are constructed in contradiction to their own claims.

The first part, "Retheorizing National Cinema: The Classical Period," reveals the extent to which the national industries that developed before the 1960s did so through engagements with the dominant "foreign" cinematic styles of the silent and studio periods, the transnational migration of talent within the region, the rise of an international "film art" culture centered in Europe, and the intervention of U.S. foreign policy. Charles Ramírez Berg reconsiders the advent of a unique "classical" narrative style in Mexican cinema through a close textual analysis of Enrique Rosas's twelve-episode serial *El automóvil gris* (*The Gray Automobile*, 1919).[15] The impressive docudrama provides a chronological account of a series of high-profile robberies of Mexico City's wealthiest families at the height of the Revolution in 1915, ending with actual footage of the criminals' execution before a firing squad. Rather than promote a "pure" national style, Ramírez Berg explores the diverse international influences—Italian melodramas, French crime serials, and the Hollywood narrative paradigm—which Rosas incorporated into Mexico's unusually long emphasis on documentary production (1896–1917). In this manner, Ramírez Berg establishes the positivist and documentary origins of Mexican narrative cinema.

In "Crossing Nations and Genres: Traveling Filmmakers," Ana M. López continues her earlier challenge to rethink the "old" Latin American cinemas outside their purely antithetical position within the paradigm of the New Latin American Cinema.[16] In particular, she rejects the national-international binarism that has constituted these cinemas as "discrete national phenomena" subject to state policies, expressive of national culture, and bounded by international forces, most notably Hollywood and the U.S. State Department. Instead, as a critical and historiographic counterbalance, López explores the "inter-continental forces" and "transnational cross-fertilizations" that attended the development of national film industries in Latin America. Offering the provocative example of regional coproductions, with their liminal "national" status, López then focuses on the traveling creative personnel involved in foundational "national" films. Their "foreigner's gaze," she argues, provides the basis for a transnational analysis of the emergence of national cinemas. As an example, López considers Carlos Hugo Christensen, who, starting in the 1940s, has worked in Argentina, Chile, Venezuela, and Brazil. Her reading of Christensen's *La balandra Isabel llegó esta tarde* (*The Isabel Arrived This Afternoon*, 1949), the self-proclaimed first Venezuelan "super-production," reveals a complex negotiation between margin and center, self and other, wherein the nation becomes represented through the internal "foreignness" of its own "primitive" African-based folklore and transnational bourgeois culture. Here, the nation is made visible through the slippage and paradox of its mercenary imaginings.

Julianne Burton-Carvajal provides an important counterpart to López's examination of the "traveling filmmaker," shifting focus to a comparative analysis of critical reception and the writing of national, continental, and global film histories. In particular, Burton-Carvajal examines nearly four decades of critical discourse on Margot Benacerraf's *Araya* (1957), a scripted documentary with European postproduction and a protracted exhibition history, which strikingly depicts the seemingly timeless and endless "subsistence rituals of three communities of salt gatherers and fishermen on Venezuela's remote and barren northeastern coast." Here, Burton-Carvajal draws out the paradoxes and politics of all critical taxonomies, arguing that the most important thing about the film is not deciding where it belongs— that is, determining who is right in either claiming or rejecting the film from a particular history: subaltern, national, regional, foreign, or global. Instead, Burton-Carvajal argues that the structure of that debate is itself found in the film's engagement of conflicting temporalities, epistemologies, and cinematic modes. It is in this way, contrary to the epistemological certainty of most aesthetic genealogies, that *Araya* is an heir to the Flaherty tradition, a foundational Venezuelan film, a precursor of New Latin American Cinema, and a masterpiece of world cinema. As another form of movement, reception, like travel and like the cinema itself, produces the irony of not being in any one place.

In "Transcultured Anticommunism: Cold War Hollywood in Postwar Mexico," Seth Fein extends the research into the role of the United States in the Golden Age of Mexican cinema, exploring the confluence of U.S. anticommunist policies and the emerging Mexican political economy in the post–World War II period. Drawing upon extensive production files and governmental documents, Fein reveals the extent to which U.S. foreign policy continued to affect Mexican film production after the more widely known support provided as part of wartime propaganda efforts. Fein then examines two films produced at Estudios Churubusco in Mexico and distributed by RKO that represent a "transnational and state-to-state mass-media collaboration" that attempted to serve the different needs of the Mexican state (and state-controlled cinema), U.S. foreign policy, and Hollywood: John Ford's *The Fugitive* (1947) and Alejandro Galindo's *Dicen que soy comunista* (*They Say I Am a Communist,* 1951). These films combined U.S. anticommunist propaganda with Mexican political symbols for commercial dissemination throughout Latin America, representing the economic and ideological congruence between the two national cinemas and their respective states in the postwar decade.

The second section of the book, "Desire and the Nation: Contemporary Cinema," examines national cinemas since the 1970s, considering the function of desire within the imaginings that define the nation-state as sovereign and limited. These essays posit desire as the fulcrum through which cinema registered a social critique of the nation-state during a period in which hemispheric neoliberalism walked hand in hand with an unsteady and uneven democratization. Given the weakness of both the state and civil society—vis-à-vis the military, the elite classes, and international debt / global capital—a national cinema of social change necessarily turned to the carnivalesque realm of desire. The reason was quite practical. Often, as in Brazil and Mexico, state censorship remained almost entirely political, so that, for better or worse, pornography and the erotic became a default arena and symbol of the combined interests of the free market and freedom of speech.

Laura Podalsky and Monica Hulsbus each examine contemporary directors in Brazil whose work coincides with the transition from military rule to democracy, providing close readings of films in which female desire serves as political allegory for the nation-state. These films represent the breakdown of the authoritarian state's institutions, especially schools, which typically perform the task of inculcating nationalism and regulating desire. And as both authors demonstrate, these two functions are by no means unrelated. That both narratives focus on young male-identified women and use reflexive and experimental styles signals a liminal moment within which the state has lost its tight grip on the nation.

In "Fulfilling Fantasies, Diverting Pleasures: Ana Carolina and *Das tripas coração*," Podalsky explores the "multisensorial" pleasures of Carolina's parody and subversion of the patriarchal fantasy within its authoritarian institutions: state, school, church, family. Insofar as Carolina's critique of the social needed to circumvent political censorship, she draws upon the erotic genre of *pornochanchadas* and the melodramatic realm of the family, foregrounding young women within the narratives. This nexus of sexuality and the family in the body of the young woman allows the films at once to escape censorship and to expose the mechanism for reproducing such power relations. For Podalsky, sexuality and the family become the site for both the law (using psychoanalytic film theory) and its subversion (à la Bakhtinian carnivalesque), suggesting how it is that Carolina "effectively turned the rules of the dominant political order against themselves to critique political repression."

In "Performing the Nation in Sergio Toledo's *Vera*," Hulsbus considers Toledo's narrative about a young woman who wants to pass as a man in terms of its political allegory of Brazil's democratization following military rule. Hulsbus explores the "performativity" of nation, state, and subject and how the discourses and practices associated with these categories become disarticulated in the body of Vera Bauer, a young woman whose public appearance and private desires are unable to exist outside a boarding school for girls. Although the film "queers" gender and sexual normativity—something the director calls the film's "indisputable homosexual and transsexual issue"—it also equates Vera herself with the nation, a nation whose "liminality" has produced a crisis within the state apparatus. In *Vera,* this crisis is itself mapped onto the formal distinction between film and electronic images. But if the film privileges the latter over the former, it does so without recourse to a historical teleology: video allows heterogeneity and simultaneity, not redemption, whereas the cinema narrates the conflict between desire and social order.

Claire F. Fox and Harmony H. Wu each examine contemporary directors in Mexico whose work signals—in Fox's words—"the history of Mexican intellectuals and their conflicted roles as intermediaries between the state and popular struggles." Both scholars delineate the historical resonances between the contemporary period—as a period of "national" crisis—and the 1940s during which the state, culture industry, and bourgeoisie consolidated their power beneath the articulation of a Mexican national identity. In both instances, the representation of women emerges as that which both mobilizes and remains outside the films' social critique.

In "Pornography and 'the Popular' in Post-Revolutionary Mexico: The Club Tívoli from Spota to Isaac," Fox examines Alberto Isaac's *Tívoli* (1974) in light of the eponymous cabaret's place in Mexican cultural history since the late 1940s. Alfonso Arau, who stars in the film as a burlesque actor (a self-referential role for the comedian who would soon become a director), plays a populist figure who offers a problematic compromise between the state and social change. Near the end of the film, as the cabaret is about to be closed down, he forces the archetypal woman (named Eva or Eve!) to strip onstage in expression of his bitter defiance of state censorship. His act thereby obscures the (male) political struggle taking place behind closed doors. For Fox, the cultural history of the Club Tívoli reveals the imbrication of the pornographic with political discourse since the early 1950s: "women's bodies became a screen upon which conservatives projected all kinds of anxieties about social class, popular struggle, and national identity." In its own use of the female nude, Isaac's *Tívoli* "evokes those 'invisible' anxieties without naming them," thereby offering a partial critique that maintains the use of women's bodies as the lingua franca of male political discourse.

In "Consuming Tacos and Enchiladas: Gender and the Nation in *Como agua para chocolate*," Wu examines how Alfonso Arau's *Como agua para chocolate* (*Like Water for Chocolate*, 1991) engages the Revolutionary melodrama of the 1940s to reimagine the nation around the metaphor of its international consumption. Although the film has been seen as a "liberal, feminist treatise," Wu reveals its connections to the genre's conservative politics. In this respect, the film extends the genre's earlier nation-building project, wherein the social contradictions of the Revolution were resolved through the melodramatic imaginings of the romance-as-family-as-nation. But in *Como agua para chocolate,* if female agency and desire remain central to the narrative, they are also disarticulated from the genre's earlier concerns with class conflict and land redistribution. Instead, the genre and the question of female desire serve as an allegorical template for other concerns. For Wu, the film's international success explains the failure of U.S. and Mexican critics to account for its patriarchal, conservative discourse. Instead, consumption—figured around female desire—becomes the trope for "ersatz multiculturalism" in the United States and pre-NAFTA aspirations in Mexico. Whereas *Tívoli* revealed the persistence of women's bodies as a screen for (male) national politics, *Como agua para chocolate* suggests the way in which representations of female desire now resituate those politics within a global village.

In Cuba, of course, things have been somewhat different in the contemporary period, because of both its leftist political culture and its role as the institutionalized location for a cinema of social change in the Americas. In "The World according to *Plaff:* Reassessing Cuban Cinema in the Late 1980s," Gilberto M. Blasini examines Juan Carlos Tabío's comedy, *Plaff, o Demasiado miedo a la vida* (*Plaff, or Too Afraid of Life,* 1988), as a rereading of the "classical" Cuban film tradition associated with New Latin American Cinema and the critique of Hollywood-style narratives. The film follows upon a tradition of parodic and self-reflexive critique in post-Revolutionary Cuban cinema, a tradition that is in part a response to Fidel Castro's "words to the intellectuals" in 1961, wherein he warned: "Within the Revolution, everything. Against the Revolution, nothing." But here Blasini points to the specific social, economic, and ideological conditions facing Cuban filmmakers since the 1980s. These included the emergence of cross-generational tensions with respect to the Revolution, something signaled by the rise of Tabío and other young filmmakers within the Cuban Institute of Cinematographic Art and Industry. But *Plaff, o Demasiado miedo a la vida* is less a case of self-referential cinema than a reworking of the terms of melodrama itself, whereby such issues as sexism, racism, syncretic beliefs, and the bureaucratization of the state are located within the travails of the family. For Blasini, such a project navigates the limits of political critique vis-à-vis both the state and popular audiences. Thus cinema responds to Castro's "words to the intellectuals" with its own rewording: Within the melodrama, everything. Against the melodrama, nothing.

The third section of the book, "Local as Global Politics: Alternative Media," looks beyond the realm of theatrical-release narrative cinema, not at the global mass media but at the rise of community-based and independent media. To some extent, at least if we follow the careers of certain directors, New Latin American Cinema gave way to more-popular genre films that could circulate within the national, regional, and global marketplace. In contrast, recent local uses of video adhere more closely to the leftist premises and goals articulated in New Latin American Cinema manifestos. But here the nation is imagined as both local and transnational, especially insofar as community-based and independent production often participates with the state and nongovernmental organizations—and not without conflict—in the construction of a civil society around locally articulated needs. In this respect, its complicity is more pronounced, but its promise comes closer to praxis.

Patricia Aufderheide provides a critical overview of grassroots video in Latin America, assessing its value as a "strategic tool" for intervening in social processes. She considers narrowcast as well as off-air uses within local settings, institutional support within the nation, and the role of nongovernmental organizations and transnational social networks. Aufderheide's essay suggests historiographic parameters for studying grassroots video vis-à-vis both New Latin American Cinema and national media industries. The necessity of such an approach is made difficult by the lack of documentation other than "glowing" reports to granting agencies. Nevertheless, grassroots video offers a space from which to critique the relationships between communication technologies and social-cum-political power. For Aufderheide, the "grassroots" is not the negation of other spaces but a particular way in which the local, national, and global can be configured for the purpose of information equity and democratization.

Ilene S. Goldman and Brian Goldfarb each provide in-depth historical accounts of individual alternative media groups in, respectively, Colombia (Bogotá's Cine Mujer, since 1975) and Brazil (São Paulo's TV Anhembi, 1989–92). In both instances, alternative film and video production relied upon governmental support and agencies, representing a significant shift in the nature of community-based media, one wherein the usual emphasis on social change and cultural identity came into alignment with the idea of citizenship. Both histories challenge the broader contexts within which they are told, offering distinct "local" examples that complicate national, regional, and global histories of leftist social movements, feminist cultural politics, and alternative film and video production. In this respect, for example, Cine Mujer's longevity—not to mention the consequent changes in the group's structure, style, and support—is notable as a local, national, regional, global, and feminist achievement. On the other hand, TV Anhembi represents an instructive, if also short-lived, example of the local reconfiguration of "community" in the shadow of global mass media. Here, under a leftist mayor's aegis, local video activists, government agencies, and popular television forms produced that which both the national and global media seem most insistent on destroying: a public sphere.[17]

In the final essay, "Steadfast Love and Subversive Acts: The Politics of *La Ofrenda: The Days of the Dead*," Kathleen Newman engages in a close reading of Lourdes Portillo's 1988 documentary on the Mexican celebrations in remembrance of the dead that take place on the first and second days of November. In the latter part of the documentary, Portillo explores the transformation of these celebrations in San Francisco through their Chicano and Anglo participants. In this manner, the documentary examines the carnivalesque "potentiality" of difference on both sides of the border, while it implicitly links Mexico and the United States through the "politics of exclusion" that define each nation.

At first glance, *La Ofrenda: The Days of the Dead* is an example of U.S. independent documentary production: foundation funded, shot on film, broadcast on PBS, then made available on home video. But Portillo's concerns are binational and bicultural—also demonstrated in her feature-length documentary *El diablo nunca duerme* (*The Devil Never Sleeps,* 1995)—in such a way that her work cannot be reduced to the U.S. independent sector within which she works. Nor can her concerns be limited to those of a "Chicano cinema" that correlates identity to civil rights within the nation-state. But it would be just as incorrect to go to the other extreme and claim her as a Latin American producer.

If anything, Portillo reveals how the liminality within the nation relates to liminality across nations; in short, how the national and the transnational are not alternatives to each other but rather part of an interrelated set of cultural and economic structures. The inclusion of Portillo's work in this volume, then, speaks to a challenge to the national that nevertheless exists within and as part of a nation as well as to an articulation of pan-Americanism that exists within the nation against which it is predicated, the United States. But I do not want to suggest that Portillo represents an endpoint, lest I endorse a teleology rooted in the United States. Instead, Portillo suggests an open-ended approach to the nation in the Americas. As one of her narrators says regarding the Days of the Dead: "people mock death and gender and whatever else needs a little push." To mock such things is never to believe that they can go away, only that they can change. Furthermore, the requisite "little push" suggests that the impetus for change must come from within an arm's length. Thus, the "little push" that makes for visible nations brings the critic very close to his or her object of study.

Notes

1. Patricia Aufderheide, "Latin American Cinema and the Rhetoric of Cultural Nationalism: Controversies at Havana in 1987 and 1989," *Quarterly Review of Film and Video* 12.4 (1991): 62.

2. For a partial selection that suggests the theoretical and critical range of this work, see Julianne Burton and Jean Franco, eds., "Culture in the Age of

Mass Media," *Latin American Perspectives,* no. 16 (winter 1978); Julianne Burton, ed., *The Social Documentary in Latin America* (Pittsburgh: University of Pittsburgh Press, 1990); John King, Ana M. López, and Manuel Alvarado, eds., *Mediating Two Worlds: Cinematic Encounters in the Americas* (London: British Film Institute, 1993); and under the rubric of a global multiculturalism, Ella Shohat and Robert Stam, *Unthinking Eurocentrism: Multiculturalism and the Media* (London: Routledge, 1994).

3. See, for example, David A. Cook, *A History of Narrative Film,* 3rd ed. (New York: W. W. Norton and Co., 1996 [1981]); and Kristin Thompson and David Bordwell, *Film History: An Introduction* (New York: McGraw-Hill, 1994).

4. Ana M. López makes this point in "The Melodrama in Latin America: Films, Telenovelas, and the Currency of a Popular Form," *Wide Angle* 7.3 (1985): 5–13. For a critical overview of Latin American scholarship in the 1980s, see Alan O'Connor, "The Emergence of Cultural Studies in Latin America," *Critical Studies in Mass Communication* 8 (1991): 60–73.

5. See, for example, Jesús Martín-Barbero, who locates the nation in the "strategic space" between the transnational and the popular, in "Communication from Culture: The Crisis of the National and the Emergence of the Popular," trans. Philip Schlesinger, *Media, Culture, and Society* 10 (1988): 447–65. For a recent consideration of the global influence of U.S. mass media that uses the North American Free Trade Agreement as its starting point, see Emile G. McAnany and Kenton T. Wilkinson, eds., *Mass Media and Free Trade: NAFTA and the Cultural Industries* (Austin: University of Texas Press, 1996).

6. See Kathleen Newman, ed., "Latin American Cinema," *Iris,* no. 13 (summer 1991); Ana M. López, "Celluloid Tears: Melodrama in the 'Old' Mexican Cinema," ibid., 29–52; and idem., "A Cinema for the Continent," in *The Mexican Cinema Project,* ed. Chon A. Noriega and Steven Ricci (Los Angeles: UCLA Film and Television Archive, 1994), 7–12. This concern likewise motivates John King's *Magical Reels: A History of Cinema in Latin America* (London: Verso, 1990). Of related interest is López's "A Short History of Latin American Film Histories," *Journal of Film and Video,* no. 37 (winter 1985): 55–69.

7. Ann Marie Stock, "Introduction—Through Other Worlds and Other Times: Critical Praxis and Latin American Cinema," in *Framing Latin American Cinema: Contemporary Critical Perspectives,* ed. Ann Marie Stock (Minneapolis: University of Minnesota Press, 1997), xxi–xxxv.

8. Zuzana M. Pick, *The New Latin American Cinema: A Continental Project* (Austin: University of Texas Press, 1993); and Michael T. Martin, ed., *New Latin American Cinema,* vol. 2, *Studies of National Cinemas* (Detroit: Wayne State University Press, 1997). Volume 1, however, reprints the major manifestos, theoretical essays, and revisionist critiques related to the New Latin American Cinema.

9. See Ana M. López, "An 'Other' History: The New Latin American Cinema," in *Resisting Images: Essays on Cinema and History,* ed. Robert Sklar and Charles Musser (Philadelphia: Temple University Press, 1990), 308–30; and idem., *Third and Imperfect: A History of New Latin American Cinema* (Minneapolis: University of Minnesota Press, forthcoming).

10. The definition of the nation as imagined, sovereign, and limited comes from Benedict Anderson, *Imagined Communities: Reflections on the Origin and Spread of Nationalism,* rev. ed. (New York: Verso, 1991 [1983]).

11. On social movements, see J. Craig Jenkins and Bert Klandermans, eds., *The Politics of Social Protest: Comparative Perspectives on States and Social Movements* (Minneapolis: University of Minnesota Press, 1995); and Hank Johnston and Bert Klandermans, eds., *Social Movements and Culture* (Minneapolis: University of Minnesota Press, 1995).

12. Recent book-length works in English include Robert Stam, *Tropical Multiculturalism: A Contemporary History of Race in Brazilian Cinema and Culture* (Durham, N.C.: Duke University Press, 1997); Ismail Xavier, *Allegories of Underdevelopment: Aesthetics and Politics in Modern Brazilian Cinema* (Minneapolis: University of Minnesota Press, 1997); Randal Johnson and Robert Stam, eds., *Brazilian Cinema,* expanded ed. (New York: Columbia University Press, 1995 [1982]); Joanne Hershfield, *Mexican Cinema/Mexican Woman, 1940–1950* (Tucson: University of Arizona Press, 1996); Paulo Antonio Paranaguá, ed., *Mexican Cinema,* trans. Ana M. López (London: British Film Institute, 1995); Noriega and Ricci, eds., *The Mexican Cinema Project;* Charles Ramírez Berg, *Cinema of Solitude: A Critical Study of Mexican Film, 1967–1983* (Austin: University of Texas Press, 1992); David William Foster, *Contemporary Argentine Cinema* (Columbia: University of Missouri Press, 1992); and John King and Nissa Torrents, eds., *The Garden of Forking Paths: Argentine Cinema* (London: British Film Institute, 1991). In addition, Julianne Burton-Carvajal is working on an anthology on Mexican melodrama. Also of note is Karen Schwartzman's dissertation research on Venezuelan cinema, which resulted in an extensive U.S. exhibition at the Museum of Modern Art and elsewhere. See her account, "National Cinema in Translation: The Politics of Film Exhibition Culture," *Wide Angle* 16.3 (1995): 66–99.

For a recent Spanish-language anthology on research and pedagogy related to Latin American cinema, see Julianne Burton-Carvajal, Patricia Torres, and Ángel Miguel, eds., *Horizontes del segundo siglo: Investigación y pedagogía del cine mexicano, latinoamericano, y chicano* (Guadalajara, Mexico: Universidad de Guadalajara and Instituto Mexicano de Cinematografía, 1998). See also Timothy Barnard and Peter Rist, eds., *South American Cinema: A Critical Filmography, 1915–1994* (Austin: University of Texas Press, 1998). For extensive bibliographies and other resources on Latin American cinema, visit the following Web sites: the Cinemedia Project http://humwww.ucsc.edu/cinemedia/

index.html; and the Latin American Cinema Home Page http://www.libs.uga
.edu/humaniti/ltamcine.html.

13. Stock, "Introduction," xxiii.

14. Néstor García Canclini, "Will There Be Latin American Cinema in the
Year 2000? Visual Culture in a Postnational Era," in Stock, *Framing Latin
American Cinema*, 257.

15. The film was twice reedited as a feature and rereleased with sound in 1933
and 1937. Ramírez Berg's essay continues a revisionist project on Mexican cinematic style that he started with Emilio "El Indio" Fernández and Gabriel Figueroa's collaborations between 1943 and 1956. See Ramírez Berg, "The Cinematic Invention of Mexico: The Poetics and Politics of the Fernández-Figueroa
Style," in *The Mexican Cinema Project,* ed. Noriega and Ricci, 13–24.

16. See López, "Celluloid Tears."

17. For an excellent study of Latin American social movements and the
struggle for democratization over the past thirty years, see Jorge G. Castañeda,
Utopia Unarmed: The Latin American Left after the Cold War (New York: Vin-
tage Books, 1993).

Part I
Retheorizing National Cinema
THE CLASSICAL PERIOD

■ ■ ■ ■

1

El automóvil gris and the Advent of Mexican Classicism

Charles Ramírez Berg

■ ■ ■ ■

One of the few surviving examples of Mexican silent narrative film, and one that has been called "the most famous [Mexican] movie of the period,"[1] is *El automóvil gris* (*The Gray Automobile,* 1919; produced by Enrique Rosas, directed by Rosas, Joaquín Coss, and Juan Canals de Homes). Originally released as a twelve-episode serial with an estimated running length of between three and four hours, it was based on a notorious series of robberies that occurred in Mexico City in 1915. These crimes were celebrated because of the robbers' distinctive modus operandi. Taking advantage of the chaos brought on by the Mexican Revolution, the thieves disguised themselves as soldiers and displayed signed search warrants to gain entry to the houses of some of the wealthiest families in Mexico City. They terrorized the inhabitants, robbed them, and made their escape in a gray Fiat.[2]

Though it is the first Mexican docudrama, *El automóvil gris*'s re-creation of actual events is impressive. It was based on two sources: newspaper accounts of the affair by Miguel Nicoechea, a reporter who covered the crimes; and case notes taken by Juan Manuel Cabrera, the assistant chief of police for the military's Special Services, who was in charge of the investigation and was said to have made most of the arrests in the case.[3] Nicoechea and Cabrera coscripted the film with Enrique Rosas, and Cabrera played himself in the film. Furthermore, according to the film's prologue, it was shot in the locations where the events had occurred.[4] Finally—and most dramatically—rather than staging the climactic execution of six of the bandits, Rosas, who oversaw the editing, inserted documentary footage of the actual firing squad execution, which he himself had photographed in 1915.[5]

This canny combination of authenticity and sensationalism evidently appealed to audiences, doubtless contributing to the film's enormous popularity. It broke all of Mexico's established box office records, including those for most theaters to exhibit the same film on one day (19), most single-day admissions (40,233), and biggest opening day outside of Mexico City (4,012 pesos, in Veracruz).[6]

After the coming of sound, the serial was reedited twice, in 1933 and 1937. Dialogue, music, and sound effects were added, and it was condensed to feature length (111 minutes). This renewed its popularity and extended its exhibition life considerably, making it one of the longest-running, most-viewed films in Mexican cinema history.[7] In the process, however, this reconstruction completely destroyed the original. In order to conform with emergent two-hour feature-length norms, Rosas's heirs deleted scenes, characters, plot threads, and the entire last episode. What remains for today's viewers can be confusing, especially if they are not familiar with the events depicted.[8]

But even given all the problems with the film that survives, it is a seminal text in which a number of formative cinematic currents converge, making it crucial to the understanding of the development of Mexican cinema. To begin with, because of its subject matter, it conveniently satisfied the nationalistic urge central to Mexican arts at the time. Moreover, *El automóvil gris* contains an early expression of twin themes—the corruption of Revolutionary ideals and the accompanying remorse over the loss of the unique opportunity the Revolution afforded—that would haunt the nation's cinema for the next seven decades.[9] Additionally, the symbiotic relationship between political leaders and the film's producer set a precedent for state involvement in motion picture production that characterizes Mexican filmmaking to this day.[10] Finally, the film reveals how the classical Mexican cinema resulted from the blending of four national filmmaking models: (1) Mexico's rich documentary tradition that thrived for twenty years by feeding its audience's appetite for Mexican images; (2) Italian cinema, known for its attention to period detail and its mobile camera; (3) French cinema, especially, in the case of *El automóvil gris,* the crime serials (such as Georges Feuillade's *Fantomas* [1913–14], *Judex* [1916], and *La nouvelle mission de Judex* [1917]), with their extensive use of location shooting, their fast-paced cops-and-robbers narratives, and their characters' reliance on disguises; and (4) the emerging Hollywood paradigm, with its goal-driven protagonist, its causally linked narrative, and its rules of editing, lighting, and shooting based on character psychology. A formal analysis of *El automóvil gris* makes clear that, despite Mexican cinema's near-exclusive concentration on documentaries for the medium's first two decades, Mexican narrative film was remarkably well developed by 1919. But before undertaking that formal analysis, we must first familiarize ourselves with the beginnings of cinema in Mexico, with the infamous crimes themselves, and with the production of the film.

Mexican Film Culture, 1896–1917

Owing to a unique convergence of factors, Mexican cinema developed unlike any other national cinema. As I mentioned above, one key difference was that until 1917, Mexican film production was almost exclusively a documentary practice. Representatives of the Lumiérè brothers shot and exhibited their *actualités* (brief documentaries) in Mexico in 1896, and when Mexican film entrepreneurs like Salvador Toscano Barragán and Enrique Rosas began producing their own films, they found a lively market for such views of the nation. In contrast, both European and North American cinemas would gradually gravitate toward narrative; in the case of U.S. films, this was especially true after 1907.[11] And while these foreign films commanded more and more attention from filmgoers in Mexico, apart from a few isolated attempts at *el filme de argumento* (scripted fiction films), Mexican cinema production remained staunchly documentary.[12] The onset of the Mexican Revolution (1910–20) was an impetus to continue in this vein, as newsreel footage brought the civil war to life for thousands of Mexican spectators.

But interest in such films waned after 1915, and by 1916, Revolutionary documentaries were almost completely absent from Mexican movie screens.[13] One possible reason was that by this time documentaries had dedicated themselves to chronicling a Revolution that Mexicans were growing increasingly tired of. Another was that the availability of European films was dwindling because of World War I. Hollywood films took up the slack and increased their Mexican market share, although this was not without its problems. Often captivated by Hollywood cinema, Mexican viewers were also distressed by its derogatory representation of Mexico and Mexicans.[14] Such imagery helped foster the desire to create a national cinema that could compete with Hollywood's on the one hand and could counter these negative images on the other. An additional factor leading to the decline of the nonfiction film may have been the dawning sense on the part of Mexican moviegoers that documentaries were increasingly becoming political propaganda for those in power.[15] In any case, the Mexican audience's hunger for narrative films and declining interest in newsreels provided the catalyst for the rise of Mexican narrative filmmaking.[16]

El automóvil gris was only the thirty-ninth Mexican feature (defined as a film longer than 40 minutes) produced in Mexico, and only the twenty-fourth narrative film.[17] Still, it demonstrated a sure grasp of narrative and a sophisticated understanding of cinematic form. There were two principal reasons for this. One was the filmmaking expertise of former newsreel cinematographer Enrique Rosas, who was not only the film's codirector, but also its producer, coscriptwriter, chief editor, and promoter.[18] The other was that *El automóvil gris* was the perfect narrative vehicle for a film practice steeped in the documentary tradition. For a filmmaker like Rosas, skilled in reportage, it is hard to imagine a more suitable project than the cinematic reconstruction of the scandalous case of *"la banda del automóvil gris"* ("the Gray Car Gang").

The Infamous Impostors in the Gray Getaway Car

The crimes that served as the basis for Rosas's film were a series of assaults and robberies that began in April 1915 and lasted until eighteen alleged members, accomplices, and associates were arrested, tried, and variously pardoned, imprisoned, or executed in December of that same year.[19] The criminals exploited the disorder caused by the Revolution, as rival factions fought over control of the government and the capital city, which changed hands five times in the first five years of the Revolution. In the year the robberies took place, 1915, the government—and the capital—was directed first by Zapata, then by his rival, Carranza, whose counterrevolutionary forces gained control in August.[20]

The bandits' successful operation during the rule of two opposing leaders is significant because of the widely held suspicion that they were in league with high-level government officials. This was based on the bandits' possession of two signs of authority that gave them carte blanche: authentic military uniforms and signed search warrants. Thus one of the most fascinating elements of the case, one that added to the notoriety of the crimes and to the success of the film, is completely lost to modern viewers—the belief that the thieves were associated with government officers of two competing regimes.[21] In fact, although it is not clear how high the government cooperation went, it did occur.

Whether or not this collusion led to police negligence in the pursuit and capture of the gang is unknown, but other factors hampered the investigation. Chief among them was that Mexico City's infrastructure had, for all intents and purposes, collapsed. For example, because of a coal shortage, the capital's city council ordered that streetlights be lit only from 7 to 10 P.M.

This allowed the band an ideal cover for their crimes: pretending to be protecting the peace, they could ride the dark streets late at night unimpeded.

But there was mounting public pressure to find the criminals, and, all things considered, arrests were expeditiously made. By 1 June, four ringleaders had been arrested. Here fate, in the form of the shifting winds of the Revolution, intervened. Gen. Pablo González, the leader of Carranza's troops, engaged Zapata's army several times in June and July within Mexico City's limits. During one of those battles, the jail and penitentiary were damaged, and all the prisoners, including the band members, escaped. This led to a second wave of robberies by the Gray Car Gang.

When General González finally occupied Mexico City for Carranza in August 1915, he found a weary citizenry on the verge of starvation, and a society on the brink of collapse. His occupation did not improve the situation. Carranza's soldiers were probably feared more than they were respected by *capitalinos,* because renegade military units were known to sack houses almost at will. Higinio Granda, a member of the original gang, exploited the general lawlessness and the pervading ambivalence toward authority for his own ends; he headed a new gang that began its criminal activities soon after González's occupation. They were probably aided by the chief of Special Services of the military police, who likely provided them with search warrants signed by General González. As a result, rumors began spreading that González was the evil genius behind the gang's operations. Some even claimed that stolen jewelry was worn by his lover, stage diva Mimi Derba.[22]

This second series of robberies lasted from August until 12 December 1915, when Federal District police arrested thirteen male and five female suspects in the crimes. Although more suspects would be arrested in the following days, including Rafael Mercadante, Granda's second-in-command, Granda would not be among them (he was arrested and imprisoned nine months later). A few were not implicated and were released. The five women, evidently the lovers of some of the gang members, were sentenced to ten years in prison; the remaining ten men were sentenced to death. At the last minute General González pardoned four of the condemned prisoners, including Mercadante; the remaining six were executed by firing squad on 20 December.

The Making and Release of *El automóvil gris*

The major shift in the Mexican filmmaking paradigm that occurred in 1916–17, away from documentary and toward narrative, called for a corresponding change in the Mexican mode of cinematic production. No longer could a single enterprising individual fulfill all the necessary roles of producer, cinematographer, distributor, and promoter. Narrative films required the collaboration of specialists in a number of key areas: acting, writing, cinematography, editing, directing, producing, and set design, construction, and decoration. The entrepreneurs who made the first Mexican cinema were forced either to leave the business or, like Enrique Rosas, to join with others to form production companies.

Together with singer and stage star Mimi Derba, Rosas formed Azteca Films in 1917. General González, romantically involved with Derba at the time, was a silent partner. Azteca Films was a significant enough concern to have its own studio and to release five melodramas in 1917. These films were evidently influenced by Italy's "diva genre," "stories of passion and intrigue in upper-middle-class and aristocratic settings."[23] Rosas photographed them and Derba starred in four of the five, and they shared the other creative duties, both contributing as screenwriter, producer, director, and editor. The company's production of narrative films ended soon afterward; Derba returned to the stage, and Rosas returned to documentaries. For example, he released a documentary on Zapata in April 1919, one week after the assassination of the rebel leader.[24]

Rosas had already begun shooting *El automóvil gris* in March, having once again secured the backing of General González. Drawing on the experiences of Nicoechea and Cabrera, he had written the script with the poet Juan Manuel Ramos.[25] Filming continued until November, and the film was released on 11 December 1919. Though it appears that he was assisted in directing by two of the actors, Joaquín Coss (who played one of the victims, Vicente González) and Juan Canals de Homes (who played the gang leader, Granada, as he was called in the film), Rosas appears to be the film's auteur, since he personally contributed to and oversaw all stages of the production: creative (scripting and directing), technical (shooting and editing), financial, and promotional.[26] But his artistic autonomy was compromised, first by his association with General González, and second by Carranza's government.

In 1919, González was entertaining presidential ambitions. Probably not coincidentally, on the very day that *El automóvil gris* premiered in Mexico City, he accepted the candidacy in the upcoming elections. Naturally, González would have wanted to set the record straight with a filmed illustration not only of his innocence but also of his active pursuit, capture, and punishment of the gang. No doubt Rosas was eager to demonstrate that his friend and business associate was in no way implicated in the crimes. He had already produced a documentary film in 1916 celebrating González (which included the same execution footage that ends *El automóvil gris*),[27] so it is not surprising that *El automóvil gris* exonerates González by showing that Granda acted independently of high-ranking government officials. In one fictionalized sequence, Granda refers to a mastermind who planned and coordinated the gang's activities from a secret office. But this "Mr. Big" is later revealed to be merely a mannequin in a back room, thus "proving" that Granda acted alone.

Political exigencies and governmental censorship—either direct or indirect—must have colored Rosas's film. In subtle ways, the responsibility for the crimes was shifted to the Zapata regime. For one thing, the activities of the gang were condensed to five robberies, revising history so that three were depicted as having occurred during the Zapata era (though official records revealed that of the eleven robberies attributed to the gang, five occurred during Zapata's rule and six during Carranza's). For another, *la banda*'s escape from prison was portrayed as resulting from a rapacious act of the retreating Zapata troops ("On their way out of the capital," a title card relates, "the Zapatista forces open the penitentiary doors") rather than from the destructive vicissitudes of war.[28] Moreover, the military abuses of the Carranza era were glossed over. General González and the other Carranzista officials were seen as proactively engaged in the investigation, and the police were portrayed as tireless public servants working for the betterment of society. Furthermore, the film posited that the search warrants the gangsters used were fraudulent (which was not the case) and did not mention that Granda ingratiated himself with the police in both Zapata and Carranza administrations to gain inside information and/or signed documents. The reconstruction of the film in the 1930s blurred some of this propagandizing. González's influence had declined considerably since 1919 (he was not elected president), and his role in the sound version of *El automóvil gris* was reduced to one scene in which he was not identified. However, the feature still presented the Carranza government in a positive light.

Rosas, who knew the value of well-orchestrated ballyhoo, announced in September that the film he was preparing would be unprecedented in Mexican cinema: a serial with forty-five episodes requiring three successive evenings of screenings. Though the twelve-episode serial that he actually released by year's end was much more modest, it was striking nonetheless.[29] Along the way, Rosas also had to fight off competition from distributors and exhibitors who were eager to capitalize on the well-known case of "*la banda del automóvil gris*." Consequently, a flurry of films were released with that or similar titles in the fall of 1919. The most serious challenge came from another enterprising filmmaker, Germán Camus, whose company began filming its own serial. Since the film no longer exists, it is difficult to say how similar it was, but based on the chapter titles (for example, "The Robbery of the Banker's House"), Camus's appears to be a thinly disguised knockoff of Rosas's serial. The two films were even scripted by the same screenwriter, Juan Manuel Ramos. Rosas tried to shut down Camus's project through legal means but was unsuccessful. Camus's film, entitled *La banda del automóvil (La dama enlutada) (The Automobile Gang,* or *The Lady in Mourning)*, was finished and exhibited on 11 September, well before Rosas's was completed and, from all indications, had a successful run.[30]

In addition, a twelve-episode Vitagraph serial, *The Scarlet Runner* (1916), was being distributed by Jacobo Granat under the title *El automóvil gris (The Gray Automobile)*. Rosas immediately published a protestation, announcing that Granat's *El automóvil gris* was a U.S. film that had nothing to do with the nefarious crimes of 1915 and was in violation of patent laws, and that Rosas's "real" *Automóvil gris* would soon be available for viewing. When the exhibition of the U.S. film with the title *El automóvil gris* was suspended by a judge's order, Rosas may have thought he was vindicated. But the wily Granat responded by simply changing the name of the American serial to *El automóvil rojo (The Red Automobile)*.[31]

With this background in hand, I will provide a close reading of the formal characteristics of the actual film—or what remains of it—in order to examine the state and significance of Mexican film narrative in 1919.

Mexican Classicism: Synthesizing Four Cinematic Traditions and Consolidating National Film History

In her penetrating analysis of the stylistic evolution of early U.S. cinema, Kristin Thompson delineates a progression of formal tendencies that will help us understand the development of Mexican cinema and the advent of classicism. Thompson proposes three successive, if overlapping, stages. Primitive films (1895–1909) adhered to the theatrical, proscenium arch tradition and filmed their action from a front-row-center vantage point. Filmmakers gradually left primitive filmmaking behind in the transitional phase (1909–16), as they established narrative norms for the new medium. By the classical era (1917–60), Hollywood filmmakers had formulated a distinctively cinematic narrative form.[32]

As Thompson relates, U.S. narrative film developed through an extensive process of trial and error, eventually blossoming into classicism by making thousands of *actualités,* split-reel, one-reel, two-reel, serial, and feature films from 1895 to 1917. Given the evidence of *El automóvil gris,* Mexican cinema leapfrogged to roughly the same point in narrative filmmaking at roughly the same time by completely different means. It produced far fewer films than Hollywood or European cinemas, most of them short documentaries, and, by 1919, only two dozen story films. But by blending four different cinematic traditions—Mexican, Italian, French, and North American—it established its own storytelling norms. Following Thompson, we can think of Mexican cinema as also evolving in three stages. The first stage (1896–1915) consists of the native documentaries.[33] The transitional stage (1915–23) was heavily influenced by Italian cinema of the time and is represented by films such as the Rosas-Derba melodramas.[34] The classical stage (1919–60) was initiated by *El automóvil gris* and was influenced by French crime serials and by Hollywood's burgeoning narrative paradigm. The prototypical classical film, *El automóvil gris* consolidated the gains of the Mexican cinema up to that time and set the stage for the classical era that was to follow. But because Mexican film production virtually disappeared by the late 1920s, classicism would not bear fruit until the national cinema was revived by sound in the early 1930s. A profitable way to reveal how Mexican cinema arrived at a classicism of its own is to compare *El automóvil gris*'s formal characteristics with the elements enumerated by Thompson.

To try to avoid the ethnocentric trap of positing Hollywood cinema as a formal ideal to which Mexican cinema was obliged to conform in order to earn legitimacy, I will organize my comments around the question of narrative intelligibility. Since record numbers of Mexican viewers—familiar with Mexican documentaries as well as U.S. and European fiction films—obviously made sense of the film, it seems fair to ask how and by what cinematic means this narrative clarity was achieved. My one caveat is that I am forced to make my analysis based on the fragments that remain: the feature version of *El automóvil gris,* an incomplete draft of the original treatment,[35] contemporary accounts of the film, and stills from the serial that offer clues to scenes that were later omitted. Obviously, this is dangerous. To begin with, we cannot know if the missing sequences in the treatment were ever written or, if written, ever filmed. Furthermore, the shooting script prepared from the treatment is lost; presumably it would have incorporated numerous changes. Simply because an incident was described in the treatment does not mean it found its way into the finished script, that it was filmed, or that, if filmed, it was included in the finished serial. On the positive side of the ledger is that, on the whole, the integrity of the original film seems to persist in the feature. Although some threads of the narrative were deleted and others abbreviated, on the whole the story remains intact and is presented in the same order. And although some shots are extremely brief, making it appear that they may have been trimmed or that frames from the original were lost, no new footage is known to have been shot or added. Thus, the 644 shots that comprise the extant feature film probably exhibit enough of the cinematic characteristics of the original for us to judge the state of Mexican cinema in 1919.

The Poetics of *El automóvil gris*
NARRATIVE

From their taking of a criminal oath of allegiance (fig. 1.1), through a series of robberies and police chases, to their eventual capture and execution, the story of Granda (named Granada in the silent film but called Granda in the sound version) and his band is a standard crime-does-not-pay melodrama. Understanding the need to condense the complex real-life events into a streamlined narrative, Rosas and his screenwriting team produced a taut, highly intelligible film with a straightforward story line.

Multiple Protagonists / Multiple Narrative

Perhaps modeled after Feuillade's crime serials, *El automóvil gris* contains two sets of goal-oriented protagonists, the bandits and the police, which provides a built-in multiple narrative and necessitates crosscutting between them. Layered over the cops-and-robbers story lines is a third: the romantic subplots of three of the bandits and their lovers. The most prominent one in the feature film is that of Angel Chao and Carmen, which develops from courtship to imprisonment. Based on photographs of the film that have survived, at least two other romances were depicted, including that of Santiago Risco and an unnamed woman, who has a child by him. This is the couple who are married in jail just before Risco is executed. The other relationship involves Ernestina, a woman kidnapped by the gang in an early sequence. Before the action of the film begins, she has fallen in love with a man named Oviedo; only after she is kidnapped by the bandits does she discover that Oviedo is a member of *la banda*.

Adding more complexity to the narrative is the use of the motivated flashback. For instance, in an early sequence, the gang returns to their hideout with the booty from their latest robbery. But since the narrative remains with the kidnapped Ernestina and her guard, the specifics of the gang's

FIGURE I.I. *The gang take their loyalty oath; Granda is in the center. Courtesy of the Agrasanchez Archive of Mexican Cinema.*

latest job are unknown to us. At the behest of the bandit who guards Ernestina, Granada relates the adventure, which the film depicts via a flashback. In sum, these elements produce an eloquent narrative that is complex but economical, rich in texture, detail and nuance.

Causality

The narrative proceeds by rough causal linkages, as one crime leads to the next, and as the detectives and a victim, Don Vicente González, join forces to pursue and capture the bandits. For the most part the narrative develops clearly and classically—shot by shot, scene by scene, one well-elaborated causal link at a time.

Characterization

The film's most complex characters are the bandits; their pursuers, Vicente González and Inspector Cabrera, remain one-dimensional good guys. One reason for this imbalance is the decision to include the romantic relationships of the gangsters, which gives them psychological and emotional depth, helps humanize them, and provides dimensions to what could have easily been stock characters.

EDITING

The film follows the classical analytical pattern. Interior scenes usually begin with a long shot (LS) or medium long shot (MLS) to establish location. As the scene proceeds, there eventually is a medium close-up (MCU) or close-up (CU), usually of one key character as he or she speaks or notices something. Then there is a return to the original LS or MLS to close the scene. Scenes may end there or add a coda: a medium shot (MS) detail of some kind. A good example is a sequence of five shots (186–90) in a police detective's office.[36] As Vicente González makes his complaint to the Zapata-era detectives, he discovers that Granada is working for the police. The scene follows this analytical shot progression:

SHOT 186 [length, in minutes:seconds, 1:08[37]] MLS—Detective's office. A very long take that begins with Granada's assistant alone in the room, rifling through the detective's desk. Using his key to open a drawer, he takes out several sheets, and he stamps them with a seal from the desktop. Granada enters and sends the accomplice out, and the detective, González, and other agents enter. As González displays some papers, he surveys the men in the room.

SHOT 187 [:04] MCU—A surprised González spots Granada.

SHOT 188 [:03] MCU—Granada turns away nervously.

SHOT 189 [:12] MLS—González jumps Granada, attempting to strangle him. Granada takes out his pistol, but González strikes his arm and the shot is wild. The other agents hold Granada while González explains that he is one of the bandits (fig. 1.2).

SHOT 190 [:05] MS—González accuses Granada; pan right to MS of Granada as González points an accusing finger at him and the agents lead him out of the room.

Exterior sequences exhibit a similar analytical editing pattern. An example is the sequence that a reviewer at the time called "the best scene in the film,"[38] in which Vicente González happens to spot one of the bandits, Rubio Navarrete, walking behind him on a sidewalk:

SHOT 220 [:11] LS—González walks along the sidewalk toward the camera. Glancing back, he notices Navarrete and stops and hides behind a wall at a corner.

FIGURE 1.2. *Shot 189: Vicente González struggles with Granda in the police inspector's office. Courtesy of the Agrasanchez Archive of Mexican Cinema.*

SHOT 221 [:02] MCU—González with a revolver in his hand, waiting for Navarrete to approach.

SHOT 222 [:03] LS (same setup as shot 220)—Navarrete continues approaching.

SHOT 223 [:08] MCU—Navarrete stops at the street curb to light a cigarette.

SHOT 224 [:24] LS—González hides behind a fence as Navarrete begins walking down the sidewalk again. As Navarrete passes by, González, pistol in hand, confronts him. The two struggle and fight. When Navarrete tries to escape, González shoots him. Navarrete falls to the ground.

SHOT 225 [:07] MCU—Navarrete, with a head wound, bleeds on the sidewalk.

From experience, and probably from the study of U.S. and European films, Rosas understood and commanded a knowledge of the incipient shot-by-shot method for conveying narrative. And Rosas the cinematographer provided Rosas the editor with an appropriate array of shots to present a clear, coherent, and comprehensible film narrative.

CONTINUITY

El automóvil gris demonstrates the consistent use of shot–reverse shot editing that usually, though not always, preserves screen direction by adhering to the dramatic axis standardized by Hollywood films. But even when screen direction is reversed from one shot to the next, it is seldom disorienting, because common elements help link shots across a cut. Consider the example of shots 167 and 168, of four bandits approaching the Martel house. In shot 167, they walk at an angle toward the camera, screen right to left, and clear the frame. In shot 168, they are walking in the opposite direction—screen left to right—but the common subject (the same four bandits) and the continued motion (walking along the street at the same pace) is enough to confirm for the viewer that these are the same characters in the same location in contemporaneous time.

Eyeline Match and Point of View

Eyeline match is well utilized to maintain spatial orientation and direct viewer attention. Point of view is less well developed. The end of the just-mentioned sequence of the robbery of the Martel house is a good example of the film's use of eyeline match and point of view:

SHOT 172 [:27] MLS—The bandits are hurrying to make their getaway and load a heavy safe into the car (fig. 1.3).

SHOT 173 [:02] LS—Martel turns the corner to his street and stops when he sees *la banda* at his house, preparing to leave.

SHOT 174 [:02] MCU—Martel is shocked.

SHOT 175 [:08] LS—The gate, patio, and main entrance to Martel's house are shown, with bandits rushing out and boarding the car.

SHOT 176 [:03] MCU—Martel is astounded.

SHOT 177 [:04] MLS (same setup as shot 175)—The gang boards and rushes off in the car.

SHOT 178 [:11] LS—Martel is in the same position on the sidewalk, but the shot is from behind him, showing his home in the background as the car drives past him in the middle distance. Slight pan left as he watches the gang get away, then reframe to original shot as Martel runs toward his house.

With this sequence of shots, Rosas maintains screen direction and incorporates eyeline matching. And although the sequence does not exhibit

FIGURE 1.3. *Shot 172: The gang loads Martel's safe into the car in front of Martel's house. Courtesy of the Agrasanchez Archive of Mexican Cinema.*

classical point-of-view practice, it is not disorienting. Despite the shift in point of view in shots 175 and 177—long shots of the Martel house taken not from Martel's perspective but from a high angle directly across the street—the relationships among Martel, his house, the bandits, and the hastily loaded *automóvil gris* are clear throughout. Though plainly not from Martel's vantage point, these two shots are not jolting, because, as the only comprehensive shots of the robbery in the sequence, they provide important information.

CROSSCUTTING

As already noted, crosscutting is organically motivated by the dual protagonist structure. The best example of this is a stunning set piece, 43 shots long (shots 335–78), of an ambush of the gang by the detectives and the subsequent chase and shoot-out in the streets (figs. 1.4 and 1.5). This rousing action sequence not only cuts back and forth between the two sides but also intercuts the lovers of two of the fleeing bandits, Ernestina and

FIGURE I.4. *The beginning of the long shoot-out sequence: two bandits recognize they are stepping into a trap. Filmed at an angle. Courtesy of the Agrasanchez Archive of Mexican Cinema.*

Mercedes Gutiérrez. They wait in a nearby room at Ernestina's family's house, terrified as they listen to the gun battle raging outside.

ACTING STYLE

The acting in *El automóvil gris* is a combination of the exaggerated early-to-transitional style and the more measured classical. The former is particularly evident in the pointing and gesturing in the robbery scenes. But to be fair, even in sound films the acting in holdup scenes typically reverts to broad gestures because the bandits are demonstrating what they wish their victims to do. Much of the acting in *El automóvil gris,* however, is more restrained and is consistent with contemporary European and Hollywood cinema.[39] One indication of the naturalism of the acting is that the added dialogue still plays naturally and harmoniously with the actors' gestures.[40] A good example is the performance of the actor playing Martel in the scene in which Martel and his valet go to the police detective's office to report the robbery of his house (shots 183–85). Though the actor employs agitated gestures to show Martel's outrage, the scene is lighthearted, and his excitability is played for laughs. This is underscored by the three-part gag that ends the scene. Martel is so stirred up that he leaves and returns to the office three different times: once to give the inspector his card, once to fetch the hat he left on the inspector's desk, then finally to hand the inspector another business card, which the inspector indicates he doesn't need.

Dora Vila's performance as Ernestina is further evidence that the acting in the film conforms to established norms of the time. Vila conveys Ernestina's desperation after she has been kidnapped by a series of contained gestures and looks. This compares favorably with what was deemed sophisticated acting in contemporary Hollywood films. For example, Vila's performance, particularly the CUs in shots 40, 42, 45, and 66, is careful and subdued, falling comfortably between, for example, Mae Marsh's kinetic gesticulations in D. W. Griffith's *The Birth of a Nation* (1915) and *Intolerance* (1916) and Lillian Gish's more restrained style in Griffith's *Broken Blossoms* (1919) and *Way Down East* (1920).

FIGURE 1.5. *From the extended shoot-out sequence. Courtesy of the Agrasanchez Archive of Mexican Cinema.*

CINEMATOGRAPHY

Many of the interior shots are static and frontal, with the mise-en-scène presented for a front-row-center camera. But even these shots exhibit important, cinematically advanced features. First, the camera was positioned nearer the action, consistent with classical cinematic practice. This, together with the film's analytical editing, brings the viewer into *El automóvil gris*'s narrative space. Second, Rosas's location shooting authentically displayed depth. To further accentuate the depth of the real space and enhance the composition, Rosas often had characters walk toward or away from the camera. Third, Rosas typically used pans to capture a character's movement (as in shot 579, when the camera pans with a bandit's father as he crosses the bedroom to convince his son to give himself up to the police) or to survey a scene (as in shot 184, in which Martel is making his complaint to the police inspector, and the camera pans left to capture the expressions of Martel, his valet, and González). If Rosas's interior shots are admirable, his exterior compositions are exceptional. Outdoors, Rosas was liberated from the stiff proscenium style, and his exterior shooting exhibited all that Rosas, called "the dean of Mexican cinematographers" by a film critic at the time,[41] had learned at his craft.

An inventory of his shooting techniques is a primer of Rosas's cinematographic aesthetic.

Angled Shots

Rosas almost never shot an exterior action flat on but instinctively photographed from an angle, creating diagonal lines in the frame that suggested (or depicted) a vanishing point and made depth a crucial compositional element. That this carried over from his documentary style is revealed in the documentary execution scene, in which he photographed the condemned prisoners at an angle.

Moving Camera

Rosas understood the dynamism that moving the camera brought to a shot. Here he may have been influenced by Italian filmmakers who had made elaborate tracking shots a key element of their ebullient style.[42] Besides his favored medium shot pans mentioned above, *El automóvil gris* contains several other instances of a moving camera. The shots (410–11) showing the Mexican landscape outside the windows of a moving train as two bandits flee to

Puebla are one example. Then there is the tracking shot (197) that follows the gang along a sidewalk as they approach a victim's house. But the film's most impressive moving shot by far is a long (eighteen-second) tracking shot (157) that follows alongside the speeding gray automobile after the gang has robbed the Toranzo house and kidnapped a male servant. As the car rushes away, a group of gangsters taunt the bound servant in the backseat. The entire action is captured in a single, steady, well-composed shot.

Reframing

Even in the comparatively static interior shots, Rosas would follow action, reframe, and recompose. In shot 146, a long take in which the bandits badger Toranzo, forcing him to check a cedar chest in one part of the room, then a desk on the opposite side, the camera recomposes as it follows Toranzo and the bandits to each location, then reframes as they return to the center of the room. Rosas does the same in exterior shooting, as in shot 178, for example, discussed above, in which Martel spies the robbers outside his house.

Clearing the Frame to End a Shot

As I will demonstrate, Rosas had an excellent eye for composition, lighting, and perspective. He also grasped the importance of movement within the frame, and from frame to frame. Besides panning, he allowed the movement to empty from a stationary frame, and that became a favorite shot-ending device. This occurs in the aforementioned shot 167, of the gang gathering to rob the Martel house.

By providing two options in the shooting of moving characters—panning with the action or stopping and letting the actors clear the frame—Rosas adds variation and heightens interest. Furthermore, ending one shot with motion dynamically anticipates a matching action in the following shot. As was discussed with respect to continuity, the walking bandits who clear the frame in shot 167 flow smoothly into the same action in shot 168, despite a change in screen direction.

Composition in Depth

Clearly, Rosas understood that the most interesting frames contain information in all compositional planes: foreground, middle ground, background. Accordingly, he endeavored to compose his shots in depth whenever possible. One noteworthy interior example is shot 137, in which González gives his statement to the police in the inspector's office. In the foreground, the left edge of the composition is framed by the secretary's shoulder, in the middle distance is the inspector at his desk, and in the background is González.

Nearly every exterior scene takes advantage of the additional depth of field afforded by daylight. A memorable example is González's shooting of Navarrete (shots 220–25) discussed above, in which Rosas displays one of his favorite techniques: having characters advance toward or retreat from the camera. This becomes an important element of his mise-en-scène.

"Cinematographic" Mise-en-scène

Besides reframing by moving the camera, Rosas moved his actors to alter the nature of the shot. By blocking the actors toward (or away from) a static camera, Rosas would, for example, transform a LS into a MS (or vice versa), as exemplified by the González-Navarrete confrontation (shots 220–25), in which the actors move from an extreme long shot (ELS) to a MLS.

A marvelous example of this comes in the robbery of González's house. To get González to tell where his money is hidden, Granada and company take him out to the patio and threaten him. In a LS and in one long take (shot 126, 52 seconds), González is given an ultimatum, then blindfolded and readied for execution (fig. 1.6). Suddenly Mercadante, Granada's second-in-command, pulls Granada aside to discuss torturing González instead. Without cutting to a different shot, Rosas has them walk into the foreground—and into a MS—as they discuss the matter, while the other gangsters and González remain in the background. Once Granada agrees, they join the others, walking back into a LS. As a director, then, Rosas staged the action with both the camera and editing in mind. That is, his mise-en-scène was designed for interesting compositions and for shot variety within the same take, giving new meaning to the term "editing in the camera."

The Play between Light and Dark

Capitalizing on his extensive documentary background, Rosas was daring in his willingness to shoot in low-level lighting conditions. The risk paid

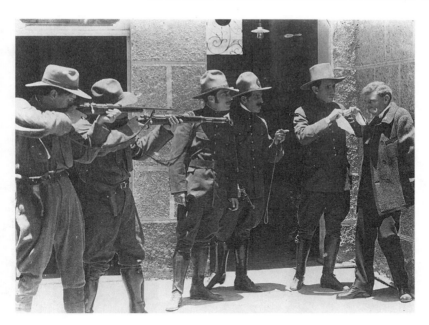

FIGURE I.6. *The gang threatens Vicente González with death. This long shot will convert to a medium shot when Granda and Mercadante (center) approach the camera. Courtesy of the Agrasanchez Archive of Mexican Cinema.*

off in a number of richly textured shots that are exceptional for the wide range of lights and shadows captured in the frame. One stunning example is of Carmen praying in a church (shot 94) that appears to be completely illuminated by natural light. Kneeling in prayer, the key light falls on her through a stained glass window to her right, the soft fill light from a single candle flame to her left.

Other examples are several establishing shots at the police station that occur throughout the film. Rosas places his camera at the near end of a short tunnel that leads from the street to the main station entrance. There his camera records the entrances of the various characters in a LS as they walk from the distant daylight of the street into the darkness of the tunnel. Approaching the camera, the characters move into a MS. Simultaneously, they pass from normal exposure into a silhouette that stands out in bold relief against the normally exposed traffic in the background. Then, as they reach the entrance, they exit the archway and fall back into normal exposure. Rosas is evidently working from the assumption that interest in the

FIGURE 1.7. *Frame within a frame: the detectives interview a witness. Courtesy of the Agrasanchez Archive of Mexican Cinema.*

shot increases as the action approaches the camera, as the figures become larger, and as the lighting on them changes. The first technique adds immediacy, the second commands viewer attention, and the third enhances visual texture.

Frames within the Frame

Another repeated technique is positioning characters within frames (doorways, windows, gate entrances, archways). In addition to mimicking the camera's framing, placing characters within a rectangle "doubles" the image, the frame within the frame (figs. 1.7 and 1.8), efficiently directing viewer attention and accentuating depth. Though this technique is not by any means as well developed or as extensively used as it would later be in sound films, its appearance so early in Mexican cinema is noteworthy. The most prominent examples are the various tunnel shots of different characters approaching the police station, discussed above.

Long Takes

The use of long takes probably stemmed from Rosas' documentary background, in which part of the drama of recording real events is seeing them play out in real time. In *El automóvil gris,* Rosas's rule of thumb was that detailed information (MSs and CUs) were given less time than establishing LSs. In analytically edited scenes, for example, the briefer shots (3–4 seconds) were typically MSs and CUs, and the longer and very long takes were LSs. Examples of lengthy LSs are the bandits' threatening to kill González in his patio (shot 126, 52 seconds), the tracking shot of the escaping car (shot 157, 18 seconds), the loading of Martel's safe into the car (shot 172, 27 seconds), the González-Navarrete fight (shot 224, 24 seconds), and the theft of the search warrants from the police detective's desk by Granada's accomplice (shot 186, 1:08). Combining the long take with a moving camera and composition in depth, Rosas creates an intricate, unbounded diegetic world. In it, narrative action has the potential to extend spatially

FIGURE 1.8. *Frame within a frame: as one of the bandits is arrested, his father and wife watch from the background. Courtesy of the Agrasanchez Archive of Mexican Cinema.*

beyond the "here" (into the distance with deep focus photography; into off-screen space with camera movement) and temporally beyond the "now" (with the long take, the content at the end of a shot is as a rule very different from its beginning).

Incorporation of Local Color

Rosas was not only a gifted filmmaker but also an experienced showman who knew how to attract a crowd. The enduring success of Mexican documentaries, several of which he filmed, promoted, and exhibited (he had projected films in *carpas* [theatrical tent shows] as early as 1899, and he opened his own nickelodeon in 1908),[43] confirmed one thing: Mexican audiences liked seeing Mexico on the screen. Thus *El automóvil gris* included sequences shot in Puebla, Ápam, and Almoloya, as police tracked down fleeing gang members. While some of these scenes were motivated by the facts of the case, others, particularly an extended, to-the-death cock fight near the end of the film, seem to be included mainly for their value as Mexican spectacle. In the bargain, such scenes helped validate local folkways and boost national pride. As early Mexican cinema struggled to differentiate itself from Hollywood and European film, such sequences stamped *El automóvil gris* as uniquely *mexicano*.

The Legacy of *El automóvil gris*

As has been said, the film was an immediate, unqualified, and unprecedented popular success. But perhaps a surer sign of its stylistic maturity was the critical acclaim it garnered in its time. Silvestre Bonnard (Carlos Noriega Hope), the astute film reviewer for *El Universal,* was thoroughly impressed by the film, commenting that it augured well for the future of Mexican filmmaking. Comparing it with other—and in his mind lesser—recent Mexican films, he singled out its "splendid cinematography" and ended his review by saying that he looked forward to Rosas's producing the definitive Mexican film in the future.[44]

But that was not to be. Rosas died on 20 August 1920, without directing another film, and *El automóvil gris* would have to stand as his definitive filmmaking statement. It was certainly up to the task, and its impact was unmistakable. To Juan Bustillo Oro, a prolific director of Mexico's Golden Age cinema (he scripted the early Revolutionary sound film *El compadre Mendoza* [1933], and directed, among many others, the hit Cantinflas comedy *Ahí está el detalle* [1940] and the classic family melodrama *Cuando los hijos se van* [1941]), Rosas's film was an "everlasting triumph."[45] More recently, *El automóvil gris* has been called the most notable movie of its time, a singular film that surpassed all the cinema that preceded it.[46] And in the introduction to their *Filmografía general del cine mexicano (1906–1931)*, historians Federico Davalos Orozco and Esperanza Vazquez Bernal call *El automóvil gris* "the most ambitious and perhaps the most important [Mexican] film of the silent era."[47]

But besides being an impressive example of early Mexican filmmaking, the film also sheds light on the complex nature of media dependency in the development of Third World cinemas. In the case of Mexico, *El automóvil gris* reveals a robust mix of native creativity with foreign influence, rather than the crushing result of First World cultural imperialism. Indeed, this study demonstrates how deterministic and oversimplified media imperialism theory can be.[48] As we have seen, Enrique Rosas was not simply copying the emerging Hollywood paradigm nor the declining European ones. On the contrary, this analysis of Rosas's poetics argues from internal evidence that this experienced documentary filmmaker was no doubt influenced by Italian cinema's exuberance, the jaunty unpretentiousness of French crime serials, and Hollywood's narrative economy. And Rosas combined these influences in such a way that *El automóvil gris* became far more than the derivative sum of its parts—it was the first dawning of Mexico's unique cinematic classicism.

Notes

I thank the UCLA Film and Television Archive for allowing me the opportunity to view and study this film.

Unless otherwise noted, translations from Spanish texts are the author's.

1. Emilio García Riera, *Historia del cine mexicano* (Mexico City: Secretaría de Educación Pública, 1986), 45.

2. Gabriel Ramírez, *Crónica del cine mudo mexicano* (Mexico City: Cineteca Nacional, 1989), 117.

3. Aurelio de los Reyes, *Cine y sociedad en México 1896–1930: Vivar de sueños* (Mexico City: Universidad Nacional Autónoma de México, 1983), 245; Federico Serrano and Antonio Noyola, "Nota a *El automóvil gris*," in *El automóvil gris* (Mexico City: Cuadernos de la Cineteca Nacional, no. 10, 1981), 10.

4. The prologue title card reads as follows: "The story that is presented here takes place in the same locations where the events actually took place. The scenes of the robberies, the homes where the criminals lived, and the locations where they were apprehended or where they confessed their guilt are rigorously authentic. The action takes place in 1915."

5. Aurelio de los Reyes, *Medio siglo de cine mexicano (1896–1947)* (Mexico City: Editorial Trillas, 1987), 75–76.

6. *Excelsior,* 25 January 1920, rpt. in Luis Reyes de la Maza, *Salon Rojo (programas y crónicas del cine mudo en México), vol. 1 (1895–1920),* Cuadernos de Cine no. 16 (Mexico City: Dirección General de Difusión Cultural, UNAM, 1968), 230. The newspaper *El Universal* reported on 11 December 1919 that on the opening day of the film in Mexico City, it premiered at eighteen theaters; rpt. in Helena Almoina, *Notas para la historia del cine en México (1896–1925), vol. 2* (Mexico City: Colección Documentos de Filmoteca, UNAM, 1980), 100. Ramírez reports that on one afternoon after its premiere it showed at 23 theaters; Ramírez, *Crónica del cine mudo,* 119.

7. Emilio García Riera and Fernando Macotela, *La guia del cine mexicano: De la pantalla grande a la televisión* (Mexico City: Editorial Patria, 1984), 36; Ramírez, *Crónica del cine mudo,* 121.

8. De los Reyes, *Cine y sociedad,* 256; Federico Davalos Orozco and Esperanza Vazquez Bernal, *Filmografía general del cine mexicano (1906–1931)* (Puebla: Universidad Autónoma de Puebla, 1985), 55–56.

9. I have written about the thematic darkness that pervades sound-era Revolutionary films. See my discussion of a classic film of the genre, *Vámonos con Pancho Villa,* in *Cinema of Solitude: A Critical Study of Mexican Film, 1967–1983* (Austin: University of Texas Press, 1992), 201–2. David Maciel has recently argued that one of the defining features of Mexican filmmaking of the late 1980s and 1990s is that its filmmakers have at long last been able to shake off this languishing postrevolutionary guilt. See his "El imperio de la fortuna: Mexico's Contemporary Cinema, 1985–1992," in *The Mexican Cinema Project,* ed. Chon A. Noriega and Steven Ricci (Los Angeles, CA: UCLA Film and Television Archive, 1994), 33–44.

10. For a discussion of the state's support of Mexico's Golden Age cinema, see my *Cinema of Solitude,* pp. 12–15; for the effect it had on the Golden Age's decline, see pp. 37–42; for an account of state support in the postclassical era, see pp. 44–54. See also Maciel, "El imperio de la fortuna."

11. Kristin Thompson, "From Primitive to Classical," in *The Classical Hollywood Cinema: Film Style and Mode of Production to 1960,* ed. David Bordwell, Janet Staiger, and Kristin Thompson (New York: Columbia University Press, 1985), 159–60. See also Eileen Bowser, "The Films: Alternate Scenes," chapter 4 in her study of early cinema, *The Transformation of Cinema: 1907–1915* (New York: Charles Scribner's Sons, 1990).

12. De los Reyes, *Medio siglo,* 36.

13. De los Reyes, *Cine y sociedad,* 202.

14. For example, an early Mexican film critic, Silvestre Bonnard (Carlos Noriega Hope), asked that Mexico's Department of Censorship step up its protests of Hollywood's anti-Mexican filmmaking. See "La censura de las películas cinematográficas ¡Es necesario hacer algo!" ("Film Censorship: It's Time to Do

Something!"), published in *El Universal,* 17 February 1920; rpt. in Almoina, *Notas para la historia del cine,* 132–35. See also an unsigned, undated article, presumably published in a Mexico City newspaper in 1920, that complained about the denigrating representation of Mexico in U.S. films; rpt. in Reyes de la Maza, *Salon Rojo,* 227–28.

15. De los Reyes, *Medio siglo,* 66; de los Reyes, *Cine y sociedad,* 204.

16. Both de los Reyes, *Medio siglo,* 20, and Carl J. Mora, *Mexican Cinema: Reflections of a Society, 1896–1980* (Berkeley: University of California Press, 1982), 16, have termed the period of Mexican filmmaking from 1915 to 1923 the Silent Golden Age. This is not to be confused with the Classical Golden Age, which lasted roughly from 1936 to 1956.

17. Davalos Orozco and Vazquez Bernal, *Filmografía general del cine,* 25–52. See also Moisés Viñas, *Índice cronológico del cine mexicano* (Mexico City: Dirección General de Actividades Cinematográficas, Universidad Nacional Autónoma de México, 1992).

18. Aurelio de los Reyes comments on the difficulty of ascertaining the initiation of the project in *Cine y sociedad,* 245.

19. However, other opportunistic criminals are suspected of having imitated the method of *la banda del automóvil gris,* and similar robberies probably occurred during the nine-month period. Even after six members of the gang were executed, some copycat crimes were reported.

Except where noted, this section summarizes the historical research published by Aurelio de los Reyes in the chapter entitled "Gangsters contra charros" ("Gangsters versus Cowboys") in *Cine y sociedad,* 174–91.

20. See Ricardo Pozas Horcasitas, "Del infierno al purgatorio, del fin de la dictadura a la promesa de la democracia (1910–1920)," in *Filmoteca 1: El cine y la revolución mexicana* (November 1979), 4–21; Jan Bazant, *A Concise History of Mexico: From Hidalgo to Cárdenas, 1805–1940* (Cambridge: Cambridge University Press, 1979), 123–46; Anita Brenner, *The Wind That Swept Mexico*, 2nd ed. (Austin: University of Texas Press, 1971), 3–61.

21. According to published accounts, the robberies were extremely lucrative for the thieves, netting them jewels, clothes, and cash. At one house, they took 200,000 pesos, at another 78,000 pesos' worth of bank notes. But the assaults could turn extremely violent. Just after midnight on 25 May, for example, Manuel Taliabue surprised two gang members as they were about to break into a house. They killed Taliabue, robbed him, and proceeded to enter the house. There they murdered a young boy in front of his mother and sister. See de los Reyes, *Cine y sociedad,* 176–77.

22. Ramírez, *Crónica del cine mudo,* 117. Five years after the crimes, and after the opening of the film, Higinio Granda declared that he had not acted alone in committing the crimes, and that "high officials" had been his accomplices; de los Reyes, *Cine y sociedad,* 243.

23. Kristin Thompson and David Bordwell, *Film History: An Introduction*

(New York: McGraw-Hill, 1994), 58. According to Davalos Orozco and Vazquez Bernal, *Filmografía general del cine,* 30–40, all five of the Derba-Rosas films were "in the Italian style."

24. De los Reyes, *Cine y sociedad,* 202–8; Davalos Orozco and Vazquez Bernal, *Filmografía general del cine,* 18–19, 33–48.

25. Ramos was one of the most prolific screenwriters of Mexican silent cinema. Among his credits are *Tepeyac* (1917), *Confesión trágica* (1919), *Viaje redondo* (1919), *Hasta después de la muerte* (1919), *El zarco* (1920), *Carmen* (1920), *Amnesia* (1921), and *La parcela* (1921). He even adapted the script for the film that competed with *El automóvil gris,* called *La banda del automóvil (La dama enlutada).* See Serrano and Noyola, "Nota a *El automóvil gris,"* 11, 14.

26. See de los Reyes, *Cine y sociedad,* 245–46. Likewise, the credit page for the film in the published screenplay gives Rosas sole credit as director; see *El automóvil gris* (Cuadernos de la Cineteca Nacional, no. 10, 1981), 119.

27. García Riera, *Historia del cine mexicano,* 46.

28. De los Reyes, *Cine y sociedad,* 247–56.

29. Ramírez, *Crónica del cine mudo,* 118–19. Rosas's choice to make a serial rather than a feature in the first place may seem unusual today, but for more than a decade after the inception of the form in 1913, the serial was extremely popular. In 1922, for example, 35 percent of movie theaters in the United States were exhibiting them. See Anthony Slide, *Early American Cinema* (Cranbury, N.J.: Barnes, 1970), 157–70; and Richard Koszarski, *An Evening's Entertainment: The Age of the Silent Feature Picture, 1915–1928* (New York: Charles Scribner's Sons: 1990), 164–66. Moreover, a serial is sensible in that it was a useful bridge between the short film and the feature (p. 164). For an international perspective on silent serials, see "The Brief Heyday of the Serial," in Thompson and Bordwell, *Film History,* 61–62.

30. De los Reyes, *Cine y sociedad,* 246–47; on Ramos's participation, see note 25. See the various announcements for and newspaper criticism of the film in Almoina, *Notas para la historia del cine,* 59–72.

31. De la Maza, *Salon Rojo,* 215–16; Ramírez, *Crónica del cine mudo,* 114.

32. See Kristin Thompson's chapters 14–17 and David Bordwell's chapters 1–7 in Bordwell, Staiger, and Thompson, *The Classical Hollywood Cinema.*

33. I will refrain from using "primitive" to describe the first phase of Mexican cinema because, besides implying an uncritical notion of progress, the word denotes not just "early" but "crude." In the case of Mexican cinema, this was not always the case in the period 1896–1915. Most of the films made during that time were documentaries, and based on the ones that survive, some of them were fairly accomplished films. I prefer to think of this stage of Mexican cinema as simply the initial period, without assigning a priori aesthetic value to it as compared with later stages.

34. An impressionistic insight into one Mexican viewer's estimation of Ital-

ian silent cinema may be found in director Juan Bustillo Oro's memoirs, *Vida cinematográfica* (Mexico City: Cineteca Nacional, 1984), 33–35. Among the more memorable elements of silent Italian cinema noted by Bustillo Oro were the "idyllic and sometimes licentious" stories, the historical spectacle of early epics such as *The Last Days of Pompeii* (1913), *Quo Vadis?* (1913), and *Cabiria* (1914), and the beauty of Italian film actresses. Another way to gauge the impact on Mexican cinema is to note that many of the films produced in Mexico in 1917, the first year of sustained Mexican narrative filmmaking, were inspired by Italian melodramas. The first Mexican narrative feature, *La luz* (*The Light,* 1917) was a remake of the Italian film *Il fouco.* In addition, the five Rosas-Derba films made that year were in the "Italian style." See Davalos Orozco and Vazquez Bernal, *Filmografía general del cine,* 30–40.

However, both Italian and French films were popular in Mexico in the 1910s, though their prominence gradually gave way to Hollywood cinema, especially during and after World War I. Bustillo Oro imagined a "battle" between Italian and French cinemas over the Mexican movie market. According to him, the French cinema dominated the marketplace early in the decade, until Italian spectacles and melodramas rose in popularity. The French "countered" with detective serials such as Feuillade's. The prominence of both French and Italian cinema in Mexico is evident in the newspaper accounts of the day and is chronicled in both de la Maza's and Almoina's compilations.

35. "El automóvil gris: Argumento original," in *El automóvil gris* (Cuadernos de la Cineteca Nacional, no. 10, 1981), 19–57.

36. In designating individual shots, I will refer to the shot numbers given in the published script, *El automóvil gris* (Cuadernos de la Cineteca Nacional, no. 10, 1981), 59–117.

37. Since I viewed a video copy of this film to prepare this article, I could not count actual film frames. Therefore, I could not make precise determinations of shot length. The lengths that I offer were made with a real-time counter, however, and, though approximate, are probably accurate ± 1 second.

38. Silvestre Bonnard, *"El automóvil gris"* (review) in *El Universal,* 13 December 1919, rpt. in Almoina, *Notas para la historia del cine,* 103.

39. David Cook comments on the relatively restrained acting of the Italian silent cinema. See his *A History of Narrative Film* (New York: W. W. Norton and Co., 1990), 60.

40. García Riera disagrees, saying that the addition of sound frequently made the actions look ridiculous and the acting look theatrical; *Historia del cine mexicano,* 47.

41. Bonnard, *"El automóvil gris,"* 102.

42. Commenting on camera movement in silent Italian cinema, Kristin Thompson and David Bordwell note that *Cabiria*'s tracking shots were the most influential of the period. Slow tracking shots became common elements in cinema of the mid-1910s and were known as *"Cabiria* movements." See

Thompson and Bordwell, *Film History,* 58. See also Pierre Leprohon, *The Italian Cinema* (New York: Praeger Publishers, 1972), 31, and Cook, *A History of Narrative Film,* 59–60.

43. "Enrique Rosas: Nota biofilmográfica," in *El automóvil gris* (Cuadernos de la Cineteca Nacional, no. 10, 1981), 121.

44. Bonnard, *"El automóvil gris,"* 103.

45. Juan Bustillo Oro, *Vida cinematográfica* (Mexico City: Cineteca Nacional, 1984), 44.

46. Ramírez, *Crónica del cine mudo,* 121.

47. Davalos Orozco and Vazquez Bernal, *Filmografía general del cine,* 19.

48. This view is elaborated in Ella Shohat and Robert Stam, *Unthinking Eurocentrism: Multiculturalism and the Media* (New York: Routledge, 1994), 27–31.

2

Crossing Nations and Genres

TRAVELING FILMMAKERS

Ana M. López

■ ■ ■ ■

Within the general trajectory of Latin American filmmaking, the big moment of pan-continental travel and collaboration is generally said to have happened with the New Latin American Cinema in the 1960s. As this accepted historical narrative would have it, filmmakers who had been working independently to produce "new" cinemas in their respective countries began to meet on foreign and Latin American soil, to share ideas, and to think of themselves as a united—if not necessarily unified—movement. Thus under the banner of the new cinema movements and the new national cinemas of the 1960s (especially Cuba's), intercontinental cinematic collaborations were heralded as one of the central strategies of the new pan–Latin American movement. Even in this period, however, although there was indeed much cinematic collaboration among the various Latin American nations, the tendency of most film histories has been to treat the cinemas of each nation as discrete phenomena, framed primarily by the sociopolitical vagaries of each state and only incidentally linked to continental social changes and movements.[1]

Thus it is hardly surprising that the ostensibly far more insular "classical" or "Golden Age" cinemas of Latin America produced in the 1930s, 1940s, and 1950s have also been understood primarily as discrete national phenomena. Although historians have recognized and analyzed these cinemas' susceptibility to shifts in international politics and economics (for example, the oft-cited U.S. embargo of raw film stock shipments to Argentina during World War II and the Spanish Civil War) and the effect of the presence of Hollywood and other imports upon local markets and production, the classical cinemas have nevertheless been analyzed as circumscribed primarily by state cinema policies and national cultural characteristics. Thus most histories and analyses (in English, Spanish, and/or Portuguese) of this period of Latin American filmmaking have dealt almost exclusively with the national forces and players that shaped the "national" cinema.[2]

This focus on nation has unfortunately obscured important intercontinental forces in the classical period. Although not defined by the unified ideology of a pan-continental social movement like the New Latin American Cinema, the classic cinemas were also marked by often intense and significant agenda and standard-setting transnational cross-fertilizations. The most obvious evidence of these cross-fertilizations are the coproductions among Latin American producers that became de rigueur in the 1950s but existed as early as the 1940s. Most often engineered through the Mexican or Argentine industries, these films have a curious status: in Mexican and Argentine film histories they tend to be included, although designated as inferior works, whereas in "other" contemporary national histories (for example, accounts of pre-Revolutionary Cuban film) they are, with few exceptions, highlighted as indigenous achievements and as evidence of the energy and potential of the nascent local cinema industry.

Although less evident than the recognized coproductions, traveling film personnel also provided for rich transnational exchanges. Of course, it goes without saying that Latin American filmmaking was profoundly influenced by travel across the Rio Grande. For example, many of the sound cinema pioneers of Latin America—especially from Mexico—learned the craft in the United States, especially in the days of the "Hispanic" cinema boom in the late 1920s and early 1930s. Although many only appeared as extras in "Hispanic" films or worked within the industry in secondary roles (assistants, makeup artists, translators, etc.), they later returned home bitten by the cinematographic bug and went on to produce the "national" cinema: Emilio Fernández, Gabriel Soria, Miguel Zacarías, Alejandro Galindo, Alberto Gout, Chano Urueta, Raphael Sevilla, Fernando Méndez, Raúl de Anda, Gilberto Martínez Solares, René Cardona, Tito Davison, and others.[3] In Mexico, *Santa* (1931), the first successful national sound film, was produced by a compendium of Hollywood-trained talent: director Antonio Moreno had worked in a number of silent films and early talkies, actress Lupita Tovar had also worked in silent films and starred in the Spanish-language version of *Dracula,* Donald Reed (aka Ernesto Guillén) was a silent film actor, the Russian-born cinematographer Alex Phillips had already worked on many Hollywood silent features and had been Greg Toland's assistant. In fact, Alex Phillips, like many other expatriates, arrived in Mexico in this period to stay and became one the most celebrated cinematographers of the Mexican cinema, with hundreds of films to his credit. Like Phillips, other U.S. expatriates joined the nascent industry, crossing the Rio

Grande in the "wrong" direction: David Kirkland, John H. Auer, Robert Curwood, Robert O'Quigley, Jack Lauron Draper, Ross Fisher. Others like Paul Strand traveled to Mexico for short periods or for specific projects, such as Strand's work for *Redes* (*Nets,* 1934).

But travel across the Atlantic was also fruitful: some of the most celebrated cinematographic travelers to Latin America came from Europe. Sergei Eisenstein's trip to Mexico in 1930 left a significant imprint upon the nascent Mexican cinema, and Luis Buñuel's extended and productive stay continues to be the source of much debate. Alberto Cavalcanti's sojourn in Brazil as director of the Vera Cruz Studios in São Paulo in the late 1940s and the 1950s, although less discussed, was no less significant. The Vera Cruz experience—the failure of high-budget studio-based filmmaking in Brazil—gave rise to important debates about the national cinema in the mid- to late 1950s that set the stage for the emergence of the Cinema Novo movement.

Despite the fascination of these already fairly well tracked international trails, what interests me most is the history of *intra*continental travel and cinematic exchanges in this period: that is, the effect and influences of filmmakers and actors who traveled within Latin America and participated in collaborative film projects with nations other than the one with which they were professionally affiliated. The issue of intracontinental influences in the classical period is not only a fascinating historical puzzle but also one that questions the viability of the "national" as the signpost of classical Latin American film histories by highlighting the hybridization inherent to all national cinemas. Against the prevailing myth of national cinematic insularity and histories of national achievements and failures, I want to argue for the need to look at the history of Latin American cinema from a continental perspective that includes, but mediates, the national. This will require an analysis of official international agreements and collaborations but, more important, much research into the networks of intellectual and cinematic exchanges established unofficially through interpersonal relationships and work-related travel. Thus, in this context, the figure of the traveling filmmaker—and the foreigner's gaze—as a site for tracing the mediation of nation is potentially a key for opening up a space for transnational analyses of the classic Latin American cinema.

Of the intracontinental travelers I have been able to track down, Carlos Hugo Christensen stands out because of the persistence of his pan-national efforts. He began his filmmaking career as a very young man in Argentina in the 1940s, worked in Chile and Venezuela, and ended up settling in Brazil in the mid-1950s, where he thrived despite his relative marginalization from the emergent (and later institutionally powerful) Cinema Novo crowd.

Christensen began his film career at a time of great growth for Latin American cinema. Both the Argentine and Mexican cinemas were thriving, having totally eclipsed the Spanish cinema (in crisis because of the civil war) in the internationally strong Spanish-language market: in 1940 there were 5,160 movie theaters in Latin America—Brazil had 1,450, Argentina 1,021, Mexico 823, and Cuba 375. Of the 17,829 theaters in the United States, 360 regularly played Spanish-language films.[4] In Brazil the sound industry had found a firm commercial footing with carnival-inspired variety films and comedies. Simultaneously and inspired especially by the Mexican and Argentine examples, other nations had begun their efforts to produce national cinemas in the late 1930s and continued to do so—with various degrees of success—throughout the early 1940s (Peru, Uruguay, Cuba, Chile, Venezuela).

In Argentina, although there were approximately thirty functioning production companies (in 1942), most filmmaking revolved around two studios: Argentina Sono Films, the oldest, and Lumiton, founded in 1932 by three radio pioneers.[5] In the early 1930s, both studios produced an essentially "popular" cinema, with great emphasis on tangos and popular singers, melodramas set in the *arrabales* (popular neighborhoods), and populist comedy. Lumiton became well known for its tightly knit technical and artistic teams, quick production schedules, and efficient—if not minimal—budgets.[6] In this period, its principal director was Manuel Romero. Firmly convinced of the commercial potential of the new industry and attempting to attract middle-class and upper-class audiences, which disdained the national cinema, in the late 1930s Lumiton began to focus on more-sophisticated subject matter and settings, producing a more romantic "bourgeois" cinema and highlighting the work of director Francisco Mugica.[7] When Christensen directed his first film for Lumiton in 1940, the studio was again searching for new models and subject matter, still with an eye to the more elite sectors of the audience but also looking to make further inroads internationally via "universal" stories and styles.

In the mid-1940s, Christensen presented Lumiton with a viable option: explicit sexuality in either comedic or melodramatic scenarios. His 1943 film *Safo: Historia de una pasión* (*Safo: Story of a Passion,* 1943), a melodrama about a young boy enslaved by the sexual power of a much older prostitute, is credited for introducing "the erotic" into the Argentine cinema. It was an immediate success, transforming Roberto Escalada, the male lead, into an overnight star and consolidating the career of Mecha Ortiz, who played the prostitute. The film played for more than a year in Buenos Aires and was widely seen throughout the continent. In 1944, Christensen's *La pequeña señora de Pérez* (*Little Mrs. Perez*, 1944) duplicated the success of *Safo* in the realm of comedy. Thus began what Argentine historian Domingo di Núbila has handily dubbed the "Christensen era" at Lumiton.

However, alongside Christensen's successes, the Argentine industry was beginning to feel the effects of the war and the U.S. embargo on raw film stock imports. Although the studios set up a film black market (through third countries, especially Chile and Uruguay), the high costs of these transactions led to production cutbacks: from a high of fifty films in 1940, production dropped to a low of twenty-three in 1945. Despite stentorian efforts to control production costs (via even tighter production budgets and frenetic schedules), Lumiton had to cut back severely. Meanwhile, the Mexican industry had quickly filled in the gap in the international market created by the decrease in Argentine production. After the war, the Argentine industry was also affected by Juan Perón's rise to the presidency in 1946 and the subsequent political polarization of the nation. The cinema was placed under the jurisdiction of the Subsecretaría de Informaciones y Prensa de la Presidencia de la Nación (a sort of ministry of propaganda) and its director, Raúl Alejandro Apold, who subsequently became known as the "cinema czar." As a result of Apold's tight control over scripts and all facets of production and of modifications of the state protection laws between 1947 and 1950, the industry changed greatly in character, several studios closed (Lumiton stopped producing in 1952), and many actors and directors left to pursue their careers elsewhere (most notably, Libertad Lamarque, whose hostile relationship with Eva Perón led to her departure for Mexico in 1946).

While Mexico still had the strongest and most far-reaching cinema after the war, the overall market for Latin American films had begun to contract. Hollywood had very quickly reestablished its absolute dominance over all international markets, including the Spanish-language one, and all Latin American producers faced stiffer competition. Nevertheless, other Latin American nations—still awed by the accomplishments of the Mexican and Argentine industries in the 1930s and early 1940s—remained eager to tap into what was still perceived as a potentially lucrative and prestigious "national" enterprise. In these instances, state support for industrial development was often made available. Thus in 1946, Christensen was invited to direct in Chile by the recently established state-funded national producer Chile Films, initiating his continental filmmaking with *La dama de la muerte* (*The Lady of Death,* 1946). Accustomed to the industrial limitations of working for Lumiton, Christensen recalls that he was shocked by how Chile Films did business:

> The Chile Films studios were more modern than the Argentine and were excellently equipped. The personnel was also very professional. But they spent too much money: the manager used to come to work in the morning in a nineteenth century horse-drawn carriage.[8]

Christensen's assessment of the inefficiency of the Chile Films setup is shared by Chilean film historian Alicia de la Vega, who dismisses this period of "importing talent" to build a national industry—of the nine films produced, only two were directed by Chileans while Argentines directed the remaining seven—as a "complete failure" because of poor scripts, the imported talent (which did not include big-name recognizable stars), the attempt to "internationalize" the content, and excessive production budgets.[9] It is interesting to note that Chile Films had contracted with Argentina Sono Films for "commercial, administrative, and technical" advice and that its model of studio organization, already causing difficulties nationally, was hardly appropriate for the Chilean scenario.[10] Although *La dama de la muerte* was among the best-received of the studio's films, contemporary critics in the weeklies *Ecran* and *Ercilla* regularly lambasted all the Chile Films productions for the lack of "Chilean-ness resulting from their pancontinental creative and technical crews."[11] In this instance, then, the national context ostensibly precluded the "traveler's gaze" from even being heralded as a contribution to the formation of a national cinema, although the period decidedly merits further research on just this account.

Shortly thereafter, following the extraordinary success of *El angel desnudo* (*The Naked Angel,* 1946), which featured the first female nude of the Argentine cinema and transformed Olza Zubarry into its first "sexy" star, Christensen was once again invited to travel and encountered a vastly different scenario. His description of this experience provides interesting insights about the paradoxes of the formation of a national film industry:

> Some Venezuelans came to Lumiton and invited me to work at new studios that would be inaugurated with my film. They said that they wanted to develop a *Venezuelan* cinema and were willing to go to great lengths to achieve their objective. According to them, they had everything there. So, I went. Although the studios existed, there was nothing in them. I remember that I said to them, "But you said you had everything!" And they responded, "If we had told you the truth, you would not have come."

Then, the owner of the studio, Villegas Blanco, told me to make a list of what they needed to import. Lights, cameras, everything necessary to make a feature-length film was brought in *by air*! Since there was no technical infrastructure, I brought technicians in from *Argentina*.[12]

The studio that brought Christensen to Venezuela was Bolivar Films. Owner Villegas Blanco had purchased the equipment and studios of Condor Films (a firm started in 1940 by Rafael María Zambrano that had produced only two films before disappearing in 1942), then had contracted with the state to produce documentary, publicity, and newsreel shorts. Gradually, the company forged important alliances with other smaller producers and distributors until, in 1948–1950, it came to be perceived as the preeminent national producer and received funding from the state to finance feature-length fictional projects.

Why was the Venezuelan state interested in fostering a national cinema at this particular conjuncture? For one thing, after the 1945 coup, there had been a concerted movement to define a singular national identity. Echoing the foundational work of the characters of Rómulo Gallegos's novel *Doña Bárbara* (1929), who embody and act out the struggle between a primitive and violent past (Doña Bárbara) and the modernizing force of civilization (Santos Luzardo), the national culture was identified with the attributes of a subsector of the nation: the culture of the llano, or plains, with its mythical *llanero*-cowboys wearing spats and boots, and peasants shod in espadrilles. Within this paradigm, a national cinema was perceived as a modernizing force, but one that could still highlight the cultural elements being promulgated in other cultural realms as the marks of national identity.[13] In the period 1948–1958, the decade of the dictatorship (and especially after dictator Pérez Jiménez took over in 1950), this tendency was exacerbated: the officially promulgated *nuevo ideal nacional* included as one of its central dimensions an explicit celebration of folkloricism—especially the image of the *llanero* as the essence of national culture.

Christensen's second project for Bolivar films, the feature *La balandra Isabel llegó esta tarde* (*The Isabel Arrived This Afternoon,* 1949) was, in many ways, a perfect synthesis of the Venezuelan state's cultural and national agenda. As an adaptation of Venezuelan writer Guillermo de Meneses' 1934 short story of the same title, it was by default positioned as a celebration of national culture. Although Meneses would fall from grace during the decade of the dictatorship, in the late 1940s he was recognized as one of the principal voices of the national literature. His work in this period, including "La balandra Isabel," followed the realist tradition of Gallegos but with a difference. While Gallegos's positivist foundational fictions used the "local" referent—that is, regional settings and characters—as a source of national stability and an access to universal values, Meneses' work reconfigured similarly folkloric referents within radically unstable fictional universes. His focus on the power of sexuality to determine and drive human action and, even more significantly, his fascination with Afro-Venezuelan culture (rather than rural *llanero* culture), simultaneously marked his work with a "new" vanguard spirit while celebrating—and exoticizing—some of the most traditional, yet mysterious, aspects of the national imaginary. Much more indebted to Freud and Bergson than to nineteenth-century positivism, Meneses' fictions are peopled with characters who are adrift in, rather than grounded by, their regionality. Thus refigured as liminality, the regional/folkloric gives rise to doubts and uncertainties that threaten the social and psychic integrity of the individual. Having already been adapted for the stage in 1943 by Meneses himself, "La balandra Isabel" was thus positioned as a perfect symbol of a new Venezuelan national cultural identity.

Adapted to the screen by another Venezuelan writer, Aquiles Nazoa, and Christensen himself, the film version of *La balandra Isabel* pulled together a literary work of recognized national importance whose subject matter also addressed those folkloric elements in the forefront of official definitions of the nation, and with the same exoticizing impulse. *La balandra Isabel* was the most talked-about and awarded film of the period. Billed as the first Venezuelan "super-production," the film and its production were widely publicized. That its budget of 900,000 bolivares (approximately U.S.$270,000) was "suicidal" and almost double that of any other previous Venezuelan production was in itself a guarantee of prestige seconded only by the fame of the Mexican actor Arturo de Córdova, who received the then unheard-of salary of $10,000 per week.[14] *La balandra Isabel* was widely heralded as the beginning of the national film industry. For example, Miguel Otero Silva in the newspaper *El Nacional* claimed that the film was "a revelation for natives and foreigners of all the grandeur and potential that the Venezuelan cinema can achieve." He went on to say:

> Can a cinematography like this be ignored or stagnate? A nation that produces a film like *La balandra Isabel* will not remain on the margins and has the duty to continue offering us such works of art.[15]

The film's pan-national cast—not only Arturo de Córdova but also the Argentine actress Virginia Luque and a host of other secondary characters—and genesis disappeared under the pressure to highlight its foundational characteristics, especially after the film won the best cinematography award at the Cannes Film Festival for the work of its Spanish-born cinematographer José María Beltrán.

Of course, exoticizing the nation via folklore as a strategy for foundational national cinemas had already proven to be a viable strategy in Latin America, as the success of the Mexican *ranchera* genre had proven in the late 1930s. Here, however, more than a decade later, joined to the focus on sexuality in Meneses' story and to Christensen's already-established reputation as a "sexy" director, the folkloric nation is reinscribed as a locus for desire and a melodramatic engine. Rather than focus upon couple formation—the family romance—within a folkloric allegory of the nation, *La balandra Isabel* invokes the folkloric as an explicitly erotic subtext tinged with foreignness and with the potential to destabilize the family and the nation.

In the best Latin American melodramatic tradition, *La balandra Isabel* tells the story of Segundo, a captain from Isla Margarita who owns the ship *La Isabel.* Happily married and with a preadolescent son who is eager to follow in his seafaring footsteps, Segundo is introduced as a stable patriarchal figure with great authority. But when he goes off to sea, we discover that he is in fact unstable and obsessed by a powerful sexy woman, Esperanza, with whom he spends time in the port town of La Guaira. Esperanza wants Segundo to herself, and when her own sexual wiles seem insufficient to the task, she engages the help of Bocú, an Afro-Cuban / Venezuelan *santero* who puts a spell on Segundo to force him to return. The spell works. Segundo, even though accompanied by his son on this particular trip, is drawn inexorably to Esperanza, until he discovers that she is betraying him with Bocú. After he fights with Bocú, the power of the spell and of Esperanza's sexuality are dispelled and he is able to return to his son and his ship and to head home to Isla Margarita, his wife, and a "normal" social order.

To read *La balandra Isabel* simultaneously as foundational for the national cinema and through the lens of a traveling filmmaker is thus especially apropos, because the film is itself, in part, about traveling. Furthermore, both impulses, although ostensibly contradictory, find cinematic expression in a similar kind of formal gesture: a double-voicedness or dual focus that mediates the melodramatic through an appeal to the documentary power of the image and its potential ethnographic truth.

The film begins with a documentary-like move. The credits are superimposed upon a freeze-frame of waves violently crashing on a jagged rock and accompanied by dramatic orchestral scoring that approximates the sound of the ocean. Following the director's name, the frozen image is animated and dissolves into a sailboat upon which a rather crudely drawn map of northern Venezuela is superimposed. On the upper half of the map is Isla Margarita, and while the camera slowly reframes to center the small island, an obtrusive authoritarian male voice-over (with a marked Venezuelan accent) identifies and describes the locale where the story will be set: "Land of sailors, at other times a mecca for greedy adventurers attracted by the fame of its pearls, Margarita dazzles like an invocation to the world of fauna." As the narrator finishes his poetic description, a series of dissolves show the "land of sailors" and the cycles of the "world of fauna": nets drying on the beach; a large group of men, women, and children pushing a boat out to sea; the women and children standing on the beach as the boat sets off; pulling a net in (shot from three different directions); pulling the boat out of the water; the men using baskets to transfer tiny little fish to buckets; a closer shot of the leaping fish in the basket. Thus the film interrupts the trajectory of its very melodramatic credit sequence to begin with a minidocumentary treatise—in almost perfect travelogue style—that succinctly introduces and describes the life cycle of the island with images that scream out their "authenticity." The people here are obviously nonactors and the action is clearly unstaged. Furthermore, we can briefly see the bemused glances of several of the participants who occasionally look at the camera and smile shyly amidst all their activity. Formally embracing this "other" island into the nation but through the eye of the foreign traveler, this documentary introduction simultaneously exalts and exoticizes Isla Margarita and the humble "natives" who work the sea by inserting them into diegesis as little else but the "world of the fauna" of the island.

Echoing this gesture, the first dramatic scene of the film is also marked by a traveler's gaze. Following a fade to black after the close-up of the tiny fish leaping in a basket, a high-angle shot shows a bunch of kids paddling in the water yelling, "¡El último, mister, el último!" ("The last one, mister, the last one!"). A man visually coded as a foreigner—sweating profusely and wearing a white linen suit and hat, a loud flowered shirt, a camera around his neck, and a smoking cigar—stands on the pier and pitches coins into the sea for local kids to dive for. Identified as "Monsieur" (one of the kids even yells out to him, "¡Monsieur-cito!"), this character is a typical "foreigner," like many others in Latin American films of the period, and his actions those of a typical visitor to a colonial outpost. After one last big pitch, one of the kids gets a cramp, and a handsome man, observing the foreigner disapprovingly, dives in to pull him out. The man is the boy's father, Segundo, played by the easily recognized (especially after a strikingly beautiful close-up) Arturo de Córdova. When he comes out of the water, Segundo squares off with the foreigner, pushes him off the pier, and walks off with his son.

Narratively, this sequence serves to introduce two of our principal characters—Segundo and his son—and to characterize the father-son relationship and patriarchal lines of descent as central and linked to the sea and seafaring. But beyond its service to the plot, it also begins the film with a curious, determining, and very telling gesture. What can we make of the figure of the foreigner here? He is of no further narrative significance and never reappears, but his presence—like that of the map—is an index of the film's necessarily ambivalent position vis-à-vis its problematic, if not impossible, national commitments. By focusing on the diegetic foreignness of "Monsieur," the film can relativize the extra-diegetic otherness of Arturo de Córdova as a Venezuelan ship captain into a cinematic imaginary structured by the melodramatic. Recognized and displaced, foreignness itself becomes the principal source of melodramatic excess. Thus the film sets the terms for Segundo's redemption—he must reject the foreign, the other, his own foreignness—wherein the national becomes a question of taming the excess of foreignness rather than only a battle over emotions, passion, and desire.

This initial insistence on highlighting "otherness" is echoed, narratively and visually, throughout the rest of the film. For example, early in the film, after we have been introduced to his idyllic and quite bourgeois home life with wife and son, Segundo leaves Isla Margarita for La Guaira, a port town where he himself is a stranger and a traveler, an outsider.[16] His earlier locatedness and integrity—the source of his authority—begin to wane while still at sea. He is haunted by a song—identified by his noticeably Argentine first mate, Martinote, as "Esperanza's song"—and stares at the sea longingly while his sailors joke about the women waiting for them in La Guaira (in Venezuelan slang). When they arrive at La Guaira (a crowded prototypical port town in which nationalities, races, classes, and genders seem to coexist easily), Segundo dons a dapper white linen suit and straw hat and goes ashore, where he is greeted warmly by a series of women asking after his sailors. Reenacting "Monsieur's" stance and clothing, he is jovial and self-assured with all of them, a man completely in control of himself and his element, *un capitán*. Before entering El Cuerno de la Fortuna (The Horn of Plenty), the bar where Esperanza sings, he runs into a crazed old woman, María, who prepares him for what he is about to find: Esperanza is with another man. Inside the bar, Esperanza is next to an older man in a card game and singing with her back to the door; she does not see Segundo enter. Our first close-up of her discloses a beautifully excessive face, markedly sensual, already glistening with desire (the complete opposite of his wife's proper beauty). Segundo waits until the end of her song and then moves in to take her away. When challenged by the old man, they first duel at cards (Segundo wins), and finally they fistfight. At the end, the old man is beaten to a bloody pulp and gives up, while Segundo is barely mussed (only a little strand of curly hair has fallen onto his forehead). When he comes to Esperanza, they kiss passionately and leave the bar after Segundo throws the bartender a golden coin. Literally repeating "Monsieur's" actions in the first sequence, Segundo's aggressiveness and conquering spirit are not that different from those of the prototypical foreigner. Like Monsieur, he watches the natives bemusedly and has no respect for the life of this "other" world. He has money and, as he tells Esperanza, no man there is "man" enough to take her away from him. Subsequently, Esperanza begs him to stay with her, and in the throes of passion, he promises to stay with her forever. But after spending three days in her messy, crowded, and noisy apartment—surrounded by flypaper, bottles of liquor, and squabbles among neighboring women—he is utterly disgusted by the exotic, yet squalid, banality and vulgarity of her life.[17] When subsequently confronted by his first mate's song—a folk ballad with the refrain "la mujer margariteña siempre tiene su nobleza" ("the woman from Margarita is always noble")—he orders his men to set sail.

A similar layering of otherness occurs when on the way back home, after Bocú's spell begins to affect Segundo, a storm forces the ship to stop at Carenero, another island port. In this even more exotic locale—an other to the other of La Guaira—the primarily Afro-Venezuelan natives are celebrating the feast of San Juan with *santería* drumming, singing, and dancing. Here there is no "normalcy"; it is night and the otherness is explicit and all-encompassing. And Segundo is no longer in control: he is driven to drink and into a mad frenzy—beautifully photographed in canted medium and close-up shots—by Bocú's spell and by the powerful ritualistic festivities. The otherness here is utterly foreign, excessive, dangerous, unmediated, intolerable.

Later, when Segundo seems to have moved permanently to La Guaira, where Bocú's spell keeps him enslaved to Esperanza's sexuality, he becomes a complete moral weakling and physical bully. The formerly dapper *capitán* becomes a besotted drunk; all he can do is hang around Esperanza, listen to her singing, and bully the bar patrons to be as entranced by her as he is.

Here, Segundo has been completely depersonalized. His passion has denuded him and transformed him into a caricature of his former powerful self. Driven only by a mad desire and sweating rather unbecomingly (again, like Monsieur in the first sequence), he ignores his work, his sailors, certainly the memory of his wife waiting for him back home, but, most significantly, even his own son. He has become an other to himself.

Finally, a further layering effect is produced by the film's curious international mix of professional and nonprofessional actors and of extraordinarily popular stars and relative unknowns. Alongside Arturo de Córdova, arguably the most recognizable male star of the period,[18] are a series of lesser-known actors and a large number of nonactors who, with few speaking parts, provide a significant "authentic" backdrop for the unfolding melodrama. In his first screen appearance, Nestor Zavarce, the child who plays the son, mediates between the professional actors and the nonactors who provide local color: his more awkwardly delivered lines are touchingly sincere, appropriate to a child, and help diminish the difference between the two groups.

The international provenance of the actors and the curious mix of their various accents is similarly elided, but through an additional displacement that further complicates the work of nationality in the film. First of all, the location for most of the action—La Guaira—is established as remote and distant, far from the national stability and belongingness of Isla Margarita. Although cartographically La Guaira is on the mainland and centrally located (and the port for the capital city of Caracas), in the melodramatic geography of the film La Guaira is other: it does not appear on the map and is figured as an uncharted national territory, a Caribbean contact zone. Although races and nationalities seem to mix with impunity (one of the La Guaira women we see early in the film is called Olga and speaks with a European accent), the dominant thread of La Guaira is carried by a specific "foreign" influence: African religious rituals. Handily ignoring all demographic evidence to the contrary,[19] the film carefully confines *santería* to the cinematic outposts (La Guaira and, later, Carenero). In Isla Margarita, the furthest region of the cartographical nation of the introduction, Segundo's wife, Isabel, is a proper Catholic who has pictures of saints on her walls, makes son and husband say grace and cross themselves before dinner ("¡Santígüense, herejes!" ["Cross yourselves, heretics!"] she tells them), and attends Sunday mass dutifully. She even gives Segundo a small medal of the Virgin of the Valley on a chain for "protection." Despite its cartographical distance—or perhaps precisely because of it—Isla Margarita is the haven for the pure national values that will win the day: home,

church, and patriarchy. The source of La Guaira's otherness is clearly identified: Bocú is described as the son of a powerful and well-known Cuban
santero, who sired him as well as the madwoman María. By displacing the
source of the supernatural force that threatens the stability of man, patriarchy, and family onto a Cuban black man and onto Afro-Cuban—rather
than Afro-Venezuelan—rituals, the film is able to simultaneously present
pan-national movement as a given while reinforcing the desire and need for
a national stability centered on its rejection. *Mestizaje* may be an unavoid-
able given, but the terms of its incorporation into nationness will be closely
regulated.

The scenes of the film that focus on *santería* activities are effective in yet
another register, for they echo all too well the substance of authentic *santería* practices as well as their performative power and visual excess. Ranging
from the detailed (and dramatically filmed) presentation of Bocú's house
and altar when he puts the spell on Segundo in the cigar smoke ceremony—using the religious medal that Isabel had given Segundo for protection—to the festivities of San Juan in Carenero, the "folkloric" scenes
were orchestrated by Juan Liscano, a well-known Venezuelan folklore expert whose name features prominently in the credits and whose collaboration grants these aspects of the film an even greater legitimacy. Presenting Afro-Venezuelans who, with the exception of Bocú, are obviously
nonactors, these sequences are explicitly linked to the film's initial documentary and distancing gesture as yet additional evidence of the authenticity of its national representation. But they also further the film's pecu-
liarly ambivalent position vis-à-vis the nation's internal otherness: despite
the film's emphasis on "folkloricism," the nationness it promotes is not
itself folkloric. How else can we read the existence of a folklore "expert"?
Why would a folkloric national imaginary shared by all citizens require that
an expert's testimonial evidence be explicitly acknowledged? Unlike the
Mexican *comedia ranchera*'s effortless production of a folkloric world as national allegory—in which the autoreferentiality of an expert would be absurd—*La balandra Isabel* needs this mediating presence in order to constitute a specific paradigm of nationness vis-à-vis multiple and multicultural
referents.

But what is at stake in *La balandra Isabel* is not simply positioning certain cultural elements as "foreign" within the national space of the narrative
(this is obviously worked out diegetically) but a slippage of foreignness itself
as a category. The crux of nationness here is not really the issue of foreign
versus native but rather a question of two kinds of foreignness: primitive

(erotic, uncontrollable, dangerous) and bourgeois (Catholic, patriarchal, stable). In this way, the nation sees itself as exotic-erotic from a "foreigner's" perspective.

In the short story upon which the film is based, Meneses focused exclusively on painting a rich portrait of the Afro-Venezuelan life of his characters in the spirit of primitivism. The story lacks the film's crucial second tier of foreignness: we learn that Segundo is married and has children but we never meet them, and furthermore Segundo is called a "negro verde," a ladies' man with women in every port. Similarly, all of the characters are explicitly black (and address each other as "negrito" and "negrita") and working-class poor, so there is no class or racial difference implicated in the drama. Most tellingly, in the story the spell upon Segundo doesn't work: he does not return to La Guaira, and Esperanza is left waiting for him at the docks. Although it does function as a sketch of a familiar yet implicitly distant other, the story's power is derived from its treatment of eroticism and sexuality. Frankly depicted and described, the erotic is what the story's location in otherness enables. In the film, however, which is aided by an internationally recognized melodramatic mode and star system, Segundo/ Arturo de Córdova can overcome the primitive, for the film ultimately subordinates it to the ideals of a transnational bourgeois culture premised upon patriarchy and Catholicism.

Quasi-documentary naturalism, melodrama, and exoticized/eroticized folklore come together in *La balandra Isabel* at the intersection of the nation with pan-national forces, coding an auteurist impulse, star presence, and hybrid generic allusions as national and necessarily pan-national, foundational, and destabilizing. Straddling the difficult crossover of national and international aspirations, influences, and effects, *La balandra Isabel* highlights, above all, the paradoxical work of nationness in "national" cinemas and the impossibility of separating the "foreigner's" gaze from the nation's own best-intentioned introspections. That this perverse configuration was ostensibly designed to allow for the formation of a national cinema leads us to question to what degree other Latin American cinemas, and perhaps national cinemas in general, have been enabled by a figural or literal foreigner's gaze.

Despite all its complex slippages and national paradoxes, *La balandra Isabel* did not magically engender a national film industry in Venezuela. That dream was postponed—after a detour through the New Latin American Cinema of the 1960s—until the oil boom of the 1970s and 1980s. But it did generate a significant series of further pan-Latin American cinematic collaborations and imbrications. Cinematographer José María Beltrán remained in Venezuela, while Arturo de Córdova continued his prolific traveling career. Christensen returned to Argentina, where he directed, among other films, *Si muero antes de despertar* (*If I Die before Awakening,* 1952), an adaptation of a short story by the U.S. detective/thriller writer William Irish. A critically well received and successful film, it was, according to Domingo di Núbila, not only one of the best films of the year but also the indirect cause of Christensen's subsequent exile to Brazil: given the Peronist climate, "it was [politically] dangerous to make great films." [20] Christensen's career in Brazil, an indirect extension of *La balandra Isabel,* will constitute another chapter in the saga of Latin American traveling filmmakers and the persistence of the foreigner's gaze in national cinemas.

Notes

Research for this essay was made possible, in part, by grants from the Roger Thayer Stone Center for Latin American Studies at Tulane University.

Unless otherwise specified, all translations from Spanish and Portuguese sources are my own.

1. Thus, for example, although it is impossible to consider the phenomenon of post-Pinochet Chilean exile without taking into account pan-continental collaborations, the pan–Latin American influences upon the seemingly far more insular Cuban ICAIC (Instituto Cubano del Arte e Industria Cinematográficos) cinema or the Brazilian Cinema Novo movement have yet to be investigated.

2. One exception to this rule is Paulo Antonio Paranaguá's *Cinema na América Latina: Longe de Deus e perto de Hollywood* (Porto Alegre, Rio Grande do Sul: L&PM Editores Ltda., 1985). Albeit brief, this is to my knowledge the only comparative, continental historical study of Latin American cinema to date.

3. For the most detailed account of the Hollywood "Hispanic" cinema, see Juan B. Heinink and Robert G. Dickson, *Cita en Hollywood: Antología de las películas norteamericanas habladas en castellano* (Bilbao, Spain: Ed. Mensajero, 1990). See also Emilio García Riera, *Mexico visto por el cine extranjero*, 6 vols. (Mexico City: Era-CIEC, 1987–90) and *Historia documental del cine mexicano*, vol. 1 (Guadalajara, Mexico: Universidad de Guadalajara, 1993).

4. Statistics from the *Segundo anuario cinematográfico cubano: 1941–42* and the *Anuário cinematográfico cubano no. 5 (1944–45)*, cited in Silvia Oroz, *Melodrama: O cinema de lágrimas da América Latina* (Rio de Janeiro, Brazil: Rio Funda Editora, 1991), 121, 137.

5. The history of the creation of the Lumiton studios is an interesting one. Four friends (César José Guerico, Enrique Telémanco Susini, Luis Romero

Carranza, and Miguel Mugica) who owned a radio company received a large cash payment from ITT (International Telegraph and Telephone) to give up the business. With the funds, they decided to go into movie production. They bought a camera in the United States, bought a lot in the Buenos Aires neighborhood of Munro, and built a studio from the ground up. At its peak, the studio had more than four hundred employees. See interview with Lumiton set designer Richard Conord in Homero Alsina Thevenet, ed., *Reportaje al cine argentino: Los pioneros del sonoro* (Buenos Aires, Argentina: Editorial Abril, 1978), 189–209.

6. Four-week shooting schedules were the norm for a feature film. During production, it was common for employees to sleep on the studio grounds. The top talent had the use of a special "chalet" on the property that had been acquired with the original lot and retained for this purpose. See Mecha Ortiz, *Mecha Ortiz* (Buenos Aires, Argentina: Editorial Moreno, 1982), 206–7.

7. According to Domingo di Núbila, *Historia del cine argentino,* vol. 2 (Buenos Aires, Argentina: Editorial Cruz de Malta, 1959), 591.

8. Cited in Oroz, *Melodrama,* 139.

9. See Alicia de la Vega, *Re-visión del cine chileno* (Santiago, Chile: Editorial Aconcagua, 1979), 32–33, 379–80.

10. For an assessment of this process, see also Jorge A. Schnitman, *Film Industries in Latin America: Dependency and Development* (Norwood, N.J.: Ablex, 1984).

11. See citations of reviews in Julio López Navarro, *Películas chilenas* (Santiago, Chile: Editorial La Noria, 1994).

12. Cited in Oroz, *Melodrama,* 164; emphasis mine.

13. See, for example, Enrique Alí González Ordosgoitti, *Diez ensayos de cultura venezolana* (Caracas, Venezuela: Fondo Editorial Tropykos, 1991), 69–75.

14. Ricardo Tirado, *Memoria y notas del cine venezolano* (1988), cited in *Literatura latinoamericana en cine,* ed. Steve Solot (New York: Motion Picture Export Association of America, 1991), 11.

15. Miguel Otero Silva, cited in *Literatura latinoamericana en cine,* ed. Solot, 11.

16. In terms of the imaginary geography of the film, La Guaira is clearly figured as a more remote outpost than Isla Margarita and is a place where wild forces and desires take root and where social mores and customs are wildly dislocated. However, geographically, La Guaira is in fact more central to the nation, as it is the port for the capital city of Caracas. Ostensibly La Guaira should have been a modernizing force even in the late 1940s rather than, as in the film, an almost anachronistic site for the occult, the forbidden, and the foreign. It is interesting to speculate how geographical consciousness might have affected the Venezuelan viewer in 1949.

17. The scene when Segundo awakens in Esperanza's less-than-bourgeois

abode may well be one of the most effective and elegantly constructed in the film, conveying its complex message economically via pointed glances, reframings, rack focus, and excellent editing.

18. De Córdova was, himself, a traveler. He appeared in a number of Hollywood films in 1939–1947, including *For Whom the Bell Tolls* (Frank Tuttle, 1943) and *Frenchman's Creek* (Mitchell Leisen, 1944). Domingo di Núbila claims that in 1947, de Córdova's star had begun to wane ("His star was in complete decadence. . . . Despite the success of his Hollywood films, Mexican producers were no longer interested in him," p. 94). But as Emilio García Riera argues in *Historia documental del cine mexicano,* vol. 3, *1945–1948* (Mexico City: Ediciones Era, 1971), 238, given how extraordinarily busy de Córdova was in 1947, this hardly makes sense: he filmed *La diosa arrodillada* (Roberto Gavaldón) and *Algo flota sobre el agua* (Alfredo B. Crevenna) in Mexico; *New Orleans* (Arthur Lubin) in the United States; a U.S.-Mexico coproduction, *The Adventures of Casanova* (Roberto Gavaldón); and finally, *Dios se lo pague* (Luis César Amadori) in Argentina. Whatever the case may be, this last film, the most popular Latin American film of the decade, transformed him into the most recognizable and bankable male star in the continent. In subsequent years he continued his pan-continental travels, filming regularly in Mexico, Argentina, and even Brazil (in two other films with Christensen).

19. See Angelina Pollak-Eltz, *Vestigios africanos en la cultura del pueblo venezolano* (Caracas, Venezuela: Universidad Católica Andres Bello, 1972).

20. Di Núbila, *Historia del cine argentino,* 157.

3

Araya across Time and Space

COMPETING CANONS OF NATIONAL (VENEZUELAN) AND INTERNATIONAL FILM HISTORIES

Julianne Burton-Carvajal

■ ■ ■ ■

Araya, a 90-minute scripted documentary filmed in 1957, depicts a 24-hour cycle in the subsistence rituals of three communities of salt gatherers and fishermen on Venezuela's remote and barren northeastern coast (figs. 3.1 and 3.2). The unusual reception trajectory of this self-consciously poetical social document has been marked by bursts of rekindled interest at ten-year intervals. Honored with two important prizes at the 1959 Cannes Film Festival, commercially released in France in 1967, premiered in Venezuela in 1977, featured selection of the ambitious Latin American Visions retrospective organized in Philadelphia in 1987, it generated enthusiastic critical response at the 1995 Chicago Latino Festival and was honored with tributes in Venezuela and Colombia in 1997.

Despite this remarkable resilience, *Araya*'s historical place in the formative history of both Venezuelan national cinema and the New Latin American Cinema movement is still contested. Over the decades, European and North American critics have not hesitated to celebrate the film as universal masterpiece, authentic national product, and exemplar or precursor of regional cinema's highest capabilities. Upon its long-deferred Venezuelan release in 1977, a number of commentaries in the press likewise heralded *Araya*'s preeminent position in national—and in Latin American—cinema: "the crowning achievement of national cinema" (Matías Carrasco, *El Universal,* 17 May); "national cinema's most important film" (Alfonso Molina, *El Nacional,* 18 May); "a cinematic work of authentic national expression with universal projection" (RAS, *El Nacional,* 1 June); "precursor of all Latin American cinema" (Penzo, *Momento,* 23 May). For these writers, *Araya*'s earlier European success, its "universal" appeal and "worldwide" acclaim, confirmed and enhanced its national import.

FIGURE 3.1.   *Parallel landscapes of Venezuela's Araya peninsula, natural and man-made. Reprinted courtesy of Margot Benacerraf.*

In marked contrast, a pair of Venezuelan film historians and critics writing in specialized journals over a twenty-year period disputed *Araya*'s status as a foundational film and as a national and Latin American product. For these writers, formed within a Marxist, anti-imperialist tradition, European exhibition was not a valid point of entry into national and continental production histories. The very precariousness of these still-emerging genealogies dictated that all taint of dependency be rejected. Its European post-production and the nearly twenty years that elapsed between its filming and its reception in its country of origin [1] made *Araya* tangential to the evolution of national and continental cinema. As we shall see, the readings of the film elaborated by these critics emphasized an understanding of history effectively circumscribed by its own historical moment.

Araya's director, Margot Benacerraf, was born in Caracas in 1927 to Sephardic immigrants from North Africa who accumulated great wealth in their adoptive land. The young Margot was educated in literature and art history under the tutelage of a number of illustrious refugees from the Spanish civil war. She subsequently studied drama in New York and film-making in Paris, editing *Reverón* (1953) as well as *Araya* (1959) in the latter city, where her extended residence put her in close contact with many of the foremost international artists of the period, including Pablo Picasso, Henri Cartier-Bresson, Roberto Rossellini, and Luis Buñuel. It is not unusual for Latin American filmmakers, including the more militantly engaged ones, to come from families of means, to develop close ties with leading international artists, and to seek European coproduction funds or facilities. Judging from the examples of Margot Benacerraf and Argentina's María Luisa Bemberg, however, the "original sin" of class privilege seems to be less pardonable in a woman filmmaker.

I can only speculate on the role of class and gender in Benacerraf's marginalization by film critics and historians identified with the militant left, while acknowledging that there may be other contributing factors imperceptible from my current vantage point. Any attempt to understand *Araya*'s anomalous inclusion-exclusion status—its inclusion in a transnational canon and its persistent exclusion from national and continental film histories—must therefore be centrally located in the film itself.

What insights into processes of canon formation and the writing of national and supranational film histories does a comparative look at the film's critical reception in three countries—France, Venezuela, the United States—across five decades yield? The comparative rereading of critical responses that follows will make apparent how inextricably *Araya*'s place *in*

FIGURE 3.2. *Persistent versions of "pharaonic labor." Reprinted courtesy of Margot Benacerraf.*

history is tied to its stance *toward* history, as well as to the time and place—
the historical moment and geocultural location—of its reception.

Narratives of National Cinema

Venezuelan film historian Julio E. Miranda begins his 1989 history of documentary in Venezuela by deliberating the generative status of the Benacerraf film:

> This history could have begun, perhaps, with *Araya* (1959). Venezuelan
> documentary filmmaking . . . would thus have its origin in the discovery
> of "distant lands" more in the lyric manner of a Flaherty than following
> the inquisitive approach of Chris Marker or Joris Ivens. But Margot Bena-
> cerraf's beautiful and dense feature-length film was not seen in Venezuela
> until 1977. Though it took prizes at Cannes in 1959 and is mentioned
> in Sadoul's *Diccionaire,* it was an exotic flower, a true hothouse bloom—
> a myth more than a film.[2]

Upon the Venezuelan release of the film in 1977, Tomás Eloy Martínez,[3]
in an intricately crafted essay suffused with literary flair, conferred foundational status on a continental scale while at the same time (by his use of
the participle "colonized") marking an ironic distance. Miranda's "exotic
flower" metaphor, with its heavily gendered mildly xenophobic undercur-
rents, can be traced to this 1977 text:

> Eighteen years [had to pass] for *Araya* to cease being an exotic flower in
> the little movie theaters of Rue de l'Harpe or King's Road and to make its
> appearance at last on the salt flats where its story began. . . . Eighteen years
> had to go by for *Araya* to be recognized as the first forerunner of a con-
> tinent which would later be colonized by the films of Miguel Littín, San-
> tiago Alvarez and Patricio Guzmán.[4]

That same year, 1977, Venezuelan film critic Alfredo Roffé dismissed
Araya as "alien to the historical and cultural process of Venezuela." His
highly critical essay concluded that *Araya*'s deferred national exhibition
meant that "it lost its chance to serve as point of reference for the national
film movement" as well as "having lost what at the moment of its making
would have been its great merit: to demonstrate that high-level cinema
could be made in Venezuela." His perception of the film's remoteness and

disconnectedness from the "genuinely national" has a softened echo in Miranda's reference to "distant lands." This coincidence suggests that both critics subscribed to the embedded assumption that the "true" nation is urban and centralized. Might they have subscribed as well to the even more deeply embedded assumption that the face of the "true" nation does not reveal itself in cinema except to male directors—like those they both list in abundance as the authentic producers of the national documentary tradition?

Intimations of Universality

In marked contrast to these Venezuelan commentators' refusal to accept *Araya* as a genuinely national expression, European critics and film historians did not hesitate to see it as the first, formative instance of Venezuelan filmmaking within an unself-consciously universalized, though not always Eurocentric, frame of reference. Luis Buñuel is quoted in several sources as saying upon the film's festival premier, "I have not seen images as beautiful as those of *Araya* since Eisenstein's *¡Que viva México!*—a canny association that fuses the old and the new worlds within the historical frame of two political and aesthetic revolutions, the Russian and the Mexican.[5] After noting that the only other "Venezuelan" film previously honored in France (Carlos Hugo Christensen's *La balandra Isabel llegó esta tarde,* 1950) had been directed by an Argentine, leading French film commentator Marcel Martin, writing in 1967 upon *Araya*'s French release, asserts: "It does not go against historical truth to affirm that *Araya* is the first authentically Venezuelan film that deserves to become part of posterity along with the name of its author." At the same time that he finds *Araya* "a dazzling revelation of Venezuelan cinema," Martin also judges it in terms of universal, transgeographical criteria, dichotomizing the film medium into two basic, complementary functions: "*Araya* is a film that realizes one of the two essential functions of cinema: to render reality visible." (The other essential function: "to give a face to dreams.")

Another leading French film critic, Georges Sadoul, then regarded as the world's foremost historian of international film, singled out *Araya* upon its initial Cannes screening in 1959, taking the festival jury to task for not awarding it a prize. (The two prizes it won were from the International Society of Film Critics [FIPRESCI] and the Technical Commission of French Cinema.) His article concludes with the same universalizing critical discourse: "Sooner or later, I am sure, among audiences who love and understand film, *Araya* will demand recognition as a great work." Eight years later, upon *Araya*'s French release, Sadoul reiterated his earlier prediction and then quoted at length from a 1921 text by experimental filmmaker and theorist Jean Epstein on the heretofore imperceptible and spontaneous synchronization of movement—be it of human, animal, or machine—that the invention of the movie camera at last rendered capturable:

> . . . [T]here exists a sort of symphony or orchestration whose causes are obscure to say the least. We know how crowd scenes in the cinema produce a rhythmic, poetic, photogenic effect. The reason is that the cinema, better and differently than our own eye, knows how to set that cadence free, to inscribe that rhythm which is fundamental to its harmonics.

Sadoul goes on to assert: "This program-text, which impressed me greatly in 1921, has been in my opinion better realized by *Araya* than by any other film."

The collection of quotes assembled thus far reflects some of the critical leitmotifs frequent in the *Araya* reviews and commentaries across decades and nationalities and shifting historical, cultural, and ideological paradigms. The self-validating invocation of masters and masterpieces and the equally self-authorizing invocation of theoretical criteria serve different functions, depending on the context in which they are invoked. While French critics, Sadoul foremost among them, voice the opinion that *Araya* is an innovative work, ahead of its time, Venezuelan critics perceive only a debt to past masters that reinforces *Araya*'s marginal status in the evolution of an authentically Venezuelan documentary tradition. The taxonomical debate privileged by several of the film's critics—what kind of documentary is this?—again generates more anxiety in the national context than in the extranational one.

Other aesthetic and thematic concerns do not seem to be the product of the different positioning of Venezuelan and European commentators. Both national and extranational commentators display a tendency to dichotomize formal beauty and social concern, for example, as if convinced that the former necessarily undermines the latter. *Araya*'s visual and aural address of its human subjects in relation to their physical environment and their present, past, and future generates responses ranging from awe to outrage. The film's engagement with—or alleged failure to engage—processes of historical transformation thus resonates relentlessly, if unpredictably, in its reception.

The Social, the Historical, the Aesthetic

Miranda compresses several of these concerns into the second of the two paragraphs which he dedicates to *Araya* in his 1989 study of Venezuelan documentary:

> *Araya* did not just register the reality of a "distant land" but registered it in a way that made that land even more distant. Perhaps because of its landscape-centered lyricism which inserts the inhabitants of the Araya Peninsula into the order of the elements, attenuating and even dissolving the social order within the natural one. Perhaps because the film's discourse is always the filmmaker's discourse and the overloaded voice-over text does not "give voice" to the concrete men and women whom we see on the screen. Perhaps because, when in spite of everything the problem of the harsh and underpaid work in the salt marshes has been laid out, the concluding images confer closure by presenting the mechanization of that labor process in an epic manner, without questioning in the least the new conditions of exploitation that this mechanization will engender, the unemployment that it will occasion, etc. The film's "denunciation" is relegated in the end to the museum of images and its overall thrust is concentrated in its visual splendor.

Alfredo Roffé, writing shortly after the Venezuelan release of the film in 1977, expounds the most ideologically infused critique:

> Benacerraf deliberately and expressly excludes all reference to socio-economic and political structure and relations of production. . . . Who owns the salt marsh, who owns the trucks or the salt, who reaps the profits . . . is not known. The sudden industrialization of the salt marsh lacks any connection with any operational mechanism—private, collective or public. . . . No one gives an opinion, expressing satisfaction or protest—neither the inhabitants of Araya nor the voice-over commentator. . . . Just as the people represented are denied speech, they are also denied all possibility of non-verbal communication. . . . [They] are inter-changeable. . . . Just as speech becomes noise or, in the best case, musical accompaniment, human beings are transformed into viewable objects.
>
> Story, social relations, individuality are all eliminated. What replaces them? *Araya* proposes a closed, static, ahistorical world in which everything is infinitely repeated without changes, without conflicts, eternally. . . . This climatological determinism is the ontological basis of the

universe without possibility of escape which is *Araya*. . . . The basic conception that suffuses and configures the entire film is the representation of
a closed, autonomous system in which men are fixed coefficients and any
variation, when variation exists, comes from an external mandate. Human
beings are transformed into immutable parameters, without will, impotent
and incapable of inserting themselves . . . into the process of change.

Moving from *Araya*'s content to a brief consideration of its formal structure, Roffé asserts: "The film's much admired figurative elaboration is organized, with astonishing consistency, according to the same generative
principles." He offers two examples: the "unnatural pattern of movement"
that requires subjects "to walk in lines" rather than allowing more sponta-
neously irregular human groupings, and the use of depth of field as a "decorative device." Roffé then concludes:

Rather than resonance between signifiers and signified, we have a voiceless,
untranscendent repetition . . . of the reigning natural order, presented as
eternal, the product of superhuman authority and human submission to
that divine/natural order. In other words, the validation of the existing
state of things, the beautification of that state, and the negation of any possibility of change resulting from man's voluntary action. *Araya* is practically the filmic manifesto of the defenders of the status quo.

In summary, then, Miranda contends that the filmmaker's discourse
displaces the voices of the social actors, while *Araya*'s "epic" style and
"landscape-centered lyricism" create a "museum of images" that "dissolve
the social order within the natural one" and submerge sociopolitical concerns and consequences beneath "visual splendor." Roffé also deplores
the absence of socioeconomic references and the relegation of social actors
to "viewable objects" denied not only speech but "all possibility of nonverbal communication." In his view, *Araya* presents history as *separate* from
human beings whom it depicts as subject to an "eternal . . . divine/natural
order" and "incapable of inserting themselves . . . into the process of
change." More impervious to the film's aesthetic impact than Miranda,
Roffé dismisses its "figurative elaboration" as artificial and "decorative." For
him, *Araya* is insubstantial in form as well as content. He attributes political
partisanship to the film (and, not too indirectly, to the filmmaker herself)
suggesting a starkly dichotomized political horizon: those who do not sub-
scribe to the same account of historical change as he must be reactionary
defenders of the status quo.

At the head of the last column of the four-column essay that he wrote upon *Araya*'s French release in 1967, Georges Sadoul, no less Marxist-identified than the Venezuelan critics just cited, confronted a possible form-content dichotomy in his assessment of the film:

> I am perhaps insisting too much on the formal beauty of this symphony of rhythms, images, and natural sounds. I should then say that the film is first and foremost a painful and measured record of the medieval servitude to which the salt producers of Araya are still subjected in 1958. For them, the labor and exploitation were no less horrible than in the sixteenth century just after the Spanish colonizers discovered that natural, inexhaustible salt-marsh. Association with the pyramids of ancient Egypt is prompted by more than the shape of the mounds of salt. The slaves of Ramses II were no more badly treated than the peons of the Araya Peninsula, where the equatorial sun and the permanent contact with the salt eats away the skin.

Significantly here, it is not the film that Sadoul finds lacking in political dimension but rather his own analysis that has been too prone to emphasize *Araya*'s formal beauty, thereby downplaying its denunciative dimension.

"*Araya* has already become an historic film," Sadoul continues. "A little after its shooting, enormous bulldozers invaded the peninsula. . . ." He acknowledges the ambiguity of liberation from pharaonic labor as inferred from the film's dramatically inserted concluding images of heavy industrial machinery: the families may "end up in the atrocious slums of Caracas" (slums that Sadoul had glimpsed in a Leacock-Pennebaker collaboration, *Yankee no,* 1960). "The salt flat sustained its workers badly, it's true, but it did allow their subsistence," he observes clear-sightedly, concluding this paragraph with a rather impressive, even prescient, sociohistorical synthesis: Latin America's huge army of unemployed, the preponderance of regimes based on feudal colonialism, the presence of U.S. military experts in countries like Bolivia (Che Guevara would be tracked down and killed there later that same year), and the Vietnam conflict. Sadoul was clearly very attuned to his historical moment, yet his sense of *Araya* as "historic" seems more a function of its relation to a vanished past than to a process of ongoing transformation. He does not read the apparition of the machine at the conclusion of the film as a deliverance but rather as a potentially definitive dispossession and displacement. However, he implies, the advent of the industrial machine begins another phase, another story, another film.

In the same essay, Sadoul also attempts to locate *Araya* within the changing historical panorama of filmmaking practices. Acknowledging how quickly films age, he begins this essay by noting the marked shift in preference away from extensive voice-over narration in documentary. He judges Benacerraf "well ahead of her time in terms of her sound montage" because of her incorporation of multileveled ambient sound along with the poetic voice-over narration: "the sound of the waves on the shore, the oars in the water, the seashells being piled one on the other, the magisterial orchestration of ambient sound with the music of composer Guy Bernard." [6]

Tendentious Taxonomies?

Marcel Martin is less troubled than other writers by *Araya*'s ambiguous relationship to conventional taxonomies of film:

> A document that is both almost raw and yet very carefully crafted, [*Araya*] is a poetic film . . . which seeks to be not so much a documentary as a work in which the beauty of nature, human activity, camera movements, the recurring motif of the sea and the strong sonorities of the musical accompaniment all have an essential role to play. *Araya* is a *musical* film in which [sound] variations play against light and movement.

Alfredo Roffé begins his essay by citing Paul Rotha's 1936 text, *Documentary Film,* because one category it posits, the "naturalistic-romantic," is "perfectly applicable to *Araya*." Laying out in considerable detail the characteristics of this approach—which has, in Roffé's estimation, been in decline since the mid-1930s and "survives only in tourist and publicity films"—Roffé specifies the characteristics that make *Araya* a late example.

For Tomás Eloy Martínez, the filmmaker's structuring intervention is decisive in categorizing her work as "precursor of the great Latin American documentary novels." From his perspective, only critical naiveté explains the prevalent tendency to receive the film as an unmediated documentary recording of daily life. "Criticism did not yet know how to discern the degree of deliberate artifice and efficient reconstruction of daily life that informs apparently trivial scenes like the selling of the fish, the mid-day meal, the walk to the cemetery," he explains.

Michael Wilmington, writing in the *Chicago Tribune* in 1995, obviates the taxonomical debate that has engrossed so many of the film's commentators when he categorizes *Araya* simply and aptly as a "prime example of the lyrical social documentary," recognizing that lyricism and realism are not incompatible modes of expression.

Since Venezuelan painter and onetime filmmaker Angel Hurtado wrote the essay on *Araya* for the Latin American Visions compendium while head of the audiovisual unit of the Museum of Contemporary Art of Latin America in Washington, D.C., we can infer that he was highly conscious of his mediating role in the transcultural and transhistorical (re)reception of the film. His opening sentence claims for *Araya* the status of "a classic of both Latin American and world cinema." He characterizes the film's subject as "the very symbol of the human condition": "the painful struggle to make a living." He finds a "timeless and universal pathos" in the depiction of this "odyssey of physical resistance," stressing that the film's "denunciation of mindless human exploitation is made soberly, without resort to melodramatics or demagoguery." He concludes by rhetorically subordinating history and politics to poetry and art: "Today, its value is found not in social protest but in the hymn it sings to human endurance in the struggle against adversity." In Hurtado's view, taxonomies are beside the point. *Araya* is a genuine classic because it was made by a "true documentary artist," someone who "delves into fundamental aspects of our world, seeking out the characteristics peculiar to each region—characteristics which the artist then transforms into images of universal impact."

Attributions of Influence

Benacerraf and her film have been subject to numerous canonical comparisons. Georges Sadoul seems to have set the comparative parameters for *Araya* with the first piece he wrote in 1959: "A film in the tradition of Flaherty *(Nanouk of the North)*, Eisenstein *(¡Que viva México!)*, Paul Strand *(The Rebellion of Alvarado)*, Joris Ivens *(Borinage)*, and Luis Buñuel *(Land without Bread)*." Writing in the mid-1960s, Marcel Martin reached beyond the documentary canon when he stated that *Araya* warrants comparison to the best work of Jean Renoir as much as to that of Flaherty and the Visconti of *La terra trema*. For Tomás Eloy Martínez, writing one decade after Martin and two decades after Sadoul, *Araya* exemplifies "a cinema of description and memory, like that of Alain Resnais," as well as "of communication and celebration, like that of Robert Flaherty and Joris Ivens." Roffé cites Visconti's *La terra trema*, Chris Marker's and Alain Resnais' *Les statues meurent aussi*, the latter's *Nuit et brouillard*, and Lindsay Anderson's *O Dreamland* as comparable examples of the naturalistic-romantic documentary— a list more original than many, not to mention more laudatory than his vehement critique seems to warrant. Angel Hurtado compares Benacerraf's film to Eisenstein's *¡Que viva México!*, (unspecified) Flaherty, and Grierson's *Drifters* and contrasts it with Buñuel's "aggressive realism and focus on horror and abjection ultimately smacking of pamphleteering in *Land With-out Bread*." Michael Wilmington invokes Flaherty and Ivens, returning the context of comparison to the two principal documentarists originally invoked by Sadoul, so strikingly divergent in their documentary practice. The consistency of this latter comparative pairing across time and space underlines *Araya*'s combination of the descriptive and the sociohistorical.

Other potential constellations of comparison exist. If the Eisensteinian comparison still seems apt, arguably Orson Welles' Brazilian experiment, *It's All True,* is equally so. Shot in the early forties but only recently edited and released, Welles's unfinished film was thus detached much longer than *Araya* from both generalized reception and its geohistorical site of production. Now partially reconstructed (as *Three Men on a Raft*) and incorporated into a documentary, *It's All True: Based on an Unfinished Film by Orson Welles* (1993), which contextualizes the entire suspended project, it offers another pole of comparison. All three films—*¡Que viva México!, It's All True,* and *Araya*—relate the human figure and "primitive/traditional" communities to vast, austere, imposing landscapes in formalistic ways that problematize the relations of both individual and group to nature, culture, and history. All three challenge simplistic polarizations of documentary and fictional modalities.

However, though such a comparative configuration inserts Benacerraf into an elevated pantheon, it also risks reinforcing the insidious suggestion that, even as a Venezuelan filming in Venezuela, she was somehow "making distant lands more distant." Certainly the distance between Benacerraf and the inhabitants of Araya was no greater than, for example, that between Bolivian director Jorge Sanjinés and the members of the Andean community he filmed in *Blood of the Condor* (1969).[7] The critical practice of associating Benacerraf and *Araya* exclusively with European or American referents arbitrarily cuts off the film and its maker from their national and hemispheric context.

Glauber Rocha's seacoast drama *Barravento* (*The Turning Wind,* 1961) arguably owes a debt to *Araya,* which, if recognized formalistically and historiographically, might allow the Benacerraf film a stronger claim to the foundational status that has eluded it to date. Though chroniclers have long recognized Rocha's pivotal role as visionary promoter and polemicist of Brazil's Cinema Novo movement, forerunner of the New Latin American Cinema movement, they seem unaware that he saw *Araya* in 1959 as a journalist covering the Cannes festival, and that he interviewed its director and kept in subsequent touch with her until his death in the early 1980s because he was so profoundly affected, personally and aesthetically, by the example of what she had accomplished in such independent and artisanal fashion.[8]

Like *Araya,* Rocha's *opera prima* (edited by the director who was to become the other pillar of Cinema Novo theory and practice, Nelson Pereira dos Santos) emphasizes the natural setting through a similar virtuosity of camera angles, movements, and montage. In *Barravento*'s intricate parable, it is not the machine but the ambiguous promise of the remote city that rends the cohesive fabric of tradition in this Edenic, predominantly Afro-Brazilian fishing community. Rocha's film brings to the foreground narratively and visually what Benacerraf's relegated to one level of her multi-leveled soundtrack: music, dance, religious ritual, patterns of belief, and cultural expression. In *Barravento,* the seacoast setting and the determining impositions of nature are figured into an intricate emplotment of human and metaphysical impulses, materialist and mythical epistemologies.

Arguably a much more intricate and accomplished work than the celebrated *Tiré dié* (1960), which Fernando Birri produced in collaboration with the students at the incipient Documentary Film School in Santa Fe, Argentina—a film that is generally regarded as the first expression of (Spanish-language) New Latin American documentary—*Araya* deserves to be re-viewed in the context of all the important Latin American works of that formative 1950s decade, renowned or obscure, features and documentaries, including Alex Viany's *Agulha no palheiro* (*Needle in a Haystack,* 1953), Linduarte Noronha and Rucker Viera's *Aruanda* (1959), Paulo César Saraceni's *Arraial do Cabo* (1959), Nelson Pereira dos Santos's *Rio 40 graus* (*Rio, 100 Degrees,* 1956) and *Rio, zona norte* (*Rio, Northern Zone,* 1957), and Roberto Santos's *O grande momento* (*The Great Moment,* 1958)—all from Brazil; Bolivian Jorge Ruíz's *Vuelve, Sebastiana* (*Come Back, Sebastiana,* 1953); Chilean Sergio Bravo's *Mimbre* (*Wicker,* 1957) and *Trilla* (*Thresher,* 1958); the Cuban collaboration *El mégano* (*The Charcoal Worker,* 1954); as well as (trans)national "superproductions" like *La balandra Isabel llegó esta tarde* (1952), other Venezuelan-made films like the Shell Film Unit's documentary *Llano adentro* (1956), and features like César Enríquez's *La escalinata* (1950) and Román Chalbaud's *Caín adolescente* (1959). Not to reinsert *Araya* into its contemporaneous context leaves the film in a genealogical limbo: an enduring and artful anomaly, the somewhat fortuitous product of a fragile talent that, three decades later, has still not fulfilled Sadoul's exhortation that she "owes world cinema a second feature worthy of *Araya,* that would likewise make its mark on film art and film history."[9] Such a limbo is disturbingly consistent with a critical and historiographical tradition that has persistently elided women's contributions to national and regional cinematographies.

The Poetics of Evocation

Though all the writers of the chain of essays examined here recognize *Araya*'s intricate formal and temporal structuration, Tomás Eloy Martínez's essay stands out because it replicates rather than simply describes that intricacy. It begins with a carefully choreographed invocation of two locations "then" and "now," rhetorically negating the passage of time in both the scattered communities of the Araya peninsula and the crowded streets and Festival Palace of Cannes. It concludes by projecting the reader into Araya's sole movie theater at an unspecified present-future moment: "Every Saturday night a different life in order to silence the echoes of their other life that was always the same. Every Saturday night embracing an alien identity in order to flee one's own, monotonous identity." Here, "some other Saturday night," these viewers of interchangeable Westerns "may see themselves in the perfect mirror of a film called *Araya*."

Between these "unchanged" locations, the body of this essay "locates" itself and its reader "in" the film with a recollection of *Araya*'s opening moments that is more effective than evocations by other commentators because its paradoxical, synesthetic play of contrasts mimics the film's own poetics:

> You will see a heavy chorus of clouds. You will hear a light wash of the sea. You will witness the progress of the rising sun across a lunar landscape. You will hear the sparkling salt crystals under the silence of Araya. "On this earth nothing grows," another voice will intone. And this will be the door through which you will enter into a perfect film and remain in it (or it in you). . . . Not for an instant in *Araya* will that counterpoint cease between the barrenness of what is seen and the fertility of what is heard.

Like Araya the place, *Araya* the film and, by the metathesis just invoked, the viewer/reader become locations impervious to temporality and as such capable of apprehending a timeless, universal creation:

> Eighteen years have not passed for *Araya* either because this work was conceived with the structure of a classic in order that it be immune to corruption and death. It is the story of 24 hours (unity of time) in the life of a town (unity of place), the saga of men who are condemned to repeating the same tasks (unity of action).

Martínez evokes visual poetry with verbal poetry. Deeply invested in the notion of the timelessness of art, he engages history in order to poetically negate it. Like Benacerraf, he invokes the machine (in this case the movie projector about to unspool a print of *Araya* for the assembled audience of the peninsula's inhabitants) as both climax and enigma:

> Who knows what will happen when they see it some Saturday. . . . Maybe they will feel that this story belongs to a remote past which is no longer theirs. Or more likely they may discover that they themselves have been for eighteen years the blind heroes of an interminable film, while life went on somewhere else.

This writer posits two incompatible eventualities for the audience/actors of *Araya* in Araya: perhaps everything has changed for them, or then again, perhaps nothing has. In the latter case, the one he deems more likely, the mirroring of *Araya* the film and Araya the place leaves both outside of history *("mientras la vida andaba por otra parte")*. If history has transformed the Arayans, they will not recognize themselves in the mirror of the film. If they do recognize themselves, it will be as "blind heroes," blind presumably to the forces of change which, like life itself, happen somewhere else. Is Tomás Eloy Martínez creating a mirror effect of his own in this perversely inconclusive conclusion by reflecting back the film's putative exclusion of the historical? Or is he simply asserting his belief in the supremacy of imagination over analysis, art over politics, poetry over history?

History and Temporality

For Angel Hurtado, writing for a U.S. audience in 1989, the importance of *Araya* hinges on the fact that Margot Benacerraf arrived on that remote peninsula just "in time to capture on film the last days of an activity" that had continued unchanged for nearly half a millennium, just before "technology replaced human effort." Hurtado here touches upon a point of interest central to the past, present, and future reception of *Araya*. Two temporalities, one preindustrial and the other protoindustrial, are embedded in *Araya*. In the former, time—like the monumental pyramids of salt and the fulsome clay vessels so strikingly photographed in the film—is molded by manual and corporeal rhythms. In the other, time is mediated by rhythms no less mechanized than the process of filmmaking itself—which in this case also stands on a historical threshold between artisanal and industrial modalities (a point that will be further explored below). *Araya*'s deliberately classical cyclicity, its carefully orchestrated unities of time, place, and action, and its elaborately layered soundtrack and poeticized narration all combine to emphasize if not actually *produce* the either celebrated or dreaded intervention of industrial technology as the intrusive instant of rupture in a prolonged but *not* uninterrupted or unchanging march of time.

In the past as in the present, where some critics discern a heroics of human endurance, others deplore the erasure of human agency. Whether one reads it as epic-heroic or, conversely, as a melodramatic inscription of imminent danger, the intrusion of industrialized mechanization is manifestly "out of key" with the rest of the film because of the shift to heavy, symbolically "modern" orchestration that accompanies it and because of the use of quick montage: three violent explosions are followed by cuts to a series of different machines—earth movers, cranes, steam shovels, conveyor belts—that progressively break up the surface of the earth, reducing it to ever smaller fragments in the process, the montage suggests, of "constructing" the steel girding of a multistory building. Whether this incongruous skeletal structure is seen as ominous or promising, whether the machinery is read as liberating or displacing, the abrupt intrusion of the machine as if sui generis violently disrupts a rhythmic cycle that the film has constructed, not as eternal but as coterminous with all of history.

The commentaries reviewed here variously reiterate the *"y de pronto"* ("all of a sudden") of the script, which both introduces the arrival of the machine and concludes the narration:

> And all of a sudden . . .
> On this desolate land . . .
> On this ancient Araya . . .
> 450 years come face to face . . .
> Will human suffering disappear?
> Will this ancient world be able to change?
> Will machines finally succeed in replacing the strong arms of Benito, Beltrán and Fortunato . . . to build the pyramids?
> Will these be the last baskets of salt?
> Is this the end of the circle-dance of the salt?
> And here one day will real flowers grow for the ancient dead of Araya? [10]

The entry of the machine, the soundtrack and montage suggest, is as abrupt and transformative as the arrival of the Spanish conquistadors nearly five centuries earlier. The film's prologue invokes a once-glorious eminence that emerged from nothingness and returned to anonymity and ruin. "One day some men set foot on this land where . . . all was desolation. And they called these lands Araya. . . . And these men returned to Spain to tell their king of salt flats as vast as human eyes had ever beheld. . . . And so great was Araya's fame that the king built a fortress to defend it, the second in importance in all the West Indies. . . . So much effort to raise this fortress . . . How many men died in the attempt? . . . Many years went by. Expensive and no longer useful, the fortress was demolished. More years, more centuries went by. . . . What remains of Araya's fame?"

This same notion of intrusive, instantaneous transformation can be found in the "Then, one day . . ." that Benacerraf used in interviews to describe the shift from ancient to modern, manual to mechanized modes of salt production: "Then, one day, a company decided to take over the salt production." [11] Such phrases ask the viewer to believe that the filmmaker "just happened" to be present at the precise instant preceding historical transformation. If documentary's central function is that of bearing witness to what exists, what more important task than the "capturing" of a mode of existence that is just about to disappear, that can *only* exist from that moment on as the (temporally frozen) product of cinematic intervention? [12]

The axis of meaning around which *Araya*'s reception revolves is precisely this liminality between kinds of historical and perceptual time. At the core of differences in responsive stance is the degree of perceived disjunction between the apprehension and the interpretation of a particular way of life. Future generations of commentators, viewing *Araya,* will not escape the film's implicit mandate: to comment on the film is to characterize how it has chosen to represent both unchangingness and its negation; to comment on the film is to take a position on, as well as in, history.

Finding a Place in History, Finding a Place as History

Film historian Georges Sadoul, the first to attempt a historiography of world cinema that reached beyond the borders of Europe and the United States to include the emerging cinemas of postcolonial regions, deemed *Araya* "a great work" and expressed confidence that "sooner or later" the film-loving public would come to share his opinion. For Marcel Martin, *Araya* was "the first authentically Venezuelan film" and as such "deserves to become part of posterity along with the name of its author." Tomás Eloy Martínez presented *Araya* to the Venezuelan public as "an unknown masterwork," "a perfect film." Angel Hurtado (re)introduced it to the American public as "a classic of both Latin American and world cinema." Yet for Julio Miranda, author of several books on Venezuelan documentary, *Araya* is the point where that national documentary history might have begun but did not; its combination of extranational renown and long-deferred national reception relegates as it elevates, rendering *Araya* "a myth more than a film." For Miranda, myths have no place in history; for those who challenge the Eurocentric rationalism of this assumption, however, myths—even (alleged) cinematic ones—are as central to historical understanding as facts. A rhetoric that excludes *Araya* from national or continental history by virtue of its legendary status only flimsily masks its author's bias.

Miranda's and Roffé's exclusionary concept of the national was anomalous on the left. As Jorge Castañeda points out in his brilliant analysis of its history and prospects, the Latin American left has characteristically believed that "[t]he destitute and excluded from society make up the people, and thus the 'real nation' . . ."[13] Margot Benacerraf's impulse to focus on one of the most remote, isolated, and marginalized elements of the national (*creole*) population anticipates or echoes the impulse that moved many of her contemporaries across the continent to venture into the remote and neglected corners of their countries in order to film the subcultures they found there—Cuban charcoal workers, Brazilian cowhands, Argentine potters, Chilean threshers, Colombian brickmakers and saltmakers were some of the provincial subcultures organized around particular modes of production that became the subjects of influential documentaries in the 1950s and 1960s.[14]

As we have seen, *Araya* concludes by juxtaposing a painstakingly depicted preindustrial temporality to a brashly introjected protoindustrial one, thus posing a contrast between "timeless" manual rhythms of labor that harmonize with the natural world and the disruptive "dissonance" of mechanization. For commentators across decades and national and cultural boundaries, this visual and aural juxtaposition mandates both filmmaker and viewer to take a stand, to identify historical forces and their consequences and to offer an interpretation of processes of change. Miranda and Roffé, Venezuelan intellectuals shaped by the heroic revolutionary discourses of the 1960s and 1970s, dichotomize the depiction of human potentiality for transformative intervention, on the one hand, and the impact of external natural or historical forces on the other, interpreting acknowledgment of the latter as "proof" of complicity with the powers that be.

It is important to clarify that the Araya peninsula has no documented preconquest history. A literal blank slate, its entry into history coincided with the arrival of the Spanish ships in 1500. The toponym is Spanish, derived from the Punta de Raya (Stingray Point) designation on the early Spanish navigational maps. Its population is the product of its inscription into an imperial economy. The Iberian ancestry of the inhabitants is manifest in their surnames and physiognomy as well as in their music.

In the historical discourse elaborated by the film, the introduction of the industrial machine at the climax parallels the moment of discovery and conquest invoked in the prologue. Both are regimes of extraction imposed from outside and above, and both mark new historical moments as violent intrusions upon a preexisting world powerless to impede their arrival. The film's analogy between colonial conquest and the neocolonial introduction of modernizing industrialization seems more aptly read as an intervention in, rather than an abdication of, political discourse. *Araya*'s discursive logic is symbolic and associative rather than explicitly didactic. Two symmetrically located constructions, both massive, looming structures devoid of human presence, symbolize two different yet analogously intrusive and transformative historical epochs. *Araya*'s montage evokes both the grandeur of the Spanish fortress and its crumbling into ruin. The hollow emptiness of the steel building skeleton in the film's climactic montage is a visual echo of Buñuel's *Los olvidados,* in which a structure connotes imposed, intrusive, incongruous modernity. The question posed by *Araya*'s structuration seems to be: Might time and history someday render this modern structure as anachronistic and "out of place" as the Spanish stone fortress crumbled to ruin?

When Roffé denounces *Araya* as "practically the filmic manifesto of the defenders of the status quo, of the present situation, of the preservation of privilege," he is separating his reading of the film as product from the film as practice—without considering the latter. In fact, the practice that produced *Araya* was consistent with, and arguably anticipated, the committed, contestational modes of filmmaking that Roffé and Miranda elsewhere exalt and that have been generally regarded as constitutive practices of the New Latin American Cinema.

Araya's mode of production hovers between the preindustrial and the postindustrial. On the one hand, the constraints of a limited budget, the use of a single camera and two-person crew, the relatively long coexistence with the members of the remote community being filmed, the impossibility of viewing rushes until the editing phase, and Benacerraf's intense personal involvement with every aspect of preproduction and postproduction all place *Araya* within the artisanal mode of cinematic production, an approach that would be embraced time and again by exponents of the New Latin American Cinema movement. On the other hand, the crane shots toward the beginning, middle, and end of the film connote a more industrialized mode of filmmaking. The fact that it was not a studio crane but construction machinery found on site and utilized in improvised fashion (fig. 3.3), while consistent with the film's artisanal mode, also suggests

FIGURE 3.3. *The fortuitous presence of the machine: the construction crane, borrowed on site, makes possible the montage of crane-shot panoramas that opens the film. Margot Benacerraf, standing; cameraman Giuseppe Nisoli, kneeling. Reprinted courtesy of Margot Benacerraf.*

cinema's congenital implication with mechanization and the "modern" world and thus signals as well the inherent contradiction of cinematic artisanality. Roffé does not take any of this complexity into account when he brands *Araya* practically a manifesto of the status quo.

In their denunciation of *Araya*'s insensitivity to human agency, neither of the Venezuelan critics takes note of the film's painstaking depiction of women's double shift of paid and domestic labor, or its touching visual emphasis on the fleetingness of childhood in an economy that conscripts all able bodies early on. The history that they accuse the film of occluding is clearly neither gendered nor sensitive to the social inscription of the very old and the very young. Those who accuse the film of lacking historical dimension also fail to recognize the unique survival of musical forms from early Renaissance Spain in the popular songs recorded on site by Benacerraf and her cameraman and later integrated into the film's complex, layered soundtrack. In short, the allegation that the film occludes history is itself historical—a product of perceptions and attitudes that bear the filtering mark of their own particular historical circumstances.

Roffé's specific criticisms can be challenged one by one. References to "socio-economic and political structure and relations of production" may be insufficient but are by no means totally absent. The narration emphasizes the deep relationship between salt and capitalism: etymologically and historically, a *sal*aried worker is someone paid in salt. The local boss *(mayordomo)* is cited twice, the second time by name. The trucks and barges that load the salt suggest integration into a larger economy, just as Isabel Pereda's itinerant selling of the freshly caught fish and the arrival of the water truck confirm the existence of a monetary rather than purely subsistence regime. However poetic, Benacerraf's montage provides a concrete, step-by-step account of a labor-intensive production process: the chopping, loading, transport, unloading, washing, reloading, hauling, weighing, piling, drying, bagging, and carrying of the salt to the barges. Other processes of production—the netting, sorting, washing, selling, and salting of the fish; the throwing and firing of clay pots—are also rendered in considerable detail (figs. 3.4 and 3.5). A more neutral Marxist criticism would certainly acknowledge if not commend this meticulous, production-centered materialism.

Though Roffé insists that *Araya*'s social actors are denied speech and

FIGURE 3.4. *The visual poetics of human toil. Reprinted courtesy of Margot Benacerraf.*

FIGURE 3.5. *Women-made vessels from the unyielding soil of the Araya peninsula. Reprinted courtesy of Margot Benacerraf.*

nonverbal communication, close attention to the soundtrack reveals fragments of many conversations. The women in particular are highly communicative among themselves. It bears keeping in mind that synchronous sound recording was a luxury that few artisanal filmmakers had access to in the late 1950s. Roffé also denounces the elimination of "social relations and individuality," yet the three (reconstituted) families—the Salazars, the Ortizes, and the Peredas—are carefully delineated, as are some of their social relations with relatives and neighbors, though admittedly in a highly controlled manner.

However subtly, *Araya* presents gender relations as paramount. It is the women who guide the viewer in making the transition from the open-air workplace into the enclosure of the home. (And as they do so, they move in spontaneous groupings, not the regimented formations that Roffé censures.) The young boys enjoy many kinds of active play—marbles, kites, swimming, scrambling up the pyramids of salt. The young girls engage in more serious pursuits: Carmen Ortiz contemplatively gathers seashells destined to adorn the family gravesites in lieu of flowers; Petra's preadolescent daughter dutifully carries coffee to her father on the docks while the younger brothers in her charge frolic. The "double day" of the women is made clear in myriad ways. Returning from a night of labor, Dámaso, the Salazar *paterfamilias,* is served his meal and then takes his rest, while his wife Petra, initially viewed operating the scales that weigh the salt, undertakes her home shift, preparing food and washing the family laundry as her counterpart, Isabel Ortiz, sells and salts fish, nurses her youngest child, and chops and gathers firewood. Perhaps there is no contradiction in the fact that though the narrator makes reference to the cock fighting ring at Manicuare, the director does not see fit to include visuals of this hypermasculine entertainment. Finally, the symbology of the courtship sequence is strikingly gendered. Petra's son Fortunato chooses as his courting site "the well of brackish water." In the first "two-shot" of the lovers, his intended remains unseen, substituted by the water jug she carries on her shoulder. (What was empty has now been filled.) The entire sequence is framed by cutaways to sperm-shaped kites dancing in the sky.

Roffé finds Benacerraf's depth-of-field compositions "decorative," citing the example of Petra Salazar's framing at the scales while two men in the distant background above and behind her shovel salt (fig. 3.6). In fact, this composition is part of a larger montage that begins by framing and

FIGURE 3.6. *Composition in depth: Petra Salazar weighs the baskets of salt. Third shot in a sequence. Reprinted courtesy of Margot Benacerraf.*

reframing Petra alongside the profiled belly of a very pregnant woman. By ignoring the context of the shot that he singles out, Roffé also ignores how the entire montage simultaneously invokes women's productive and reproductive labor, raises implicit questions regarding adequate prenatal care (women forced to work through late-stage pregnancy), and queries what the prospects will be for the next generation of Arayans.[15]

Roffé reads in *Araya* the denial of human agency and the defense of "a closed, static, ahistorical world." Another perspective might perceive an organic, integrated way of life that, despite its harshness, celebrates concerted, collective effort between and across generations. Explicit denunciation and protest may be omitted from Benacerraf's depiction, but irony— intentional or inadvertent—is not. As the narrator informs us in his opening monologue that "nothing grows here," an aerial shot of a landscape sporadically dotted with trees qualifies his assertion. His claim that "all was desolation" is belied by its companion shot of surf breaking along a pristine beach, an image no less evocative of "tropical paradise" in the 1950s than today. As the prologue concludes, the first crane shot carries us over perfect pyramids in the foreground as the narrator intones, "Another day is about to begin." What the crane's progress reveals, however, is not the faltering beginnings of a new day's labor but a veritable human anthill of activity already well under way, not the daybreak of the soundtrack but a more advanced hour (compare figs. 3.2 and 3.1).

A history prior to the designated moment of inception is what is being emphasized in this ironic juxtaposition of sound and image tracks. Likewise, the "today just like yesterday" repeatedly intoned on the soundtrack may be read ironically, given how both narration and visuals affirm early on that this day is not like the yesterday of Araya's long-lost glory. The repeated aural invocation of "gestures that never cease" is ironic, given the imminent possibility that they will cease forever due to the abrupt intrusion of another historical epoch.

What *Araya* seems to be reaching toward is the depiction of a development-of-underdevelopment cycle like those Eduardo Galeano re-created so poignantly in his 1971 chronicle, *The Open Veins of Latin America,* a boom-and-bust syndrome that Benacerraf evokes but cannot yet name. Her emphasis is on the *longue durée,* the time in between the apogee of colonial exploitation and the inception of (neocolonial) modernization through mechanization. Her pessimism regarding this impending phase is registered, I believe, in the initial quick cutaways within the climactic montage of the machine, cutaways to the human work rhythms of community members chopping wood, grinding corn, pounding salt with poles. The survival of these ancestral rhythms and the Arayans who perform them, Benacerraf seems to suggest, is made precarious by the violent (re)introduction of outside forces of historical transformation.

Conclusion

Araya's place in film history is secure or contested, depending on what kind of film history it is being located within. A historiography that encompasses a global (though not necessarily Eurocentric) purview implicitly privileges auteur and text over nation and reception context while tolerating all kinds of hybridities. In contrast, narrators of national film histories and the "continental project" of New Latin American Cinema are notably anxious about hybridity, hypostatizing "authenticity" instead and privileging national and regional reception context over text and auteur. *Araya*'s national reception is therefore paradoxical: to receptive Venezuelans (as exemplified by several writing in the popular press), this "exotic flower" long on display abroad was finally, triumphantly returned to its natural habitat, while to resistant Venezuelans (as exemplified by left-identified intellectuals writing in more-specialized publications), the species appears alien on native soil. Is a national consciousness that welcomes extranational validation less authentic than a stance that posits an uncontaminated national essence, refusing to acknowledge that the phenomenon of interregional as well as transatlantic transculturation lies at the root of all Latin American cultural expression—local, national, and hemispheric?

Araya is neither the first nor the only Latin American work to be consecrated abroad before achieving recognition at home. What was true for fiction writers like Jorge Luis Borges or Gabriel García Márquez, whose books began to be read widely in their home countries only in response to their success abroad, has been true for many filmmakers. Numerous landmarks of Latin American cinema, "new" and otherwise, achieved that status only through their prior European consecration—among them Emilio Fernández's *María Candelaria,* Luis Buñuel's *Los olvidados,* Fernando Solanas's and Octavio Getino's *The Hour of the Furnaces,* and several early Cinema Novo works, Glauber Rocha's included. The virtual impossibility of viewers from one Latin American country familiarizing themselves with the films of a neighboring country without traveling to Europe or North America is a notorious holdover from hypercentralized colonial administrative practices, only very recently mitigated by the proliferation of video (and video piracy). Thus it remains curious that *Araya* should be excluded from the national and continental pantheon ostensibly for reasons over-looked in countless other instances.[16]

Araya elicits dichotomies because it engages them. Both implicitly and explicitly, the film juxtaposes historical temporalities, modes of cinematic production, ways of representing continuity and change, linear and syn-chronic worldviews, evocative and analytical epistemologies. It should come as no surprise, then, that its reception trajectory is also characterized by conflicting modes of response—national versus supranational, politi-cized versus poetic—and that it has been variously heralded as a timeless, transcendental, universal masterpiece and dismissed as an alien, anachro-nistic, and reactionary aberration. In straddling the borders between mu-tually exclusive terms whose very polarization now appears to be an effect (rhetorical?) of ideological and epistemological factors, *Araya* as product, practice, and reception trajectory calls these very dichotomies—and the historiographic and critical practices that produce them—into question. This phenomenon is one source of the film's persistent interest, impor-tance, and impact (fig. 3.7).

Postscript

Publication of this essay, written in 1995, was delayed by the demise of the journal for which it was originally intended. In October 1996, months after revisions were completed, I received by fax two unidentified clippings from the Caracas press. "Margot Benacerraf Winner of the 1995 National Film Prize," both headlines announced. According to one text, the five-person jury unanimously agreed that "In the dawning moment of our national cinema, Benacerraf's work managed to give Venezuelan cinema a place in world film history, a place that it has maintained in succeeding decades." The other clipping invoked her two documentaries as "decisive in local film history" while the first observed that both "continue to be an exemplary register of the history of Venezuelan filmmaking." The unidentified writers of both notices did not hesitate to confer on *Araya* (as well as on Bena-cerraf's earlier experimental documentary, *Reverón*) the foundational status whose elusiveness prompted the foregoing reflections. In addition to her filmmaking credits, both articles noted, the award was conferred in recog-nition of Benacerraf's "efforts to promote national film culture, her cre-ation of such landmark institutions as the Cinemateca Nacional de Vene-zuela and the Filmmaking Workshops offered by the Ateneo de Caracas,

FIGURE 3.7. *Margot Benacerraf with her local "assistant" on the pier during the filming. Reprinted courtesy of Margot Benacerraf.*

and her ardent militancy in favor of all the currents of Venezuelan cinema."

These good tidings occasioned both satisfaction and doubt. Does this recognition herald a generalized revision of Venezuelan film history, I wondered, or will the guardians of the purity of both national and continental film traditions remain staunchly impervious to governmental gestures that, even four decades after the filming of *Araya,* only reinforce their conviction about the director's degree of investment in the "status quo"?

Equally belatedly, I came across a review of *Araya* by the late Marta Traba, Latin America's foremost art critic, still best known in the United States for the novels that she wrote relatively late in her prematurely and tragically truncated life.[17] When *Araya* had its Venezuelan release, this brilliant Argentine critic, long resident of Bogotá, where she left an enduring legacy in the Colombian art world, had moved on to Caracas. In tribute to her enduring perspicacity, I conclude this rumination on *Araya* across time and space by echoing words penned by another female artist-intellectual of Benacerraf's generation, someone long unanchored from her place of national origin, steeped in European tradition yet profoundly committed to the expressive arts of Las Américas, and above all exquisitely sensitive to the temporal atemporality and transcendent sociality of art:

> It seems logical that the response to Margot Benacerraf's film would be an apotheosis. This is how Venezuela's cultured sector redeems its share of guilt or negligence that an excellent documentary, awarded prizes at Cannes in 1959, inexplicably only now arrives in its own country. . . .
>
> Of course this coincidence of opinion converges on beauty, since the intense and perfect beauty of *Araya* deserves to be called by name. In order to accentuate it, Margot Benacerraf has made every act, situation, and real-life character into the servant of that beauty. Her clear intention to impose a normative visual structure—ordering objects in such a way that their deep beauty is revealed, synchronizing movements, and adjusting both landscape and human beings to a rhythmic canon, silencing her protagonists so that they do not interrupt beauty's murmur—is rightly considered an estheticizing vision.
>
> . . . The startling thing about *Araya* is that it articulates two generally incompatible elements, reality and estheticism, allowing each perspective to "irrigate" the other. The film's estheticism does not rise above its reality, depriving it of verisimilitude in ways that go beyond the fashion and circumstances of the period (. . .) but rather dramatizes and underlines a social situation that it accepts as real, a situation of such inherent vigor that it is not dissipated in the poetic aura of the film's estheticism. This exceptional fact clearly rests upon the equally exceptional personality of Margot Benacerraf, on the maniacal curiosity of her eye as well as the sincere emotion of her temperament, on her will to appropriate her theme in a global way and to possess it emotionally until it becomes a part of her, transformed into the *amormundo* (world love) that [Peruvian novelist José María] Arguedas talked about.
>
> This is what accounts for the permanent rupture deep within *Araya,* a rupture produced within the classic equilibrium between emotion and creative freedom that occurs when estheticism is superimposed upon real life. Through that crack, one can breathe the breath of life, so different from the ponderous air that aspires to contain all things. . . . The esthetic equilibrium of *Araya* does not culminate in the construction of a perfect poem as would occur in a classical work . . . [because] from the first image, the mirror of classicism in *Araya* is clouded by hidden turbulences. . . .
>
> Paradigmatically, *Araya* will always be the condensation of an awesome human experience (not a socioeconomic study of relations of production,

obviously, nor a means of identifying the guilty capitalists) filtered through the admirable visual language of film. . . . Great photography, great editing, the inflamed quest for modulated greys amid unforgettable extremes of black and white—that is what accounts for the visual pleasure that *Araya* offers. A period text and period music accompany a film that knows no period, a definitive work.

> —EXCERPTED FROM MARTA TRABA, "MIRAR EN CARACAS: PLACER
> VISUAL FRENTE A *ARAYA,*" *EL NACIONAL* (CARACAS; 6 MAY 1977)

Notes

1. From development of the negative through the final cut, which reduced 3 hours of edited footage by half, all postproduction was done in Paris. Even the film's voice-over narration was written and spoken in French because of the requirements and pressures of preparing for the Cannes competition. Despite various attempts, a Spanish version was not produced until 1977, when the film had its Venezuelan premier. A combination of factors seems to have contributed to this prolonged delay, both personal (the director's ill health) and circumstantial (the difficulty of finding distributors and exhibitors of feature-length documentaries).

2. Sources are listed at the conclusion of this text. All translations are my own.

3. This now prominent Argentine film critic and novelist (*La novela de Perón, Santa Evita*) lived in exile in Venezuela during the 1970s.

4. Littín is best known as a feature filmmaker, first in his native Chile *(The Jackal of Nahueltoro, The Promised Land)* and later in exile *(Letters from Marusia, Montiel's Widow, Viva el presidente, Alsino and the Condor, Sandino)*. He returned to his native Chile in the early 1990s, after filming the clandestine *Actas de Chile*. Fellow Chilean Guzmán is the director of the epic three-part historical documentary, *The Battle of Chile* as well as, in the 1990s, *La cruz del sur* and *La memoria obstinada*. The career of Santiago Alvarez, Cuba's foremost documentarist, spanned the history of the Cuban Film Institute, from its 1959 founding to his death in 1998.

5. According to Benacerraf, the source of this quote was in fact Eli Lotar, cameraman for Luis Buñuel.

6. French critic Marcel Martin, writing the same year as Sadoul, is the only commentator among those assembled here to pose a ("minor") criticism. This has to do with the film's voice-over text (written in French by the poet Pierre Seghers and the filmmaker), which he finds "pompous" and "over-written," the expression of a "vain lyricism" exacerbated by the "too perfect" diction of the narrator (Laurent Terzieff).

7. For Sanjinés's account of how he and his crew unwittingly provoked and subsequently overcame the rejection and hostility of this indigenous community, see "Revolutionary Cinema: The Bolivian Experience" in my *Cinema and*

Social Change in Latin America: Conversations with Filmmakers (Austin: University of Texas Press, 1986), 35–47.

8. Benacerraf worked with a single cameraman, Giuseppe Nisoli, and no other crew; she scripted the film, recorded the sound, cast and directed the social actors, supervised the editing and sound-mixing, cowrote the narration—all with minimal, though consistently top-notch, collaboration.

9. For a full recounting of Benacerraf's subsequent career as founder and promoter of a number of important Venezuelan film institutions, see my translation of Karen Schwartzman's "Interview with Margot Benacerraf" in *Journal of Film and Video* 44.3–4 (fall 1992–winter 1993), 51–75, and part 2 of my forthcoming book, *Three Lives in Film,* which details Benacerraf's life and career.

10. My translation from the Spanish script. A new print of *Araya,* with English subtitles based on a new translation done at Benacerraf's request by Karen Schwartzman with assistance from me, is currently being made in France under the director's supervision.

11. As quoted for example in "La quinzaine cinématographique" edition of *Dossiers Art et Essai* (12 April 1967): 7.

12. The projected modernization of the Araya peninsula was announced in 1956 and well covered in the national press *(El Universal, El Nacional)* in March, April, and May of 1957. The bulk of a 1957 issue of the magazine *Mundo Social* was dedicated to the Pérez Jiménez government's projected "Salaraya: A New City in Venezuela's Industrial Geography," with dozens of photographs showing the traditional labor methods accompanying a text touting the arrival of resorts, tourism, and a hospital as well as a modern residential complex for employees of the projected salt factory. As was typical of many of these national development projects, this one was only realized on a limited scale, though sufficient to destroy the traditional ways of life on the peninsula, creating widespread unemployment and all the accompanying social problems.

13. Jorge Castañeda, *Utopia Unarmed: The Latin American Left after the Cold War* (New York: Knopf, 1993), 273.

14. Respectively: *El mégano* (1955), by Julio García Espinosa; *O homen de couro* (1969), by Geraldo Sarno; *Los alfareros de Chimbayo* (1954), by Jorge Prelorán; *Trilla* (1958), by Sergio Bravo; *Chircales* (1968, 1972), by Marta Rodríguez and Jorge Silva; *El hombre de la sal* (1969), by Gabriela Samper.

15. Reevaluating the film in 1995, Julio Miranda ("*Araya*: Notas contradictorias sobre un film mítico," *C de cine* 1 [May]) strikes two newfound notes of praise. He commends the film's attention, first, to work and workers, given a subsequent national film tradition that has preferred to depict "rogues, delinquents, prostitutes, guerrilla fighters, and policemen . . . ," and, second, to feminine agency *(protagonismo feminino),* though he cannot resist taking its director to task for not emphasizing this aspect on the soundtrack, given the narrator's general "indefatigability." The rest of the essay plays the same tune as

his earlier responses, emphasizing the same shortcomings—the absence of socioeconomic and sociopolitical contextualization; the inattention to festivity and leisure, feelings, and beliefs—as part of its director's deliberately deceptive withholding of information for the sake of excessive, essentializing exoticism and pretentious auteurism.

16. The inclusion of *Araya* in the retrospective of works by Latin America's women filmmakers at the 1987 Havana Festival of New Latin American Cinema may or may not have been indicative of a disposition to admit it into the NLAC canon, since the very context of this exhibition framed the selected films on the basis of their prior exclusion (gender difference) without providing a context for comparison outside that framework.

17. Born in Buenos Aires, Argentina in 1930, Marta Traba had traveled and lived in several Latin American cities before eventually requesting U.S. residency in the early 1980s, a request that the Reagan government denied. Reluctantly relocated to Paris, she was killed in an airplane crash outside Madrid in 1983, along with her second husband, the esteemed Uruguayan-born literary critic Angel Rama, and a number of other prominent figures in Latin American arts and letters, all en route to Colombia for a symposium on the role of art in the twenty-first century.

References

Hurtado, Angel. *"Araya,"* in *Latin American Visions: A Half Century of Latin American Cinema, 1930–1989,* ed. Patricia Aufderheide (Philadelphia: International House, 1990), 7–8.

Martin, Marcel. "Découverte de Vénézuéla" and *"Araya:* Le sel de la mer," *Cinéma 67: Le Guide du Spectateur* (Paris), no. 117 (June 1967), 19–20, 115–16.

Martínez, Tomás Eloy. "La segunda vida de *Araya*: Margot Benacerraf, a la vuelta de 18 años ante el estreno de una obra maestra desconocida," *El Nacional* (Caracas; 15 May 1977).

Miranda, Julio E. "El cine que nos ve (Para una historia del documental venezolano)," chapter 1 of *El cine que nos ve: Materiales críticos sobre el documental venezolano* (Mérida, Venezuela: Letra Viva, 1989; reprinted by the Controloría General de la República, Caracas, n.d. [1990]).

Roffé, Alfredo. *"Araya,"* *Cine al Día,* no. 22 (Caracas; November 1977).

Sadoul, Georges. "Le sel de la terre vénézuélienne," *Les Lettres Françaises* (Paris; 27 April–3 May 1967).

———. "Ne maudissons pas les juges," *Les Lettres Françaises* (Paris; 21–27 May 1959).

Wilmington, Michael. "Film Notes," *Chicago Tribune* (2 February 1995).

4

Transcultured Anticommunism

COLD WAR HOLLYWOOD IN POSTWAR MEXICO

Seth Fein

The only suggestion I have is to emphasize the Communist angle a bit more. If the Germans are beaten our job is going to be fighting communism and we might as well start getting ready for that now.

—NELSON ROCKEFELLER, to John E. Abbott, director of
Museum of Modern Art's Film Library, 1940

■ ■ ■ ■

During the late 1940s two distinct political patterns converged in Mexico: one global, the cold war, and the other national, the institutionalization of rightist development. Each reinforced the other; the cold war did not determine postwar Mexican development as much as it interacted with the socioeconomic and political model imposed by the ruling one-party regime, which appropriately renamed itself the Partido Revolucionario Institucional (PRI) in 1946. Mass culture reproduced this convergence and was itself decisive in forming the ideological environment that guided the popular politics of the period. For Mexico, in the early postwar period, film was a pervasive form of national culture connected to the state's project. It was closely integrated into the structures of official power through the Secretaría de Gobernación's expanding mass-culture bureaucracy. As the government of Miguel Alemán (1946–56) pursued its private-sector-oriented agenda at home, reinforced by its deepening transnational pact with the United States, Mexican mass media reconfigured nationalist discourse to support the rightist triumph within the state party that drew strength from the deepening cold war.[1]

Although Mexican cinema of the early 1950s was an important cultural and commercial counterweight to Hollywood throughout the Western Hemisphere, it was not a nationalist film industry (artistically or industrially). The context for Mexican production was transnational. In terms of commercial development, that context made the Mexican film industry more vulnerable to postwar Hollywood competition than had been the developing prewar (sound) movie sector. The logic of U.S.-Mexican relations, established under the political alliance forged during World War II, decreased the Mexican industry's economic and ideological autonomy vis-à-vis the United States and made it increasingly difficult for the Mexican state to intervene to protect national cultural production during the early cold war (which coincided with the apex of Mexican cinema's so-called Golden Age).[2] These limits were imposed less by the dynamics of capitalist competition than by those of collaboration. Moreover, economic structures conformed to broader political ones: the convergence of the Mexican state's postwar project with the anticommunist crusade led by U.S. foreign policy. Those who challenged the regime's retreat from social reform, Alemanismo's institutionalization of authoritarian control in the name of modernization and national progress, were branded unpatriotic.

Wartime programs instituted by the Motion Picture Division (MPD) of the Roosevelt administration's Office of the Coordinator of Inter-American Affairs (OCIAA), headed by Nelson Rockefeller, not only modernized and expanded Mexican film production, within a Hollywood-led industrial framework, but also strengthened ideological collaboration between both states and film industries. Working through Hollywood functionaries, the MPD sought to develop the Mexican film sector as an ostensibly autonomous and culturally "authentic" source of Latin American propaganda. While, as I have shown elsewhere, this economic collaboration brought about the rise of the so-called Golden Age of Mexican cinema (i.e., aggregate and artistic growth within a U.S.-dependent framework), it also created the industrial infrastructure for production of transcultured propaganda. Even as economic collaboration slowed with the war's end, the integration of the two film industries persisted, cementing institutional arrangements that accelerated the simultaneous use of transnational mass culture as an instrument of postwar U.S. foreign policy and of American state formation.[3]

Hollywood's integral role in planning and executing U.S. government wartime film programs in Mexico meant that its involvements in Mexican film production deepened as the Mexican industry grew. And just as World War II strengthened the overall transnational and interstate links between Mexico and the United States, especially in the area of mass media, it also modernized Hollywood's relationship to U.S. foreign policy.[4] Movies were no longer viewed by Washington simply as commodities to be promoted internationally with special vigor, owing to their importance to overall U.S.

ideological and commercial interests; by the postwar period, commercial cinema was an integral weapon in the U.S. government's plans to wage cultural cold war. In Mexico these patterns intersected with the unusually complex form of mass media development involving transnational private-sector contacts as well as the intervention of the Mexican state. These wartime projects—combined with the U.S. industry's independent commercial links to Mexican studios, producers, and exhibitors—provided infrastructure for new forms of collaboration that reproduced the ideological convergence between the postwar Mexican state's project and U.S. cold war culture policies.[5]

As is evident from Nelson Rockefeller's statement in this chapter's epigraph, even before the OCIAA's film activities got under way, U.S. authorities viewed film as crucial to the pursuit of U.S. cultural hegemony in Latin America (regardless of the protean nature of global U.S. policies).[6] Dominant ideas might fluctuate, but the means to disseminate were to be constant. Early on, Rockefeller, who understood better than most U.S. elites the danger posed by Latin American social inequities to U.S. interests, viewed anticommunism to be as important for postwar ideological hegemony as antifascism was for wartime control. And the U.S. government's wartime project to deliver technical and material aid to the Mexican film industry—begun as a program focused on developing a client foreign film sector to carry out ideological projects—metamorphosed into RKO's partnership with a group headed by Mexican media magnate Emilio Azcárraga in the construction of the Latin America's most modern motion-picture studio, Estudios Churubusco.[7]

RKO's involvement in the U.S. government's Latin American film propaganda during the war exceeded that of other U.S. studios and often ran counter to short-term economic interests, as it pursued the U.S. government's ideological agenda. Nelson Rockefeller had a major economic stake in RKO at the start of the war, and that influence served the OCIAA's film initiatives.[8] Laurence Duggan, a leading figure in the planning of the State Department's Latin American cultural initiatives, reported in 1944: "Nelson says that of all of the motion-picture producers RKO has been the most cooperative. It has interested itself in Latin American matters in a way which no other company has done. Its interest has not been financially remunerative; it has lost a good deal of money."[9]

In fact, RKO sought to use its new studio to coopt Mexico's lucrative wartime production and to preempt what it viewed (correctly) as inevitable postwar protectionist measures by the Mexican government. Commercial ambitions aside, what was not in doubt was the cultural infrastructure that the Mexico City studio would provide the U.S. government. At the time of the U.S. studio's initial deal with Azcárraga, Ambassador George Messersmith noted that "while [RKO] may take in some Mexican participation, even as much as 50%, it is going to be, in fact, an American studio with a high-powered company behind it." [10] In providing a transnational mode to produce Mexican mass culture, the U.S. studio's investment in Estudios Churubusco would be central to U.S. propaganda production. And in planning propaganda projects to be carried out as entertainment films, RKO executives at Estudios Churubusco not only worked on behalf of their company but also collaborated with the U.S. government, which had been instrumental in facilitating the studio's Mexican venture. Estudios Churubusco became the locus of U.S.-Mexican transnational and state-to-state mass-media collaboration, in ways that exemplified and transcended instrumental financial links. During the cold war it was the site of transcultural propaganda production that married U.S. and Mexican antisubversive discourses with Hollywood and Mexican cinematic conventions for inter-American dissemination as entertainment.

This essay analyzes two examples of that collaboration. In so doing, it seeks to unite the intertwined histories of production and representation (or political economy and signs) within a framework that explores transcultural processes at work in U.S.-Mexican relations. As Mary Louise Pratt reminds us, "While the imperial metropolis tends to understand itself as determining the periphery . . . it habitually blinds itself to the ways in which the periphery determines the metropolis." [11] Although scholarship on both sides of the U.S.-Mexican border has acknowledged the importance of international interactions between the neighbors in the development of cinema in both nations, little work has moved beyond the screen, theoretically or empirically, to investigate that relationship. [12] Similarly, in the broader field of film studies, attempts to "historicize" cinema have generally produced compelling criticism but very little of it based on original research about the connections of film to state and society, economics, and ideology. [13] This is a call not for simple empiricism (i.e., a historian's fetishization of archives) but for more-developed (and -informed) contextualization in historical writing about national and transnational film cultures, that is, the self-proclaimed subject of much recent scholarship. [14]

Mexican Cinema as Hollywood: Anticlericalism as Communism

The Fugitive (1947)—directed by John Ford and starring Henry Fonda, Dolores del Río, and Pedro Armendáriz—demonstrates how economic

and ideological objectives (or Hollywood and U.S. government goals) reinforced each other in early cold war transnational film production. The
first film produced by Ford's independent Argosy Company, *The Fugitive*
was made in Mexico at Estudios Churubusco and distributed by RKO (a
company with close connections to all of the talent involved).[15] Adapting
Graham Greene's *The Labyrinthine Ways* (1940),[16] Ford presented a severe
anti-anticlerical message about the danger that communism posed to peasant values, traditions, and beliefs. In doing so, his antileftist agenda converged with Hollywood's censorship machinery to remake Greene's tale of
personal salvation as political allegory.[17] The film depicts an anonymous,
supposedly fictional Latin American nation controlled by a totalitarian state
that brutally oppresses Catholic peasants in the name of social egalitarianism and modernization. Political police dress in fascist-style uniforms that,
like much early cold war culture, drew upon visual signs (such as pseudo-
fascist political emblems) and other historical references that had been dis-
seminated widely in U.S. and Mexican antifascist wartime film propaganda.
Now residual symbols of rightism were redeployed to combat leftism.[18]

A transnational hybrid, the film shrewdly combined Mexico City and
Hollywood talent.[19] The U.S.-reared Armendáriz portrayed the police lieutenant (Juan Rafael) in charge of the state's anticlerical pogrom.[20] The
movie's pressbook pointed out to U.S. audiences that the Mexican star
was "a prime favorite with moviegoers south of the border."[21] Armendáriz starred in an earlier binational production backed by RKO. *La perla*
(FAMA, 1945), based on John Steinbeck's original screenplay, was shot bi-
lingually (to produce separate English and Spanish versions) at Estudios
Churubusco and on location in Mexico. And following *The Fugitive*'s distribution, in 1948 RKO released *The Pearl* in the United States (three years
after its Mexican premiere). Teamed with Armendáriz was another transnational figure, Dolores del Río (who played María Dolores: the priest's
protector and the lieutenant's ex-lover and, unbeknownst to him, mother
of his child). In promoting *The Fugitive*, RKO exploited the Mexican actress' presumed cross-cultural appeal, since her film career had begun in the
United States in the 1920s (where she later appeared in RKO sound features) and had been transformed in Latin America, when she repatriated to
Mexico during World War II to star in major films. A studio press release
highlighted the former Hollywood star's newfound south-of-the-border
fame, explaining that recently "she has been making pictures for the Latin-
American trade, and she is a high favorite from Laredo to Cape Horn."[22]
Where earlier she had been, at different moments, compelled by Holly-

wood to conceal or redirect her *mexicanidad*, now RKO promoted del Río's Mexican fame as a sign of the authenticity of its Latin American production.[23] (Other prominent Mexican actors—including Fernando Fernández and Miguel Inclán—played supporting roles.)

The Fugitive not only involved stars recognized throughout Latin America but also reproduced the distinctive visual style that had come to define Mexican cinema during the height of its Golden Age in the 1940s. In search of further authenticity, as well as the cooperation of Mexican authorities, Ford involved talent behind the camera who was central to Mexico's emerging motion-picture canon: cinematographer Gabriel Figueroa and director Emilio "El Indio" Fernández (who served as the movie's associate producer).[24] In addition to collaborating on RKO's earlier binational experiment *La perla/The Pearl*, both had worked extensively with Armendáriz and del Río. The actors had been paired in major Fernández-Figueroa films—including their monumental wartime production *María Candelaria* (1943), del Río's first Mexican feature—and were widely recognized as an acting team throughout the Spanish-speaking Americas. Carlos Monsiváis has described this collaboration (in front of and behind the camera) as the essence of Mexico's cinematic construction of national identity.[25] Hence, the two principal architects of the film culture that helped to construct the post-Revolutionary Mexican state's pseudonationalism (working with two of its principal icons) served, too, the anticommunist cinematic crusade of Hollywood (and the U.S. State Department).

Economically, *The Fugitive* was an attempt by RKO to find a transnational mode of production that would result in films appealing to combined U.S. and Latin American markets by appealing to hemisphere-wide audiences. Shooting in Mexico furthered this effort by providing an "authentic" setting to be exploited in advertising. Also the film's producers sought to take advantage of lower costs at a time when the modernizing Mexican film industry, especially Estudios Churubusco, was promoting itself as a convenient and economical site for Hollywood production (which, in turn, would generate capital for Mexican producers). In part to reach a cross-cultural audience, without relying on costly and controversial dubbing, the film relied on minimal dialogue.[26] Ford utilized techniques perfected in his long experience as a director of silent films, as well as Figueroa's dramatically expressionist cinematography, to craft a visual narrative that depended as little as possible on spoken words (and therefore subtitles) to convey its meanings.[27]

Despite the film's Good Neighbor intentions, its subject was controversial for the Mexican government. The U.S. industry's censorship agency, the Production Code Administration (PCA) of the Motion Picture Association of America (MPAA), was instrumental in shaping the most politically sensitive portions of *The Fugitive* for Mexico-U.S. relations. The PCA, whose cooperation with U.S. foreign policy had been institutionalized during World War II,[28] emphasized that the producers must make clear that the story had no relevance for the Mexican state's contemporary ideology or policies. Early on in the project's development, PCA chief Joseph Breen, who had overseen many of Hollywood's wartime projects in Mexico, warned Ford of "the danger which this story suggests from the standpoint of the Mexican government." He continued:

> It may be possible to change the locale of this story into an unidentified tropical country and possibly establish affirmatively that the locale is not Mexico. It may, also, be possible, with proper guidance from responsible Mexican government authorities, to retain the Mexican locale and at the same time present the story in such a way as to keep it free from any possible offense to the Mexican government and people.[29]

The PCA suggested the insertion of a prologue disclaiming identification with Mexico. Following this idea, the film's opening narration underlined that the story was not about Mexico, even as it emphasized that it was filmed there. It noted its international production—as a sign of cold war good neighborliness—while denying any relationship to recent Mexican history: "This picture was entirely made in our neighboring republic Mexico, at the kind invitation of the Mexican government and the Mexican motion-picture industry. Its locale is fictional, it is merely a small state a thousand miles north or south of the equator. Who knows?"

Instead of the Mexican state's post-Revolutionary anticlericalism, the prologue linked the film's events to developing cold war geopolitics, by describing the "timeless and topical story" as "still being played out in many parts of the world." In the final script submitted to the PCA for review, the prologue's contemporary references had been even more explicit, warning against the Communist presence in "Yugoslavia, Poland, Russia, Germany, China, and God help us, in some parts of the United States," which threatened the same loss of freedom depicted in *The Fugitive*. In addition to more overt allusions to communism, the shooting script's final draft was also more insistent than the produced film in disclaiming any relevance to contemporary Mexico. It instructed: "[*The Fugitive*'s] locale must not be confused with Mexico, nor is there to be anything in the costumes or characters to indicate Mexico. In fact, every effort will be made to show that it is not Mexico."[30] (No doubt because it would draw too much attention to what it sought to deny, the studio diluted the prologue's intensity in the actual film.)[31]

More than dominant cold war U.S. ideology, *The Fugitive* reproduced the postwar alteration under way in official Mexican discourse, which in the 1930s had equated anticlericalism with a broader collective struggle for social justice but in the 1940s linked progress with individual advancement through capital accumulation and antileftism. Similarly, state-sanctioned nationalism (and history) no longer focused on defending sovereignty against gringo intervention and economic imperialism but on defending it from subversion by the same foreign and domestic enemies defined by the emerging U.S. security state. Although the film's opening insisted that the depicted nation was fictitious,[32] Greene's indictment of anticlerical policies in Tabasco during the 1930s was explicit. The participation of Mexican talent combined with the publicized location shooting underlined the story's connection to Mexico. It is significant that the Mexican government, historically hypersensitive about Hollywood representations, cooperated in the film's production, including oversight of the actual shooting by a censorship official from the Secretaría de Gobernación's Dirección General de Cinematografía.[33] Moreover, during the film's shooting in Mexico, Ford, del Río, and executives from Estudios Churubusco met with Alemán to explain the project to him, which the Mexican president endorsed.[34]

This support was a strong statement that the Alemanista state decisively renounced the anticlerical policies pursued in the 1920s and 1930s, which not only alienated church hierarchy but also had provoked popular rebellion led by activist priests and fought largely by rural folk. As the state party reconfigured itself publicly in 1946, cultural policies represented recent changes in church-state relations. As recently as July 1945, the Secretaría de Gobernación's Departamento de Censura had refused to authorize a production proposed by prominent filmmaker Raúl de Anda (a close collaborator of the state, and U.S. foreign policy, during World War II), because the story was sympathetic to the Cristiada (the popular struggle against state anticlericalism in central western Mexico that climaxed in the late 1920s). De Anda, president of the Asociación de Productores Nacionales, went forward with production of *Sucedió en Jalisco o los cristeros* and gained authorization for release of his film with the ascension of the Alemán administration in 1946.[35] The consolidation of such conservative cultural policies under Alemán was the context for *The Fugitive*'s Mexican production.

The Fugitive's portrayal of a popular struggle against an oppressive state married anti-anticlericalism and anticommunism (each fundamental to the devoutly Catholic and politically conservative Ford's own beliefs). By equating social egalitarianism with totalitarianism, and religious resistance with freedom, *The Fugitive* provided a message that simultaneously served U.S. and Mexican state ideologies. As its commitment to social justice waned, the Mexican regime's need to justify the social status quo as consistent with its revolutionary heritage necessitated equating radicalism with subversion and as being inconsistent with popular culture. At the very moment that the state publicly abandoned its anticlerical legacy—signaled by Avila Camacho's 1940 presidential campaign declaration "soy creyente" [I am a believer]—it also suspended another part of its revolutionary creed, agrarian reform. Popularizing its abandonment of unpopular religious policies would help conceal its related abandonment of popular radical reforms. In the postwar period, the government invested in infrastructure to develop large-scale commercial agriculture in the north of the country that produced export crops for the U.S. market, while it suspended support for the *ejidal* holdings of peasants concentrated in the center and south of the nation.[36]

This strategy—backbone of Mexico's so-called postwar economic miracle—supported import substitution industrialization with foreign exchange earned from agricultural exports (while swelling cities with landless peasants who were forced into poverty of the urban informal sector). This relationship between religious freedom and capital accumulation, drawn by the PRI, converged with U.S. discursive maneuvers to marginalize foreign radical reforms in the name of individual liberty and national progress.[37] The film's prologue—a binational endorsement of its message—expressed to audiences the Mexican state's ideological stance during the cold war: fighting radical subversion at home (in order to promote "progress") and willing to engage in the production of U.S. images supporting that mission. The timing fit well with the U.S. government's efforts in 1947–48 to reconfigure the Monroe Doctrine as an inter-American, anti-Soviet alliance expressed by the newly formed Organization of American States.[38] Notable is that the Mexican government was concerned not with the film's condemnation of anticlericalism (key tenet of its earlier post-Revolutionary project) but rather with being historically linked to authoritarian practices, which, although condemned by the film, resonated the PRI's own repressive tactics.[39]

After *The Fugitive*'s U.S. release, Mexican officials concerned over the representation of the ruling regime, and particularly of the army, considered censuring the film. A Mexican official in El Paso, Texas, advised Alemán's personal secretary that the film was "contrary to the good intentions and desires that the president has for national unity," owing to its denigrating portrayal of the Mexican military. In the end, the Mexican government rejected such action, because it would call more attention to the tale's parallels with Mexican history than would allowing the film to be distributed without disruption. In any case, Mexico could not limit distribution beyond Mexico, and cultural bureaucrats felt that *The Fugitive*'s relevance to cold war politics outshone its connections to contemporary Mexican affairs.[40]

The Fugitive presents a proselytizing police lieutenant as the embodiment of totalitarian oppression. He is a zealot who views religion as an impediment to social progress. Juan Rafael's sincerity represents the danger of radical thought: it warps the perspective of otherwise good men. By contrast, the corrupt police chief (played by Mexican American character actor Leo Carrillo)—who is the political crony of the state's governor—is motivated by lust for power and money (not ideas) as he coordinates his government's anticlerical crusade. If Armendáriz's character is the brutal face of a revolutionary regime, Carrillo's is its hypocritical heart. In the end, radicals like the lieutenant are themselves manipulated by rapacious elites. This is underlined by the film's representation of race: The lieutenant's facial features physically link him to the peasants he terrorizes (he insists, "I am an Indian like you"), even as he outwardly rejects their creed. By contrast, the decadent police chief appears as a light-skinned *criollo*.[41]

Unlike the cynical state that he naively serves, the lieutenant expresses heartfelt contempt at the religious beliefs of peasants. In trying to convince townsfolk to reveal the identity of the fugitive priest (Fonda) they are hiding in their midst, he offers the film's characterization of Communist atheism:

> You superstitious fools. Do you still believe what the priests told you? All they ever wanted was your money. They took your money and what did they give you? Anything to eat? Did they feed your children? No! They filled you full of lies. They talked to you about heaven. They told you to be meek and humble. Everything would be fine when you die. They want you to die, these priests, not live. They preach against the revolution, because we want you to live, not die.

Unsuccessful in his appeal, the lieutenant randomly arrests one of the assembled villagers; as his wife pleads for mercy, he is roped around the neck and dragged off to be held hostage as a means to extract information from the other members of the pueblo. Even more brutally, when the priest is finally captured, the state executes him (which only strengthens popular resistance and religious resolve).

Praised by U.S. critics for its stylistic achievements (especially Figueroa's cinematography), *The Fugitive* failed economically in the United States and Latin America.[42] Despite its equivocal reception, Estudios Churubusco remained involved in the transnational production of anticommunist propaganda but strictly in the form of Mexican entertainment films—rather than overtly international collaborations like *The Fugitive*. The more culturally authentic the production, the better for U.S. government propaganda specialists. RKO executives continued to facilitate such productions.

As Secretario de Gobernación in the administration of his predecessor, President Alemán had overseen U.S. aid to the Mexican film industry, including RKO's partnership in Estudios Churubusco. And RKO and the Mexican government also collaborated in producing commercially distributed U.S. documentaries that highlighted the Alemán regime's achievements for Latin American and U.S. audiences, such as the studio's 1949 entry in its *This Is America* documentary series.[43] Transnational production in Mexico itself revealed the complexity and contradictions of U.S.-Mexico mass-media collaboration. RKO chairman N. Peter Rathvon appealed directly to President Alemán for state subsidization of Estudios Churubusco, which had never proved profitable. The studio accepted the possibility that the Mexican government might merge Estudios Churubusco with other film facilities to rationalize domestic production, but it demanded that, until that step was taken, the regime supply financial aid in the form of tax relief. Without this support, Rathvon argued, the studio would have to shut its doors, canceling several planned projects for the U.S. market, including the "possibility for large film production for English-language television," a potential economic stimulus for Mexico's film sector.[44] Even as conflicts between the Mexican government and Hollywood escalated in 1949 over state intervention designed to protect Mexican film production from Hollywood competition, RKO maintained collaborative relations with the Alemán administration over matters concerning its Mexican interests.[45]

Estudios Churubusco was, then, the locus of U.S.-Mexican transnational and state-to-state mass-media collaboration, in ways that at once exemplified and transcended instrumental financial links. With the deepening of the cold war, it became the site of entertainment production that merged Mexican and U.S. discourses and cinematic practices, producing

"Mexican" films for international dissemination in Latin America. These projects were undertaken with the unattributed support of the U.S. State Department (and by the mid-1950s the U.S. Information Agency. We consider one such example in the following section.

Hollywood Cinema as Mexican: Nationalism as Anticommunism

Intertextual images and ideologies illuminate transnational economics and production. In Latin America, as elsewhere, U.S. propaganda took a new turn in the wake of the Korean War. That conflict transformed U.S. mass-media initiatives as it did so much else in U.S. foreign and domestic policies. In the Latin American field of engagement, this meant much more overt political messages; anticommunism became the singular theme in combating perceived neutralism, as the U.S. approach to Soviet containment became increasingly globalized in scope and militarized in operation. International U.S. culture programs focused less on the virtues of the "American way" of doing things, and more on the immediate threat posed by communist subversion.[46] In Mexico this merged with the host state's own midcentury "frenetic search for 'lo mexicano' [the authentically Mexican] that," in the words of Roger Bartra, "accompanied the *boom* to modernize in the postwar period."[47]

Dicen que soy comunista (1951), directed and cowritten by Alejandro Galindo, merged the emplotment, themes, and characterizations of Hollywood anticommunism, well honed by the early 1950s, with Galindo's own nonradical populism:[48] self-professed radicals reveal themselves to be rapacious criminals who hypocritically invoke socially progressive rhetoric to gain the sympathies of naive, hardworking folk (a Mexican analogue, perhaps, for the anticommunist, cold war populism of Elia Kazan's *Viva Zapata!* of 1952).[49] RKO executive Richard Tompkins, working in coordination with the U.S. State Department, oversaw the movie's production and distribution. As director of Estudios Churubusco-Azteca (the two studios merged in 1950 as RKO began to pull out of its Mexican venture), Tompkins produced the film directly with the studio's own resources, although his role went unattributed in the movie's credits.[50]

The film offers a morality tale about the life of Benito Reyes (Adalberto "Resortes" Martínez), a typesetter in a print shop. The business's owner is a compassionate and honest man who treats his workers with dignity. For example, instead of dismissing the habitually late Benito, don Federico

(Augusto Benedico) accepts his employee's excuses, allowing him to make up missed work rather than fire him. Labor conflict is absent in this example of beneficent small-enterprise capitalism. The business's owner also is democratic. He accepts an order to print posters for the Partido Radical de las Juventudes Revolucionarias de Vanguardia (Radical Party of Vanguard Revolutionary Youths), a supposedly ultra-leftist group whose gruff leaders appear in their stylized suits and hats as stereotypical gangsters (a representation typical of Hollywood's cold war films).[51]

Benito, who earlier has demonstrated his working-class consciousness in a dispute over the price of sugar with a local bodega owner, becomes intoxicated by the propaganda he prints. Stimulated by the party's rhetoric, he daydreams about political protests and social revolution; he exemplifies the danger that ideological seduction posed to well-meaning but ingenuous proletarians, who were susceptible to subversive propaganda. His enthusiasm spills over from the workplace into the street. Excited by the new ideas, he involves himself in an altercation with a police officer, who has detained his son, El Huicho (Joaquín Roche Jr.) and several of his paperboy friends for vandalizing the Cadillac of two clownish, arrogant national deputies (Salvador Quiroz and Arturo Castro). Benito makes a speech indicating his class consciousness. The very same gangster-radicals who brought the broadside to the print shop witness the brawl and set their eyes on Benito for recruitment.

Benito joins their party, although its internationalist rhetoric at first clashes with his nationalist inclinations. When he takes an oath of allegiance, in a contrived ceremony (beneath a poster depicting a likeness of Lenin) at the Partido's headquarters/hideout, he flinches when commanded to proclaim himself a "citizen of the world" but then goes ahead with the ridiculous ritual (involving the use of a telephone directory as a supposedly sacred political text). Convinced he is serving the working classes, Benito enthusiastically enlists. After he departs the meeting, the gang's boss (Miguel Manzano) cynically jokes that the party needs more men like Reyes: "pure, honest, innocent, and afraid of the devil."

Benito's girlfriend, Berta (María Luisa Zea), is a beautiful *morena* waitress in a working-class café who has demonstrated maternal love (i.e., her goodness despite her evident sensuality) for Benito's son. She is a contestant to be named Reina de los Maceros (Queen of the Waiters) in the beauty pageant at the restaurant workers' annual ball. Berta's main competition is a *rubia* cigarette girl, appropriately named Olga (Josefina del Mar). She works at the elegant Champs Elysées restaurant, meeting place of prominent politicos and gangsters, including the corrupt forces behind the Partido Radical. Like much U.S. cold war film propaganda, Olga's name suggests the hand of Soviet influence; while her blond good looks mark her as a *malinchista* from Mexican cinema, a threat to Mexican womanhood as well as the nation. She is thus doubly (and cross-culturally) damned, as sinister and subversive. Moreover, Olga is sexually aggressive and conniving. And she seeks out powerful suitors at the Champs Elysées, which caters to members of the upper classes who abide by foreign models of elegance. By contrast, Berta is the ideal image of working-class femininity: romantically loyal and enthusiastically engaged with Mexican popular culture. She works in a neighborhood *lonchería* and enjoys *danzón* and other popular entertainments.

Benito arrives at the Champs Elysées intending to intimidate Olga by presenting himself as a representative of the supposedly 28,000-member Partido Radical (the figure cited by his new bosses), who he promises will vote for Berta. In the course of his encounter with the cigarette girl, Benito is mistaken for an important politico by the same two buffoonish national deputies with whom he earlier had the street altercation over El Huicho. They invite him to eat with them, and hours later the three emerge from the club drunk. The deputies loan him their Cadillac (preeminent symbol of affluence and political corruption in the era of Alemán) to accompany Olga to her apartment. Convinced that Benito is indeed secretary general of an important political party, Olga seduces him in order to gain the allegiance of his presumed minions, in her quest to be Queen of the Waiters.

His newly acquired self-importance, as radical politico, alienates Benito from his community. The Cadillac parked in the courtyard of his apartment complex attracts the scorn of his neighbors, who mock his newfound leftism. Corrupted by his sense of power and his infatuation with Olga, he is haughty with Berta, no longer committed to her nor her quest to win the beauty contest. As he rejects Berta, Benito, a widower, also neglects his son. El Huicho mourns the lost possibility of a restored family but finds comfort from Berta, who acts as a surrogate parent for the abandoned youth.

Benito is slow to recognize his handlers' duplicity, which is first revealed to the audience through their illegal acts and hoodlum manner (recognizable from not only Hollywood films but also popular Mexican gangster movies of the period).[52] Cajoled into participating in the robbery of a food warehouse, supposedly to redistribute its goods for the welfare of "the people," Benito recoils at the violent destruction of private property when, after the theft, the gang members defy their promises of a peaceful operation by blowing up the building and, unbeknownst to Benito, murdering two security guards forced to remain in the exploding edifice. In another scene, the gang shakes down the local merchant with whom Benito had argued earlier, forcing him to buy wholesale goods from their syndicate at inflated prices or risk personal harm and the destruction of his small business.

In addition to the gang's violence, the plot also attacks the motivations of radical organizations, revealing them to be treasonous. The Partido Radical is really a front for a gangster who is exporting the stolen foodstuffs, demonstrating not only the lawless hypocrisy of self-proclaimed radicals but also their lack of patriotism, by stealing food from their country's needy. Drawing on well-known Mexican and U.S. World War II cinema stereotypes, as in *The Fugitive,* a symbol of rightist foreign subversion transmutes into a leftist one. The gangster behind the Partido is named Wilhelm Ribendurf (Charles Rooner), suggesting an ex-Nazi.[53] Further conflating fascist with communist identities, the film uses satirical names to mock contemporary pro-Soviet Mexican politicians, including Vicente Lombardo Toledano, the Marxist ex-chief of the powerful Confederación de Trabajadores Mexicanos (CTM), which was founded with the support of President Lázaro Cárdenas in 1936 and had been crucial to Cardenismo's survival. A supporter of Mexico's antifascist partnership with the United States at the start of World War II, Lombardo Toledano became a prominent postwar enemy of U.S. foreign policy, as leader of the anti-imperialist Confederación de Trabajadores de América Latina (CTAL), which the CIA and USIA covertly and overtly opposed throughout the Americas.[54] Likewise, Lombardo came to be a thorn in the side of the state he had helped build; in 1948 he founded the nationalist-leftist Partido Popular (PP) to oppose the ever-more-rightist regime of his former ally, Miguel Alemán, whose PRI continued to benefit from the support of the increasingly conservative (and docile) CTM. The film parodies Lombardo with a character named Leobardo Tolentino, who authors the Partido Radical's hypocritical "manifesto." Similarly, the Secretary General of the Partido Comunista Mexicano (PCM), Dionisio Encinas, is satirized by another character, called Dionisio Robles, who plans the mob's electoral fraud. These political markers grounded fiction in current events, conveying the message that contemporary leftists, who positioned themselves outside the state-party's corporatist structure, were antinationalists.[55] The PCM and PP represented subversive forces not only to the PRI but also to the U.S. State Department, which saw both groups as instruments of Soviet mass-culture initiatives; Mexico City embassy officials typically described Lombardo as "a recognized leader of Communist and anti-U.S. propaganda efforts," as they justified their own propaganda initiatives as countersubversion.[56]

The Partido Radical sends Benito to a political luncheon to assassinate Ribendurf's nemesis, Gildardo Molina, an honest state governor who does not tolerate the transport of contraband through his (unnamed) state. Branding the governor an "enemy of the people," the Partido provides Benito a gun and explains that his act will bring him glory, as a champion of the working classes. Arriving at the Champs Elysées, he encounters the two deputies, who still believe that he is secretary general of an important party. Disrupting Benito's plan to sneak into the affair and fire a fatal shot, they insist that he sit with them at the banquet table headed by the governor. Molina represents the liberal, integrationist intentions of the ruling regime, in contrast to, on the one hand, the soft corruption of the two buffoonish deputies (which conformed to popular perceptions regarding PRI legislators during the Alemán years) and, on the other, the violence and deceit of the Partido Radical's leaders. The governor rises to speak of his administration's dedication to "social progress" and above all the creation of a society with equal "opportunity for poor and rich alike." After listening to the politician's sincerely spoken words, Benito abandons the conspiracy. Class struggle is unnecessary in a society governed by such a progressive state. The governor articulates his party's (i.e., the PRI's) commitment to efficient, honest government administered by compassionate pragmatists (in contrast to ideological extremists who promise utopias but inevitably exploit the masses). Yet this scene's message was ambiguous; it opened ways to alternative, subversive readings by audiences. For example, Resortes's easy manipulation by the (seemingly honest) PRI governor, like his earlier seduction by rogue radicals, could indicate the susceptibility of the masses not just to subversive ideas but also to the dominant party's rhetoric.[57] In this way Galindo's work here, as elsewhere, offers a critical perspective, albeit one wrapped in an ultimately pro-PRI narrative.

Having returned to his political senses, Benito is now targeted for assassination by his betrayed comrades. His son is kidnapped in order to lure Benito to his death. Meanwhile, the suddenly sober Benito tries to win back Berta's love, begging her to allow him to escort her to the Waiters' Ball. As the printer pleads for the waitress's forgiveness, his neighbors (the local bodega owner and El Huicho's street friends) rush into the restaurant to inform Benito of his son's abduction. Upon hearing the news, Berta demonstrates her true love for Benito and his son by dropping her cool facade and willingly casting aside her chance to win the evening's contest; she joins the barrio clan's rescue of El Huicho. When Benito does not emerge from the gang's headquarters, Berta further demonstrates her loyalty by rushing in, leaving the others waiting outside (fig. 4.1). Inside, Ribendurf

FIGURE 4.1. *El Huicho, Benito (second adult from left), and Berta held captive in the headquarters of the Partido Radical de las Juventudes Revolucionarias de Vanguardia, while the gang's public political leader, played by José Pulido (far right), and its clandestine criminal master, Ribendurf (second from right), look on. The mise-en-scène frames the film's principal characters with readily recognizable Communist propaganda. Courtesy of Filmoteca, Universidad Nacional Autónoma de México.*

orders that Berta, Benito, and El Huicho be murdered in his organization's warehouse, where its stolen goods are stored for sale on the black market. While they are forced into cars, the band of barrio friends go for help. Upon entering the warehouse, the newly savvy Benito sarcastically comments on all the good the party has done with the supplies it supposedly redistributed to the poor.

Dicen que soy comunista is a farce. Inside the warehouse, Benito, Berta, and El Huicho confound their dim-witted captors in a slapstick chase sequence. Finally, they are rescued by their neighbors, the police, and the two national deputies (no longer presented as decadent and corrupt satraps but as brave defenders of national sovereignty). Inside this comedy there are sober messages about state and society. The police, for example, are represented, as they are in other urban-set Mexican Golden Age films—such as Galindo's *Campeón sin corona* (1945), *¡Esquina bajan!* (1948), and *México nunca duerme* (1958)—as apolitical guarantors of justice. Also, the demise of radical subversion restores *la familia chica;* [58] following the rescue, Benito demonstrates this when he announces his intention to marry Berta, introducing her to his new friends, the legislators, as "the future doña." The stability of "normal" family life is reinforced by local cross-class community ties, linking small-property owners, like the print-shop owner and the neighborhood shopkeeper, to workers, like Benito. The *bodegero* and Benito's boss each show how personalist bonds of place supersede class or ideological differences. This social organization is, in turn, supported by a progressive state, that, as the governor pointed out earlier, expands social opportunities for rich and poor alike, defended against subversion, and contained class struggle within officially sanctioned, i.e., state-controlled (corporatist) politics.

As in other Mexican films of the 1950s, family, community, and the state are the true allies of the working classes. This reproduced Alemanismo's populist rhetoric during Mexico's push toward capital accumulation through protected import substitution industrialization following World War II. The film's negative message, however, is less clear than its positive one. Foremost, its representation of communism is, on at least one level, ambiguous, since the radicals are in reality gangsters and not Soviet agents. But there is no ambiguity about the fact that radical rhetoric, which challenges the authority of the postwar Mexican state, is not only antinationalist but also corrupt. The class-conscious political aspirations of organic progressives like Benito can best be fulfilled by "legitimate" authorities, i.e., by the PRI.

The film's final scene amplifies these themes. Benito and Berta rush to the Waiters' Ball, where Olga is about to be crowned queen. Flanked by the ruling-party deputies, symbols of state approval, Benito addresses his working-class peers. He explains that he has brought the votes of the supposed 28,000 members of his political party, but, before he utters the name of the now defunct Partido Radical de las Juventudes Revolucionarias de Vanguardia, he turns for advice to one of the state's representatives. The deputy whispers in Benito's ear, and the printer confidently announces the name of his *new* political organization, the Partido Revolucionario de las Juventudes Democráticas (Revolutionary Party of Democratic Youth). The comedy's conclusion displays the state's invocation of nationalism as a means to demonize, marginalize, and suppress independent political movements that did not accept the ruling regime's authoritarian structure; in official ideology, rational development and social progress could only be legitimately carried out through alliance with the dominant political system.

For contemporary Mexican spectators, surrounded by official rhetoric,

Dicen que soy comunista equated democracy with the politics of single-party rule, and leftism with illegality, greed, and violence. Class-struggle was anti-nationalist, and leftist radicalism masked exploitation by corrupt domestic interests and their unnamed "foreign" allies. Its message, therefore, also synthesized the U.S. State Department's early cold war, Latin American cultural policies (that simultaneously sought to contain external Soviet influence and curtail internal radically nationalist movements, especially independent labor currents) with those of Alemanismo (that sought to suppress dissent as it redefined nationalism to justify supposedly short-term proletarian social sacrifices for aggregate economic gains asserted as essential for long-term development).

Behind the film's ideological engagement lie more instrumental international interactions. *Dicen que soy comunista* was backed by the U.S. government, which utilized RKO's Mexican operation to produce transnational propaganda during the early cold war. As soon as the film was completed, the U.S. embassy sent a safety print of the twelve reels to the State Department as an example of the kind of film propaganda that could be produced in Mexico.[59] Reports of the movie's reception, as a huge ideological and commercial success, particularly popular with urban workers, led Mexico City embassy officials to lobby the State Department for development of an independent production company headed by Richard Tompkins, the U.S. executive in charge at Estudios Churubusco (and a nephew of the RKO president N. Peter Rathvon).[60] Based on his collaboration with the State Department on *Dicen que soy comunista,* Tompkins established an "independent" production concern in Mexico City to produce other anti-communist films, including animated shorts and newsreels, with unattributed U.S. aid. This would be part of the mass-cultural cold war that came to be directed globally by the U.S. Information Agency, after its establishment as the full-time custodian of U.S. propaganda in 1953.[61]

Conclusions

It is unlikely that audiences accepted the intended message of *Dicen que soy comunista;* that is, its alleged popularity does not, of course, signify anything meaningful about reception. There are limits, too, to what this film, or *The Fugitive,* can tell us about Mexican popular politics and society. But their history does open a window on the production of transcultured discourse that served an ideological alliance between the United States and Mexican governments as they jointly pursued cultural cold war, aimed to undermine independent political organization, in the name of antisubversion. It allows us to visit processes well-described by Bartra, who writes: "[I]t seems that cinema, television, radio, comics, and *fotonovelas* . . . have taken fuller advantage of the possibilities of a defining national culture vis-à-vis the specifically Mexican subject. The terrible paradox is that they have achieved this despite being at the same time, the principal purveyors of so-called cultural imperialism and, in most cases, having an openly foreignizing vocation."[62] But this was the paradox of Mexican cinema as well as political economy and official ideology during the 1950s (and since then): how to render national the outside of a system whose inside is thoroughly transnational.

In different ways *Dicen que soy comunista* and *The Fugitive* show the growing transnationalization of the U.S. government's mass-cultural foreign policies facilitated by Hollywood's international structure. Although part of a global system, this was not, naturally, the same universally. In Mexico, this process rested on a particular foundation of political and economic relations, initially built during World War II and reinforced in the early cold war. This foundation supported the postwar structure connecting Hollywood and the Mexican film industry at Estudios Churubusco. Moreover, the films analyzed here demonstrate the ideological congruence between the postwar projects of the U.S. government and the Mexican state, when the anticommunist crusade pursued internationally by U.S. foreign policy coincided with Alemanismo's nationalist rightism. This international convergence reflected broader and deeper bilateral patterns, during a period when less visible (but extremely significant) structural and institutional, transnational, and state-to-state links between the United States and Mexico strengthened in ways that reinforced the PRI's increasingly reactionary project, which looked to suppress radical challenges without losing ideological control of its nationalist heritage nor the appearance of international independence vis-à-vis its northern neighbor.[63]

The Fugitive appropriated Golden Age Mexican cinema to disseminate Hollywood anticommunism. Conversely, *Dicen que soy comunista*'s message conformed to the Mexican state's domestic and international project that appropriated U.S. forms of cold war rhetoric in order to impose a reactionary political economy at home. Together these films show the two-way flow of cultural production, even within a U.S.-dominated economic structure.[64] They represented popular interests—peasant values in *The Fugitive,* proletarian ones in *Dicen que soy comunista*—in cold war terms. To revisit Bartra: "The principal problem that all political structures of mediation resolve is how to transfer social antagonisms to arenas where the class struggle can be domesticated, thereby guaranteeing the continuity of the system. The imagery which defines the Mexican as subject to history and politics—that is, as subject to a specifically Mexican domination—has managed to transfer the territory of national culture to the two massive social classes that form the basis of the modern state: the peasants and the workers." [65]

While Wallerstinian determinism should be resisted, we can safely observe how Mexican cinema's position in the cultural cold war conformed to the semiperipheral characteristics of its industrial development: its mass-media system produced national signs within an environment created by its collaboration with Hollywood and U.S. foreign policy. Mexico, then, played an intermediary role culturally, as an exporter of transcultured propaganda to the rest of Latin America. In both their form and content, *The Fugitive* and *Dicen que soy comunista* demonstrate what Néstor García Canclini has termed, in analyzing a somewhat different historical situation, the "oblique powers" created by the forces of transnational hybridization in Latin America.[66] Rather than an instance of cultural imperialism imposed by a foreign power, the films' histories untangle the dense transcultured web woven by U.S. and Mexican elites that facilitated not simply cinematic collaboration but also transnational state formation in the cold war.

Notes

For assistance with the research in this article, the author thanks Francisco Ohem, Salvador Plancarte, and Celia Barrientos of the Filmoteca Nacional de la Universidad Nacional Autónoma de México; Sam Gill of the Margaret Herrick Library of the Academy of Motion Picture Arts and Sciences; and Brigitte Kueppers of the Special Collections of the Arts, Architecture and Urban Planning Library of the University of California at Los Angeles.

1. My conception of postwar ideological congruence in U.S.-Mexican relations concurs with patterns discerned by Alan Knight in *U.S.-Mexican Relations, 1910–1940: An Interpretation* (La Jolla: Center for U.S.-Mexican Studies, University of California at San Diego, 1987), 1–20. Recently Knight has extended this model chronologically to include the cold war; see his essay "Dealing with the American Political System: An Historical Overview 1910–1995," in *Bridging the Order: Transforming Mexico-U.S. Relations,* ed. Rodolfo O. de la Garza and Jesús Velasco (Lanham, England: Rowman and Littlefield, 1997), 1–31. I explore the "on the ground" interplay of U.S. and Mexican political projects and mass-media regimes in "Everyday Forms of Transnational Collaboration: U.S. Film Propaganda in Cold War Mexico," in *Close Encounters of Empire: Writing the Cultural History of U.S.–Latin American Relations,* ed. Gilbert Joseph, Catherine LeGrand, and Ricardo Salvatore (Durham, N.C.: Duke University Press, 1998).

The connections between Latin American rightism and U.S. cold war foreign policy are examined in Leslie Bethell and Ian Roxborough, "The Postwar Conjuncture in Latin America: Democracy, Labor, and the Left," and Roxborough, "Mexico," in *Latin America between the Second World War and the Cold War, 1944–1948,* ed. Bethell and Roxborough (Cambridge: Cambridge University Press, 1992), 1–32 and 190–216, respectively. In this vein, a recent work that comprehensively relates transnational to state-to-state relations in Mexico is Steven Niblo, *War, Diplomacy, and Development: The United States and Mexico, 1938–1954* (Wilmington, Del.: Scholarly Resources, 1995). Good general overviews of the regime's postwar project are Tzvi Medin, *El sexenio Alemanista: Ideología y praxis política de Miguel Alemán* (Mexico City: Era, 1990); Luis Medina, *Historia de la revolución mexicana, 1940–1952: Civilismo y modernización del autoritarismo* (Mexico City: El Colegio de México, 1979); Blanca Torres, *Historia de la revolución mexicana, 1940–1952: Hacia la utopía industrial* (Mexico City: El Colegio de México, 1979). For relations in the 1950s, see Olga Brody Pellicer, *Historia de la Revolución Mexicana, 1952–1960: El entendimiento con los Estados Unidos y la gestación del desarrollo estabilizador* (Mexico City: El Colegio de México, 1978).

On the relationship between state ideology and representation of North Americans, see John Mraz, "Lo gringo en el cine mexicano y la ideología alemanista," *La Jornada Semanal,* no. 297 (19 February 1995), and Ignacio Durán, Ivan Trujillo, Monica Verea, comps., *México–Estados Unidos: Encuentros y desencuentros en el cine* (Mexico City: Universidad Nacional Autónoma de México/Instituto Mexicano de Cinematografía, 1996).

2. For the economic consequences of wartime collaboration with the U.S. government and Hollywood for the Mexican film industry, see my article "Hollywood, U.S.-Mexican Relations, and the Devolution of the Golden Age of Mexican Cinema," *Film Historia* 4.2 (June 1994): 103–35; a revised version published in Spanish is "La diplomacia celuloide: Hollywood y 'la edad del oro' del cine mexicano," *Historia y Grafía* 4 (spring 1995): 137–76.

3. Recent multidisciplinary historical works that deal with the particular nexus among the cold war, U.S. foreign policy, and commercial cinema are Kyoko Hirano, *Mr. Smith Goes to Tokyo: Japanese Cinema under the American Occupation, 1945–1952* (Washington, D.C.: Smithsonian Institution Press, 1992); and Reinhold Wagnleitner, *Coca-Colonization and the Cold War: The Cultural Mission of the United States in Austria after the Second World War* (Chapel Hill: University of North Carolina Press, 1994), 222–74. About the broader connections between international mass culture, including film, and U.S. anticommunism, see Fein, "Everyday Forms of Transnational Collaboration"; Walter Hixson, *Parting the Curtain: Propaganda, Culture, and the Cold War, 1945–1961* (New York: St. Martin's Press, 1997); and for a case study, Gerald K. Haines, *The Americanization of Brazil: A Study of U.S. Cold War*

Diplomacy in the Third World, 1945–1954 (Wilmington, Del.: Scholarly Resources, 1989).

4. The best overview is Emily Rosenberg, *Spreading the American Dream: American Economic and Cultural Expansion, 1890–1945* (New York: Hill and Wang, 1982). See also Clayton Koppes and Gregory Black, *Hollywood Goes to War: How Politics, Profits, and Propaganda Shaped Movies during World War II* (New York: Free Press, 1987); Holly Cowan Shulman, *The Voice of America: Propaganda and Democracy* (Madison: University of Wisconsin Press, 1990); Allan Winkler, *The Politics of Propaganda: The Office of War Information* (New Haven, Conn.: Yale University Press, 1978). For an outline of the evolution of mass-culture policies that originated in wartime inter-American relations but remains, like the above books, generally an institutional history focused on Washington rather than an international study, see Frank Ninkovich, *The Diplomacy of Ideas: U.S. Foreign Policy and Cultural Relations, 1938–1950* (New York: Cambridge University Press, 1981).

5. A few important examples of Mexican entertainment features that addressed themes in ways serving U.S.-Mexican wartime political collaboration are *Soy puro mexicano* (1942), *Cinco fueron los escogidos* (1942), *Espionaje en el Golfo* (1942), *De New York a Huipanguillo* (1943), and *Escuadrón 201* (1945). On this mode of wartime entertainment production see Seth Fein, "Transnationalization and Cultural Collaboration: 'Mexican' Cinema and the Second World War," *Studies in Latin American Popular Culture* 17 (1998): 105–28. I address nontheatrical wartime film propaganda in "Proyectando México: La segunda guerra mundial y la representación de México en propaganda fílmica estadounidense," in *México–Estados Unidos: Encuentros y desencuentros,* 31–49.

6. Rockefeller to John E. Abbott, director of the Museum of Modern Art's Film Library, 9 September 1940, Rockefeller Archive Center (Pocantico Hills, New York), Record Group III 4 L (Nelson Rockefeller papers Personal Projects), Box 139, Folder 1367.

7. In 1943, RKO became partners with Emilio Azcárraga, already Mexico's most important mass-media capitalist, the owner of an important radio network and movie theaters and later the founder of Televisa. His own empire expanded greatly, owing to his partnership with the U.S. government in wartime propaganda programs and his own connections to the Mexican state. For Azcárraga's film relations with the United States, see Seth Fein, "Hollywood and United States–Mexico Relations in the Golden Age of Mexican Cinema" (Ph.D. dissertation, University of Texas at Austin, 1996), 354–72. See also José Luis Ortiz Garza, *México en guerra: La historia secreta de los negocios entre empresarios mexicanos de la comunicación, los nazis, y E.U.A.* (Mexico City: Planeta, 1989). For an overview of the studio's development and comprehensive filmography, see Tomás Pérez Turrent, coord., *La fábrica de sueños: Estudios Churubusco, 1945–1985* (Mexico City: Instituto Mexicanos de Cinematografía, 1985).

8. See Betty Lasky, *RKO: The Biggest Little Major of Them All,* 2d ed. (Santa Monica, Calif.: Roundtable Publishing, 1989), 161. Independent Hollywood producer John Hay Whitney (the money behind *Gone with the Wind* and the OCIAA's Motion Picture Division's first director) had a prewar distribution agreement with RKO for the films from his company Pioneer Pictures, and almost took over RKO in the mid-1930s, ibid., 104–6. Whitney also had directed the Museum of Modern Art's Film Library, a Rockefeller family project like the museum itself, in the late 1930s.

9. Laurence Duggan to Guy Ray, 7 July 1944, U.S. National Archives Record Group 84, General Records Mexico Embassy, Washington National Record Center, Suitland, Md., 840.6. Rockefeller's liberal vision of the relationship between U.S. capital and Latin American development has increasingly received attention from historians of inter-American relations. Elizabeth Cobbs examines how this carried over into private-sector endeavors, when Rockefeller left the government after World War II, in *The Rich Neighbor Policy: Rockefeller and Kaiser in Brazil* (New Haven, Conn.: Yale University Press, 1992).

10. Messersmith to Laurence Duggan, 26 February 1944, Central Files, Department of State, National Archives Record Group 59, U.S. National Archives, Washington, D.C., 812.4061–Motion Pictures/320.

11. An important comparative application of this concept, for my own thinking, is Mary Louise Pratt, *Imperial Eyes: Travel Writing and Transculturation* (New York: Routledge, 1992).

12. The international literature about Golden Age Mexican cinema is large and growing. Important comprehensive works include Emilio García Riera's encyclopedic *Historia documental del cine mexicano,* 2d ed., 17 vols. (Guadalajara: Universidad de Guadalajara, 1992–95), and concise *Historia del cine mexicano* (Mexico City: Secretaría de Educación Pública, 1985); Jorge Ayala Blanco, *La aventura del cine mexicano en la época de oro y después* (Mexico City: Grijalbo, 1993); Aurelio de los Reyes, *Un medio siglo de cine mexicano (1896–1947)* (Mexico City: Trillas, 1987). An important anthology of translated writing is Paulo Antonio Paranaguá, ed., *Mexican Cinema,* trans, Ana M. López (London: British Film Institute/Instituto Mexicano de Cinematografía, 1995). About Mexico's representation by Hollywood, crucial for understanding the interaction of both cinemas, see Emilio García Riera, *México visto por el cine extranjero,* 6 vols. (Mexico City: Ediciones Era, 1987–90). Important works by U.S. scholars include Joanne Hershfield, *Mexican Cinema/Mexican Woman, 1940–1950* (Tucson: University of Arizona Press, 1996); Carl Mora, *Mexican Cinema: Reflections of a Society, 1896–1988,* 2nd ed. (Berkeley and Los Angeles: University of California Press, 1988); and Charles Ramírez Berg, *Cinema of Solitude: A Critical Analysis of Mexican Films, 1967–1983* (Austin: University of Texas Press, 1992), which juxtaposes later production to the Golden Age epoch.

13. Two important recent collections are Ann Marie Stock, ed., *Framing Latin American Cinema: Contemporary Critical Perspectives* (Minneapolis: Uni-

versity of Minnesota Press, 1997), and John King, Ana M. López, and Manuel Alvarado, eds., *Mediating Two Worlds: Cinematic Encounters in the Americas* (London: British Film Institute, 1993). See also the essays collected in *Studies in Latin American Popular Culture* 17, ed. Ana M. López., devoted to "Popular Cinemas/Popular Cultures." For a comparative international history, see John King, *Magical Reels: A History of Latin American Cinema* (New York: Verso, 1990).

14. I develop these ideas in "El cine mexicano a la luz de las relaciones internacionales," in *Horizontes del segundo siglo: Investigación y pedagogía del cine mexicano, latinoamericano, y chicano,* ed. Julianne Burton-Carvajal, Patricia Torres, and Angel Miguel (Guadalajara: Universidad de Guadalajara and Instituto Mexicano de Cinematografía, 1998), 94–100. Recent works, from a variety of disciplinary perspectives, that demonstrate the reciprocal benefits of history and film studies include Leo Charney and Vanessa R. Schwartz, eds., *Cinema and the Invention of Modern Life* (Berkeley and Los Angeles: University of California Press, 1996); Thomas Doherty, *Projections of War: Hollywood, American Culture, and World War II* (New York: Columbia University Press, 1993); Heidi Fehrenbach, *Cinema in Democratizing Germany: Reconstructing National Identity after Hitler* (Chapel Hill: University of North Carolina Press, 1995); Hirano, *Mr. Smith;* Randal Johnson, *The Film Industry in Brazil: Culture and the State* (Pittsburgh: University of Pittsburgh Press, 1987); Marsha Kinder, ed., *Refiguring Spain: Cinema/Media/Representation* (Durham, N.C.: Duke University Press, 1997); Marcia Landy, *Cinematic Uses of the Past* (Minneapolis: University of Minnesota Press, 1996); Gina Marchetti, *Romance and the Yellow Peril: Race, Sex, and Discursive Strategies in Hollywood Fiction* (Berkeley and Los Angeles: University of California Press, 1993); Robert Rosenstone, ed., *Revisioning History: Film and the Construction of a New Past* (Princeton, N.J.: Princeton University Press, 1995); Thomas Saunders, *Hollywood in Berlin: American Cinema and Weimar Germany* (Berkeley and Los Angeles: University of California Press, 1994); Robert Sklar and Charles Musser, eds., *Resisting Images: Essays on Cinema and History* (Philadelphia: Temple University Press, 1990); Eric Smoodin, *Animating Culture: Hollywood Cartoons from the Sound Era* (New Brunswick, N.J.: Rutgers University Press, 1993); Vivian Sobchack, ed., *The Persistence of History: Cinema, Television, and the Modern Event* (New York: Routledge, 1996); Janet Staiger, *Interpreting Films: Studies in the Historical Reception of America Cinema* (Princeton, N.J.: Princeton University Press, 1992); Robert Brent Toplin, *History by Hollywood: The Use and Abuse of the American Past* (Urbana: University of Illinois Press, 1996); and Denise Youngblood, *Movies for the Masses: Popular Cinema and Soviet Society in the 1920s* (Cambridge: Cambridge University Press, 1992).

15. Ford's partner in his Argosy Company was his longtime friend and former RKO production executive Merian Cooper, who had also been a partner with Whitney at Pioneer Films in the 1930s. The script's author, Dudley Ni-

chols, was also a personal friend and professional collaborator of Ford's who, like the director himself, had worked at RKO prior to the war.

16. In the United Kingdom, Greene's story was published as *The Power and the Glory*. As a member of the Navy's Signal Corps, Ford had spent the war years making propaganda films for the U.S. government, including the Academy award–winning *Battle of Midway* (1942).

17. See Joseph Breen to Merian C. Cooper, MGM, Culver City, 29 May 1940, "The Fugitive," Production Code Administration collection (PCA), Margaret Herrick Library of the Academy of Motion Picture Arts and Sciences, Beverly Hills, Calif.

18. See Fein, "Transnationalization and Cultural Collaboration," for the earlier rendering of these symbols in U.S./Mexican cinema during World War II.

19. The passing interpretation of *The Fugitive,* as well as other U.S. cold war films set in Mexico, by Richard Slotkin, demonstrates the international short-comings of conventional scholarly research and writing about film. Unaware of how the Mexican film industry, state, and political culture contributed to the movie's content and form, Slotkin imposes a U.S.-centered interpretation that locates the film's central themes and modes of representation as derived strictly from U.S. discourses. Archival research as well as a more international contextualization of the film's historical formation undermine this breezy read-ing. See *Gunfighter Nation: The Myth of the Frontier in Twentieth-Century America* (New York: Harper Perennial, 1993), 417.

20. For a brief interpretation of the actor's transnational career, see Seth Fein, "Pedro Armendáriz," in *Encyclopedia of Mexico: History, Society, and Culture,* ed. Michael S. Werner (Chicago: Fitzroy Dearborn Publishers, 1997), 101–2.

21. "The Fugitive" Pressbook, New York Public Library for the Performing Arts, Lincoln Center (NYPLPA), Film Collection, p. 5.

22. Ibid.

23. See Ana M. López, "Are All Latins from Manhattan? Hollywood, Eth-nography, and Cultural Colonialism," in *Unspeakable Images: Ethnicity and the American Cinema, ed.* Lester D. Friedman (Urbana: University of Illinois Press, 1991), 404–24, for an analysis of the sociocultural forces that forced del Río from Hollywood.

24. For an important recent contribution to understanding the national qualities of Figueroa's work, see Charles Ramírez Berg, "The Cinematic Inven-tion of Mexico: The Poetics and Politics of the Fernández-Figueroa Style," in *The Mexican Cinema Project,* ed. Chon A. Noriega and Steven Ricci (UCLA Film and Television Archive, 1994), 13–24; see also *El arte de Gabriel Figu-eroa,* special issue of *Artes de México* (winter 1988).

25. "Notas sobre la cultura mexicana en el siglo XX," in *Historia general de México,* 3d ed., vol. 2, coord. Daniel Cosío Villegas (Mexico City: El Colegio de México, 1981), 1516–17.

26. On conflict between Mexican motion-picture labor and Hollywood over dubbing in the mid-1940s, see Fein, "Hollywood and United States–Mexico Relations," 372–80.

27. See Alberto Isaac, *Conversaciones con Gabriel Figueroa* (Guadalajara, Mexico: Universidad de Guadalajara, 1992), 34–40, for Figueroa's work with Ford on *The Fugitive*.

28. For example, PCA chief Joseph Breen was the first director of the wartime council of Hollywood executives that coordinated the U.S. industry's Latin American activities with the OCIAA, the Motion Picture Society of the Americas.

29. Joseph Breen to John Ford, 27 November 1945, "The Fugitive," PCA.

30. "The Fugitive," Final Script, 26 October 1946, RKO Scripts, Collection 003, UCLA Performing Arts Library (RKO Collection 003), Box RKO-S-1586, Folder 1778.

31. See "Cutting Continuity on 'The Fugitive,'" 30 June 1947, UCLA RKO Collection 003, Box RKO-S-1586, Folder 1778.

32. A geographical reference, in the final script's prologue, that this fictitious land could be "a thousand miles north or south of the Panama Canal" was changed no doubt to remove a prime symbol for Latin Americans of U.S. imperialism. "The Fugitive," Final Script, 26 October 1946, UCLA RKO Collection 003, Box RKO-S-1586, Folder 1778.

33. "Memorandum sobre la película 'El Fugitivo,'" from Arturo Ortíz Múgica in Ernesto P. Uruchurtu, Secretaría de Gobernación to Rogerio de la Selva, Secretario Particular del Presidente de la República, 20 January 1948, AGN, Ramo Alemán, 523.3/26; Don Vasque, Economic Assistant, to SD, 22 January 1948, NARG 84, Security-Segregated General Records, Mexico Embassy, 840.6.

34. Pérez Martínez, Departamento de Supervisión Cinematográfica de la Secretaría de Gobernación, "Memorandum sobre 'El Fugitivo,'" pp. 1–2, January 1948, Archivo General de la Nación, Mexico City (AGN), Ramo Alemán, 523.3/26.

35. See Arturo Ortíz Múgica, "Memorandum sobre la película 'Los Cristeros,'" AGN, Ramo Alemán, 523.3/26. The state's intervention with *Los Cristeros* represented the way in which official ideology was in flux in the 1940s. See Jean Meyer's interpretation of the Cristero Rebellion as popular antiauthoritarianism in *La Cristiada,* 3 vols. (Mexico City: El Colegio de México, 1973–75), and *The Cristeros: The Mexican People between Church and State, 1926–29* (Cambridge: Cambridge University Press, 1976); see also his similarly sympathetic portrait of Sinarquistas in *El Sinarquismo: ¿un fascismo mexicano?* (Mexico City: Cuadernos de Joaquín Mortiz, 1979). On popular reaction to local anticlerical practices, see Marjorie Becker, *Setting the Virgin on Fire: Lázaro Cárdenas, Michoacán Peasants, and the Redemption of the Mexican Revolution* (Berkeley and Los Angeles: University of California Press, 1995).

36. The best overview of the state's economic policies in this period remains Clark Reynolds, *Mexican Economy: Twentieth-Century Structure and Growth* (New Haven, Conn.: Yale University Press, 1970). On the Mexican state's rightward movement in the post-Cárdenas years, see Luis Medina, *Historia de la revolución mexicana, 1940–1952: Del cardenismo al avilacamachismo* (Mexico City: El Colegio de México, 1979), and Alan Knight, "The Rise and Fall of Cardenimo, c. 1930–c. 1946," in *Mexico since Independence,* ed. Leslie Bethell (Cambridge: Cambridge University Press, 1991).

37. A recent study that compellingly explores the transnational operation of U.S. discourses (particularly in Latin America) in the early cold war, is Arturo Escobar, *Encountering Development: The Making and Unmaking of the Third World* (Princeton, N.J.: Princeton University Press, 1995).

38. For a recent synthesis of cold war uses of the Monroe Doctrine, see Gaddis Smith, *The Last Years of the Monroe Doctrine, 1945–1993* (New York: Hill and Wang, 1994).

39. Antonio Castro Leal, Director of the Departamento de Supervisión Cinematográfica de la Secretaría de Gobernación, "Memorandum sobre 'El Fugitivo,'" 20 January 1948, AGN, Ramo Alemán, 523.3/26; and Pérez Martínez, "Memorandum sobre 'El Fugitivo,'" 3–4.

40. Gustavo A. Rovirosa, representative of the Secretaría de Salubridad y Asistencia to the Panamerican Sanitary Commission in El Paso, to Rogelio de la Selva, AGN, Ramo Alemán, 523.3/26.

41. This conflation of rightist prejudice and leftist egalitarianism was a staple of cold war U.S. westerns; see Slotkin, *Gunfighter Nation,* 369.

42. See "The Fugitive," Production File, MHL and Clippings File, NYPLPA. See also Ronald L. Davis, *John Ford: Hollywood's Old Master* (Norman: University of Oklahoma, 1995), 198. *The Pearl* also did not succeed economically in the United States. As with *The Fugitive,* reliance on the expressive visual images of Figueroa to convey the story did not sit well with U.S. audiences, who were used to more conventional narratives.

43. Jerome Bronfield, RKO Pathe, Inc., New York, to Alemán, 2 August 1949; and Luis García Larrañaga to Bronfield, 9 August 1949, AGN, Ramo Alemán 523.3/62. Bessie Galbraith de Reyes, Regional Director of the Mexico City Office of the New York Advertising/Public Relations firm Foote, Cone and Belding to Alemán, 14 October 1949; and Galbraith de Reyes to Roberto Amoros, 24 October 1949, AGN, Ramo Alemán, 523.3/65.

44. N. Peter Rathvon to Alemán, 15 July 1948, AGN, Ramo Alemán, 523.3/47. Other notable English-language features produced by RKO at Estudios Churubusco include *Mystery in Mexico* (1947) and *The Big Steal* (1949).

45. N. Peter Rathvon to Miguel Alemán, 17 January 1949, AGN, Ramo Alemán, 523.3/47. For 1949's conflicts, see Fein, *Film-Historia,* 119–24.

46. For an example of how this developed in Mexico, relevant for other areas of the world, see Fein, "Everyday Forms of Transnational Collaboration."

47. *Oficio mexicano* (Mexico City: Grijalbo, 1993), 32; translation is mine, italics in original.

48. Galindo and Gunther Gerszo wrote the script, which was shot in July and opened at Mexico City's Cine Palacio in November 1951.

49. For a discussion of *Viva Zapata!*'s ideology, and the Mexican government's attempt to shape Twentieth Century Fox's representation of Mexican history, see Fein, "Hollywood and United States–Mexico Relations in the Golden Age of Mexican Cinema," 722–39. See also Paul J. Vanderwood, "An American Cold Warrior: *Viva Zapata!* (1952)," in *American History/American Film: Interpreting the Hollywood Image,* ed. John E. O'Connor and Martin A. Jackson (New York: Continuum, 1988), 183–201.

50. "Film Dicen Que Yo Soy Comunista," Rankin to State Department (SD), 18 October 1951, NARG 59, 511.125/10–1851; "Transmitting Further Advertising Material in Connection with Film DICEN QUE YO SOY COMUNISTA," Rankin to SD, 19 October 1951, 511.125/10–1951.

51. This formula characterized Hollywood's contemporaneous representation of working-class organizations as fronts for the mob. The most famous example is, of course, *On The Waterfront* (1954). Directed by Kazan and written by Budd Schulberg, two artists whose public demonstrations of their anticommunism (in their cooperative testimonies before the House Un-American Activities Committee) allowed them to prosper in 1950s Hollywood. For a succinct and perceptive analysis of this cultural equation in U.S. cold war films, see Stephen Whitfield, *The Culture of the Cold War* (Baltimore: Johns Hopkins University Press, 1991), 130–44.

52. An introduction to Orol's work, including a comprehensive filmography, is Eduardo de la Vega Alfaro, *Juan Orol* (Guadalajara, Mexico: Universidad de Guadalajara, 1987).

53. Casting Rooner reinforced this reference, since he earlier had played a Nazi agent, Rudolph Hermann von Ricker, in Raúl de Anda's prowar propaganda film, *Soy puro mexicano* (1942). For an analysis of this latter film's message and production, see Fein, "Transnationalization and Cultural Collaboration," 118–20. See also note 41.

54. See Niblo, *War, Diplomacy, and Development,* 283.

55. At the same time that the state tried to marginalize radical movements like the Partido Comunista Mexicano and Partido Popular, it also tried to coopt their messages. Interestingly, Lombardo himself did not directly challenge the state's authority as much as he tried to influence its policies and enhance his own political power. For an excellent exploration of both dynamics, see Barry Carr, "The Fate of the Vanguard under a Revolutionary State: Marxism's Contribution to the Great Arch," in *Everyday Forms of State Formation: Revolution and the Negotiation of Rule in Modern Mexico,* ed. Gilbert M. Joseph and Daniel Nugent (Durham, N.C.: Duke University Press, 1994), 326–52.

56. "USIE Country Paper for Mexico," 6 August 1952, NARG 59, 511.12/

8–652. See also the early depiction of Lombardo as a dangerous international leftist in the otherwise mainly pro-Mexican, *March of Time* pseudodocumentary "Mexico's Dilemma" (1940) analyzed in Seth Fein, "El cine y las relaciones culturales entre México y Estados Unidos durante la década de 1930," *Secuencia* 34 (spring 1996): 188–89.

57. Too, Galindo splits the image of the PRI by contrasting the self-absorbed deputies with the compassionate governor.

58. The idea of Communist subversion as a threat to family values dominated cold war U.S. mass culture. See Elaine Tyler May, *Homeward Bound: American Families in the Cold War Era* (New York: Basic Books, 1988), especially 92–134. Jean Franco examines the way in which two Golden Age films, Emilio Fernández's *Enamorada* (1947) and Luis Buñuel's *Los olvidados* (1950), confronted the central position of women, mothers, and the family in the postwar Mexican state's liberal ideology, in *Plotting Women: Gender and Representation in Mexico* (New York: Columbia University Press, 1989), 147–59. See also Julia Tuñón, "La silueta de un vacío: Imágenes fílmicas de la familia mexicana en los cuarenta," *Film-Historia* 4.2 (June 1994): 137–47.

59. O'Dwyer to State Department, 17 August 1951, NARG 59, 511.125/8–1750.

60. Forney A. Rankin, Counselor for Public Affairs, to SD, 18 October 1951, NARG 59, 511.125/10–1851. Rathvon, who also had been involved with other OCIAA film-production activities during the war, directed similar private-sector propaganda production in postwar Europe on behalf of U.S. foreign policy.

61. See Fein, "Hollywood and United States–Mexico Relations," 684–722.

62. Roger Bartra, *The Cage of Melancholy: Identity and Metamorphosis in the Mexican Character,* trans. Christopher J. Hall (New Brunswick, N.J.: Rutgers University Press, 1992), 167.

63. Yet, while institutional links between Hollywood and the Mexican film industry served U.S. cold war ideological initiatives, Good Neighbor–era cultural cooperation over censorship ended with World War II. After the war, two contradictory patterns coexisted: continued U.S. influence in Mexican production but less bilateral cooperation over issues of national representation; see Fein, "Hollywood and United States–Mexico Relations," 720–39.

64. For an enlightening exegesis of the discourses of cultural imperialism, see John Tomlinson, *Cultural Imperialism: An Introduction* (Baltimore: Johns Hopkins University Press, 1991.)

65. Bartra, *The Cage of Melancholy,* 167.

66. Néstor García Canclini, *Hybrid Cultures: Strategies for Entering and Leaving Modernity,* trans. Christopher L. Chiappari and Silvia L. López (Minneapolis: University of Minnesota Press, 1995), 206–63.

Part II
Desire and the Nation
CONTEMPORARY CINEMA

■ ■ ■ ■

5

Fulfilling Fantasies, Diverting Pleasures

ANA CAROLINA AND *DAS TRIPAS CORAÇÃO*

Laura Podalsky

■ ■ ■ ■

In the last decade, women filmmakers have emerged as a potent force in the Latin American film industry, winning both critical and commercial favor. Recent scholarship has focused on the work of directors like María Luisa Bemberg (Argentina), Tizuka Yamasaki (Brazil), the collective Cine Mujer (Colombia), and even figures from the old cinema like Matilde Landeta and Adela Sequeyro (Mexico). Unfortunately, critics have largely ignored the work of a provocative Brazilian filmmaker, Ana Carolina.[1] Like the films of other contemporary women directors, Ana Carolina's work critiques the patriarchal basis of the social formation. Unlike films by other contemporary women directors, *Mar de rosas* (1977), *Das tripas coração* (1982), and *Sonho de valsa* (1987) eschew the principles of realism in favor of a carnivalesque aesthetic in order to critique the dominant social order. This may account to a certain extent for the difficulty of dealing with her films within the critical tradition of Latin American film scholarship, which has often stressed the social and political aspects and functions of films. While scholars have explored the ways in which films like Yamasaki's *Patriamada* (1984) and Bemberg's *Camila* (1984) address specific historical situations, they seem to be stymied by what some have labeled Ana Carolina's "surrealism"[2] and by the absence of explicit historical references. Liberally sprinkled with absurd elements, her films relentlessly parody patriarchal order and interrogate its relation to dreams and fantasy.

Ana Carolina's films deploy the type of strategies discussed by Robert Stam in his 1989 book *Subversive Pleasures: Bakhtin, Cultural Criticism, and Film,* in which he explores the subversive potential of Mikhail Bakhtin's formulations of carnival and the carnivalesque. By "turning the [everyday] world upside down," by privileging boisterous polyphony over authoritative monologue, and by celebrating the lower body, carnivalesque articulations challenge (if not subvert) established hierarchies (political, social, aesthetic) and, consequently, the dominant order. As Stam notes, Bakhtin's theories "promote . . . the subversive use of language by those who otherwise lack social power" and are particularly useful for an "analysis of opposition and marginal practices, be they Third World, feminist, or avant-garde."³ The carnivalism of Latin America, and particularly of Ana Carolina's Brazil, is both literal and metaphoric—present in the familiar mixing of cultures (African, European, indigenous) in the country's annual celebration and in its more general cultural life.⁴ Although Stam does not explicitly discuss Ana Carolina's films,⁵ their polyphonic soundtracks, emphasis on "lowly" voices (of disempowered groups) and speech (about sex and other bodily functions), and general sense of inverted order clearly call for such an analysis. This essay argues that the use of carnivalesque strategies in Ana Carolina's *Das tripas coração* enables Carolina to critique patriarchy in a way that other women filmmakers working within the domains of realism cannot.

This analysis challenges theoretical tendencies in both Latin American and feminist film criticism. Latin American film criticism has on the whole overlooked the potential usefulness of psychoanalytically informed film theories. The critique of psychoanalysis in Latin American cultural studies often rests on the assumption of the region's break with "Western" traditions of the individual and the nuclear family that form the context behind the origin and applicability of psychoanalysis as articulated by Freud and Lacan.⁶ While perhaps convincing in regard to the cultural expressions of indigenous groups, this assumption is unwarranted in relation to the work of artists like Ana Carolina who clearly develop and circulate in a cultural field heavily influenced by "Western" concepts.⁷ The films in her above-mentioned "trilogy" focus on the development of the individual female subject through "adolescence, youth, and maturity."⁸ They play precisely with the relations between sexuality, the family, the Law, and the subject at the heart of psychoanalytic theory. In *Mar de rosas,* a young girl from a middle-class family tries to kill her mother, who had tried to kill her husband. In *Sonho de valsa,* a young woman grapples with her incestuous desires for her brother and her simultaneous yearning for independence. Conversely, in *Das tripas coração* these concerns are presented as the object of a patriarchal state fantasy about female education.

At the same time, Ana Carolina's films make evident certain blind spots in feminist film theory as it has been articulated on the basis of an analysis of U.S. and European cinema. The carnivalesque strategies deployed in her films problematize critical paradigms that focus on an analysis of the gaze and the image to the exclusion of the soundtrack. Although Laura Mulvey, E. Ann Kaplan, and Mary Ann Doane,[9] among others, persuasively attack the conventional visual mechanisms used to represent women, they retain a specular bias and fail to give an adequate account of the role of aural mechanisms in establishing gender hierarchies in the cinema. The first major text to take up that issue and to argue for the progressive potential of voice in cinematic texts was Kaja Silverman's *The Acoustic Mirror: The Female Voice in Psychoanalysis and Cinema* (1988).[10] Silverman's discussion of voice in cinematic texts forms an immensely productive complement to Bakhtin's formulations, which often favor aural metaphors like polyphony and heteroglossia. As Stam notes, "Bakhtin's insistence on the presence of 'voices' as well as 'images'" can function as a critique of "the Western masculinist imagination [which] is strongly 'visualist,' positing cultural facts as things observed or seen rather than heard, transcribed, or invented in dialogue."[11] The role of voice is central to Ana Carolina's project of creating a different type of cinematic pleasure. While filled with spectacle, *Das tripas coração* does not depend on the reproduction of a privileged patriarchal / masculine gaze for its comic effects. Instead of offering self-reflexive representations as the only adequate alternative to this phallocentric visualism (or assuming that the only alternative to patriarchal pleasure is unpleasure), *Das tripas coração* and the other two films in the trilogy articulate the pleasurable as multisensorial. Like Lizzie Borden's *Born in Flames* (1983), *Das tripas coração* creates a complex soundtrack that solicits spectator pleasure and laughter through its inventive polyphony.[12] Its parody of patriarchal fantasy depends first and foremost on its aural play, which is perfectly in keeping with the etymological roots of the word "parody." Often thought of as "double-voicedness," the word comes from the Greek *paroidia* or Latin *parodia,* meaning "mock song." As discussed below, the pleasure of Ana Carolina's film results from its articulation of subversive voices that unsettle authoritative discourses.

Patriarchal Projections and Disruptive Voices

At the opening of *Das tripas coração,* a government bureaucrat walks into a girls' school with the intention of closing the institution because of what he characterizes as the female directors' administrative and financial mismanagement. While waiting for the faculty in a conference room, he asks a cleaning woman if the teachers are young and beautiful. After receiving her affirmative response, the official promptly dozes off in front of a clock at 4:55 P.M. This sequence functions as a narrative frame that reappears in the last minute of the film, when the man awakens at 5 P.M. as the school faculty enters the conference room.

The body of the film is the official's dream about the events in the school on the day before its permanent closure. He fantasizes about the obsessive love affair of two female teachers (Miriam and Renata), of the undisciplined behavior of the students who talk and sing about cocks and masturbate en masse, of the carnal desires of the school priest who can barely contain his own bodily fluids when a girl pees in the aisle during mass, and of the misguided administration of the ascetic headmistress and her assistant who characterize the suspected orgiastic behavior of their students as "communist." He imagines the girls' school as the site of unbridled passions where the students overrun all authority, terrorizing Olivina, the chemistry teacher, until she collapses. Taking over another class, the students invite not only their instructor but also Flanela, the maintenance man, and the school's female cleaning staff to join in their exuberant revelry of song and dance. As dreamed by the state bureaucrat, the girls' undisciplined behavior levels all hierarchies between teachers, staff, and students and thus disrupts clear lines of authority and social control. In other words, the school is a "world turned upside down." The hyperbolic nature of these sequences clearly points to the absurdity of the official's fantasy. On an allegorical level, the framed narrative ridicules the projections of the patriarchal state about the consequences of relaxing its vigilance.

The narcissistic nature of those projections becomes obvious when the official imagines himself as Guido, the single male professor at the school. The film represents Guido as a self-absorbed egotist who roams the hallways mumbling an unending monologue about heterosexual love while trying to place himself at the center of sexual desire and conflict within the school. Guido's self-positioning is a mirror for the role taken by the state official who describes his job as *interventor* (a mediator, or, more literally, he who intervenes) when he first enters the school. Just as the bureaucrat's arrival reorders the school hierarchy by placing him in control, Guido's proclamations attempt to interpolate his students as functions of his desire. During his last class, Guido pontificates, "Madness is the best way to boast. . . . Here I'm showing you my madness and you will act it out." [13] Guido proceeds to lecture the girls about the need to liberate their inner madness and to release themselves from social constraints.

The sequence parodies the self-absorbed nature of his monologue through its multilayered soundtrack. Guido's words are punctuated by the giggles and whispers of his students, who both engage and deflect his admonitions. While Guido rambles on about himself, the students ask each other for clarification ("What is he saying?" "I don't know."), sing dirty ditties ("My mother's dead, she needs a mass. Yours is alive, she sells her ass."), and whistle, giggle, and whisper. The girls' irreverent enunciations contest Guido's position as authority. Although some are responses to his words, others create a discrete circuit of articulations among the girls themselves. At the beginning of the scene, Guido's words compete with the girls' voices, which issue at almost equal volume. As the sequence opens with a track right past several rows of students, the visual images do not direct the spectator-auditor's attention to Guido any more than the soundtrack does. The sequence highlights polyphony, the term Bakhtin uses for the orchestration of a plurality of voices that "do not fuse into a single consciousness but exist on different registers, generating dialogical dynamism among themselves." [14] While Guido does not appear to recognize any voice but his own, the girls (and the spectator-auditor) clearly do. Their polyphonic exchanges engender a carnivalesque atmosphere that disrupts and impedes Guido's attempt to indoctrinate them in the/his social order. Thus, the film undermines the attempts of Guido/the state official to position himself as the speaking subject whose enunciations inscribe the girls as "other," mere objects of his desire.

The scene in the classroom echoes another that takes place during the last church service. As the priest intones about the "joys of being a woman," various voices are audible, once again creating a polyphonic atmosphere. At the beginning of this sequence, a Hassidic man enters the church; his protracted argument with the school director about whether or not he has the correct address drowns out the words of the priest. Minutes later, the cleaning women discuss a fictional entertainer's sexual orientation. In both of these occasions, the priest's presence is registered only in a muffled voice-off. The authoritativeness of the priest's ardent assertions about the saintliness of women is further undercut by images that contradict his words. As his voice-off compares the "little hands" of the young women in the church with those of the Virgin Mary who bathed the brow of Christ, the image track shows a shot of a girl's hands taking a pornographic prayer card (with the Virgin Mary on one side and a close-up of fellatio on the other) from Flanela to pass it to her companions. This sequence and the one in the classroom suggest that while the discourses of state education and of the Church set the terms of desire and rebellion, neither effectively fixes the female subject in a submissive position.

In *The Acoustic Mirror,* Silverman argues that classical Hollywood films stave off the threat of the male subject's lack by displacing it onto the female subject through aural conventions as well as through the visual ones first outlined by Laura Mulvey.[15] Silverman argues that Hollywood films do this by anchoring the female voice to a female body inside the diegesis while associating the male voice with the enunciatory power of the cinematic apparatus itself. Allowing only the male voice to serve as a disembodied voice-over, Hollywood let the female voice speak only from "within" one of several enclosures: (1) from a text within the diegesis (a musical spectacle, a film-in-the-film); (2) through hypnosis and the mediation of a male doctor who compels her to confess; or (3) through a heavy accent that marks the materiality of the voice. These three strategies position the female voice within the diegesis at "a point which can be overseen and overheard."[16] Thus, the female voice, like the female body, is held in place by a masterful male subject.

This paradigm is not adequate to address the function of the soundtrack in *Das tripas coração,* which actually "encloses" female voices without producing the effects Silverman attributes to Hollywood films. Ana Carolina's film has a Chinese-box structure. The female characters speak from within a male fantasy (i.e., through his mediation). In fact, at the beginning of the official's dream, Miriam and Renata recall the events of the last day of school in a voice-over; thus, the official dreams of Miriam and Renata remembering the last day. While situated as projections of a male subject (i.e., in the position of being overheard and overseen by him), the female subjects in *Das tripas coração* do not conform to his (Guido's/the official's) injunctions. Rather, they act in visual and aural terms to make the inadequacy of the male subject both audible and visible (as I will argue in the next section). Thus, Ana Carolina's film problematizes Silverman's equation of enunciatory enclosure and the disempowerment of the female subject.

At the same time, Silverman's analysis of the radical acoustic strategies employed in feminist experimental films—namely the detachment of the female voice from a specific diegetic body—is particularly useful for unpacking the subversive charge of the soundtrack of *Das tripas coração.* In the sequence in Guido's classroom, the girls' voices are quasi-disembodied. While seemingly issuing from that diegetic space, the shots rarely match voice with on-screen image. Instead, the voices issue from sources that are not visually identifiable as discrete units. They function as a type of maenadic chorus that surrounds Guido. Even more disturbing is the frequently asynchronous soundtrack. While attributable on some level to poor post-synchronization, I would argue that the "bad" dubbing of certain sequences in *Das tripas coração* is self-conscious, given Ana Carolina's background as sound director on Rogério Sganzerla's 1969 underground film, *A mulher de todos,* in which the provocative mix of U.S. rock and samba is central to the film's transgressive message.[17] In the opening of her film, one of the students runs alongside the official and repeatedly asks him what he is doing there while an extradiegetic female chorus encourages the "Students of Brazil" to "work for truth and their generation" and to "fight unceasingly for illumination." Not synchronized to the movements of her lips, the girl's voice undercuts the admonitions of the extradiegetic chorus by upsetting the realist pretensions of the visual track.

One final example further demonstrates how the soundtrack helps to break down the gender roles established by dominant ideology. In a particularly absurd sequence, Joana, a young student played by a male actor, speaks to the priest about a grave dilemma that no one at the school recognizes. S/he exclaims in a high-pitched voice, "I'm a man, Father," and pulls up her skirt to prove it. The sequence highlights multiple incongruities: Joana's dress (female) does not match her body (male) and Joana's voice (sounding like a male voice's high-pitched imitation of a female voice) is asynchronous with her/his body. Thus, the film confuses both the visual and aural gender codes that would identify Joana as either a boy or a girl. While the priest tries to persuade Joana that she is a girl who has simply overidentified with her "masculine side," his promise, "Let's be *close* friends, Joana," after she pulls up her skirt suggests that he "recognizes" Joana as a man and a possible homosexual partner. Through the priest's doublespeak, the scene pokes fun at the precarious basis of the gender divisions deployed in dominant discourses. The sequence highlights gender as an aural and visual performance rather than as an unmediated reflection of an "inner" coherence that is always already constituted. As Judith Butler notes in *Gender Trouble,* drag parodies the very notion of an "original or primary gender identity."[18] Thus, the priest's ambiguous response mocks the apparent fixity of patriarchal gender divisions that he himself tries to impose.

The Spectacle of Male Desire

Up to this point, I have argued that the film's use of parody offers a successful critique of patriarchal fantasy. However, parody does not necessarily disrupt and disable dominant ideology. Linda Hutcheon's definition of parody—"repetition with difference"—questions the degree to which it constitutes a break with convention.[19] Stam makes a similar qualification when he notes that the carnivalesque is not essentially or necessarily subversive. While emphasizing the subversive potential of drag as parody, Butler notes that parody "has been used to further a politics of despair, one which affirms a seemingly inevitable exclusion of marginal genders from the territory of the natural and the real." [20] Given these qualifications, what are the limits of *Das tripas coraçao*'s parody? While I have been arguing for the subversive function of the film's soundtrack, what about its images? Does the way the film toys with the spectacle of the female body unwittingly reinscribe woman as object? Does the spectator identify with the official's "voyeurism" because s/he sees through his eyes/dream? While infrequently displaying naked bodies, the film piles sexual spectacle upon sexual spectacle to the—perhaps—scopophilic delight of the spectator. The girls caress themselves and each other; two of the teachers (Miriam and Renata) participate in a ménage à trois with Guido; and the female cleaning staff rub themselves against Flanela. In fact, the film's foregrounding of sexual spectacle links it to the *pornochanchada,* a type of soft-core porn in Brazil that arose in the 1970s only to be replaced by a more hard-core variety in the subsequent decade when *Das tripas coração* appeared. [21] While hyperbolic, these visual depictions might also encourage traditional patterns of spectatorial pleasure and undermine, or at least lessen, the subversive potential of the soundtrack. However, there are at least two ways in which the film avoids this and instead celebrates deviant pleasures.

As theorized by Silverman among others, classic Hollywood cinema re-enacts and assuages certain psychic traumas that reaffirm gender hierarchies by firmly associating lack—a necessary condition of male as well as female subjectivity—exclusively with the latter. [22] Central to this process is the films' construction of a male ego ideal with whom the spectator can identify. The male character's ability to master his diegetic world (to reach his goal and fulfill his desire) and the stylistic mechanisms that support this mastery seal over the male spectator's awareness of his own lack. Clearly not a part of the Hollywood tradition, *Das tripas coração* associates lack with the male subject.

In the framed narrative, male heterosexual desire is an impediment to pleasurable unions; only lesbian liaisons are represented as satisfying. When Guido repeatedly and literally places himself between Miriam and Renata, who are lovers, the conflict culminates in a threesome that fails to sexually satisfy any of them. After Miriam and Renata move away from Guido, each responds to the question "Gozou?" ("Did you enjoy it/come?") with a resounding "No." The unfulfilling conclusion to the ménage à trois mocks Guido's (or the official's) phallocentric notions of sexuality. [23]

The outcome of the ménage à trois anticipates the disappointing attempt by another male professor, who returns to the school briefly to say his good-byes, to screw a cleaning woman in the boiler room. Despite his efforts to put her where he wants her (literally placing himself on top of her and metaphorically doing so by chanting "criada, domestica, mucama" ["servant"]), the professor finds himself impotent. Through these sequences, *Das tripas coração* undermines the cinematic male's traditional omnipotence. While Guido and the other professor try to satisfy their desires by controlling women, the film relentlessly dramatizes male lack. It mocks Guido's earlier claim to his students that the penis is the fountain from which sprout both gods and mortals by underscoring the difference between the penis and the phallus. Rather than assuaging the male spectator's awareness of his own lack, the film/dream's central protagonist exacerbates it.[24] Consequently, there can be little sense of pleasurable complicity between the spectator and the official/Guido.

While foregrounding the male characters' lack, *Das tripas coração* also manages to undermine conventional spectating by "dirtying" the spectacle and diminishing its "to-be-looked-at-ness" by employing another carnivalesque strategy: reveling in *all* bodily emissions. The film overturns conventional hierarchies that valorize certain parts of the body over others. This leveling effectively prevents the fetishization of the female body and thus furthers the film's subversive project.

To transgress representational conventions, Ana Carolina's film reworks some of the strategies used by the underground, or *udigrudi*, filmmakers in Brazil in the late 1960s and early 1970s. Their films, otherwise known as garbage cinema, attempted to create a "dirty screen" by aggressively violating canons of good taste. Sganzerla's *A mulher de todos* mocks the type of soft-core porn that dominated Brazilian screens. The film chronicles the adventures of a sexually voracious woman who screws one of her various male partners in a bathroom stall. In this and other ways, Sganzerla's work disregards norms of the "presentable" and plays with the notion of "dirty pictures." Like Sganzerla's irreverent display of the transgressive, *Das tripas coração* makes a spectacle of the act of vomiting and peeing as well as the act of making love. When Olivina, the chemistry teacher, collapses in class after being harassed and ultimately physically attacked by her students, she is sent home. Helped to a waiting car by Guido, Olivina vomits all over the front steps of the school. After the cleaning women wave good-bye to the departing car, the camera follows their subsequent efforts to remove the vomit. Through a gradual tilt down, the camera records the progress of the vomit as it is pushed down the steps. The camera's "refusal" to turn away demonstrates the film's unconventional framing of the body as spectacle. The sequence is a fine example of the film's grotesque realism, the term Bakhtin used to refer to an "anti-illusionistic style which remains physical, carnal, and material."[25] The materiality of the sequence is less a product of its unmediated "presencing" of vomit than of its refusal to deliver the expected. Its insistence on "crossing the line" between "suitable" and "unsuitable" representations evokes unanticipated, visceral responses from spectator-auditors unaccustomed to such displays.

The film also establishes unconventional links between bodily functions to mock the titillating power of female bodies on display. The coup de grace to the priest's sermon about the saintliness of women comes when one of the students makes a spectacle of herself by peeing in the aisle in front of the altar in order to win a bet. As the girls file out of the chapel shouting "She won her bet. She won her bet," the headmistress and her assistant have to restrain the priest who threatens to relieve himself in the same place. Having been unable to control his bodily urges earlier in the film (when he urinated behind a nearby statue), the priest's reaction to the situation here can be read in two ways. Either he is trying to urinate—in which case the scene foregrounds the priest's inability to control his own body—or he is trying to ejaculate—in which case the sequence disturbs the conventional link between spectacle and sexual pleasure by positioning urination as sexual stimulus. In either case, the film "dirties" the screen by placing profane acts in sacred spaces. In so doing, it either de-eroticizes the female body or places that eroticized body in the realm of the perverse.

A later scene further "levels" bodily pleasures in a decidedly profane space when Flanela, the maintenance man, begins to clean a bathroom while several girls are inside the stalls. An overhead track reveals a pair of girls smearing lipstick on their faces; another pair caressing and kissing each other; and a fifth girl smoking alone. As Flanela becomes excited by the girls' behavior—i.e., by his aural (and visually imagined?) perceptions of it—he enters a stall to masturbate. Shots of the girls leaving the stalls are interspersed with medium shots of Flanela becoming increasingly excited inside his stall. Encouraged by the girls, who throw a pair of panties into the stall, Flanela finally ejaculates. As he comes with one off-screen hand, he flushes the toilet with the other on-screen hand. In a particularly carnivalesque move, the sequence de-eroticizes Flanela's increasing excitement by comically drawing a parallel between the liberatory power of different types of lower body emissions. By timing his ejaculation to the flush of the toilet, *Das tripas coração* undercuts the conventional positioning of the ejaculating cock as the climax of the film. The scene deflects what Stam calls the "monologic" nature of conventional sexual imagery "which subordinates everything to the masculine imagination" and, in the end, to the "veneration of the ejaculating penis/phallus as the measure of all pleasure." [26] While Flanela's climax "resolves" the tension between himself and the girls who are provoking him, it is not the singular focus of the sequence, which spends more time on the girls' interactions with each other. The peak moment actually occurs in the water fight that breaks out among them before the abrupt entrance of the ascetic headmistress ends their frolicking and the sequence itself.

Deviant Allegories

The film's subversive charge is apparent not only in its polyphonic sound-track and dirty spectacles but ultimately in the way it functions as an alle-gory about the contemporaneous situation in Brazil and about the relation-ship of desire and power. Made in 1982, during the waning of the military government that had ruled the country since 1964, *Das tripas coração* cri-tiques that regime's economistic logic and repressive tactics. When the state official first enters the school, he justifies his presence as a response to the school's economic failure and promises to replace it with a new business. His preoccupation with financial matters and his bureaucratic language al-lude to the discourse of developmentalism favored by the military govern-ment, while his closure of the school symbolizes its repressive actions against sectors it characterized as subversive. Ana Carolina commented on the film's allegorical function in an interview with sociologist Vivian Schel-ling, comparing Brazil to "a big school—when the teacher is there every-one behaves and as soon as the teacher leaves, chaos breaks out." [27] Her comment addressed the inability of the military regime to successfully in-doctrinate the Brazilian people who did not internalize its ideology and the inability of civil society to provide alternatives. Consequently, the gov-ernment had to retain constant vigilance and surveillance through various social institutions. Ana Carolina's films celebrate the breakdown of those institutional imperatives. *Mar de rosas* focuses on the collapse of a middle-class family, *Das tripas coração* on the disintegration of state and religious education, and *Sonho de valsa* on the failed socialization of the female subject.

Ana Carolina's films demonstrate a particular interest in relating the function of these institutions to the establishment and maintenance of gen-der hierarchies. Her trilogy explores the way in which structures of desire operate through the exercise of power and how social control acts as an aphrodisiac for certain dominant groups. In *Das tripas coração*, the priest becomes aroused precisely by the taboo (e.g., peeing in front of the altar) and by transgression (Joana, the girl-boy). He is excited by things/acts that defy the borders erected by the Church (between the sacred and the profane, between woman and man) to effectively discipline unproductive libidinal impulses deemed dangerous to the social order. In Buñuelian fashion, Ana Carolina's film suggests that the repressive force of social institutions like the Church actually provokes the libidinal desires they ostensibly seek to control.[28] In the ménage à trois sequence, an eyeline match links Miriam's gaze (over the shoulder of Guido whom she is embracing) to a life-size Christ figure hanging on the wall above them. In place of the thin figure previously there is Guido/the official, who tells her to "suck it." Rather than castigating her for her actions, the Christ-figure encourages her to perform for him (and) Guido (and) the official. The shot clearly aligns various patriarchal institutions (state, school, and church) through the figure of the official/Guido/Christ to reveal their complicity in soliciting the female behavior they seemingly condemn.

Finally, *Das tripas coração*'s attack on the Brazilian military government has a very specific target in its censorship laws. After 1968, the military government established strict controls over political expression through the implementation of the Fifth Institutional Act. During the same period, independent filmmakers began to flood Brazilian theaters with *pornochanchadas*. Ana Carolina's film ridicules the state's acceptance of pornography and simultaneous censorship of political criticism by "using the conventions of pornochanchadas to escape censorship while making disguised criticisms of the social order."[29] By reveling in bodily imagery, *Das tripas coração* effectively turned the rules of the dominant political order against themselves to critique political repression.

Notes

I thank Julianne Burton-Carvajal for her many helpful suggestions on this paper.

1. There are a small number of relatively brief articles that deal with her work, including John Mosier, "The New Brazilian Cinema: Ana Carolina," *Americas* (May–June 1983): 58–59; Barbara Kruger, "Ana Carolina, Mar de Rosas," *Artforum* 25 (April 1987): 129–30; Simon Hartog, "Ana Carolina Teixeira Soares: A Conversation," *Framework* 28 (1985): 64–69; and João Carlos Rodrigues, "Das tripas coração," *Framework* 28 (1985): 77–81.

2. See David França Mendes in a review of Ana Carolina's work in *Programação TABU* 39 (July 1989): iv, the guide to monthly programming for Cineclube Estação Botafogo in Rio de Janeiro; Luis Trelles Plazaola, *Cine y mujer en América Latina: Directoras de largo metraje de ficción* (Rio Piedras: Editorial

de la Universidad de Puerto Rico, 1991), 88; and Rodrigues, "Das tripas coração," 77.

3. Robert Stam, *Subversive Pleasures: Bakhtin, Cultural Criticism, and Film* (Baltimore: Johns Hopkins Press, 1989), 18, 21–22.

4. Ibid., 126–29.

5. Stam does mention Ana Carolina briefly in a footnote in his chapter "The Grotesque Body and Cinematic Eroticism," in which he characterizes her work and that of Luis Buñuel and Pedro Almodóvar as having "mined th[e] vein of sexualized sacrilege," p. 254.

6. This logic seems to be behind Teshome Gabriel's theorization of Third Cinema as antipsychological. While never specifically naming psychoanalysis, Gabriel's formulation characterizes analytical frameworks that focus on the individual as inappropriate for Third World texts. Gabriel, *Third Cinema in the Third World: The Aesthetics of Liberation* (Ann Arbor, Mich.: UMI Research Press, 1982). See also Julianne Burton's "Marginal Cinemas and Mainstream Critical Theory," *Screen* 26.3–4 (1985): 16–18; and Gabriel's response, "Colonialism and 'Law and Order' Criticism," *Screen* 27.3–4 (May–August 1986): 140–47.

7. See Ana Carolina's specific use of psychoanalytic references in the Hartog interview listed above.

8. Vivian Schelling, "Ana Carolina Teixeira: Audacity in the Cinema," *Index on Censorship* 14.5 (1985): 60.

9. While Doane's recent work focuses on the visual track, she did some important earlier work on sound. "Voice in the Cinema: The Articulation of Body and Space" (first published in *Yale French Studies* 60 [1980]: 33–50) addressed the role of sound in a film's ideological work and briefly discussed its relation to gender. Doane's article can be considered an important precursor to the work of Kaja Silverman and Amy Lawrence (see note 11).

10. Kaja Silverman, *The Acoustic Mirror: The Female Voice in Psychoanalysis and the Cinema* (Bloomington: Indiana University Press, 1988). More recently, Amy Lawrence has taken up this project in *Echo and Narcissus: Women's Voices in Classical Hollywood Cinema* (Berkeley and Los Angeles: University of California Press, 1991) and in "Women's Voices in Third World Cinema," in *Sound Theory, Sound Practice,* ed. Rick Altman (New York: Routledge, 1992).

11. Stam, *Subversive Pleasures,* 19. There are also divergences between Silverman and Stam. While Stam links Bakhtin's project to that of Luce Irigaray (both stress the plurality and multiplicity of the subject and, more important, favor the voice as liberatory), Silverman critiques the French feminist extensively for suggesting that the voice is somehow less culturally mediated than the visual register. Silverman also argues that French feminists participate in the Western tradition of associating voice with presence and with the speaker's inner essence (p. 43).

Silverman's critique of Irigaray does not diminish her interrogation of the visualist prejudice of film theory (pp. 200–1); it merely cautions against facile celebrations of the voice as somehow "outside" ideological constraints. Bakhtin understands voice as socially constituted at all times and therefore his formulations remain in sync with those of Silverman.

12. See Teresa de Lauretis, "Aesthetic and Feminist Theory: Rethinking Women's Cinema," in *Technologies of Gender* (Bloomington: Indiana University Press, 1987), for a discussion of the way the polyphonic soundtrack of *Born in Flames* addresses an audience that is female and heterogeneous.

13. The film models Guido on Paulo Martins, the intellectual who unceasingly ponders his own madness in Glauber Rocha's *Terra em transe* (Land in Anguish, 1967). Rocha's film criticizes Paulo for his failure to reject utopian dreams and to act decisively within a concrete political realm. *Terra em transe* represents Paulo's vacillations between a reactionary senator and a populist governor as an unresolved struggle between two fathers. Ana Carolina's film reactivates the figure of the male narcissist to explore what was implicit yet unexamined in Rocha's film: the phallocentric logic of traditional political regimes.

14. Stam, *Subversive Pleasures,* 229.

15. Laura Mulvey, "Visual Pleasure and Narrative Cinema" and "Afterthoughts on 'Visual Pleasure and Narrative Cinema' inspired by *Duel in the Sun,*" reprinted in *Feminism and Film Theory,* ed. Constance Penley (New York: Routledge, 1988).

16. Silverman, *The Acoustic Mirror,* 62.

17. The influence of Glauber Rocha's work on Ana Carolina's is also evident in her complex sound mixes. Rocha created complex mixes of, for instance, Villa Lobos and African-Brazilian rhythms in his films. See Bruce Graham, "Music in Glauber Rocha's Films," *Jump Cut* 22 (May 1980): 15–18, rpt. in *Brazilian Cinema,* ed. Randal Johnson and Robert Stam, (East Brunswick, NJ: Associated University Presses, 1982), 290–305.

18. Judith Butler, *Gender Trouble: Feminism and the Subversion of Identity* (New York: Routledge, 1990), 137–39.

19. Linda Hutcheon, *A Theory of Parody: The Teachings of Twentieth-Century Art Forms* (New York: Metheun, 1985), 32.

20. Butler, *Gender Trouble,* 146.

21. Randal Johnson argues that "between 1981 and 1988, hardcore pornography accounted for an average of almost 68 percent of total production." See "The Rise and Fall of Brazilian Cinema, 1960–1990," *Iris* (1994): 98, 110.

22. Kaja Silverman, *The Subject of Semiotics* (New York: Oxford University Press, 1988).

23. The low-key lighting and the bared breasts of the actresses playing Miriam (Xuxa Lopes) and Renata (Dina Sfat) might point toward a different reading as they fall within the conventions for eroticizing the female body. How-

ever, as shots of the ménage à trois are cross-cut with shots of events in two other diegetic spaces, the spectator's voyeurism is continually interrupted.

24. Silverman's book *Male Subjectivity at the Margins* (New York: Routlege, 1992) deals with films like *Best Years of Our Lives* and *It's a Wonderful Life* that foreground male lack. However, unlike *Das tripas coração*, those films eventually displace male lack.

25. Stam, *Subversive Pleasures,* 236.

26. Ibid., 167.

27. Schelling, "Ana Carolina Teixeira," 60.

28. See Stam's discussion of Buñuel as carnivalesque in *Subversive Pleasures,* 102–7.

29. Schelling, "Ana Carolina Teixeira," 59.

6

Performing the Nation in Sergio Toledo's *Vera*

Monica Hulsbus

■ ■ ■ ■

Sergio Toledo's significance as a filmmaker cannot be separated from the Brazilian struggle for social and economic justice, since his life, education, and work reflects on the social events that culminated in the gradual return to a democracy in Brazil by the mid-1980s. Toledo was born in 1956. In 1970, while still a student in sociology at the São Paulo University, he met Hector Babenco. Impressed by Babenco's work, Toledo began making Super 8 films. In 1975, he started working professionally as an editor and assisting directors such as Walter Hugo Khoury, Maurice Capovilla, Jorge Bodansky, and Ana Carolina. During the period of 1975–83, Toledo produced some short films: *Parada geral* (*General Strike,* 1975); *A história dos ganha-pouco* (*A History of Earning Little,* 1977); *A luta do partido dos trabalhadores* (*The Struggle of the Workers' Party,* 1982); and *Communidade* (*Community,* 1983). In 1978 he made, in collaboration with Roberto Gervitz, his first full-length feature, *Braços cruzados, maquinas paradas* (*Crossed Arms, Stopped Machines),* a documentary that dealt with the Brazilian worker's situation before the return to democracy. It was awarded Best Director's prize at the Leipzig Festival, and it represented Brazil in the Forum of Young Filmmakers at the Berlin Festival in 1980.

Sergio Toledo's early success and subsequent move to feature-length narratives coincided with a serious decline in Brazilian cinema that was brought about by the petrol crisis, massive foreign debt, and the enormous increase in international interest rates that shook the national economy in the early 1980s. Toledo's first feature project, *Vera,* won a prize from the São Paulo Department of Culture in 1983 and a prize from EMBRAFILM in 1984–85. These awards allowed him to engage in research for a year while having two other people write the script. But because EMBRAFILM was unable to provide sufficient funds for the completion of the film, Toledo had to postpone production for another year and raise the necessary funds from private entrepreneurs. Although Toledo was eventually able to complete the film, the industry itself suffered further setbacks. By 1988, according to John King, after maintaining an annual average of sixty films for a number of years, the industry released just ten, and EMBRAFILM went bankrupt.[1]

It was also during this time when, after a period of sixteen years of military rule (particularly brutal between 1968 and 1974), a gradual period of liberalization began to pave the road to democracy in Brazil. In 1979, under the administration of Gen. João Batista Figueiredo, a number of opposition parties congregated in the Partido do Movimento Democrático Brasileiro, putting the military on the defensive. The 1982 elections, after five years of social mobilization and protest—focused mainly on the factories and working-class communities of São Paulo and coordinated as much by the Catholic Church as by parties and unions—gave the opposition the government of the leading states and a majority in the Chamber of Deputies. Three years later, after considerable deterioration in the government party (the Partido Democrático Social), the military lost the presidency to Tancredo Neves, who, because of precarious health, was succeeded shortly thereafter by José Sarney, marking the first stage in the transition to a full democracy.

Toledo's description of the film can be read in its allegorical function as a transition from the institutional terror imposed on the nation by the military to the gradual process of democratization that followed the election of Tancredo Neves as president:

> Vera is a girl who struggles to convince people that she is a man, that she is the opposite of what she is. The one question I asked myself from the outset was: what made her feel the need to negate her own body and build a masculine persona? I did not want to discuss the subject in the light of an indisputable homosexual or transsexual issue. What attracted me was what one might call the symbolic quality that represents a certain contemporary way of thinking in which fear and pretense play important roles.[2]

The plot focuses on the transition of Vera Bauer, the protagonist, from a boarding institution for girls to her insertion into the larger metropolitan world. In her struggle to survive the brutality she encounters in the institution, where she has spent most of her life, she develops a tough masculine persona, "Bauer," as she demands to be called. Through this impersonation, she demands obedience and respect from her peers. When she turns eighteen, she must leave the institution because by law she is now an adult.

Assisted by a sympathetic sponsor, Vera finds a job in a research center. There she meets Clara, a beautiful young woman with whom she initiates an intense relationship. Overwhelmed by the realities of life outside the institution where she grew up, Vera's behavior becomes more extreme, culminating with her showing up to work wearing a men's suit. Subsequently, she is fired from the research center and is rejected by Clara, with whom she has fallen in love. These events precipitate a crisis in which she is forced to realize not only that her impersonation is not yielding the desired respect and obedience but also that it is in fact harming her.

Although Toledo's career developed mostly during the years of Brazilian military rule and throughout the return to democracy, offering a case study of the transition, my particular investment in Toledo's *Vera* stems from the symbolic signification with which the protagonist is endowed. Vera—or Bauer, as she calls herself—is a character who condenses within herself the greatest possible number of social relations or links with the historical moment of the Brazilian transition to democratization. The ambivalence she embodies, coded as a misalignment of gender and sexuality, can be read in connection to the contradictory social forces that characterized Brazil's domestic policy in the period that preceded democratization. Vera's impersonation of masculinity both invokes and destabilizes authority when she appropriates a discourse of power and yet fails to compel belief in its representation. Her enactment of authoritarian masculinity incites a crisis of signification and discursive address when the travesty of her appropriation exposes her as a thief—a walking scandal. Furthermore, it eventually brings about the collapse of her entire self.

Within the scope of this essay, I will construct a textual reading of Toledo's film elaborated from the following premises: (1) In Toledo's text the nation is staged as a site of liminality between a discourse of authority and the failure of its performativity. (2) The liminality of the nation is condensed within a single character who simultaneously flouts authority and compels its crisis, allowing the narration to circumvent the problems of speaking in the voice of "the people." Before undertaking a close reading of the film, it is important to note how Toledo's stylistic rhetoric questions the authority manufactured by a linear representation of history when he establishes a link between the performativity of gender/video and nationness. As part of a visual rhetoric targeted to the reconstruction of popular memory, Toledo establishes a tension between film and electronic images. Whereas all the events of the story world are contained within the film, the film is itself haunted by video monitors. These video images reflect Vera's deterioration, screening apocalyptic images of failing technology as an anticipation and reinforcement of the events of the story world and linking them with Vera's subjectivity. In addition, they also screen images of civilian warfare and resistance, suggesting an infiltration of social events as images into the personal, private, and work environment, where these are received as televisual representations. Such representations were familiar and wide-spread among a Brazilian audience, since the social upheaval of the early 1980s could no longer be suppressed by the military. Moreover, 70 percent of Brazilian households possessing television sets were by then connected nationwide through satellite communication, reception dishes, and networks of retransmitting ground stations.

The film is framed by electronic images, starting with the opening shot and later resolving the tension between both media when closing the narrative. The film's opening shot is a video image of the launching of the *Challenger* space shuttle, connecting the image to a phallic technical iconography—displayed in its highest degree of performativity as well as in its uttermost measure of failure. The destruction of the *Challenger* was broadcast worldwide as a U.S. national catastrophe when it exploded into flames on 28 January 1986, killing among the crew a woman named Christa MacAuliffe, the first and only civilian to participate in a national competition sponsored by NASA to be part of a launch. Following the opening shot, a frontal shot in which Vera and her mentor, Professor Trauberg, walk along a corridor—whose round, narrow shape replicates the *Challenger*'s—situates the video image of the launch within the realm of the story world, mapping its allegorical function onto Vera's character. In the next section, I will engage in a close reading of the film, after which I will discuss the stylistic elements, resuming analysis of the film's significance within the sociopolitical context of the day.

A Different Space: Vera/Bauer's Story

Within the order of the story, the film is engaged in the struggle to stabilize two disparate modes of perception within the protagonist. Vera contains the knowledge of the violence exerted upon "woman" experienced within the juvenile institution that delivers her into the larger social realm. She knows that in there, as a woman, she is forced to submit, that her vulnerability lends itself to abuse, and that even when a certain degree of participation is promised by the administration, honesty and self-assertion result in more abuse. Vera stores the knowledge of captivity, of powerlessness. Bauer, on the other hand, refuses to be called Vera and, by the same token, refuses to be interpellated as "woman." She carries her family name as a sign of resistance, while in a similar fashion she holds within herself the intricate family network that the girls in the orphanage have designed in order to survive.

The network in which the girls at the institution establish relationships is a carefully stratified system in which they become fathers, sons, grandfathers, mothers, daughters, and lovers to each other. Gender is reassigned according to personal makeup and in relation to a fixed referent whereby masculinity and authority are conflated. Hence, the toughest butch is grandfather to the most vulnerable femme, and also father to the second-toughest butch. Along with this reterritorialization of gender, there is also a precarious space for ambivalence, a place wherein Vera, after being initiated into the "family," rehearses an androcentric posture and yet preserves a certain degree of vulnerability. This space she will continually refer to as "different."

Her difference shapes her movement from the one institution associated with the military state—the orphanage where she was raised—to another institutional space, associated to the emerging democratic state—her new work environment at the Advance Research Center. Whereas the function of the Advance Research Center in the film remains unspecified, it does clearly reflect a microworld where processing and cataloguing outside social events is mediated by specialized fields of information. In this sense, it fulfills the same functions the intellectual and the artist are expected to perform.

A video monitor is placed on the side of the corridor that Bauer and Professor Trauberg walk together; catastrophic images of war are recurrently screened by these monitors throughout the film. Saturating the narrative space, they function as a punctuation and a reminder of a universe whose brutality is deployed and contested by means of technology. An equivalent punctuation is devised around Clara and Bauer's encounter. They meet at the research center's gallery while each of them walk around a three-dimensional representation of a tortured body that hangs from the ceiling. All around the walls photographs of encounters between the forces of authority and civilians speak of abuse and oppositional struggles. Clara introduces herself: she is a young and graceful Black woman who works at the video and documentation department, where she stores and reconstructs electronic images of civilian resistance. Marked by race, memory is the property of the unprivileged, thus becoming, literally, popular memory.

Bauer's passage—from her biographical past at the orphanage to her present social environment at the video lab where she visits Clara—is both a temporal and a spatial switch but not a redeeming one, for she carries with her both the internalization of abuse and the effects of her victimization. Next, another flashback bears testimony of such abuse: the director of the orphanage has called a meeting with the purpose of improving communication between the administration and the girls. Vera solicits permission to discuss the behavior of the staff toward the girls and as a consequence is sent to solitary confinement for two days.

Later, Bauer walks with Clara, at the research center. Clara speaks about being a single parent, about being both mother and father to her son. Framed in a deep shot and against the monumental physicality of the institution, Clara articulates a project of subversion upon an androgyny of functions. Contrasting Bauer's limited repertoire, the narrative champions Clara—her androgynous youth to be the depository of images and the guardian of popular memory—as the one who is truly free. Bauer inevitably and painfully recognizes in Clara the flexibility, awareness, and multidimensionality she lacks, and hence she falls in love with her. An ominous video monitor depicting exploding objects foreshadows catastrophe, anticipating and commenting on the asymmetry of their respective positions.

A flashback to the orphanage provides more information on the transformation of Vera into "Bauer," her masculine persona. While the girls chat at the assembly line during break, someone talks about Vera's girlfriend, Thelma, having an affair with one of the male guardians. Vera volunteers to "take care of it." Harassed and physically abused by Vera, Thelma falls down on the bathroom floor, bursting into tears. The disparity of points of view becomes a spatial difference, emphasizing the split of gender roles that follows. This shot and the next one mark a major threshold in Vera's identity from her initial position of vulnerability to her newly acquired capacity to inflict pain—the emerging Bauer.

Subsequently, the camera frames a pair of legs dressed in male's clothing, transferring her transformation to the present. Bauer is stared at by the people at the research center: she has come to work in drag, dressed as a man (fig. 6.1). Her fellow workers request her dismissal, and even Clara severs their connection. Still in drag, Bauer visits Clara's home, where Clara's parents are also visiting. Bauer passes as a man: Clara's parents are not able to tell the difference. Amused, Clara asks, "How did you fool them?" To which Bauer replies: "I didn't, what they saw, they saw with their own eyes. The important thing is what one sees, not what one thinks." [3] Identity for Bauer is predicated upon appearances.

The next sequence, a flashback, depicts how Bauer authenticates her

FIGURE 6.1. *Vera Bauer, from* Vera *(1986). Courtesy of Kino International Corporation; photograph by Luciana De Francesco.*

identity as a masculine subject. The camera frames her frontally while she comes out of the shower, covering herself abruptly upon seeing Paizao, the head of the "family," staring at her. Paizao has come to pass on to Bauer the responsibility and privilege of looking after the girls, for she is now eighteen and about to leave the orphanage. Bauer agrees to take over. Returning to the present, a frontal shot of Bauer masquerading as a man while dubbing a male singer completes the illusion. She has found a job at a nightclub, after being fired from the research center.

Bauer and Clara become involved. The soundtrack previously used with the shots at the orphanage is now applied to a shot in which a naked Clara and a covered Bauer kiss. Bauer's persona is construed according to the orphanage's vertical power system—her female body is not to be seen or touched—in which to be a man means maintaining the appearance of it at all times. Clara refuses to engage sexually under those terms (fig. 6.2).

Next, a flashback depicts a confrontation taking place between the administration and the girls after the director demands that the girls wear dresses, alarmed at "this butch thing." Bauer, leader of the "family" now, initiates verbal resistance. Angered, the director proceeds to humiliate the girls by ordering them to pull down their pants and demanding that the girls prove they are real men. "To be a real man you've got to have balls," he states, "and you girls have nothing going" (fig. 6.3).

At this point the narrative has reached its climax, both rhetorically and within the diegesis. While Bauer has completed the illusion of masculinity within the restricted arena of the nightclub, appropriating its voice and gestures, rhetorically a cluster of visual associations become manifest. The story's gravitational pull is trauma, the humiliation Bauer and the other girls had to endure as "woman." The injury is in turn transferred onto others who may represent "woman," and hence, by means of displacement, an identification with the victimizer functions to assert control and fend off potential aggression from the outside. This pathological internalization of abuse is in turn conveyed to a macroworld in which multiple video screens displaying terminal destruction testify to a social framework of domination and brutality.

Torn between desire and self-preservation—that is, the preservation of her masculine persona—Bauer pays a last visit to the orphanage, now closed and partly demolished. Accepting defeat, she collapses. Her collapse figures as the precondition for a restructuring of identity, for it is from the ruins of its apparatuses—such as the institutionalization of gender and violence—that the possibility for a continuation of subjectivity is articulated.

FIGURE 6.2. *Vera and Clara, from* Vera. *Courtesy of Kino International Corporation; photograph by Luciana De Francesco.*

FIGURE 6.3. *"To be a real man you've got to have balls. . . ." Vera and the director of the orphanage, from* Vera. *Courtesy of Kino International Corporation; photograph by Luciana De Francesco.*

Next, a shot inside the video lab at the research center pans over the innumerable monitors, showing a propagation of video images of war, atom bombs, crashes, planes, rockets, and torpedoes. This dystopian universe gradually fades out, giving way to a close-up of Vera's emerging face. Multiplied through the monitors, the image of her face confronts the camera. Vanished, her face is replaced by her writing, which finally articulates a new beginning: "I have always been afraid of looking inside me . . . and finding nothing but a deep silence. But now I know that, despite everything, there is no other possible way." A new sense of history—a retrospective understanding—has made such articulation possible for Vera.

Video and the Discourse of Nationness

Rhetorically, the narrative is propelled by means of two distinct mechanisms. The editing is a key stylistic element throughout the film, by which meaning is generated. In addition to the editing, a tension within the film is created by the consistent reappearance of video screens, launching an implicit interrogation about the function and role of the two media. Moreover, this interrogation points to issues of legitimacy and representation, already dealt with within the story itself. The tension is ultimately resolved by the proliferation of Vera's writing over the video screens at the lab, ending the narration in a circular movement that closes where Vera begins to retell her story.

The editing, which links and contrasts information within the story world, structures the narrative along spatial and temporal planes, whereby the past and present are imbricated and illuminate each other. As a form of discourse, it functions to express a subjectivity not contained diegetically, by means of which the enunciation constructs a specific reading for the spectator. Such a reading travels through the narrative structure in a double movement: it is articulated within the narrative structure yet ultimately works to destabilize it. Through sequencing and a careful juxtaposition of images, the narrator's statement is filtered in between shots, working relentlessly to undermine the predicament mobilized within the story—that is, brutality and authority enforced through gender. In doing so, it formulates a subplot that is later recuperated within the story world on account of a final collapse of the terms employed by the narrator.

Toledo advances a textual discourse of nationness that is not contingent upon a historical teleology. Rather, his rhetorical strategy relies upon the production of a discourse whose guarantee is the present political relation of the spectator and his or her process of identification with the markers facilitated by the narrator within the story world. Using the protagonist as a focalizer, the narration covers a personal history whose "symptoms" push the story toward the reconstruction of memory, while stylistically proceeding through techniques similar to those of the analyst. Proposing the analytic techniques as really "situations of history," Lacan argues:

> The path of restitution of the history of the subject takes the form of the restitution of the past. That restitution is to be considered as the target at which the strategies of technique direct their aim. What is crucial is not "reliving the past," "having memories," but the *present synthesis of the past called history, and its reconstruction, re-writing the history.*[4]

Through and by the figure of Vera Bauer, both the rhetorical narration and the story world aim at a contradiction, carving for the spectator a disjunctive identification, an impasse. The spectator is immobilized in a dual strategy. On one hand, the narrative offers a critique of authority through the conflation of masculinity and brutality. On the other, it is through a deconstruction of gender that a critique of authority can actually be read as a critique of illegitimate authority, for to present a truthful image gender must be abstracted from any questions concerning its origin—such as that of the relationship between sex and gender. In other words, while gender needs to be manifest, it must at the same time owe nothing to the gesture through which it appears. Insofar as its origin is divorced from its performance, gender owes its authority to a seamless appearance. However, whereas a seamless appearance permits such divorce to be concealed, its authority will always be haunted by the fact that it is only an approximation of a normative ideal.

Metaphorically, Vera's impersonation of gender lends itself to be read as a sociopolitical impasse whose poles finally and painfully yield a threshold from whence a national identity could be reconstructed. Vera's failure to compel belief by her enactment of masculinity is not necessarily due to the asymmetry between sex and gender—an asymmetry that violates the standard of "realness"—since she is capable of passing. Her failure results from the extreme anxiety she feels regarding questions of origins—more so since she is an orphan—an anxiety that ultimately precipitates in a crisis when Clara, the object of her desire, requests that she undress. As I have mentioned earlier, for Vera "to be a man" is intimately associated with the appearance of masculinity, and hence undressing—revealing a female body—and relinquishing authority mean the same thing. Torn between desire and the compulsive need to assert control, Vera's persona collapses. Hence, Vera's crisis is a crisis of signification and representation, a crisis triggered when asked to give up what in her understanding defines masculinity: authority.

Vera's identity crisis marks a stylistic shift whereby electronic images take over cinematic images. Even though the narration closes shortly after, what the video monitors bring about in connection to the events of the story world is a delayed narrative closure into an extended present. This extended present is defined by the properties of the electronic medium through which Vera rewrites her history. Hence, Vera's history is recuperated within a technological medium that articulates the simultaneity of communication in the present. In addition, issues of origins are not within its nature, since video and television are really an instant media whose fundamental character is reproducible.[5]

Television and video are inscribed within a set of cultural readings defined by transmission and simultaneity, whereas these qualities shape the cultural perception of both media. While the broadcast image is the replica without an origin, its image is also infinitely reproducible through time and space, thus allowing it to be read as live, continuous, and immediate. Insofar as these qualities define video and electronic culture in general, their role in the "writing" of history is somehow problematized. For even though television has become a historical medium, of which Toledo's opening shot with the *Challenger* disaster is a good example, its ideology relies significantly on immediacy. Furthermore, the technology of video and television did not evolve out of a need for an archival preservation of history. Thus, the materiality of its technology negates the linear teleology of history, generating instead a text whose performativity forces us to reconceptualize our understanding of what constitutes the writing of history.[6]

As Marita Sturken argues, "[H]istory is often created as an act of preservation within specific social structures. That is, to formulate a history is to establish the legitimacy and autonomy of a particular field."[7] Video, instead, as a result of its fast development and its inconsistent association with institutional spaces and funding, has been more difficult to historicize.[8] Its strategies of intervention seem to demand a degree of separation from institutional support, a segregation that in turn has reinforced its status as a "nonproper medium" and as an effective tool in the creation and improvement of a participatory democracy.

Toledo's choice to end the narration with a proliferation of video screens back at the research center is also "an act of preservation within a specific social structure." Yet such preservation does not yield the "legitimacy" of a history, since this history, like gender and national identity, is one in the process of reconstructing itself. Furthermore, it is a history that is many, innumerable histories and that, in Homi Bhabha's words, proposes a "national life [which is] redeemed and signified as a repeating and reproductive process"[9] but whose living principle does not imply homogeneity.

Notes

1. John King, *Magical Reels: A History of Cinema in Latin America* (London: Verso, 1990), 126.

2. Kino International Release's Press Kit, September 1987. Kino International Corporation is the U.S. distributor.

3. All dialogue is this essay is from subtitles.

4. Lacan, *The Seminars,* book 1, p. 19, quoted by Stephen Heath in *Edinburgh '77 Magazine,* in connection with Foucault's interview on popular memory published by *Cahiers du Cinema,* no. 251/2.

5. Marita Sturken, "Paradox in the Evolution of an Art Form: Great Expectations and the Making of a History," in *Illuminating Video: An Essential Guide to Video Art* (New York: Aperture, in association with the Bay Area Video Coalition, 1990), 110.

6. Ibid., 120–21.

7. Ibid., 104.

8. Ibid.

9. Homi K. Bhabha, "DissemiNation: Time, Narrative, and the Margins of the Modern Nation," in *Nation and Narration,* ed. Homi K. Bhabha (London: Routledge, 1990), 297.

7

Pornography and "the Popular" in Post-Revolutionary Mexico

THE CLUB TÍVOLI FROM SPOTA TO ISAAC

Claire F. Fox

El exotismo es el último recurso de las temporadas vacilantes.
(Exoticism is the last recourse of uncertain times.)
— ARTURO MORI, "Rosita y el exotismo," *Jueves de Excélsior*, 1952

■ ■ ■ ■

Miguel Alemán Valdés was the first civil president to be elected in post-Revolutionary Mexico. During his administration, 1946–52, the national bourgeoisie that rose to power in the wake of the Revolution became consolidated under the Partido Revolucionario Institucional (PRI), the political party that continues to rule in Mexico to this day. For scholars of the Mexican cinema, the Alemán *sexenio* is a watershed; its early years marked the culmination of Mexican cinema's "Golden Age," which had begun during the previous transitional administration of President Manuel Ávila Camacho (1940–46). The stars and genres promoted by the strong Mexico City–based studio system in this period defined a nostalgic and coherent vision of *mexicanidad,* or Mexican national identity, for audiences that at the time were vastly divided according to regional, ethnic, and class identifications.

For many scholars, the end of the Golden Age is marked by the institution of the Plan Garduño in 1953. At the same time that this policy sought to wrest Mexican screens from the dominance of U.S. movies and their stereotypical portrayals of Mexican society, it also enforced a strict moral code and put an end to the more explicitly erotic Mexican genres that had flourished during the Ávila Camacho and Alemán *sexenios*.[1] That protectionism went hand in hand with censorship in the film industry is a peculiar symptom of a power struggle that was occurring within the

Mexican political system during the post-Revolutionary era. The work of historian Anne Rubenstein on the censorship of comic books in Mexico from the 1930s through the 1970s describes a tacit division of labor that evolved between conservatives and liberals on matters of cultural policy, which serves as a useful point of departure for my discussion of theater and film censorship during the same era. Rubenstein argues that popular culture was one arena in which disenfranchised Catholic conservatives were strategically permitted to gain a toehold by their moderate and secular PRIista compatriots. From the PRI's point of view, allowing moral conservatives to dominate cultural issues was the lesser of two evils, because it kept them from intervening in economic and political policy making. According to Rubenstein, moralizing campaigns on the part of predominantly middle-class conservatives were in fact reactions to Mexican modernization itself and the drastic changes that this implied for family life, gender roles, and social mobility. The form that their activism took, however, was censorship, aimed at protecting consumers from the alleged criminalizing and immoral influence of mass media. In the end, Rubenstein concludes, right-wing supervision of print media through the establishment of the Comisión Calificadora de Revistas Ilustradas and regional citizens' groups, was not altogether effective in eradicating pornography, but it did have the unanticipated effect of protecting national popular publishing industries from foreign competitors.[2]

It was this unanticipated protection from the "harmful" messages of foreign media that best served contemporary policies of the PRI, aimed at defusing the power of leftist movements within Mexico by promoting *mexicanidad,* a cross-class project for national identity.[3] At the first PRIista assembly held during the Alemán administration, the president of the party, Rodolfo Sánchez Taboada, declared Communism to be an "exotic doctrine" alien to Mexico.[4] Octavio Paz symptomatically registered the shift in his 1950 collection of essays *El laberinto de la soledad,* in which he noted "the success of the contemptuous adjective *malinchista recently* put into circulation by the newspapers to denounce all those who have been corrupted by foreign influences" (my emphasis).[5] With a little help from moral conservatives, the Alemán administration was thus free to pursue U.S. capital investment in Mexico, while simultaneously protecting *mexicanidad* through supervision of the culture industries.

It has not escaped the attention of Mexican cultural critics like José Agustín that the Alemán era's spirit of antiexoticism had an ironic double meaning, for *exótica* was also the word used to describe the female performers of the flourishing nightclub scene and *cabaretera* movies of the 1940s and 1950s and who also came under attack from moral conservatives.[6] The pun is more than coincidental, because "pornographic" images of women were explicitly associated with "foreign" ideas (i.e., undesirable political ideas) as the dual targets of censorship boards. In the years prior to the Plan Garduño, live theater and cinema found themselves subject to much the same sort of critique as comic books in the capital's conservative periodicals such as *Mañana, Hoy, Novedades, Revista de Revistas,* and *El Nacional,* which repeatedly called upon the government to clean up the film industry and Mexico City's nightclubs. In extreme cases, they attributed the moral bankruptcy of these industries to foreign-born owners and producers.[7] One editorial page in *Mañana* from 1951, for example, featured a piece denouncing the "communist student agitators" who had burned down a homage to President Alemán in the Zócalo, alongside items about the plague of *exóticas* in Mexican cinema, and the failure of the city's *campaña moralizadora* (moralizing campaign) due to the corruption of low-ranking officials.[8] In another editorial, the magazine sarcastically derided the film censorship office for allowing both *exóticas* and derogatory foreign stereotypes of Mexicans to flourish in the city's theaters:

La semana pasada un audaz reportero consiguió una sensacional declaración del subjefe de ese departamento [encargado de velar la moral pública en el cine]. En ella, el conspicuo funcionario hablaba de que en México no puede hacerse nada contra las películas pornográficas porque ello es ir "contra la libertad de pensamiento y de expresión."

¡Gloria a Tongolele, María Antonieta Pons y Rosa Carmina, defensoras ilustres de la libertad de pensamiento!

Incidentalmente, en las últimas cuatro semanas se han estrenado en los cines metropolitanos media docena de películas en las que se humilla a México y se pinta a los mexicanos como mariachis químicamente puros.

(Last week an audacious reporter obtained a sensational declaration of the subdirector of that department [in charge of overseeing public morality in film]. In the document, the conspicuous official spoke of the fact that in Mexico nothing can be done against pornographic films because that is to go "against freedom of thought and expression."

Glory to Tongolele, María Antonieta Pons and Rosa Carmina, illustrious defenders of freedom of thought!

Incidentally, in the last four weeks half a dozen movies have premiered in metropolitan theaters in which Mexico is humiliated and Mexicans are portrayed as chemically pure mariachis.)[9]

Popular theater and cinema were bound together not only by their being targets of moralizing campaigns in the early 1950s but also by the *cabaretera* genre, in which the film industry packaged the lush music and spectacle of the cabaret setting and distributed it to a national audience. These movies tended to focus upon the fall and redemption of strong, highly eroticized female protagonists played by actresses such as Meche Barba, Ninón Sevilla, Rosa Carmina, María Antonieta Pons, and Amalia Aguilar, many of whom had once worked as *exóticas* in the city's nightclubs.[10] According to Carlos Monsiváis, the *cabareteras* were among the various types of urban melodramas that functioned as a guide to city life for migrants who abandoned rural areas for Mexico City in vast numbers during this period.[11] Given the centralization of Mexico's culture industries in the capital, it is interesting to note the harmony that existed between moralizing campaigns directed at popular theater, which fell under the purview of the city's regent, and those in the film industry, which were waged at a national level. Conservative newspapers repeatedly expressed fear that nightclubs and the film industry were contaminating one another. *Mañana* summarized, "With minimal cost and even less effort, so-called '*churros*' are produced with María Antonieta Pons, Amalia Aguilar, Meche Barba, Rosa Carmina. Thus (in the cabarets) you have the 'exoticism' of the Dolly Sisters, Tongolele, Yara, Brenda Conde, *la zaguera* María Victoria, etc. Is this the cinema that one wants to promote?"[12] Mexico City itself was a microcosm in which one could see the same tensions between moral conservatives and liberals that also existed on a national scale, for example, between the conservative Catholic stronghold of Guadalajara and the secular modernity of the capital.

One Mexico City nightclub known as the Tívoli found itself at the center of debates over free speech, public morality, and control of urban space on several occasions from the late 1940s to the 1970s. The club was closed and reopened by the regent in the early 1950s, condemned and razed in the 1960s, and finally commemorated by director Alberto Isaac (1924–98) in his 1974 movie, *Tívoli*. When Isaac's movie was released, many of the capital's intellectuals were skeptical about the attempts of President Luis Echeverría (1970–76) to cultivate an atmosphere of free expression by promoting the work of young filmmakers and leftist themes in the cinema following the student massacre of 1968, which had occurred during the administration of Echeverría's predecessor, President Gustavo Díaz Ordaz (1964–70). Several prominent film critics viewed Isaac's *Tívoli* as little more than escapist nostalgia, its nudity only a token sign of *apertura* ("openness").[13] While President Echeverría praised the fact that the representation of nudity and language had relaxed a great deal under his leadership in the *Cineinforme Nacional* of 1976, Adolfo Torres Portillo, secretary of the Society of Mexican Screenwriters complained, "The cinematic 'apertura' in Mexico is for everything that has to do with sex and violence, and for nothing that has to do with social and political problems."[14]

The political nature of sexually explicit or pornographic images has in fact received scant attention in scholarly research on film censorship in Mexico, which instead has tended to focus on productions that were suppressed because of their critical stance toward the government or the Revolution.[15] Though I generally agree with Torres Portillo's assessment of the *apertura* under Echeverría, I would like to suggest that between the visible arena of the female nude and the invisible arena of (male) political struggle, a link arose during the censorship campaigns of the early 1950s, when women's bodies became a screen upon which conservatives projected anxieties about social class, popular struggle, and national identity. By recurring to that earlier era, Alberto Isaac's use of the female nude in *Tívoli* metonymically evokes those anxieties without naming them directly. Before discussing the film, however, I will briefly outline that earlier period of the Club Tívoli's rocky history.

The Club Tívoli

The apogee of the Tívoli coincides with the wave of *civilismo* that swept through Mexico during the Ávila Camacho and Alemán years. The club probably took its name from two well-known Porfirian nightspots called El Tívoli del Eliseo and El Tívoli Central.[16] But beyond their names, the clubs shared little in common. The modern Club Tívoli was situated at the corner of Santa María la Redonda (today Eje Lázaro Cárdenas) and Libertad, near the Plaza Garibaldi in Mexico City's working-class Colonia Guerrero. In the 1940s and 1950s, this district was densely populated with nightclubs, brothels, and bars, including an all-male theater called the Apolo, where many of the Tívoli's *exóticas* received their start in the business.[17] From the Tívoli, they could aspire to play classier revues such as the Follies, the Río, and the Cervantes, and perhaps they could even make it to the cinema. The Tívoli's floor shows, consisting of burlesque acts and sexual humor interspersed with comic political sketches, catered primarily to mixed audiences from the working class but were also frequented by the scions of Mexico City's upper and middle classes, for whom the club provided an informal course in sex education.[18]

The Tívoli's *exóticas,* known also as *encueratrices* or *ombliguistas* ("belly-buttonists"), based their acts upon the Gypsy Rose Lee tradition of strip-tease.[19] During the club's heyday in the late 1940s, a growing fascination with the South Pacific began to complement the existing popularity of Cuban rhythms and performers. Perhaps the best-known figure to emerge from this milieu was Yolanda Montes, or "Tongolele." This U.S.-born *exótica* of Tahitian, Swedish, Spanish, and French ancestry was famous for her forty-minute-long dance routines combining Afro-Caribbean and South Pacific motifs. Tongolele only stripped down to a bikini in her live performances and never bared her navel on the screen; in her old age she still insisted on the tastefulness, artistry, and family-oriented nature of her act.[20] Regardless of their nationality, the *exóticas* cultivated Asian- or African-inflected stage personas that were often evident in their nicknames, such as "La Muñequita China" ("The Little Chinese Doll") and "El Huracán del Caribe" ("The Hurricane of the Caribbean").[21] The Mexico-based *exóticas* shared the capital's stages with prestigious international performers such as Josephine Baker.

In order to deflect the complaints of conservatives about the Tívoli and other venues of its kind, the capital's regent, Fernando Casas Alemán, appointed a promising young writer, Luis Spota, to the newly created position of Jefe de Espectáculos (Chief of Spectacles) in 1949. Both Casas Alemán and Spota were adherents of President Alemán. Spota had covered Alemán's presidential campaign for *Excélsior,* and despite early flirtations with left-wing politics, he quickly became enamored of the president's pro-development and pro-business policies.[22] As an insider in theater and journalistic circles, Spota was a logical appointment for the position of Jefe de Espectáculos, despite his mere twenty-three years of age. His lover, actress Elda Peralta, collaborated with him on several projects for the cinema. Although Spota directed and starred in a handful of movies, his film work was never accepted by his peers in the industry; he attempted several times unsuccessfully to join the director's union (Sindicato de Trabajadores de la Producción Cinematográfica), before renouncing movies altogether to concentrate on television and writing in the late 1950s.[23] As a writer too, Spota met with mixed reactions to his work. His realist novels have labored under the category of "middlebrow" fiction, though they remain among the best-selling titles in Mexico.[24]

As Jefe de Espectáculos in 1949–1951, Spota had the job of overseeing and issuing permits for all forms of public entertainment, ranging from bullfights to circuses.[25] He tried repeatedly and unsuccessfully to get nightclubs to tone down their acts, but his efforts seem only to have converted him into an object of ridicule by the press. Arturo Mori, by far the most *exótica*-friendly critic, taunted "Luisito" mercilessly in his pieces in *Jueves de Excélsior*. At one point, Spota shut down the Club Tívoli, acting on orders from Casas Alemán, only to have his order countermanded two days later by the regent himself.[26] Elda Peralta recalls that one newspaper voted Spota and Tongolele "the two most publicized vedettes of 1950."[27]

The summer of 1951 appears to have been particularly volatile for the young bureaucrat. The troubles began in July, when Su Muy Key was found shot to death in a cheap hotel room, the victim of her lover Roberto Serna, who had then turned the gun on himself. (Incidentally, Serna was the publisher of comic books and the scandal sheet *¡Oiga!*) Carlos Denegri in *Revista de Revistas* chided, "*Exótica,* lower class hotels, traffickers in vice, etc., etc., the saddest accent of the lowest morality."[28] By the beginning of August, municipal authorities announced that those clubs presenting nudity in their acts had thirty days in which to clean up their shows.[29] Newspaper critics went on the offensive, making fun of Spota's impotence to enforce this rule. *Excélsior* described him weaving "hundreds of little dresses from his typewriter for the *exóticas* who spread their gruesomeness from the Tívoli to the Río and Cervantes."[30] From August through November 1951, all reports suggest that the ultimatum had no effect, and the Tívoli did not change its shows.[31] In October, the theater critic "El Caballero Puck" reported, "The *exóticas* keep doing their thing; by adding a ribbon to their minimal costumes, the inspectors and authorities permit them to continue acting. The Tívoli continues its nauseating and lewd work."[32] Shortly after the thirty-day period, Spota resigned his post.[33]

Spota's involvement with other projects during this period suggests that his commitment to public morality was opportunistic. In his novels, for example, he was frank about sex, if a bit lurid in his depiction of working-class sexuality. In 1949, the same year that he accepted the Jefe de Espectáculos position, he wrote the screenplay for his first movie, entitled *Hipócrita (Hypocrite),* one of many melodramas about fallen women that were produced during this era. Later in 1951, he would go on to write the screenplay for *Trotacalles (Streetwalker)* for his friend, director Matilde Landeta. Spota's personal life during this period was the very stuff these movies were made of. The epitome of the *Alemanista* petit bourgeois, he divided his time between a Catholic family life centered around his in-laws' residence, and a bohemian one, shared with his movie star mistress at the *casa chica.* In Elda Peralta's 1989 memoir about her relationship with Spota, entitled *Las sustancias de la tierra,* Peralta includes seminude publicity still photographs of herself taken by Spota, and her narrative recurs to melodramatic conventions evocative of the era's movies. It chronicles her two anguished abortions, her expulsion from polite society, conflicts with Spota over his marital status, and many nights spent crying alone.

Certainly there is ample evidence to suggest that the Tívoli's brand of entertainment scandalized Catholic sensibilities. *Mañana,* for example, rallied against Christmas season theatrical revues that presented images of the Virgin of Guadalupe surrounded by curvaceous, seminude angels.[34] The prevailing position in mainstream journalistic debates about censorship, however, was secular, class-based, and paternalist, which suggests a slight departure from the discreet alliance between Catholics and PRIistas regarding print media, as outlined by Rubenstein. In fact, many of the newspapers and magazines that strongly opposed Mexican *exóticas* regularly featured nude and seminude portraits of U.S. and European vedettes. But the need for censorship among the popular sectors was one point on which secular developmentalists and moral conservatives could agree. For although theaters like the Tívoli provided ample slumming grounds for the middle class, they were regarded by elites primarily as the domain of *léperos, pelados,* and other stereotypical lumpen and proletarian characters who were recalcitrant participants in the modernization project. Composed in large part of recent migrants to the city, these sectors were perceived as threatening, or at best as anachronistic, to the nation, though their marginal status could be linked to the spatial and economic dislocations brought about by modernization in the first place. The urban poor were visible evidence of the country's failure to forge a strong middle class based upon the nationalist myth of *mexicanidad.*[35]

According to the secular paternalist argument, education, hygiene, and exposure to the proper cultural models were required in order to inculcate middle-class values among the *gente modesta* (modest people) and *sectores humildes* (humble sectors) that so preoccupied the photoessay sections of middle-class publications. Marta Elba expressed this viewpoint well in a piece in which she argued in defense of the "artistic nude," adding nevertheless that preemptive censorship was still necessary in order for those inhabitants of "poor, dirty *colonias* of the metropolis and provincial villages" to appreciate true art:

> Cuidar que la radio no deje pasar por sus micrófonos la mas leve sugestión que incite los bajos apetitos y fomentar aquello que cultive el buen gusto popular e ilustre a los oyentes. En cuanto a los impresos, éstos deben evitar toda forma de notas rojas que despierten la morbosidad popular y que rodean de un aire atractivo a todas las formas de la delincuencia. Evitar los

casos personales del escándalo social, no dándoles publicidad, y no tratar acerca de crímenes y asesinatos que crean un estado de ánimo sombrío en el lector.

(See to it that the radio does not let the slightest suggestion pass through its microphones that might incite base appetites and encourage that which cultivates popular good taste and enlightens listeners. As for printed matter, it should avoid any lurid touches that might awaken popular morbidity and surround delinquency with an attractive air. Avoid personal cases of social scandal by not giving them publicity and by not dealing with crimes and murders that create a somber mood in the reader.)[36]

The class-based paternalism of arguments such as Elba's was unmasked in the writings of poet, playwright, and *cronista* Salvador Novo, who simply complained that theaters like the Tívoli were examples of appallingly bad taste. In one of his *crónicas* dated January 1948, Novo described a stroll along Santa María la Redonda while on his way to attend a function at the Fábregas theater. He noted that the neighborhood was in a state of flux: "the surroundings are modernized, demolished, and reemerge; they are the site of struggle between the survival of filth and the impulse towards beautification."[37] Novo's flair for the dramatic adjective and incensed rhetorical question turns his writing into a rant that is especially ironic when read against the backdrop of contemporary Mexico City. Here is a sample:

El Follies congrega a una concurrencia que se desborda por las calles vecinas, aturdidas por los megáfonos. No dan ningunas ganas de entrar en el Follies y cuando camina uno por su costado, de regreso a Donceles—¡qué asombrosa, aplastante, salvaje exhibición olfativa y visual de nuestra gula troglodita! Uno tras otro: sobre la acera, embistiendo, se instalan puestos de enchiladas y sopes, expendios de carnitas, pasteles horrendos, dulces mortecinos, panes mosqueados. . . . Y los huecos que dejarían estas instalaciones, ocupados por peines, cinturones, llaveros, tarjetas postales. . . .¿Habrá quién trague todas estas porquerías? ¿quién las apetezca? ¿Y quién compre sus peines del suelo?

(The Follies attracts a crowd that overflows into neighboring streets, deafened by megaphones. They don't make one eager to go inside, and when one walks alongside the theater, coming from Donceles—what a surprising, overwhelming, savage visual and olfactory exhibition of our troglodyte gluttony! One after the other, smashing into one another on the sidewalk, are enchilada, sope, and carnitas stands, horrendous cakes, pallid sweets, fly-covered breads. . . . And any space left by these is taken up by combs, belts, keychains, and postcards. . . . Is there anyone who would buy this junk? To whom does it appeal? And who would buy his combs off of the ground?) [38]

From today's perspective, Carlos Fuentes seems an unlikely candidate to arise as a defender of urban popular culture, but his sympathetic representation of working-class *colonias* like Guerrero and Doctores in his first novel *La región más transparente* (*Where the Air Is Clear,* 1958) is a significant intervention in the discourses of popular culture outlined above. Fuentes's novel further helped him to wage a critique against the superficiality and greed of his own cosmopolitan social background. Though the upper middle-class characters in this expansive novel are more precisely drawn than its *taxistas, ficheras, braceros,* and *ambulantes,* it is the latter characters whom Fuentes endows with cultural "authenticity." The novel's working-class characters devalue their own lives and accept adversity with resignation. Gladys, the *fichera,* is the philosopher and spiritual center of this group. In one scene she asks Beto, a taxi driver, if he "ever noticed people like us, that they're a flood, they pour along the streets and markets, all just like us, and they have no voices." [39] But the novel's structure emphasizes repeatedly that these people are the only ones who are intimately tied to Mexico as a place, often intercalating their vignettes with rhapsodic passages inspired by the capital's indigenous past.

Fuentes's Colonia Guerrero is a chaotic mixture of noise, smells, garbage, profanity, sex, and commerce. Taken out of context, his descriptions resemble those of Salvador Novo. But unlike Novo, Fuentes chooses to enter the cabaret. In another scene from the novel, the characters Gabriel, Fifo, and Beto decide to take in a show at the Tívoli before making the rounds of the whorehouses on the Calle del Órgano. The show's finale is a dwarf *exótica* who strips down to a Virgin of Guadalupe medal and a G-string, as the frantic crowd shouts *"¡Pelo! ¡Pelo!"* ("Hair! Hair!"). The narration continues, "Her hand dropped to her crotch-patch and pretended to jerk it away and the lights went out and the orchestra mounted a furious crescendo." [40] This scene is set in the early 1950s, but by 1958 when Fuentes's novel was published, the nightlife of Santa María la Redonda and Órgano was already endangered by the widening of the Paseo de la Reforma in 1957 and future beautification projects, such as the installation of the José San Martín *glorieta* in the early 1960s. [41] Fuentes's portrait is that of a people trapped in ever-shrinking neighborhoods, invisible to the country's leaders and incapable of self-representation.

In the post-1985 era, Fuentes's alliance of the intellectual storyteller figure with *el pueblo* (dramatized in the novel through the special relationship of the narrator Ixca Cienfuegos to Gladys) seems dated and patronizing. It nevertheless offered a model of relating to urban popular culture that was celebratory and, more important, opposed to censorship. It did not eschew nationalism but posited itself as a populist alternative to the *oficialista* nationalism of the PRI. As we shall see, this would be the same model adopted by director Alberto Isaac for his movie *Tívoli*.

The Movie *Tívoli*

Given the mutual interest in censorship on the part of moral conservatives and secular developmentalists at midcentury, it is not surprising that two decades later, *Tívoli* director Alberto Isaac would make the bad guys out to be a group of Alemanesque developers rather than Catholic crusaders. Isaac's *Tívoli* broached the theme of censorship and pornography in the 1950s, from a vantage point in the 1970s when it had once again become possible to make movies featuring sexual humor and partial female nudity, and when the presidential administration of Luis Echeverría was attempting to distance itself from the style of predecessors like Alemán. The periodic efflorescence of licentiousness in Mexican media always seems to invite counterattacks from conservatives, but Rubenstein points out that the public outcry regarding immorality in the media that surfaced during the period of 1972–76 was different from that of previous eras. In the case of the 1950s moralizing campaigns, the right took advantage of openings extended to it by the state, whereas in the mid-1970s the right was expressing direct dissatisfaction with the "leftist" tendencies of the government itself, at least with regard to cultural policy.[42]

Because the cultural industries were so closely allied with the state during this period, moral conservatives accused the government of endorsing immorality rather than simply of failing to regulate it. Alberto Isaac was one of the young directors who rose to prominence during the Echeverría years, and his long career basically defines the changing nature of auteur-state relations since the mid-1960s. He was a member of the influential Nuevo Cine group and won second prize in Mexico's first experimental cinema competition in 1965 for his movie *En este pueblo no hay ladrones* (*In This Town There Are No Thieves,* 1964). The award led to future movie projects and later earned him recognition and funding during the Echeverría years. From the mid-1960s through 1976, Isaac would go on to direct four more feature-length movies and two sports documentaries, including the state propaganda vehicle *Olimpiada en México* (*Olympiad in Mexico,* 1968). Isaac released few movies during the López Portillo administration (1976–82), but he once again rose to prominence in 1983 when he became the first director of the Instituto Mexicano de Cinematografía (IMCINE). Isaac stepped in at an extremely critical period for the Mexican film industry; the entire country was reeling from the petroleum crisis, movie production was at an all-time low, and a fire had recently destroyed the Cineteca Nacional while the institution was under the directorship of President López Portillo's sister, Margarita. Until his recent death, Isaac continued to direct movies in addition to other activities such as illustrating and writing; his most recent release was *Mujeres insumisas* (*Untamed Women,* 1995).[43]

Tívoli was coproduced by Corporación Nacional Cinematográfica, S.A. (CONACINE), a state-run production company designated for feature-length projects, and Directores Asociados, S.A. (DASA), a private directors' cooperative founded in 1974, to which Isaac belonged. This sort of funding profile is typical of the new breed of state-supported cinema inaugurated by the president's brother, Rodolfo, in his capacity as director of the Banco Nacional Cinematográfico. A veteran actor and industry union organizer, Rodolfo Echeverría immediately undertook the renovation of every aspect of national film production and distribution and established several state-run film production companies to fund and oversee new projects.[44] The "new" Mexican cinema was to fulfill multiple missions for multiple sectors: in addition to fomenting a political climate of *apertura* discussed previously, it represented a rejection of the old guard directors, closed industry unions, and conservative private producers on the part of a younger generation of filmmakers. The latter adopted strongly auteurist goals of producing a "cinema of quality" and achieving international recognition, while domestically their work was targeted at an urban, educated, middle-class market.[45]

In 1975, Isaac and eleven other DASA directors formed the Frente Nacional de Cinematografistas (FNC). They published a manifesto in *Otrocine* that called for further industry reforms and defined their roles as politically committed filmmakers.[46] Basically their ideas were already in line with President Echeverría's cultural policy, which was characterized by strong pan-Americanist, Third World–ist, and nationalist rhetoric. Isaac's shared commitment to these principles, however, made him vulnerable to exposing the limits of the president's sincerity. Paola Costa recounts a humorous anecdote from director Paul Leduc about a trip that he and several other filmmakers took to Santiago de Chile, while the president was there attending the UNCTAD meeting (United Nations Conference on Trade and Development). In Chile, Isaac's fellow filmmakers nominated him to broach the subject of censorship with the president. Costa writes:

> Al final, el presidente quiso hablar con los cineastas; éstos se encontraban muy nerviosos y con tensiones internas, y decidieron que a nombre de ellos hablaría Alberto Isaac, y pediría, a nombre de todos un punto sobre el cual había acuerdo entre ellos, y es que no hubiera censura. Según Leduc, Echeverría nunca contestó directamente, y cambió de tema. Más bien desvió la respuesta contestando que había visto una película japonesa, *La mujer de la arena,* y que ése era el cine que le gustaba, lo cual era como contestar que el problema no era la censura sino el talento.

> (At the conclusion, the president wanted to talk to the filmmakers; they were feeling very nervous and had internal tensions of their own, and they decided that Alberto Isaac would speak in their name, and on behalf of all, he would ask for something about which they all could agree, and that is that there should be no censorship. According to Leduc, Echeverría never answered directly, and changed the subject. Or rather, he detoured the answer, replying that he had seen a Japanese movie, *Woman in the Dunes,* and that was the kind of cinema he liked, which was like answering that the problem was not one of censorship but rather of talent.)[47]

At that moment, Echeverría cleverly resorted to a loophole within the directors' own auteurist self-presentation. By stressing the importance of individual genius over collective identity and social participation, he was able to sidestep the issue of censorship.

In published interviews, Alberto Isaac praised the brothers Echeverría for their support of the film industry and their noninterventionist stance regarding creative control of projects. He spoke frankly, nevertheless, about a more insidious form of self-imposed censorship that still plagued Mexican filmmakers, including himself, and he recognized that there were still taboo subjects in the cinema, citing the recent events of 1968 as an example. It is interesting to note that in the Mexican press, Isaac located the action of his movie *Tívoli* in the early 1960s,[48] while in a dialogue with fellow Mexican director Arturo Ripstein published in the Peruvian journal *Hablemos de Cine* in 1974, Isaac suggestively proposed that one means of compensating fear of censorship was to do something "allegorically, by situating it in a different time."[49] It is difficult not to read this as a veiled reference to *Tívoli,*

FIGURE 7.I. *Tiliches (Alfonso Arau) and Tívoli performers at the Zócalo. Photograph courtesy of Rogelio Agrasanchez.*

the film that Isaac was working on that year. Read as an *Echeverrista* movie, *Tívoli* is a celebration of the popular sectors and an attack on the *Alemanista* developmentalism of yesteryear. In this light, the destruction of the Club Tívoli at the end of the movie only underscores how much things had improved since the 1950s. Read as an allegory of that which remained unrepresentable in 1974, however, *Tívoli* alludes to more-recent popular defeats, such as that of the student movement in 1968, and the movie instead becomes an attack on the continuing problems of authoritarianism and censorship in contemporary Mexico. As I shall argue, the film sustains a constant oscillation between past and present that makes both of these interpretations possible.

Tívoli stars Alfonso Arau, veteran burlesque actor and comedian, as Tiliches, the cocky, quick-witted organic intellectual of the Tívoli troupe (fig. 7.I). Tiliches reprises a character named Lucas Lucatero, whom Arau had played in Isaac's 1972 *El rincón de las vírgenes (The Corner of the Virgins)*. The character was a provincial *merolico* inspired by the short stories of Juan Rulfo; Isaac and Arau worked together on the *Tívoli* screenplay in an effort to create an extension of Lucatero that might have resulted had he migrated to the city.[50] In the movie, Tiliches is directly compared to El Palillo, another burlesque comedian who frequently came under attack for his political humor in the 1950s. Opposite Tiliches is the club's premier *exótica* Eva Candela, played by Lyn May, who evokes the 1950s Asian-Mexican vedette, Su Muy Key (fig. 7.2).[51] The gendered division of labor between Eva and Tiliches is pronounced. Eva is associated with spectacle; she performs several striptease numbers in the movie, but she hardly speaks; as an erotic object, she is transferred up the social ladder from Tiliches to Don Quijanito, the club owner, and finally to Ingeniero Reginaldo, the building contractor who has slated the club for demolition. Such oppositions between seer and seen, politics and sex, as well as the doubling of contemporary nightclub actors with their historical counterparts, are pervasive motifs in the movie. In addition, many of the supporting actors who appear in cameo roles, such as orchestra leader Dámaso Pérez Prado, Harapos, and the Dolly Sisters, have careers spanning the 1950s through the 1970s and further serve to blend the era of the movie's representation with that of its production.

Tívoli's plot is rather simple. As part of a moralizing campaign, El Alcalde ("the mayor") orders that the northern portion of the Paseo de la Reforma be widened, and the Club Tívoli is slated for condemnation in

FIGURE 7.2. *Tiliches (Alfonso Arau) and Eva Candela (Lyn May). Photograph courtesy of Rogelio Agrasanchez.*

order to make way for a new *glorieta*. Tívoli's owner and performers rally to
the club's defense—all, that is, except for Eva, who winds up becoming the
mistress of the building contractor, though she remains on good terms with
her former comrades. In its efforts to save the Tívoli, first the troupe attempts to petition the mayor; then it turns to the press and hires a labor
lawyer. Tiliches personally improvises a protest monologue on a live television show and organizes a procession of the performers to the National
Palace on the back of a flatbed truck equipped with loudspeakers, but all of
these efforts fail. Resigned to the inevitable, Tiliches persuades some of the
capital's well-known nightclub performers to participate in a farewell benefit show at the theater before it succumbs to the wrecking ball. In one last
attempt to save the club, Tiliches and a group of performers attempt to
surprise the contractor, Reginaldo, at a hideout where he goes to watch
pornographic movies. Reginaldo is not there, but in the ensuing skirmish,
Lupe, Eva's homosexual bodyguard and a former Tívoli performer, is
murdered by another bodyguard. The Tívoli is finally destroyed as its dis-
heartened performers look on. In a final, frustrated gesture of rebellion,
Tiliches inflicts a scratch along the length of a shiny black Cadillac, ruining
its paint job.

The artists of the Tívoli are portrayed as a diverse group composed of
foreigners and little people, homosexuals and strippers, who form a make-
shift family on the basis of their own marginalization and difference with
respect to mainstream society. The movie further establishes a parallelism
between the Tívoli performers and the working-class residents of the neighborhood surrounding the club. The formation of a popular front consisting
of small business owners, workers, and lumpen who face off against the
state and big business is reinforced by a high-low dichotomy in the movie's
formal structure: here, the god's-eye view is always associated with a power
bloc of bureaucrats and politicians, and there is never a shot–reverse shot
between the two registers to imply their mutual recognition. In one memorable scene, for example, Ingeniero Reginaldo and El Alcalde study a maquette of Paseo de la Reforma and determine the fate of the club.[52] With
one swipe of his hand, the mayor topples a small matchbox-size figure representing the Tívoli and orders that it be replaced by a *glorieta*. "Another
glorieta?" exclaim several members of his retinue in disbelief.

This scene and a subsequent joke in one of Tiliche's monologues are
obvious allusions to Ernesto P. Uruchurtu, who served as regent of Mexico
City following the Alemán *sexenio* (1952–66).[53] Though *Tívoli* was faulted
by critics for its "glorification of impotence," as Jorge Ayala Blanco put it,
ironically it came closer than any other movie of the *apertura* to naming a

living political figure directly, though Uruchurtu was a fairly safe target given the political climate of the early 1970s. In the recent past, the three-term regent had become a political enemy of President Díaz Ordaz, owing to his opposition to the Metro and his zero population growth strategies for managing the capital city. Díaz Ordaz successfully had Uruchurtu removed from office in 1966 following an incident in which the regent ordered the bulldozing of a squatters' settlement, an event that is reenacted at the beginning of *Tívoli*.[54] Earlier in his career, Uruchurtu was known for his campaign to beautify the Paseo de la Reforma through the addition of *glorietas* and flower beds. He was also notoriously tough on vice; he shut down brothels and ordered nightclubs to close at 1 A.M., forcing several to go out of business.[55] Yet he stands out most memorably perhaps as one of the most corrupt regents of the city, having skimmed a fortune off shady building contracts. Before becoming regent, Uruchurtu held the position of Subsecretario de Gobernación under Alemán. Like Spota, he was a point man for morality campaigns at the national level during this period. He delivered a speech at the Ariel Awards ceremony in 1950, for example, calling for an end to movies that stressed the worst aspects of the national character.[56]

Isaac's orchestration of various historical moments represents some license on his part. As he states in the opening credits, his goal was not to reproduce a faithful portrait of the Tívoli but rather to evoke a mood: "This movie does not aspire to the documented reproduction of a period from our past, but rather to the re-creation of an atmosphere, a feeling, a vital sense of Mexican nightlife that has disappeared forever."[57] Isaac emphasized that he collected numerous oral histories from people associated with the Tívoli in an effort to re-create the feeling of that earlier era;[58] however, in many respects *Tívoli* is a historical hybrid, taking its atmosphere from the early 1950s, its plot from the 1960s, and its form from the 1970s. It does feature some of the stock figures that are key elements of the *cabaretera* genre, but the costumes and hairstyles featured in the movie are pure 1970s. Moreover, *Tívoli* rejects the *cabaretera*'s melodramatic conventions, such as moral dilemmas, strong female protagonists, and character development, in favor of the picaresque vignettes, superficial sight gags, and word play, which characterize the more contemporary *fichera* ("B-girl") and "sexy comedy" genres.[59] *Tívoli* paved the way for a brief revival of movies about Mexico City nightlife in the 1950s and, ironically, for a new wave of low-budget soft-porn movies, minus the social commentary, that were to revive private industry production in Mexico.[60]

The problem of popular sectors' resistance to modernization associated with the Club Tívoli in the Alemán era returns in a more sympathetic guise in the movie *Tívoli,* as the struggle of popular entertainment forms to persevere in a landscape of uneven urban development. *Tívoli* celebrates the spirit of resistance to authority that permeates the nightclub milieu, and it privileges the popular sectors as the heart of Mexican national culture.[61] As I have argued regarding Fuentes's work, however, this salutary attitude toward working-class culture posits that the culture represented is disappearing or already gone. *Tívoli*'s self-described re-creation of a subculture that has "disappeared forever" belies that the subculture survived for at least two more decades in order to provide the cast for Isaac's movie.[62] Some of the nightspots depicted in *Tívoli,* such as the dance hall Los Angeles, are still around today. The Salón México recently reopened to much fanfare in Mexico City and inspired an insipid remake of Emilio "El Indio" Fernández's classic movie of the same name. The real Club Tívoli did give way to the developmentalist wrecking ball—however, not until 1961, just one decade before the production of Isaac's movie.

If the representation of working-class resistance as a nostalgic mixture of subversive carnivalesque humor plus eroticism persevered to such a degree since Fuentes's novel of the late 1950s, then perhaps this indicates that the "people versus the power bloc" opposition still remained a tempting political articulation for some Mexican intellectuals of Isaac's generation. As in the case of Fuentes's novel, *Tívoli*'s populism displays itself to be a project fraught with contradictions, for by setting the story in the past and giving it a foregone conclusion (at least for audiences familiar with the fate of the real Club Tívoli), there are few routes of political identification for the spectator except to cheer for underdogs who are ennobled by their own defeat. In an interview with Jaime Shelley, Isaac gingerly handled a line of questioning about the pessimism of *Tívoli*'s ending, stating that he felt that Tiliches's futile act of vandalism at the end was indicative of contemporary Mexican society. Shelley pushed further on this issue by proposing that the tendency for social struggle to express itself in meaningless acts of violence was related to the impossibility of "political militancy" as an option in Mexican society. He went on to observe that Mexican intellectuals are faced with only two options, isolation or corruption. At this point, Isaac backed off, simply suggesting a third: "Or *apertura.* . . ."[63]

Although *Tívoli* defers any direct confrontation between the people and the power bloc, its inability to issue a direct critique about its own era of production nevertheless does create tension around two recurrent, yet "censored" tropes: the face of the president and female frontal nudity. The formal means of representing these two images (or "nonimages") is similar and suggests a subtle articulation between high and low that is denied to the viewer through more conventional cinematic means (e.g., shot–reverse shot, parallel editing, extreme long shot). I will proceed to discuss these two tropes in detail before concluding.

The goal of *Tívoli*'s characters is to preserve live performance, but the movie highlights the cabaret's relation to its sister arts, film and television, to such a degree that it can be read as an overall critique of the censorship of public intellectuals. *Tívoli* does make an important distinction between live performance and mass media, and between publically and privately consumed spectacle, suggesting that newer media such as television have become the battlegrounds on which future censorship battles must be waged. The movie's "performance within a film" structure establishes a privileged alliance between cabaret and cinema, with cinema occupying the dominant position, as in the *cabaretera* genre of the late 1940s and 1950s. The affinities between these two media are obvious: both are popular entertainment forms that are consumed in public spaces, and the spectators of both theater and cinema possess a serial relationship to one another.

Television, in contrast, is shown in *Tívoli* to be a tool of the power bloc.[64] In one of his efforts to save the Tívoli, Tiliches appears on a live television show, and to the horror of the show's producers, he unexpectedly launches into a monologue about saving the club: "like the Tívoli, for example, yeah, when one thing is finished off another thing is raised . . . a fortune is raised for a contractor and a big cut for who knows? . . . or rather, for you-know-who . . . (he points upward with his thumb)."[65] Within seconds, an irate phone call arrives from "the boss," and the producers immediately cut to a commercial. In contrast to the swift censorship that Tiliches's televised routine warrants from that upper register of power, the troupe is completely ignored when it occupies the Zócalo, a traditional site of popular protest in Mexico City. Tiliches, shot in close-up, yells in vain through a megaphone to the presidential palace: "Mr. President, do not let it be said that in the case of the Tívoli, it will be demonstrated that power is exercised from above without taking into account the poor, humble, individual person."[66] His cries are answered only by mute extreme long shots of the Palacio Nacional. This last scene is another unsettling "nonimage" that subtly evokes the era of the movie's production, for public demonstrations were indeed met with violence in 1968, and later in 1971 during the Echeverría administration.[67]

Thus *Tívoli* posits "liveness" to be an attractive, but nonviable strategy, politically or otherwise, its interpellative function having been displaced by mass media and inhibited by state violence. But the movie also seems critical of mass media consumed in the private sphere, because these lack any kind of communal element. (We see Tiliches, for example, recoil in disgust at the laugh track in the television studio.) Toward the end of the movie, members of the Tívoli troupe try unsuccessfully to ambush the contractor Reginaldo in a bourgeois home that secretly houses a porno theater. There, grainy black-and-white movies of interracial, sadomasochistic sexual acts are being screened—a fairly obvious way of exposing the double standards held by the proponents of morality campaigns. Through a gradual process of elimination, *Tívoli* proffers itself as its own perfect solution. Film becomes the happy medium between privately consumed "mediated" spectacle, such as pornography and television, and the publically consumed, but now defunct, live cabaret tradition. More important, *Tívoli's* ability to digest other media and to show them undergoing censorship, suggests in a self-reflexive manner that the state-supported movie we are watching is an act of free expression.

The ubiquitous censor in the movie has no face; however, the incidents in the television station and at the Zócalo vaguely associate censorship with presidential authority. The closest the movie comes to an embodiment of the censor occurs in one scene in which Tiliches and two other Tívoli performers are kidnapped and whisked away to a mansion where an elegant party is being held. There they are ordered to perform for a mysterious host identified simply as El Hombre ("The Man").[68] It is the Christmas season, and the trio is dressed for a Santa Claus skit. As they nervously recite their lines, each toy that comes out of Santa's bag is a political double entendre, until they arrive at the final gift, a copy of *Ali Baba and the Forty Thieves*. Uncomfortable silence ensues as both performers and guests look at one another fearfully, waiting for some reaction from their host. Then the movie cuts to El Hombre himself; seated on a regal chair, backlit and seen only in silhouette, he suddenly begins to roar with laughter. In a moment, the whole party erupts as well. Since the Alemán administration, it has taboo to ridicule the president in Mexican comedy sketches, so the mere presence of an authority figure who cannot be named or represented, such as this one, is as obvious as though the president were directly indicated. There are other clues in this scene that point to the president and specifically to Alemán: El Hombre is seated on a chair that looks suspiciously like *la silla presidencial;* also, the first Santa Claus appeared at a Sears department store in Mexico City during the Alemán *sexenio;* and finally, Alemán's intimate associates, politely known as "La Fracción de los Cuarenta" ("The Group of Forty"), were popularly referred to as "Ali Baba and the Forty Thieves." [69] This glimpse of the private life of Alemán stands in marked contrast to sanctioned cameos of the president that appeared in Golden Age classics, such as *Río Escondido* (dir. Fernández, 1948). Given the present-day elements that run throughout *Tívoli,* however, the dark form of the president in this scene ambiguously wavers between a critique of Alemán and a critique of the presidential office itself.

The delicacy with which the movie handles female frontal nudity also suggests that the figure of the censor exists in the present tense of *Tívoli*'s production. The conventions used to shoot the face of El Hombre are the same ones used to shoot Eva's genitals at the climax of her striptease numbers. On two occasions in the movie, as Eva nears the end of her routine and moves to take off her G-string, the stagehands cut the lights, just as Fuentes had described in *La región más transparente.* At this moment, the movie shows us Eva's body backlit and in silhouette as she poses suggestively a few inches from enthusiastic spectators. In contrast to the eye-level shot of El Hombre, as soon as Eva sheds her last garment, the camera switches to a high-angle shot of her body, emphasizing the lower register of the high-low hierarchy employed in the movie. Eva's final movements, including the splits, are acrobatic in contrast to the bumps and grinds that began her routine, as though Isaac were working here from a visual memory inspired by his documentary coverage of the Olympics.

Though they are separated from one another, the image of the censor (president) and that of the female sex clearly have a supplementary relationship to one another, one that operates according to a tautology: we could see Eva's genitals if it weren't for the censor (president); we could see the censor (president) if this weren't a "naughty" movie. That both of these images are visible to the "live" diegetic audiences of theatergoers and partygoers depicted in the movie is very telling. In these moments, *Tívoli* breaks with the classical narrative cinematic presentation of woman-as-spectacle in which the look of the camera at the female body is triangulated through the gaze of a diegetic male spectator. [70] Eva's routine is punctuated by close-ups of the mesmerized men in the audience, but the movie denies its own spectators any shot from their point of view, electing instead to present these sights them from a third, censored vantage point. These moments represent the movie's self-censorship before its own audience, its awareness that there are limits that cannot be trespassed even in the present climate of *apertura,* its simultaneous acknowledgment of castration anxiety and the editing room floor, as it were.

Conclusion

The relationship of Spota and Isaac to the Club Tívoli can be viewed as another installment in the history of Mexican intellectuals and their conflicted roles as intermediaries between the state and popular struggles.[71] The only way that Spota was able to remain a loyal Alemanista was by resigning his position as a civil servant and reentering the private sector. And though Isaac may have been critical of the PRIista state in *Tívoli,* he certainly benefited from the Echeverría administration. In fact, many of the DASA directors tended to rationalize their position by declaring that they were not PRIistas but rather Echeverristas.[72] Isaac's proximity to the state and his commitment to social change led him to adopt populism as a compromise position.[73] His own view of *Tívoli* as a "little guy" movie is contradicted by the various class positions that "little guy" implies.[74] Jorge Ayala Blanco pointed out that the movie does not distinguish among various social actors whose interests are fundamentally at odds with one another; the night club owner and his employees, property owners and squatters are all on the same side.[75] This is the same sort of national populism that converted the *patrón* character into a "little guy" hero one decade earlier in Roberto Gavaldón's censored movie *La rosa blanca.* Isaac is not critical of the shortcomings of populism as other intellectuals of his generation have been, and his movie provides no analysis of the troupe's political strategies.[76]

Although female performers are themselves the contested images in this ongoing debate about intellectual production and censorship, they do not escape an archetypal role in narratives about the Tívoli, even when these narratives are about freedom of expression and the right of workers to organize themselves. Throughout this essay, I have used various metaphors to talk about the nude female body, all of which emphasize it as a focal point of images and ideas about politics and morality. During the previously mentioned eventful summer of 1951, for example, one cover of *Jueves de Excélsior* featured a color illustration of an artist painting the body of a voluptuous nude woman with political slogans. Above, the caption read, "The tattooing of Mexico City begins."[77] In the early 1950s through the *apertura* of the 1970s, the cinema, cabaret, and popular press turned women's bodies into a terrain demarcating the limits of state censorship, so that female nudity came to represent minimal state intervention in the private sector as well as freedom from censorship.

I would thus argue that while nudity triumphs in texts from both eras I have discussed, women—as social actors and intellectuals—do not, which tempers any liberating reading of female nudity in either historical era. In this respect, I part ways with recent arguments in U.S.-based film studies that celebrate the potential of striptease to critique or expose the process of gender construction and challenge cultural perceptions of women's passive sexual identity.[78] Isaac's movie only reinforces the idea that there is little or no difference between its female characters and the archetypal roles of "woman" that they enact in their nightclub routines. Eva, true to her name, is a temptress and a traitor, on- and offstage. In "Naná y el diablo," another classic cabaret act from the 1950s recreated for *Tívoli,* Naná is seduced and stripped naked by the devil, also stressing the Eve persona. Given that the figure of the *exótica* fused the ideas of sexual and national betrayal, we see that this familiar and "authentic" emblem of Mexican popular culture— pace Fuentes—is ambivalently imbued with a certain foreignness, making her a *malinchista* as well.

It's through Eva's character that *Tívoli*'s tension between populist nationalism and international class-based solidarity is most visible. Hostility toward foreigners is a running joke in *Tívoli,* as Tiliches has several run-ins with an Asian acrobat from Hollywood and his partner. "Those foreigners come to take away our bread," he grumbles at one point. When he learns of Eva's betrayal, he realizes the mistake he made by turning a common girl into an *exótica*: "I even baptized her! You know what she was called before?—Loreto García. From Loreto García to Eva Candela!"[79] The penultimate appearance of Eva on the truck at the Zócalo, dressed as the U.S. Statue of Liberty in chains, therefore, is both ironic and overcoded. In her final performance, Eva's treason is underscored to the movie and theater audience by Tiliches, who forces her to disrobe onstage as he displays the club's order of condemnation to the audience.[80] Eva is thus not only the troupe's mascot in its struggle for free speech *al estilo de los gringos* but also the emblem of a sexual, racial, and national difference that fails to be incorporated into the motley crew version of "the popular" put forth by the movie.[81]

Notes

I am grateful to the Center for International Studies at Stanford University for awarding me a Hewlett Faculty Grant so that I could travel to Mexico City and conduct research for this essay. I would also like to thank the following people who had a hand in this essay: Carlos Monsiváis, Gary Keller, and Ediberto Canseco for sharing their personal experiences of the Club Tívoli with me; Seth Fein and the staff of the Hemeroteca Nacional in Mexico City for providing valuable bibliographical information; Chon Noriega and the Stanford Film Workshop for their insightful comments and suggestions regarding

Isaac's *Tívoli;* and finally, my old friend Roberto Tejada Montoya, for his moral support throughout the research phase of this project.

All translations are mine unless otherwise noted.

1. The Plan Garduño was named after Eduardo Garduño, who was appointed director of the Banco Nacional Cinematográfico under President Adolfo Ruiz Cortines. For more information, see Miguel Contreras Torres, *El libro negro del cine mexicano* (Mexico City: Editora Hispano-Continental Films, 1960); Elda Peralta, *La época de oro sin nostalgia: Luis Spota en el cine, 1949–1959* (Mexico City: Grijalbo, 1988); and Carl Mora, *Mexican Cinema: Reflections of a Society, 1896–1988,* 2d ed. (Berkeley and Los Angeles: University of California Press, 1989).

2. Anne G. Rubenstein, "Mexico 'Sin Vicios': Conservatives, Comic Books, Censorship, and the Mexican State, 1934–1976" (Ph.D. dissertation, Rutgers, 1994). Rubenstein points out that the term "pornography" enjoyed broad usage by censorship boards. It referred not only to explicitly sexual themes but also to anything that might lead to immoral behavior, such as the representation of young women living alone in the city.

3. For an excellent analysis of this phenomenon, see Tzvi Medin, "El laberinto de la mexicanidad en el sexenio de Miguel Alemán," *La Jornada* 175 (18 October 1992): 16–25.

4. Cited in José Agustín, *Tragicomedia mexicana 1: La vida en México de 1940–1970* (Mexico City: Planeta, 1990), p. 94. See also Medin, "El laberinto de la mexicanidad." The Pope was evidently on the same wavelength as the PRI; Pius XII issued an encyclical in August 1950 entitled "Concerning Certain False Opinions," in which Communists and existentialist intellectuals were threatened with excommunication; see Anne Freemantle, *The Papal Encyclicals in Their Historical Context* (New York: Mentor/NAL, 1956), 283–88.

5. Octavio Paz, *The Labyrinth of Solitude and Other Writings,* trans. Lysander Kemp, Yara Milos, and Rachel Phillips Belash (New York: Grove, 1985), 86, my emphasis. The word *malinchista* derives from Malinche, Cortés's indigenous mistress, who has been historically portrayed as a traitor figure.

6. Agustín, *Tragicomedia mexicana 1,* 94.

7. See, for example, Vicente Vila, "Falsificación del mexicanismo," *Mañana* 42, no. 420 (15 September 1951): 193–95 (ironically, Vila would like to claim Buñuel for Mexico); and P.I.N., "El imperio del vicio y la prostitución empobrecen la economía de la metrópoli," *La ciudad que ya no es,* ed. Patricia Ortega Ramírez (Mexico City: El Nacional, 1990): 143–47 (reprinted from *El Nacional,* 20 January 1950).

8. "México en Mañana," *Mañana* 39, no. 396 (31 March 1951): 5.

9. "México en Mañana," *Mañana* 42, no. 419 (8 September 1951): 4.

10. For an in-depth exploration of the *cabaretera* film, see Ana M. López, "Celluloid Tears: Melodrama in the 'Old' Mexican Cinema," *Iris: A Journal of*

Theory on Image and Sound 13 (summer 1991): 29–52; for a study of *cabare-tera* fan culture, see Fernando Muñoz Castillo, *Las reinas del trópico* (Mexico City: Grupo Azabache, 1993).

11. Carlos Monsiváis, "Notas sobre el Estado, la cultura nacional, y las culturas populares," *Cuadernos Políticos* 30 (October–December 1981): 33–44, cited in Néstor García Canclini, *Los nuevos espectadores: Cine, televisión, y video en México* (Mexico City: IMCINE/CONACULTA, 1994), 41.

12. "Con un costo mínimo y esfuerzo todavía más insignificante, se producen los llamados 'churros' con María Antonieta Pons, Amalia Aguilar, Meche Barba, Rosa Carmina. De allí parte el 'exotismo' con las Dolly Sisters, Tongolele, Yara, Brenda Conde, la zaguera María Victoria, etc. ¿Ese es el cine que quiere fomentarse?" ("México en Mañana," *Mañana* 42, no. 416 [18 August 1951]: 4–5). See also "Que el cine deje de ser una cloaca," *Hoy* 756 (18 August 1951): 6–7, written upon the recent publication of the Regulations of the Film Industry Law in August 1951.

13. Jorge Ayala Blanco, "¿Verdad Señor Obispo que así no era el Tívoli?" *¡Siempre!* 1151 (16 July 1975): xiv–xv; José de la Colina, "Y vino la piqueta y nos demolió," *Excélsior* (6 July 1975): 13. See also Emilio García Riera's reference to his initial response to the movie in his *Historia documental del cine mexicano, 1974–76,* vol. 17 (Guadalajara, Mexico: Universidad de Guadalajara, 1995), 63–68.

14. Echeverría cited in Paola Costa, *La 'apertura' cinematográfica, México, 1970–1976* (Puebla, Mexico: Universidad Autónoma de Puebla, 1988), 91; Torres cited in Agustín Gurezpe, "Apertura cinematográfica útil sólo para el sexo y la violencia," *Excélsior* (19 June 1976): 32. ("La apertura cinematográfica en México es para todo lo que se refiere a sexo y violencia, pero no para los problemas sociales y políticos.") Costa's *La 'apertura' cinematográfica* offers pessimistic readings of some of the era's more overtly "political" films such as *Canoa* (dir. Cazals, 1975).

15. I refer to productions such as *Espaldas mojadas* (dir. Galindo, 1953), *El brazo fuerte* (dir. Korporaal, 1958), *La Rosa Blanca* (dir. Gavaldón, 1961), and *La sombra del caudillo* (dir. Bracho, 1960). For discussions of censorship in Mexican cinema, see also Costa, *La 'apertura' cinematográfica;* and Alfonso Gumucio Dagrón, *Cine, censura, y exilio en América Latina,* 2d ed. (Mexico City: STUNAM/CIMCA/FEM, 1984).

16. Jesús Flores y Escalante traces the history of the earlier clubs and their more recent namesakes in his *Salón México* (Mexico City: Asociación Mexicana de Estudios Fonográficos, 1993), 333–35. See also Sergio González Rodríguez, *Los bajos fondos: El antro, la bohemia, y el café* (Mexico City: Cal y Arena, 1990), 52.

17. Arturo Mori, "El llanto de las exóticas," *Jueves de Excélsior* 1472 (16 August 1951): 16.

18. According to Gary Keller, attending the Club Tívoli was a rite of passage

for middle-class men, and the club still brings back fond memories for an entire generation of Mexican lawyers, engineers, and architects. Gary Keller, interview, 8 March 1996.

19. Carlos Monsiváis, interview, 21 December 1995. I searched Gypsy Rose Lee's autobiography for a "smoking gun" but found that it never mentioned an engagement in Mexico City. She did play a Spanish-language theater in El Paso, back in the 1920s when her family was still doing wholesome vaudeville acts, and her troupe did attempt to travel to Mexico City, but they got lost in the desert and had to turn back. Gypsy's descriptions of small-town burlesque theater in the United States, nevertheless, do resonate with descriptions of the Tívoli's floor shows. See Gypsy Rose Lee, *Gypsy: A Memoir* (New York: Harper and Brothers, 1957).

20. Elena Poniatowska, "Yolanda Montes Tongolele," *Todo México,* vol. 1 (Mexico City: Diana, 1990), 227–53.

21. These are the nicknames of Su Muy Key (another stage name, obviously) and Amalia Aguilar, respectively. Su Muy Key was described by one critic as being of "Chinese, Korean, and Aztec" heritage (Arturo Mori, "La última danza de Su Muy Key," *Jueves de Excélsior* 1468 [19 July 1951]: 12); Amalia Aguilar was Cuban.

22. Elda Peralta, *Luis Spota: Las sustancias de la tierra* (Mexico City: Grijalbo, 1990), 97–104.

23. Elda Peralta, *La época de oro sin nostalgia: Luis Spota en el cine, 1949– 1959* (Mexico: Grijalbo, 1988), 97–98. Adaptations of Spota's novels include: *Vagabunda* (*Vagabond,* 1949), made into a movie retitled *Flor de Sangre* (*Flower of Blood/Blood Flower,* 1951), dir. Zacarías Gómez Urquiza; *La estrella vacía* (*The Empty Star,* 1950), movie 1958, directed by Emilio Gómez Muriel; *Mas cornadas da el hambre* (*The Wounds of Hunger,* 1951), movie 1962 (Euro-American prod., never screened in Mexico); *La sangre enemiga* (*Enemy Blood,* 1959), movie 1969, dir. Rogelio A. González; and *Cadena perpetua* (*Endless Chain,* 1968), movie 1978, dir. Arturo Ripstein.

24. See Sara Sefchovich, *Ideología y ficción en la obra de Luis Spota* (Mexico City: Grijalbo, 1985). Spota wrote more than two dozen works of fiction. Among his best-sellers was a six-novel series about power and corruption in Mexican politics: *La costumbre del poder (The Custom of Power),* 1975–80.

25. There is some confusion about whether the concluding date of his tenure in this position is 1951 or 1952, depending upon which of Peralta's accounts one reads. According to my newspaper research, Spota held the position at least through November 1951. See Peralta, *Las sustancias,* 118; and Peralta, *La época de oro sin nostalgia,* 124.

26. Peralta, *Las sustancias,* 118.

27. Peralta, *Las sustancias,* 119. Based on my research, I believe that the events to which Peralta refers actually occurred in 1951.

28. "Exótica, hoteles de barriada, traficantes en vicio, etcétera, etcétera, el

accento más triste de la mas baja moral" (Carlos Denegri, "Temas nacionales," *Revista de Revistas* [15 July 1951]: 3). In contrast, Mori elegized the *exótica* in his piece, "La última danza de Su Muy Key."

29. Sanchis Nadal, "Nuestra ciudad: Las exóticas," *Novedades* (6 August 1951), sec. 2: 1.

30. "Spota desde su máquina de escribir tejió centenares de vestiditos para las exóticas que desde el Tívoli esparcieron su morbo al Río y al Cervantes" ("Claro de Luneta," *Jueves de Excélsior* 1472 [16 August 1951]: 8).

31. See Fernando Mota, "El Tívoli no mejora su espectáculo," *Revista de Revistas* (5 August 1951): 82; and "Claro de Luneta," *Jueves de Excélsior* 1473 (23 August 1951): 8.

32. "Las exóticas siguen haciendo las suyas, agregando un listón a su mínima indumentaria, les permiten actuar los inspectores y autoridades. El Tívoli continúa en su nauseabunda labor inmoral y procaz" (El Caballero Puck, "De telón adentro," *Jueves de Excélsior* 1480 [11 October 1951]).

33. Peralta, *Las sustancias,* 119.

34. "México en Mañana," *Mañana* 38, no. 384 (6 January 1951): 5. Gypsy Rose Lee describes a similar act in the Ziegfeld Follies, in which a *tableau vivant* of Millet's *Angelus* is visited by a flock of seminude angels. Isaac's *Tívoli* contains at least three scenes that mix sacred and profane imagery.

35. Luis Buñuel's movie of the same era, *Los olvidados* (1950), is an eloquent exposé of the social contradictions of Mexican modernization.

36. Marta Elba, "El desnudo artístico no es inmoral," *Jueves de Excélsior* 1496 (31 January 1952): 16.

37. "[T]odos sus alrededores se modernizan, demuelen, resurgen y son el escenario de la lucha entre la supervivencia de la porquería y el impulso de la pulcritud" (Salvador Novo, *La vida en México en el período presidencial de Miguel Alemán,* ed. José Emilio Pacheco [Mexico City: CONACULTA, 1994], 104).

38. Ibid., 104–5.

39. Carlos Fuentes, *Where the Air Is Clear,* trans. Sam Hileman (New York: Ivan Obolensky, 1960), 160. "¿Te has fijado en la gente igualita a nosotros, que son un chorro, que son todas las que van por las calles y los mercados, todas como nosotros, que no dejan que la voz se les oiga?" (*La región más transparente,* ed. Georgina García-Gutiérrez [Madrid: Cátedra, 1982]). Thirty years later, Fuentes would recall that he gathered inspiration for this novel during a period in his early adult life when he and his buddies "would go to a whorehouse oddly called El Buen Tono, choose a poor Mexican girl who usually said her name was Gladys and she came from Guadalajara, and go to [their] respective rooms" ("How I Started to Write," in *Myself with Others: Selected Essays* [New York: Farrar, Straus, Giroux, 1988], 21).

40. Fuentes, *Where the Air Is Clear,* 159. "La mano de la exótica se acercaba a la pantaleta y fingía el último despojo. La luz se apagaba y la orquesta lanzaba un crescendo furioso." Fuentes, *La región más transparente,* 326.

41. For more information about the history of cabarets in this neighborhood, see Armando Jiménez, *Cabarets de antes y de ahora en la Ciudad de México,* 7th ed. (Mexico City: Plaza y Valdés, 1994). Unfortunately, he does not mention the Tívoli.

42. Rubenstein, "Mexico 'Sin Vicios,'" 194.

43. For more information about Isaac's career and filmography, see David Wilt, "Alberto Isaac: One Man, Many Careers," *Mexican Film Bulletin* 4.7 (February 1998): 1–3.

44. Alma Rossbach and Leticia Canel, "Política cinematográfica del sexenio de Luis Echeverría, 1970–1976," in *Hojas de cine: Testimonios y documentos del nuevo cine latinoamericano,* vol. 2 (Mexico City: UAM/SEP, 1988), 103–12.

45. Aurelio de los Reyes, "Presentación," in Costa, *La 'apertura' cinematográfica,* 12.

46. The "Manifiesto del Frente Nacional de Cinematografistas" is reprinted in *Hojas de cine,* vol. 2, 129–132.

47. Costa, *La 'apertura' cinematográfica,* 90–91 n. Incidentally, a recent exhibition of the political cartoons in the collection of Carlos Monsiváis contains several humorous drawings by Isaac and Abel Quezada that criticize the censorship of pornography. See *Aire de familia: Colección de Carlos Monsiváis,* exhibition catalog (Mexico City: INBA/Museo de Arte Moderno, 1995).

48. See for example, Beatriz Reyes Nevares, "Alberto Isaac," in *The Mexican Cinema: Interviews with Thirteen Directors,* trans. Carl J. Mora and Elizabeth Gard (Albuquerque: University of New Mexico Press, 1976), 161–70; Josefina Millán, "Alberto Isaac: En un ambiente de corrupción, todo se corrompe," *Excélsior* (18 May 1975): 13; Jaime A. Shelley, "Entrevista con Alberto Isaac," *Otrocine* 1, yr. 1 (January–March 1975): 23–32.

49. "Entonces hace una cosa de manera alegórica, la sitúa en otro tiempo" (Alfredo Barnechea and Isaac León Frías, "Los atajos del cine mejicano: Diálogo con Alberto Isaac y Arturo Ripstein," *Hablemos de Cine* 66 [1974]: 20).

50. Shelley, "Entrevista con Alberto Isaac," 24.

51. Ayala Blanco viewed Lyn May as an inferior version of another vedette, Gema ("¿Verdad Señor Obispo?," xv).

52. This scene and an earlier scene in which Ingeniero Reginaldo holds a map in front of him as he surveys the soon-to-be-demolished barrio from atop an embankment are parodies of Juan O'Gorman's well-known mural celebrating Mexico City's modernization, entitled *La ciudad de México* (1949). Newspapers and magazines of the Alemán era were also fond of publishing aerial photoessays to show off all of the new construction going on in Mexico City (see, for example, "México visto desde el cielo," *Hoy* [13 October 1951]: 26–35). García Riera comments that this scene alludes to the widening of the Paseo de la Reforma that occurred in the late 1950s (i.e., when Fuentes was writing *La región más transparente*). The precise location of the Club Tívoli in the maquette resembles that of the Can Can, another nightclub in the same vi-

cinity as the Tívoli, which was demolished in 1964 to make way for a *glorieta* (Jiménez, *Cabarets de antes,* 69).

53. Tiliches's joke concludes with the punch line, "Siendo reanimal, era regente." Isaac himself named Uruchurtu in his interview with Reyes Nevares (165). Returning to the criticism of Torres Portillo, cited earlier in this essay, he backhandedly acknowledged this distinction of *Tívoli* in the following manner: "Hemos visto en muchas películas realizadas en las últimas fechas por el cine mexicano, pretenciosamente de denuncia, en que se acusa, se ataca, pero a regímenes pasados, a Porfirio Díaz, Victoriano Huerta y, creo, que la que más se acerca a nuestros tiempos, es posiblemente una que ataca a Ernesto P. Uruchurtu, sin mencionar su nombre, puesto que todavía está vivo. Y la más "valiente" es la que denuncia al cura de un pueblo [*Canoa*]." ("In many of the pretentiously denunciatory Mexican movies made in recent times we have seen there are accusations and attacks, but only of past regimes, such as Porfirio Díaz, Victoriano Huerta, and I believe that the movie that most closely approaches our own time is possibly one that attacks Ernesto P. Uruchurtu, without mentioning his name, given that he is still living. And the 'bravest' is the one that denounces a village priest [*Canoa*].")

54. Diane E. Davis, *Urban Leviathan: Mexico City in the Twentieth Century* (Philadelphia: Temple University Press, 1994), 164–73.

55. See Jiménez, *Cabarets de antes,* regarding the wave of nightclub closings in the early 1960s.

56. Ernesto P. Uruchurtu, "Porvenir del cine mexicano," *Mañana* 11, no. 408 (23 June 1951): 25.

57. "Esta película no aspira a la reproducción documentada de un período de nuestro pasado sino a la recreación de una atmósfera, de un ambiente, de un sentido vital de México nocturno que ha desaparecido para siempre."

58. Shelley, "Entrevista con Alberto Isaac," 24.

59. For a very useful discussion of the distinction between the *fichera* and *cabaretera* genres, see Sergio de la Mora, "Fascinating Machismo: Toward an Unmasking of Heterosexual Masculinity in Arturo Ripstein's *El lugar sin límites*," *Journal of Film and Video* 44.3–4 (1992): 83–104.

60. Mora cites *Las ficheras* (1976) and *Muñecas de media noche* (1979) as examples (*Mexican Cinema,* 133). García Riera cites *Bellas de noche* (dir. Delgado, 1974), which was released several months after *Tívoli* as the first movie of the genre (*Historia documental del cine mexicano,* 68, 84–87).

61. Francisco Sánchez, "Tívoli," *Otro Cine* 1, yr. 1 (January–March 1975): 19–22.

62. I would like to thank Shoshanna Lurie for calling my attention to the fact that at the same time Isaac was shooting the movie, residents of nearby Tepito were organizing Tepito Arte Acá, a grassroots movement aimed at revitalizing their *colonia* through projects involving art, architecture, and popular history ("Tepito Arte Acá," Stanford University, 1996, unpubl. ms.).

63. Shelley, "Entrevista con Alberto Isaac," 25.

64. The medium has its roots in the Alemán era; the first television broadcast of the station XHTV was in fact Alemán's fourth presidential address in 1950, and Emilio Azcárraga of XHW was a close associate of the president and would go on to become the head of media giant Televisa (Jiménez, *Cabarets de antes,* 134; Agustín, *Tragicomedia mexicana 1,* 87, 90).

65. "como con el Tívoli, pero eso sí, cuando se acaba con una cosa se levanta otra . . . levanta una fortuna para un contratista y una mochada para no se sabe quién . . . o más bien dicho, para sí se sabe quién (hace un gesto con el pulgar hacia arriba)."

66. "Sr. Presidente, que no se diga que en el caso del Tívoli se venga a demostrar que los poderes se ejercen por encima sin tomar en cuenta al pobre y humilde individuo individual."

67. José Agustín, *Tragicomedia mexicana 2: La vida en México de 1970–1982* (Mexico City: Planeta, 1992), 23–28.

68. There is one previous reference to El Hombre in the movie, when a character comments about having seen El Hombre's picture in the paper.

69. Regarding the Santa Claus and Ali Baba references, see Agustín, *Tragicomedia mexicana 1,* 90.

70. Laura Mulvey, "Visual Pleasure and Narrative Cinema," *Screen* 16.3 (1975): 6–18, reprinted in Laura Mulvey, *Visual and Other Pleasures* (Bloomington: Indiana University Press, 1989); Constance Penley, ed., *Feminism and Film Theory* (New York: Routledge, 1988); and Phil Rosen, ed., *Narrative, Apparatus, Ideology* (New York: Columbia University Press, 1986).

71. According to Randall Johnson, it is very difficult for many Latin American artists and intellectuals, especially those working in mass media, to position themselves wholly inside or outside of state supervision of intellectual production (Randall Johnson, "In the Belly of the Ogre: Cinema and State in Latin America," in *Mediating Two Worlds: Cinematic Encounters in the Americas,* ed. John King, Ana M. López, and Manuel Alvarado [London: British Film Institute, 1993], 204–13).

72. Costa, *La 'apertura' cinematográfica,* 98.

73. On the subject of populism and Latin American intellectuals, see William Rowe and Vivian Schelling, "Popular Culture and Politics," chapter 3 of *Memory and Modernity: Popular Culture in Latin America* (London: Verso, 1991), 151–92.

74. "*Tívoli* es la historia de un pequeño hombre, luchando contra una autoridad brutal, que los aplasta" (cited in Millán, "Alberto Isaac," 13).

75. Ayala Blanco, "¿Verdad Señor Obispo?," 15.

76. Paco Ignacio Taibo II's novel *Heroes convocados (Calling All Heroes),* in contrast to *Tívoli,* is plagued by the failure of the middle-class intellectuals of the student movement to integrate successfully with working-class movements (Mexico City: Roca, 1994).

77. *Jueves de Excélsior* 1472 (16 August 1951).

78. See, for example, Eric Shafer, "The Obscene Seen: Spectacle and Transgression in Postwar Burlesque Films," *Cinema Journal* 36.2 (winter 1997): 41–66. This is an excellent, persuasive article; however, I do not feel that Shafer's arguments hold for the Mexican context.

79. "Esos extranjeros vienen a quitarnos el pan." "¡Hasta la bauticé! ¿Tú sabes cómo se llamaba antes? Loreto García. ¡De Loreto García a Eva Candela!"

80. From the Asamblea de Barrios to sex workers unions, the spectrum of grassroots movements in Mexico City today challenges both the conservative paternalist and the progressive populist approaches to working-class culture established in the early 1950s. The older patterns of conservative backlash still exist, however, as is witnessed in the recent wave of popular protest over table dancing in Mexico City, which once again saw the immorality of female nudity linked to the "foreign" origin of the phenomenon.

81. Eva is allied with other minor characters who are expelled from the group, such as Chi, the Asian acrobat, and Lupe, the *loca*. Regarding the position of the queen in the *fichera* genre, see de la Mora, "Fascinating Machismo."

8

Consuming Tacos and Enchiladas

GENDER AND THE NATION IN
COMO AGUA PARA CHOCOLATE

Harmony H. Wu

■ ■ ■ ■

Refiguring Foundational Fictions

Latin America has a long tradition of writing and rewriting the nation through its novels and novelists, argues Doris Sommer. Capitalizing on the gaps left by historians, novelists essentially wrote, or created, the nation: "The writers were encouraged both by the need to fill in a history that would increase the legitimacy of the emerging nation and by the opportunity to direct that history toward a future ideal." [1] These nation-building novels or "foundational fictions" overwhelmingly took the form of romances, displacing the problems of forging a nation onto the successful coupling of two lovers from different races, classes, or regions. [2]

In twentieth-century Mexico, film production has inherited the role of rewriting the nation, particularly in the popular melodramas of the 1930s and 1940s that focus on the Mexican Revolution. These "revolutionary melodramas," as Deborah Mistron names them, [3] spoke to national concerns of whether or not the Revolution had sufficiently addressed the social needs of Mexico. [4] Laura Podalsky seems to draw a connection between Doris Sommer's argument and the role of the Revolutionary melodramas when she writes:

> By repeating highly conventionalized stories which the reader/spectator already knows, the texts continually work through ideological conflicts which remain unresolved in the reader/spectator's lives. . . . Revolutionary melodramas like *Flor silvestre* provided a fictional space within which to work out the meaning of the Revolution in light of contemporary circumstances. [5]

Implicit in Podalsky's analysis of the social role of these melodramas is the historically critical and revisionist function of these filmic texts in the imagining of the Revolution. Rather than writing a foundational fiction, these films were re-creating the actual historical foundational moment of the Mexican Revolution itself. In so doing, the Revolutionary melodrama re-imagines the modern nation.

The classic Revolutionary melodrama *Flor silvestre* (*Wildflower*, 1943), directed by Emilio "El Indio" Fernández and photographed by Gabriel Figueroa, is a film very much in the tradition of Sommer's foundational fictions. The problems of the Revolution and its resolution are played out in the film as romance and familial conflict, the two mainstays of melodrama. In the film, José Luis is the son of a landowner; Esperanza's family is among the peasants who work for him. They marry in secret, reconciling in romance the class conflict at the heart of the Revolution, but José Luis's father disapproves strongly when he learns of the marriage, representing in generational terms the resistance of the "old" Mexico toward the installation of the "new" (fig. 8.1). Joining the cause of the Revolution, José Luis must fight against all that his father represents. But when his father is killed as a result of Revolutionary activity, José Luis seeks to avenge his death, a move that, as Podalsky points out, places him at odds with the national interests of the Revolution.[6] Thus José Luis's familial dilemmas reflect those of the emerging nation in a state of transition.

It is the generation to follow, Esperanza and José Luis's child, who will inherit the great legacy of the Revolution (fig. 8.2). This is explicitly figured in the narrative frame with an aged Esperanza overlooking the lands that were the site of conflict in her youth but are now peaceful, with her grown son in military uniform at her side. She speaks poetically about the love of the earth being the greatest and most painful, and she espouses that every person must have his or her piece of land: "Eran muy pocos, los que tenían tanta tierra. Otros, en cambio, no tenían nada" ("Those who had land were very few. Others, on the other hand, had nothing"). The issues of class and land reform are thus explicitly indexed as the concerns of the melodrama to follow. And she highlights the continuity of the past represented in the narrative with the present of the frame (which was, of course, the "present" for the contemporary audiences). The blood spilled in the past, she says, gave birth to the Mexico of today. Her monologue gives larger, national purpose to the personal suffering about to be related in the film,[7] as well as outlining what is at stake in this text: the lionization of social justice and the ideological realignment of the meaning of the Revolution.

As seen in *Flor silvestre,* the Revolutionary melodrama is a rich form for representations of the nation. As a foundational moment, the Revolution becomes the site of multiple and changing discourses, of honor, justice,

FIGURE 8.1. *Romance between José Luis and Esperanza, from* Flor silvestre *(1943). Courtesy of the Academy of Motion Picture Arts and Sciences.*

revenge, or family. The melodramatic form, for its part, lends its strong allegorical capacity, allowing the family and the coupling of José Luis and Esperanza to be overdetermined with the issues of the nation.[8]

Revolutionary Melodrama for the 1990s?

Against this history of foundational moments and Revolutionary melodramas comes *Como agua para chocolate (Like Water for Chocolate)* in the early 1990s. The necessary question to ask for this film in relation to this context is, What is its agenda in appropriating the forms for reimagining nationness in 1991? *Como agua para chocolate,* directed by Alfonso Arau from the novel written by his ex-wife Laura Esquivel, who also adapted the screenplay, again returns to the Revolution with its own reimagining of the nation. *Como agua para chocolate* uses the Mexican Revolution as a backdrop, returning to this foundational moment in Mexican history, but it also returns to the foundational texts of the classic Revolutionary melodramas like *Flor silvestre* that first reimagined that moment cinematically. Almost as markers of narrative progression, Arau quotes the visual style of Fernández and Figueroa with low-angle shots and wide expanses of sky and sculptural clouds,[9] almost requiring that *Como agua para chocolate* be read within the diverse context of its intertextuality. It is at once revising the classic Revolutionary melodramas like *Flor silvestre,* engaging in a historical discourse (both in its own representations and in its references to the Revolutionary melodramas, which were themselves historically revisionist), eliciting comparisons with the novel from which the film is adapted, and activating a discourse of magic realism that necessarily invokes classics of this genre in the literary tradition. At the same time, its unique production and box office history—as a staggeringly expensive production in Mexican terms and at the time of its release the most successful foreign film ever distributed in the United States—graft additional considerations of capital (cultural and otherwise) in examinations of the film (fig. 8.3).

Given the complex intertextual matrix of *Como agua para chocolate,* it

FIGURE 8.2. *José Luis is sacrificed for Esperanza and their son, from* Flor silvestre *(1943). Courtesy of the Academy of Motion Picture Arts and Sciences.*

FIGURE 8.3. *U.S. promotional ad for* Like Water for Chocolate *(1992).*

is no surprise that its ideological implications and reimagining of the modern nation are quite changed from those of *Flor silvestre*. The academic and popular discourse in the United States has articulated the ideological agenda of *Como agua para chocolate* as a liberal, feminist treatise, and the film certainly suggests these possibilities. However, I argue that the text itself doubles back against its own feminist pretensions, resulting in what is ultimately a conservative text.[10]

Woman, Nation, Revolution

Before examining the film's feminine representations, however, there needs to be an accounting of the history of representations of women in Mexican cinema. Since the Golden Age, representations of women have undergone various revisions and reinterpretations. From the strict dichotomy of virgin/whore, the image of women in Mexican screens has diversified, particularly since 1968.[11] *Como agua para chocolate* must be positioned within the history of this larger movement of redefining representations of women. Indeed, *Como agua para chocolate* has been heralded by scholars of Mexican cinema as the film that has established new ground in positing "positive images" in terms of cinematic representations of women. David Maciel writes, "*Como agua para chocolate* is perhaps the most powerful and skillfully realized women's story in recent Mexican cinema."[12] And Alex Saragoza and Graciela Berkovich argue that the feminine representations in *Como agua para chocolate* constitute an ideological break with the films that portray women who are liberated but still confined within the patriarchal system.[13] However, a close reading of *Como agua para chocolate* shows that the break is not as clean or radical as it has been figured.

Continuing in the tradition of the classic Revolutionary melodramas like *Flor silvestre,* Arau's film projects ideological issues onto the individual matters of the family. Conflict between "old" and "new" is again rendered in generational terms. The narrative of *Como agua para chocolate* concerns the subversion of the rules of Mama Elena, who has decreed that according to family tradition, her youngest daughter, Tita, may never marry and is instead condemned to care for her mother until the matriarch's death. In the repression of feminine desire and its figuration as "tradition," Mama Elena and her ideas represent outdated, patriarchal ideology. But Tita falls in love with young Pedro, and their desire to consummate and marry threaten Mama Elena's social order. As in *Flor silvestre* and the foundational fictions, it is love and the union of lovers that represent a break with the past and, in *Como agua para chocolate,* the threat of subversion to the dominant patriarchal order. But the issue here is of feminine agency and desire, not class conflict as it was in classic Revolutionary texts. *Como agua para chocolate* has appropriated the form and forum for ideological change from *Flor silvestre* and other classic Revolutionary melodramas but apparently has altered the goal of change from class to gender concerns.

Even the Revolution itself as represented in *Como agua para chocolate* is no longer associated with the agendas of class justice and land redistribution at the heart of the (historical) Revolution. Tita's magical food, into which she sublimates her own repressed desires, has an erotic effect on everyone who eats it. Tita's sister Gertrudis is so turned on by the food that she sets fire to the bathhouse with her burning desire. A Villista miles away in the midst of battle smells her passion and rides off to capture a nude and burning Gertrudis and fulfill both his and her erotic fantasies. Gertrudis joins the Revolution, not for social justice as did José Luis in *Flor silvestre* but for sexual liberation. The Revolution becomes a sexual one, reinscribed as a discourse of erotics and gender, endowing these ostensibly feminist interests with historical and national importance.

Another important marker of the text's feminine/feminist point of view is the narrative voice-over. Like *Flor silvestre*, *Como agua para chocolate* charts the reimagined Revolution's impact on the present through a narrative frame set in the spectator's present. The film opens with Tita's great-grandniece chopping onions, which triggers Proust-like memories and reflections on the narrative past.[14] The great-grandniece's voice is heard throughout the master narrative, the story of Tita and Pedro, offering subjective insights and providing explanation. As narration, the voice is omniscient and powerful: this disembodied voice effectively dominates the text, suggesting that a feminine voice and a feminine perspective control the narrative.

Clearly, as demonstrated in the examples cited above, *Como agua para chocolate* figures itself as a feminine/feminist text, presenting feminine subversion of the patriarchal system in the past to realign the nation's "future ideal" (our present, figured in the frame) with feminine agency and empowerment. However, upon pressing this reading, it soon becomes clear that elements in the narrative itself frustrate this position. Sommer's paradigm of the foundational fictions is again helpful to elucidate this problem. The purpose of romances in Latin American foundational fictions, Sommer argues, is to symbolically weave together previously divided classes and races in order to produce a hybrid new generation. She writes, "Unproductive eroticism is not only immoral; it is unpatriotic."[15] Classic Revolutionary melodramas and *Flor silvestre* follow that logic: Esperanza and José Luis's child represents the fruit of their suffering and *is* the new nation, the unity of social classes. But *Como agua para chocolate* turns problematic on this point of reproduction. Tita's only moment of maternal plenitude (which suggests alternatives to a patriarchal system) are both given to her and taken

away by the patriarchal/male figures. Tita first takes on the role of productive matriarch when her virgin breast magically produces milk to feed
Rosaura and Pedro's child—but this power is bestowed on her by Pedro's
erotic gaze, which imparts the maternal flow. Tita's nurturing maternal
agency is thus sanctioned and conferred by masculine desire. Later in the
film, Tita and Pedro consummate their love for the first time, after Mama
Elena has been killed by bandits. Tita thinks she is pregnant, a thought that
is at first horrifying, but Tita and Pedro soon await the child with hopeful
anticipation. But this promise of a new generation built on their subversive,
magic love is taken away: the pregnancy was actually a hysterical one wished
upon Tita by the ghost of patriarchal Mama Elena as psychological punishment for her sexual indiscretion with Pedro. Even though the text attempts
to create an alternate feminine discourse through its magic realist aesthetic,
one outside traditional realism aligned with patriarchy, these maternal and
patriotic moments are still tightly conferred and controlled by patriarchal
power—and the supposedly alternative, feminine magic is shown to be
bound to patriarchy and the thrust of traditional, phallic narrative.

The power of the patriarch is shown to be still intact and potent in
another significant sequence. When Tita and Mama Elena hear of the death
of Rosaura's son (Elena has sent the family to live over the border so as to
separate Tita and Pedro), Tita's anguish is overwhelming, but Mama Elena
proclaims, "¡No quiero lágrimas!" ("I don't want any tears!") With this
latest frustration by the patriarchal mother of the free flow of feminine
feeling, Tita breaks down and for the first time openly accuses Mama Elena
of her injustices. Elena strikes her, and Tita sequesters herself in the dove-
cote. Days later, when the female servant Chencha goes to her, she finds
that Tita "está como loca" ("has gone crazy") and has turned mute. While
on the one hand her madness and loss of voice (or agency) are consistent
with other Mexican screen depictions of women going mad under patriarchal pressures,[16] it is her "cure" from this patriarchally imposed madness
that creates ideological disjunctures in this ostensibly feminist text.

Mama Elena sends Tita to an asylum across the border under the care
of Dr. Brown. This young widower with a son gently cares for her, and the
great-grandniece's voice-over informs us that for the first time, within the
space provided her by this new, sympathetic and North American patriarch,
Tita feels free. It soon becomes apparent that Dr. Brown is falling in love
with Tita, as he describes pedantically how every person has a box of
matches inside, which can be lit only by a true love. Tita's matches are
damp, he says, and Dr. Brown implies that he would like to dry them.

(Magically?) Tita recovers her voice in the very next scene. The juxtaposition of Dr. Brown's nurturing attitude and Tita's recovery suggests that the resolution of her "madness" is achieved through the protective care of this North American doctor, problematizing even further a feminist interpretation; with Tita under his wing, Dr. Brown gives her back her voice. Tita uses her reinstated but limited agency to consent to marriage with Dr. Brown, trading one patriarchy (Mama Elena's) for another. Here, the narrative recovers any residual doubt that it is the patriarch that retains the power to both take away and restore—and control—feminine agency.

Any remaining progressive message in this story about the power of Tita and Pedro's *amor loco* is effectively squelched in the final resolution of the master narrative. Free from the patriarchal impediments and the old order by the deaths of Rosaura and Mama Elena, Tita and Pedro make love for the first time without fear of patriarchal or social reprisals. This *should* be the foundational moment of the text: the final consummation of the new ideology of the nation. But Pedro's death during sex frustrates the fulfillment of both Tita's erotic desires and the foundational moment. The reimposition of patriarchy is made even more pronounced and assertive by the narrative voice-over of Dr. Brown, which reiterates the metaphor of the internal box of matches. The action on screen follows the narration on the soundtrack as if obeying orders, and the room explodes in fire. The film, which has relied on the feminine narrative voice throughout, in the last instance cedes control of the text to a white male North American. The ideology and the narrative are recontained within a patriarchal, conservative discourse, showing that the only thing this magical true love succeeds in ending is not a repressive patriarchy but the lives of the lovers themselves. The resolution promises that there is no danger of subversion to patriarchal order to come out of their union, making their story a cautionary tale rather than a liberating one.[17]

The film closes with the book-ending of the frame in the present tense. Both Tita and Esperanza, Tita's surrogate daughter (Pedro and Rosaura's second child), whom she rescued from the family's repressive tradition, stand behind the narrator as spectral visions, emphasizing now visually the connections of the present with the past. But this epilogue vision of the "fruit" of the narrative suffering, however, cannot recontain the memory of the patriarchal system's nullification of the power and frustration of the desires of these fictional Revolutionary protofeminists. The would-be positive, feminist frame is "disjointed"[18] by the discourse that unfolded in the narrative.

Disjointed Discourse

Given the ideological contortions of *Como agua para chocolate* around feminism, a crucial question must be asked: What is it about *Como agua para chocolate* that activates the critical blind spot to these gender dynamics in the film? Why did it inspire such feminist adulations by critics and scholars alike, as described earlier? It certainly is not that the aforementioned scholars are unaware of or unsympathetic to the kind of ideological nullification that occurs in *Como agua para chocolate.* In fact, Saragoza and Berkovich in their article "Intimate Connections" talk about this very dynamic in another Mexican film from the same year, *Danzón:*

> . . . the female character (Julia) undergoes a change of consciousness that does not rupture the dominant order. . . . The film uses gender to suggest alternatives to the ideology of the dominant masculinist order, both on individual and societal levels. The system and its rules, in short, are vulnerable to subversion. But *Danzón* eschews an abrupt rupture of the dominant order.[19]

They see something very similar going on in *Danzón* to what I see in *Como agua para chocolate,* yet they hold up Arau's film as a "ray of hope" for changing and improving parameters of cinematic representations of women.[20] If it is clear how other would-be cinematic subversions of patriarchal order are invalidated within the text, why is that very same dynamic occurring in *Como agua para chocolate* ignored and its "feminism" paradoxically praised?

A simple yet extremely important answer is the revenue and the international prestige that *Como agua para chocolate* brings to the entire Mexican film industry. *Como agua para chocolate* must be read against yet another discourse: the financial instability of Mexican film production. Grossing almost $20 million at the U.S. box office, this is the first Latin American film—indeed, any foreign film—to have this kind of popular reception in the Hollywood-immersed North American market.[21] Such a huge success is perhaps the only antidote to the worries of an industry so dependent on a government that changes its film policy every *sexenio.* As Maciel explains: "It is critical for filmmakers to find creative and aggressive ways to successfully distribute and exhibit Mexican cinema outside its borders, since international audiences are equally important for its survival."[22] The scholars and patrons of Mexican cinema assume a tricky stance in relationship to such a popular and successful film text. Marsha Kinder iterates this problematic relationship when she writes about studying a different, marginalized national cinema:

> As Christian Metz observes in *The Imaginary Signifier,* the film historian frequently finds herself becoming an intellectual publicist for the texts she describes: "Often, by unexpected paths, unperceived by those who have quite unintentionally taken them, . . . writings on film become another form of cinema advertising and at the same time a linguistic appendage of the institution itself." I cannot deny this dimension in my own work; in fact, far from being "unperceived," I hope to demonstrate that it is part of the process being described—the reconstruction of national identity through the production, promotion, and reception of popular culture.[23]

Scholars and critics, as "intellectual publicists" of Mexican film, surely cannot attack such a commercial success, on ideological grounds or otherwise; to do so would be to attack the tenuous life flow of the whole national industry. I would argue that it is within this dynamic that Kinder describes that ideological readings of *Como agua para chocolate* are realigned.

This not only is true for U.S. scholars writing about Mexican cinema but also is manifested in the press discourse in Mexico as well. In 1992, at the time of the Mexican release of *Como agua para chocolate,* the Espectáculos section of the Mexico City daily *Excelsior* ran articles expressing anxieties about the state of the national film industry almost every day. Headlines such as "El cine mexicano sufre una de sus crisis más severas, dice Cristian González" ("Mexican Cinema Is Suffering One of Its Most Severe Crises, says Cristian González," 22 September 1992), and "Considera Silvia Pinal que el cine mexicano vive un buen momento y que puede ser mejor" (Silvia Pinal Thinks Mexican Cinema Is in a Great Moment and Can Be Even Better," 16 April 1992) exist alongside headlines such as "Los cineastas mexicanos hacen gran esfuerzo para elevar la calidad de sus películas" ("Mexican Filmmakers Are Making Great Efforts to Elevate the Quality of Their Films," 20 April 1992). There is plainly a national cinematic identity crisis being worked out on the pages of the paper.

This crisis can explain in part why in spite of lukewarm Mexican reviews (Mexican critic Tomás Pérez Turrent writes: "la respuesta del público en el mundo fue el chocolate mientras la respuesta de la crítica fue el agua" ["the response to the film by the world public was 'chocolate' while the response of the critics was 'water'"]),[24] *Como agua para chocolate* walked away with ten Ariel awards on 7 April 1992, after its "chocolatey" Mexican popular reception and "watery" critical reviews, suggesting that the Mexican Academy felt pressure to compensate for the mediocre reviews in light of the popular box office reception.[25] This did not go unnoticed or uncriticized—the weekly news magazine *Proceso* reported on the Ariel awards with this article: "*La Tarea* and *Danzón,* reconocidas en el mundo, sin Arieles; falible, la selección, reconoce la Academia" ("*La Tarea* and *Danzón,* Praised throughout the World, Go without Ariels; The Academy Acknowledges That Selection Is Fallible"). This review of the awards barely mentions *Como agua para chocolate,* the film that siphoned the awards away from these other critical successes, merely listing the categories *Chocolate* won toward the very end of the article. The focus on *La Tarea* and *Danzón*'s lack of awards and the absence of substantive discussion of *Chocolate*'s Ariel successes implicitly criticize and accuse the Academy for rewarding popular success over cinematic achievement—or realigning its discourse to fit the buzz and money circulating around a surprisingly popular film.[26]

Clearly—perhaps even obviously—then, the economic factor is extremely powerful and is a necessary consideration in filmmaking and intellectual discourse, and perhaps particularly so in the Mexican situation. But this begs more questions: What reasons can we look to for *Como agua para chocolate*'s extraordinary popularity, and what problems does that popularity raise? Of Emilio "El Indio" Fernández, with whom *Como agua para chocolate* shares a continuity in the Revolutionary melodrama, Julia Tuñón writes: "It is important to recognize that Emilio Fernández constructs an image of Mexico which influences ideas about Mexico abroad as well as at home."[27] This interface of national representations with international reception is certainly in operation with *Como agua para chocolate*'s unprecedented foreign viewing audiences, all of whom are consuming an image of Mexican nationness along with the magical love story. This revised Revolutionary melodrama reimagines the Revolution and the modern nation not only for "home" audiences but for export markets, too. As a Mexican relates, "[C]uando alguien se entera de que uno es mexicano, dice reaccionando de inmediato, 'Ah, sí, *Como agua para chocolate*.'" ("When someone discovers that you are Mexican, he or she reacts immediately with, 'Ah, yes, *Like Water for Chocolate!*'").[28] So the question of nation necessarily enters into the international consumption of this film text.

Eating Magical Otherness

After the film had established a word-of-mouth familiarity and had started showing its incredible box office potential, newspaper advertisements in the United States read, "Experience the Magic" and later, "Experience the Magic—*Again*." This zippy slogan sums up what sold American audiences on the picture: the strong element of a magical realist style. Victor Zamudio-Taylor and Inma Guiu point out the following passage in Janet Maslin's *New York Times* review:

> This film, a lively family saga that is centered on forbidden love and spans several generations, relies so enchantingly upon fate, magic and a taste for the supernatural that it suggests Gabriel García Márquez in a cookbook-writing mode. (The best-selling Mexican novel by Laura Esquivel, who also wrote the screenplay, interweaves the fanciful story of "Like Water for Chocolate" with actual recipes.) Whether you approach this swift, eventful tale on the culinary or the cinematic level, prepare for a treat.[29]

Zamudio-Taylor and Guiu protest Maslin's take on the film, saying, "After all, there is more to the novel and film than magical realism and food,"[30] but their objections too easily dismiss the reality that this is the level at which a majority of U.S. filmgoers consumed the movie. In fact, the distribution and promotion of the movie actually sought this kind of reception, as can be seen in the newspaper ads and other promotional materials. Whether or not this approach was anticipated or desired by the filmmaker and the author, the promotion of the film essentially plugged into an established perception of Latinness, actively courting the art house public familiar with the best-selling magical realism of Gabriel García Márquez's *Cien años de soledad (One Hundred Years of Solitude)* and Isabel Allende's *La casa de los espíritus (The House of the Spirits)*. Arau and Esquivel's film even quotes the well-known literary image from *Cien años de soledad,* the magical encounter with the gypsy's block of ice, framing the erotic summer rendezvous between Pedro and Tita with fetishized close-ups of a huge block of ice. Magical realism and *Como agua para chocolate* are reductively commodified as identifiable markers of Latino cultural identity, obliterating national or cultural distinctions of Mexico, Colombia, Chile. As Chencha says of the exchange of Tita for Rosaura as Pedro's bride—"You can't change tacos for enchiladas!"—but the film does just this with distinct national and cultural Latin identities.

To take the second half of Zamudio-Taylor and Guiu's objection, promotion for the film did precious little to assert that there was more to *Como agua para chocolate* than food. Distributor (and notoriously aggressive marketer) Miramax convinced Mexican restaurants across the country to re-create the dishes made in the film and held a contest for "amateur chefs" to submit "seductive recipes" for a prize trip to Mexico. A New York party celebrating the film's success, with Mayor David Dinkins in attendance, had actress Claudette Maille (Gertrudis) re-create on the West Side Highway the scene where she is carried off naked by a Villista on horseback, with the festivities ending in a wedding feast identical to the banquet in the film.[31] These promotions suggest that there is nothing *but* food to *Como agua para chocolate,* with the possible exception of the spectacle of nude women riding bareback.[32]

The cross-promotion with hard-cover copies of the best-selling novel sold at the movie theaters further commodifies the *Como agua para chocolate* representation of Mexican identity.[33] As was written in *Variety,* "[T]he book, a Gabriel Garcia Marquez [*sic*] type story spiced with recipes, is really cooking."[34] With the recipes in the book to be tried at home after watching the film, *Como agua para chocolate,* both novel and movie, really does present a García Márquez "feel" in cookbook-writing mode.

One can sympathize with Zamudio-Taylor and Guiu in their desire to discredit that reading and recuperate for the film "its historical awareness, national specificity and gender construction"[35]—even though the dynamic they argue against very apparently is at work in the cultural marketplace and even though the film itself thwarts progressive/positive gender and national construction—because the usual implications for Mexican representation in the global sphere are not, to use lingo in the spirit of the film, appetizing. These implications can be deduced from the following excerpt from an article attempting to define the elusive nature of magic realist cultural production:

> . . . the strength of Magic Realism in the "periphery" (Latin America, Africa, the Caribbean) and its comparative weakness in the "core" (Western Europe, the USA), could be explained by the fact that collective myths acquire greater importance in the creation of new national identities, as well as by the more obvious fact that pre-industrial beliefs still play an important part in the socio-political and cultural lives of developing countries. Magic Realism gives popular cultures and magical beliefs the same degree of importance as Western science and rationality. In doing this, it furthers the claims of those groups which hold these beliefs to equality with the modernising elites which govern them.[36]

This passage links the magical realist mode to the production of national identities, but more significant, at the same time it unwittingly extracts the problem of reading magical realism. Magical realism, author William

Spindler argues, belongs to those cultures on the margins, in the "periphery," in contrast to the cultures at the center or the "core," whose Western scientific rationalism forecloses participation in this aesthetic discourse. He is very clear about where magic realism exists (Latin America, Africa, the Caribbean) and where it doesn't (Western Europe, the United States); one is periphery, the other the core. Magic realism, as exemplified by this academic typology, is a sign of primitive and preindustrial culture and its encounter with modernity, limited to and defining those nations on the margin.

While Spindler is arguing in some capacity for this marginal aesthetic's subversive potential, I suggest that when commodified for popular international consumption, magic realism fixes a frozen identity of Mexicanness—and then by consuming popular conception, *latinidad*. In demanding and consuming endless reproductions of magic realism, the dominant U.S. culture condemns a lumpen, undifferentiated pan-Latin culture to repetition of an aesthetic that, from the point of view of the rational, industrial, and dominant cultures that consume the images, both defines it as Third World and fixes its status there. Magic realism becomes not a challenge to Western rationality and scientific discourse but rather *reaffirms* their hegemonic position of power. Paul Willemen calls the effect of this dynamic "cultural apartheid" and the cultural "ghetto."[37] Confining the parameters of "authentic" Mexican (and in its perceived amorphous unity, Latin American) national culture in this way denies Mexican identity in the internal sphere passage to what Homi K. Bhabha calls "the living principle of the people," whereby cultural and national identities transform and evolve in the daily performances of both culture and life.[38] *Como agua para chocolate* plugs into and perpetuates this cultural apartheid of the fossilizing magic realist aesthetic and adds fuel to the exotic fire with its fetishization and eroticization of commodified, consumable images of border life and food. And as these images are bought and eaten with U.S. dollars, they are digested and become just another ingredient in the mess of the melting pot, drained of any residual Mexican specificity. Much as the disturbing intensity of Frida Kahlo's self-portraits is transformed and resituated through the endless postcard reproductions tacked on North American walls for their chic exoticism and foreign tokenism, magic realism and Latin identity are condemned to the cultural ghetto in the name of pluralism.

Finally, we arrive at an explanation for the immense success of *Como agua para chocolate* in the usually hermetic U.S. film market. Embedded in the melodrama is a representation of Mexico/Latin America that characterizes it as magic, folkloric, exotic, provincial—in short, other. Even the film's final attempt at realigning the narrative with its glossed-over but disjointed frame elicits this subordinate national relationship: Tita's surrogate daughter, Esperanza, whose name invokes Dolores del Río's famous character in *Flor silvestre,* is explicitly figured as the "hope," the success of the new ideology. Significantly, she marries the son of North American Dr. Brown, symbolically and literally crossing the border of two national communities. If we take Doris Sommer's definition of a foundational text, it is in the marriage of Esperanza and Alex Brown that *Como agua para chocolate* becomes such a text, not in the story of Tita and Pedro. Esperanza and Alex's union is productive and marries together two classes, races, and nations, but the message is quite different from the subversive feminist one that is first promised. In the context of the early 1990s political ambitions and economic troubles, the message of the final frame set in our present evokes pre-NAFTA aspirations, laying the foundations of "natural" family bonds between Mexico and the United States in the past and justifying appeals for aid and (inter?)dependency in the present. The happy ending comes when the "hope," Esperanza, trades in Mama Elena's pre-Revolutionary patriarchy for Alex Brown's and Uncle Sam's late-capitalist patriarchy.

Seeing the movie, buying the book, and maybe going to a Mexican restaurant afterward become a way of indulging in an easy but ersatz multiculturalism and a problematic political correctness. There is nothing threatening or subversive in the text; both its national and feminist messages fall in line with dominant Western/North American parameters. The film's familiar and comfortable claims to exotic otherness reassuringly reaffirm the status of the United States as the "center."

While the literary foundational fictions of the previous century sought to define and differentiate national identities, *Como agua para chocolate* as foundational fiction obfuscates boundaries and forms alliances with border nations. Alfredo Alvarez Padilla writes in the 1990s, "New images and myths have been created by the publicity industry as a means of improving the international perception of Mexican-American relations."[39] *Como agua para chocolate* certainly can be read as part of that ongoing project, and it can be argued that the film represents a new foundational fiction for our postmodern age of multinational capital and blurred cultural identities.

Alfonso Arau himself can be seen as confusing the boundaries of distinct national identities. Prized in the United States, as we have seen, for his aesthetic of "otherness," he is regarded more cautiously in Mexico and is sometimes referred to as too commercial—or by extension, too "American." Arau responds to his Mexican critics by accepting their charge of commercialism as a compliment.[40] Indeed, Arau seems to personify the ambivalence of the problem of Mexican cinema: while repeatedly returning to Latin American themes (his in-the-works *Regina* deals with the Mexican student massacre of 1968,[41] and he was instrumental in changing the protagonist family of Hollywood's *A Walk in the Clouds* [1995] with Keanu Reeves from Italians to Mexicans[42]), in interviews he comes across as mostly concerned with U.S. critical reaction to his work and being able to make "un plato para el primer mundo, hecho con gente y dinero del tercero" ("a dish for the First World, made with people and money from the Third").[43]

Scholars writing and audiences watching within the margins of U.S. national boundaries and capital must be cautious in embracing the admittedly appealing universalist message of *Como agua para chocolate*. That the film articulates (multi)nationality through discourses of gender is extremely important and must not be overlooked. What does this kind of new foundational fiction do to representations of culture and gender? What and who get distorted or forgotten in the (re)telling of the (inter)national history? Even in a magically reimagined past, the white patriarchy dominates. The dangers of fetishized fossilization on the one hand and cultural homogenization on the other are very real. Alvarez Padilla asks, "Will the Mexican artistic soul be transformed by trade negotiations?"[44] I would add that women's "souls" are also at stake here, insofar as discourses of the nation in the global village depend on representations of the feminine. We must be careful to consider what we are asked to consume: who is being shortchanged when taco is switched for enchilada?

Notes

The author thanks Ana M. López, Chon Noriega, and Marsha Kinder for their invaluable insights, criticisms, and suggestions during the writing of this essay.

1. Doris Sommer, "Irresistible Romance: The Foundational Fictions of Latin America," *Nation and Narration,* ed. Homi K. Bhabha (New York: Routledge, 1990), 76. For a book-length discussion, see Doris Sommer, *Foundational Fictions: The National Romances of Latin America* (Berkeley and Los Angeles: University of California Press, 1991).

2. Sommer, "Irresistible Romance," 81.

3. Deborah E. Mistron, "A Hybrid Subgenre: The Revolutionary Melodrama in the Mexican Cinema," *Studies in Latin American Popular Culture* 3 (1984): 47–56.

4. Laura Podalsky, "Disjointed Frames: Melodrama, Nationalism, and Rep-

resentation in 1940s Mexico," *Studies in Latin American Popular Culture* 8 (1993): 63.

5. Ibid., 62–63.

6. Ibid., 63.

7. Ibid.

8. Christine Gledhill, "The Melodramatic Field: An Investigation," *Home Is Where the Heart Is: Studies in Melodrama and the Women's Film,* ed. Christine Gledhill (London: BFI Publishing, 1987), 21.

9. For an excellent discussion of the Fernández-Figueroa cinematic style and its ideological implications, see Charles Ramírez Berg, "The Cinematic Invention of Mexico: The Poetics and Politics of the Fernández-Figueroa Style," in *The Mexican Cinema Project,* ed. Chon A. Noriega and Steven Ricci (Los Angeles: UCLA Film and Television Archive, 1994), 13–24.

10. For an excellent argument along these lines that makes a critical intervention into scholarship on film melodrama, but which I regrettably encountered only after this essay was sent to press, see Julianne Burton-Carvajal, "Mexican Melodramas of Patriarchy: Specificity of a Transcultural Form," in *Framing Latin American Cinema: Contemporary Critical Perspectives,* ed. Ann Marie Stock (Minneapolis: University of Minnesota Press, 1997), 186–234.

11. Charles Ramírez Berg, "The Image of Women in Recent Mexican Cinema," *Studies in Latin American Popular Culture* 8 (1989): 161.

12. David Maciel, "El imperio de la fortuna: Mexico's Contemporary Cinema, 1985–1992," in *The Mexican Cinema Project,* 37.

13. Alex M. Saragoza with Graciela Berkovich, "Intimate Connections: Cinematic Allegories of Gender, the State, and National Identity," in *The Mexican Cinema Project,* 31.

14. Victor Zamudio-Taylor and Inma Guiu, "Criss-crossing Texts: Reading Images in *Like Water for Chocolate,*" in *The Mexican Cinema Project,* 47.

15. Sommer, "Irresistible Romance," 85.

16. Ramírez Berg, "The Image of Women," 172.

17. Charles Ramírez Berg notes a similar dynamic at play in films set in contemporary time dealing with the sexual liberation of the woman. The liberated woman, he argues, is figured as losing both her femininity and her humanity, setting up the question, "You can have liberation, but why would you want it?" Ramírez Berg, "The Image of Women," 164.

18. I use the term here in the spirit of Podalsky's analysis of the narrative frames that do not fit and are out of synch with the rest of the narrative exposition in *Flor silvestre* and *María Candelaria.* Podalsky, "Disjointed Frames," 66.

19. Saragoza and Berkovich, "Intimate Connections," 30.

20. Ibid., 31.

21. Daniel S. Moore, "Mexico Poised for New Age," *Variety* (28 March–3 April 1994): 37.

22. Maciel, "El imperio de la fortuna," 43.

23. Marsha Kinder, *Blood Cinema: The Reconstruction of National Identity in Spain* (Berkeley and Los Angeles: University of California Press, 1993), 8–9.

24. Tomás Pérez Turrent, "Entre agua y chocolate," *Dicine* 55 (1994): 11.

25. *Como agua para chocolate* was the second most successful Mexican film in 1992 in Mexico—but it still came behind Hollywood's *Batman Returns, Beauty and the Beast, Lethal Weapon 3, Basic Instinct, Alien 3,* and the Mexican *La risa en vacaciones 3 (Laughter on Vacation 3).* Nelson Carro, "1992: Un año de cine, segunda parte," *Dicine* 51 (May 1993): 3.

26. Héctor Rivera, "*La Tarea* y *Danzón,* reconocidas en el mundo, sin Arieles; falible, la selección, reconoce la Academia," *Proceso* (4 May 1992): 58–59.

27. Julia Tuñón, "Between the Nation and Utopia: The Image of Mexico in the Films of Emilio 'Indio' Fernández," *Studies in Latin American Popular Culture* 12 (1993): 159.

28. Pérez Turrent, "Entre agua y chocolate," 10.

29. Janet Maslin, "Emotions So Strong You Can Taste Them," *New York Times* (17 February 1993): C13.

30. Zamudio-Taylor and Guiu, "Criss-crossing Texts," 51.

31. Lauren David Peden, "Big Little Movies Stand Up to Summer's Blockbusters," *New York Times* (22 August 1993): 10.

32. Interestingly, Miramax's promotional campaign for another Latin American "chocolate" film—Tomás Gutiérrez Alea and Juan Carlos Tabío's *Fresa y chocolate (Strawberry and Chocolate,* 1993)—used a similar approach.

33. See "Like Water in a Desert: Selling a Tie-In in a Theater," *Publisher's Weekly* (8 March 1993): 22.

34. D. T. Max, "Like Money for 'Water': The First Hardcover Movie Tie-in in Memory Is Selling Strong," *Variety* (3 May 1993): 59.

35. Zamudio-Taylor and Guiu, "Criss-crossing Texts," 51.

36. William Spindler, "Magic Realism: A Typology," *Forum for Modern Language Studies* 39:1 (1993): 82.

37. Paul Willemen, "The National," in *Looks and Frictions: Essays in Cultural Studies and Film Theory* (Bloomington: Indiana University Press, 1994), 207.

38. Homi K. Bhabha, "DissemiNation: Time, Narrative, and the Margins of the Modern Nation," in *Nation and Narration,* 29.

39. Alfredo Alvarez Padilla, "Perceptions on Mexican Art and Culture in the 1990s," *Voice of Mexico* 24 (July–September 1993): 73.

40. Carlos Puig, "Defiende Alfonso Arau 'Regina,' otra visión del 68," *Proceso* (8 March 1993): 48.

41. Ibid., 50.

42. Guy Garcia, "Seven Lives Later, a Director Starts His Eighth," *New York Times* (28 August 1994): 16.

43. Quoted in Pérez Turrent, "Entre agua y chocolate," 11.

44. Alvarez Padilla, "Perceptions on Mexican Art," 74.

9

The World according to *Plaff*

REASSESSING CUBAN CINEMA IN THE LATE 1980S

Gilberto Moisés Blasini

"Todo discurso tiene su reverso."

— SEVERO SARDUY

■ ■ ■ ■

The 1987 International Festival of the New Latin American Cinema in Havana, Cuba, commemorated the twentieth anniversary of the appearance of the movement known as the New Latin American Cinema. The festival celebrated the historical birth of a cultural movement that in Viña del Mar, Chile, urgently called for the examination of alternative ways of creating a distinct cinematic language that would challenge the hegemony of Hollywood's commercial paradigm in order to represent the particular social, cultural, political, and national realities and concerns of Latin American countries.[1] In subsequent years, the spirited cinematic momentum, full of exciting possibilities generated in Chile and elsewhere in Latin America, lost some of its original intensity. The Latin American cinematic project was directly affected by the either forced or necessary exile of filmmakers like Miguel Littín (Chile), Jorge Sanjinés (Bolivia), Fernando Solanas, and Octavio Getino (Argentina) from their respective countries and by the rising popularity of Latin American television, the financial difficulties associated with efficiently producing and effectively distributing films, and the decline in film attendance as well as many other social, economic, and political changes that affected Latin American countries and their film industries.[2] Furthermore, Néstor García Canclini has recently pointed out the necessity of considering the impact in Latin America of the "transnational conditions . . . in which art and communication are produced, circulated, and received."[3] In specific, he discusses "the displacement of cinema from the public arena to the home" where audiences can consume films via public television, cable television services, video satellites, laser discs, and so on.[4]

The impact of all these elements came to the foreground in the 1987 International Festival, which focused on questions concerning the success and effectiveness of the New Latin American Cinema's primary project: that of producing a distinctive cinema that would directly address and promote the social, cultural, and political transformation and empowerment of its audience. Furthermore, these concerns led to two crucial questions: (1) What in 1987 was "new" about the New Latin American Cinema? and (2) is this cinema still effective in its political agenda, specifically in terms of engaging spectators and addressing their issues? Thus, the New Latin American Cinema came under an internal "critical revision" of its cinematic practices (e.g., how films work in terms of narrative, style, and address to audiences) with the hope of maintaining the vitality of a movement directly involved in the sociopolitical struggles and processes of its audience.

Patricia Aufderheide explains this situation of a "critical revision" in her article "Latin American Cinema and the Rhetoric of Cultural Nationalism":

> What was for years a muttered undercurrent among many of the old guard New Cinema filmmakers, and a point of disaffection for many younger directors, also became public: the need to rethink the basic terms that define the New Latin American Cinema—or perhaps even to pronounce it dead and go on with something not yet imagined.[5]

Throughout the rest of her essay, Aufderheide elaborates some of the main points that dominated the dialogue among the different generations of Latin American filmmakers and theorists mainly revolving around finding effective alternatives for invigorating this cinematic movement.

Cuba, the cultural and political "guardian" of the New Latin American Cinema, had already been undergoing some internal restructuring since the early 1980s. In 1982, Julio García Espinosa became the head of the Cuban Film Institute (Instituto Cubano de Artes e Industrias Cinematográficas, ICAIC) when Alfredo Guevara left the position to become an ambassador to UNESCO in Paris. This transition at the top of the ICAIC signaled the beginning of a number of changes that included the promotion of a group of new filmmakers who had been trained in documentaries and newsreels but had not had the opportunity to make fiction films.[6] The incorporation of these "young" filmmakers mobilized ICAIC's existing cinematic discourses, generating a cross-generational dialogue that reexamined the island's cinematic practices, especially those related to making films that would simultaneously entertain and stimulate critical reflection.

In 1983, Juan Carlos Tabío's *Se permuta* became the first fiction film by a director from ICAIC's "second" generation of filmmakers to open in Cuba. *Se permuta* also initiated what Paulo Antonio Paranaguá would refer to five years later as "the young directors' . . . recovery of a comic verve likely to serve better as an underpinning for their social critique."[7] This renewed interest in comedy contrasted to the genre's neglect during the 1970s, even after the ICAIC had produced popularly and critically acclaimed comedies in the 1960s such as Tomás Gutiérrez Alea's *Las doce sillas* (1962) and *La muerte de un burócrata* (1966), and García Espinosa's *Las aventuras de Juan Quin Quin* (1967).[8] In *Se permuta,* Tabío used comedy to comment on Cuba's precarious housing conditions as well as—albeit mildly—on issues related to sexism, racism, and class elitism.[9] Five years later, Tabío returned to the comedy genre in *Plaff, o Demasiado miedo a la vida* (1988).[10] The film deals with a wide variety of issues present in contemporary Cuba: sexism, racism, the role of syncretic beliefs in the island's social imaginary, the heavy bureaucratization of the state, and the ideological tensions between two different generations of Cubans in relation to the Revolution and its accomplishments. These issues are explored through a plot that revolves around the melodramatic suffering of Concha, a middle-aged widow who is tormented throughout the film by someone who throws eggs at her with "evil spells" on them. Concha's sufferings due to these eggs are intertwined both with her fear of being abandoned by her only son, José Ramón, who marries Clarita, a woman that Concha cannot stand, and with her reluctance to accept Tomás, a suitor who wants to marry her and move with her to a house outside of Havana.

Upon its release, *Plaff* was a tremendous success with audiences and critics both at home and abroad. Carlos Galiano informs that more 500,000 spectators saw *Plaff* in Havana in its first five weeks, matching the success of Tabío's first film.[11] Galiano also asserts that the film had been unanimously praised by Cuban critics in terms of its humor and original narrative structure and the performance of popular actress Daysi Granados, as well as for its critical stance toward Cuba's situation during the late 1980s.[12] For example, Alex Fleites lauds the film for its "artistic risk" and for "bravely looking to establish a dialogue with its audience, even at the expense of attacking its already established philosophical and aesthetic conceptions."[13] Beyond the island, Maryse Condé recognized *Plaff*'s importance in the history of Cuban cinema because it broke from a "hopeless series of Cuban films attacking the reactionary bourgeois, extolling the role of women in society, and illustrating the honorable contribution of the peasant."[14] Condé finishes her reflection by stating that *Plaff* "revealed, still timidly, to viewers that in Cuba also, a number of walls are cracking, perhaps before collapsing entirely."[15] I would argue that what Condé perceives as a "revelation" has to do with *Plaff*'s departure from prior ICAIC films because its comments on contemporary society are combined with a parodic, self-reflexive narrative that reexamines cinema itself and its institutionalization in Cuba.[16]

This essay examines how Tabío uses parody in *Plaff* to mobilize a number of existing cinematic discourses that simultaneously provide an engaging and politically safe narrative frame for his commentary on Cuban everyday life in the late 1980s while putting into perspective ICAIC's history and practices. The text becomes the embodiment of a cross-generational dialogue not only in its plot, through the characters of Concha and Clarita, but also in its narrative form and cinematic style in relation to earlier ICAIC films. Thus *Plaff* constitutes a rereading of the "classical" Cuban film tradition, in other words, the films and theories of filmmaking of the 1960s and 1970s that were pivotal in the solidification of a national cinema with artists such as Gutiérrez Alea, García Espinosa, Humberto Solás, and Santiago Álvarez, among others. This parodic rereading creates an artistic alternative that seeks to broaden and invigorate the filmic and narrative possibilities of contemporary Cuban cinema. In order to understand *Plaff* as a parody, the film should be examined in relation to three different axes of ICAIC's history: the theories of Cuban filmmakers (such as García Espinosa's seminal essay "Por un cine imperfecto" and Gutiérrez Alea's "La dialéctica del espectador"), Cuban comedies from the late 1960s (such as García Espinosa's *Las aventuras de Juan Quin Quin* and Gutiérrez Alea's *La muerte de un burócrata*), and dramatic films that deal with the role of women in Cuban society (such as Solás's *Lucía,* 1968) and Pastor Vega's *El retrato de Teresa,* 1978).

"Imperfect" Theories about Cinema in Cuba

As a background to understanding *Plaff,* it is important to remember that the reasons for the existence of such a solid national film industry in Cuba are intimately related to the island's Revolutionary agenda. On 24 March 1959, just three months after Cuba's independence, the ICAIC was created with the approval of Law 169. ICAIC's mission was to develop a film in-

dustry that would help both in the education of people and in the promotion of the republic's political agenda. The relevance of this political agenda
fostered a kind of filmmaking that often emphasized the discussion of issues
over elements related to film production. For example, when talking about
films, García Espinosa stressed that the subject matter or thematic was the
principal element when it came to increasing popular awareness of relevant
social and political issues. Thus, stylistic and technical achievements were
secondary since "imperfect cinema is not interested in quality or technique
[as such] anymore."[17]

García Espinosa's position regarding imperfect cinema's style and quality
constituted an attack on the hegemonic cinematic practices of ideologically
imperialistic film industries (e.g., Hollywood) as well as a necessary tactical
response to Cuba's and Latin America's austere economic conditions. Instead of an inequitable attack against technique and technical development,
imperfect cinema's style should be understood as a filmic way of inscribing
and reclaiming Latin America's material limitations. García Espinosa was
not advocating negligent or incompetent filmmaking. In 1972 he clarified
that "imperfect cinema does not mean a carelessly or poorly done cinema"
but means one that "identifies with the development of a new culture [and]
is interested in the cultural instance that nurtures it."[18]

Part of imperfect cinema's contribution to the development of a "new"
film culture emerged from the collapse of established cinematic genres, for-
mulas, and conventions in an attempt to show sociopolitical processes
through films. This eclectic reconfiguration of cinematic genres and conventions is what Ana M. López has called the parodic operation of the New
Latin American Cinema. As she explains, "the critical juxtaposition of traditional cinematic modes—the documentary and the fictional—in the
context of realist representational strategies" constitutes one of the New
Latin American Cinema's tactics for its "fictional reconstruction or rereading [of events which] assumed the historical as the basic intertext necessary
for [cinema's] own intervention in the sociopolitical struggles of Latin
America."[19] Along with any possible cinematic "intervention in the sociopolitical struggles" of contemporary Cuba, *Plaff* adds an extra layer to its
articulation of parody by interweaving in its diegesis a number of carefully
constructed scenes that attempt to document the trials and tribulations of
the Cuban filmmaking process. Through these "documentary-like" moments, *Plaff* establishes a historical ground that can be read as a parodic,
self-reflexive comment on the working conditions for filmmakers not only
in Cuba but in Latin America in general during the 1980s.[20]

Parody as a Discursive Practice

As Linda Hutcheon defines it in her book *Theory of Parody: The Teachings of Twentieth-Century Art Forms:*

> Parody is repetition with a difference, an imitation with critical ironic distance, whose irony cuts both ways. Ironic versions of "trans-contextualization" and inversions are its major formal operatives, and the range of pragmatic ethos is from scornful ridicule to reverential homage.[21]

Parody is a dialectic between two discourses: the parodizer and the parodied. This dialogue takes place within the discursive space of the parodizer in a way that makes possible the engendering of a discursive synthesis of the two. In other words, a parody will be constituted by (1) the elements or positions of the initial discourse that are put into question, (2) a new or alternative set of elements or positions that question or challenge the initial discourse (and, in fact, do not need to challenge the initial discourse in its totality), and (3) the dialogue and (possible) outcome of the juxtaposition of the two discourses.

If this dialectical relationship of parody could be visualized in temporal terms, the parodied would represent the anterior or past, the parodizer would be the actual or present, and the dialogue between the two paradoxically represents the posterior or future. Yet how can a process that implies the present progressive tense be understood as the future? It is only through the juxtaposition of the past and the present that a possible (discursive) future can arise. In parody the important issue at stake is not the parody itself, but its consequences, i.e., the transformation of two discourses (one past and one present) into something different: an alternative discourse that does not privilege the present over the past (and possibly, but not probably, past over the present) but that opens up the space for the interaction and negotiation between them, rendering a future that acknowledges and validates both discourses. Logically, this "future" can exist only if audiences share the cultural and ideological codes that will permit them to understand the discourse as parody.[22]

Cuban audiences should not have had any problems in understanding *Plaff* as parody since they have been purposefully educated by the government about cinema and its artifices. As Julianne Burton has noted, one of the goals of the Cuban republic was to establish "a comprehensive national film program whose primary goals are universal film literacy and universal access to the medium."[23] This film program included, among other things, the publication of a film magazine *(Cine Cubano),* the creation of a Department of Cinematographic Diffusion (which consisted of screening films in rural areas outside the capital via mobile cinema units, or "cine móvil" trucks),[24] and the television program *24× Second,* a weekly show "devoted mainly to the review of major first-release films and didactic analysis of styles, genres, and filmmakers."[25] All of these venues have helped in the cultivation of an informed and critical audience potentially prepared to grasp how *Plaff* plays with the cinematic apparatus and its conventions as well as with the Cuban filmic tradition.

Plaff's recurrent references to the artifices of cinema produce a self-reflexive narrative that operates within the realm of parody by presenting "both a respectful awareness of cultural continuity and a need to adapt to changing formal demands and social conditions through an ironic challenging of the authority of that same continuity."[26] The tension between cultural continuity and its ironic challenge works in *Plaff* on at least two levels: (1) the formal and/or stylistic elements, which address elements related to the film's narrative structure, the artifice of films, and the cinematic apparatus in the Cuban context, and (2) the plot, which deals with the clash of two generations: Concha, or the generation that lived through the change from Batista's dictatorship to Castro's republic, and Clarita, or the post-Revolutionary generation whose experiences are rooted in the already consolidated republic. The ways in which these two levels work together permit spectators to pose pertinent questions about Cuban society and culture during the late 1980s. These questions include, but are not limited to, issues related to the location and configuration of women both in everyday life and in cinema, the ubiquity of governmental bureaucracy, and the tension that arises from the different ideological positions coexisting in island.

A Parodic Perspective of Cinema's Artifices

Plaff's first sequence establishes the basis for understanding the film's narrative and style as parody.[27] *Plaff* begins with an intertitle, signed by the ICAIC, that reads: "Dear audience, this film has been finished in record time so that it can debut in tribute to filmmakers on their commemorative holiday." After the intertitle, the first scene, which shows José Ramón trying to persuade Clarita to have sex while passionately kissing on a sofa, is shown upside down. Suddenly the film stops, the screen goes blank, and the sound of a projector's motor as well as the voice of a (fictional) projectionist can be heard. The projectionist says to the implied (Cuban) audience: "Caballeros, the film's first reel is defective. I will have to send it for repair to the

ICAIC. I will begin with the second reel. This is not my fault." As a result, an ellipsis is created, and the action jumps to the day when Clarita and José Ramón are celebrating their marriage.

The first important element of this sequence is the intertitle, which reveals the "supposed" intention of the film. The intertitle suggests that the motivation behind the film does not correspond to any relevant social, cultural, or political issue directly affecting the Cuban audience. Instead, the intertitle implies that the film's raison d'être is simply to fulfill a (rather trite) function that has nothing to do with the audience or their immediate issues but rather with the recognition and glorification of institutionally based filmmakers. In that respect, *Plaff* does not present itself as the kind of work that would follow the tradition of the ICAIC, that is, as a "popular film." In "La dialéctica del espectador," Gutiérrez Alea defined a "popular film" as one " that responds not only to the immediate interests (expressed in the necessity of enjoyment, play, self-alienation, illusion), but also to the basic necessity, to the final objective: the transformation of reality and the improvement of men (sic)." He continues: "A popular film is not only that accepted by the people, but also that which expresses the deeper and more authentic interests of the people, and those that respond to them." [28]

Since most of the work of ICAIC's filmmakers has consistently proven to be intricately involved with the "interests of the people," the tactic of presenting *Plaff* as a seemingly frivolous, self-indulgent, and self-serving project lays out a tone of ironic mockery characteristic of parody's "modeling process of revising, replaying, inverting, and 'trans-contextualizing' previous works." [29] *Plaff*'s ostensible "carelessness" in terms of style, performance, and technique is explained as a consequence of rushing the film's production simply to meet a deadline—the day that commemorates the role of filmmakers in society.[30] This "carelessness" also serves as a way of emphasizing that the production of Cuban films should respond to relevant contemporary issues such as the everyday struggles of a country with minimal material resources rather than vainglorious ones like the narcissistic exaltation of artists. Paradoxically, this cinematic "negligence" permits the film to comment on the island's contemporary economic and social situation as well as its cinematic practices without becoming either a propagandistic pamphlet or a subversive (i.e., anti-Revolutionary) text.

The initial sequence involving the fictional projectionist (as well as the final one when his voice reappears, informing that the repaired "first reel" will be shown) provides a framework for understanding *Plaff*'s examination of production conditions in Cuba. The projectionist, whose accidental intervention causes a rearrangement of the film's narrative order, becomes an external entity that breaks the linearity of the text and, consequently, alters its form and meaning.[31] This figure becomes the avenue for addressing the question of how much control does a director have both in the production and in the exhibition of a film under Cuba's Revolutionary government. It is relevant to notice that *Plaff* came out less than a year after the ICAIC introduced "a reform resulting in the decentralization of the examination, discussion of and the decisions regarding scripts."[32] This reform responds to a larger "rectification campaign" taking place in Cuba during the late 1980s that was looking to minimize bureaucracy and corruption and to maximize productivity. ICAIC divided all of its directors into three creative groups under the guidance of Gutiérrez Alea, Solás, and Manuel Pérez.[33] Solás explains that this decentralization of the film industry constituted an attempt "to arrange things in such a way that no bureaucratic agency was in a position to sit [in] judgment over our work."[34]

The question of bureaucracy vis-à-vis Cuban cinema is further explored in the film when the action stops and the figure of a fictional director, Juan Carlos Contreras, addresses the audience directly to explain a scene that could not be shot due both to budgetary reasons and to the film's premature deadline. The fictional director's name simultaneously invokes *Plaff*'s actual director, Juan Carlos Tabío, and a number of different characters in the diegesis who share the same last name, *Contreras*. These characters, who occupy high positions in different bureaucratic branches of the Cuban government, are all played by the same actor, Jorge Cao. A variation of this technique had already been used in García Espinosa's *Las aventuras de Juan Quin Quin,* in which Enrique Santiesteban plays four different characters, all of whom want to exploit or destroy Juan Quin Quin: a small-town mayor, a rich landowner, a sugar mill manager, and a sergeant fighting against the Revolutionary guerrillas. Whereas in *Las aventuras de Juan Quin Quin* the use of an actor to perform different characters serves to show the similarities among different agents of oppression in pre-Revolutionary Cuba, in *Plaff* it becomes a way of visualizing the ubiquity of bureaucracy in contemporary post-Revolutionary society.[35] Thus, the film attempts to show that characters like the Contreras are the reason for the existence of the "rectification campaign." Finally, the link between the figure of the director and the other six Contreras characters suggests not only that the ICAIC itself suffers from bureaucratic problems but also that the institutionalization of its filmmakers is becoming quite visible.

Plaff's use of parody also addresses elements related to the conditions under which films are exhibited in Cuba. The film's apparently erratic order caused by the defective "first reel" can be understood as an attempt to provide filmically an experience familiar to that of Cuban filmgoers. In "Death Is Not True: Form and History in Cuban Film," Timothy Barnard explains:

> With the exception of the Cinemateca and ICAIC (which have fixed-schedule archival and retrospective screening) cinema theaters project their daily programme in a continuous, uninterrupted loop. The programme generally consists of a five-minute newsreel, a ten- to twenty-minute documentary or animated short, and the feature. Cuban audiences, including the middle-class at first-run shows in downtown cinemas, seem to wander in and begin watching the show whenever they arrive (which can never be predicted when traveling on Havana's erratic transportation system). Thus the feature is often interrupted, made to straddle the short films, and viewed out of sequence.[36]

Thus, *Plaff*'s seemingly disordered narrative comments not only on Cuban filmmaking processes but also on the island's particular(ly "imperfect") film viewing circumstances.

Tabío's cinematic and narrative tactic in *Plaff* is precisely to construct a film embodying a superficial interpretation of the notion of imperfect cinema.[37] In other words, he makes a film that literally incorporates a significant number of technical and filmic "imperfections," such as the inclusion of random footage in the narrative, the distortion of the visual focus by having characters stand very close to the camera, the use of the vertical movement of a hand over the camera lens as the transition between two scenes, and so on. The incorporation of these "imperfections" becomes even more pronounced because *Plaff*'s plot sounds like the description of a typical Latin American *telenovela:* an insecure and distressed middle-aged widow, who is afraid of being abandoned by her son, constantly antagonizes her daughter-in-law. Her hostility toward Clarita in conjunction with the fear of being frequently attacked with eggs by an unknown enemy drive Concha to her death via a heart attack. Some of the primary social and political propositions implied in the film nevertheless arise from the juxtaposition of this apparently prosaic "telenovelistic" story and the film's intentional cinematic imperfections.

Tabío's use of "imperfections" can be understood as a way of playing with and reconfiguring García Espinosa's ideas about filmmaking. Rather than concentrating on the film's subject matter and its social and political function, Tabío gives equal importance to the "imperfect" elements that belong to cinematic technique and style. Marvin D'Lugo notes that this shift in emphasis as well as the self-consciousness of the film permit Tabío to avoid "the heavy-handed moralizing style of an earlier tradition of Cuban filmmaking that also dealt with important themes of the conflict and critique of contemporary society." [38] It is precisely through the deliberate inclusion of cinematic "imperfections" that Tabío introduces in *Plaff* an alternative narrative and aesthetic construction to present his criticism of bureaucracy and the question of how different generations understand what constitutes a revolutionary position, among others. Moreover, these cinematic "imperfections" constitute the devices that move the narrative forward. For example, the question of who started throwing eggs at Concha to torture her would not exist if the film had a traditional, linear narrative since the "first reel" shows that Concha herself is responsible for throwing the first spell-carrying egg. The sequence shows that Concha threw an egg at Clarita (while she was at Concha's house) hoping that the younger woman would leave José Ramón alone. However, this information is delayed through the discontinuity established by beginning with the "second reel" and ending with the sequences belonging to the "first reel." Thus, by transposing some of the concepts of García Espinosa's "Por un cine imperfecto" into a different historical moment (from 1969 to 1988), and by reworking and moderately inverting the significance of cinematic style and technique over subject matter, Tabío follows a tradition where "filmmakers use parody to criticize and renew both their craft and their world." [39]

Tabío's filmic reconsideration of García Espinosa's ideas nevertheless maintains a certain continuity with the section of "Por un cine imperfecto" that talks about entertainment. In the essay, García Espinosa clarifies that the political agenda of the imperfect cinema does not exclude the possibility of making films entertaining for both the director and the audience. He states that "the imperfect cinema can derive entertainment, precisely, from everything that denies it." [40] *Plaff*'s "imperfectly cinematic" entertainment arises primarily from the incorporation of scenes that reveal in a hyperbolic fashion the creative processes of filmmaking in Cuba, and from the use of a melodramatic *telenovela* style in the construction of the film's plot and its characters, specifically Concha.

Plaff's cinematic self-reflexivity develops through a considerable number of scenes that intermittently interrupt the film's diegesis in order to "lay bare" the devices of the cinematic apparatus (such as the one with the fictional projectionist). These scenes whimsically exaggerate not only the artifice of cinema but also the worst possible situations that can affect and interfere with the filmmaking process (especially in the context of a country with Cuba's economic means).[41] For example, during one of Concha's moments of anxiety, she accuses Clarita of being the one who is throwing eggs at her. When Clarita yells back at Concha, José Ramón sides with his mother. At this moment, Clarita decides to leave José Ramón and move back in with her family. When the scene reaches its most dramatic point, the actress who plays Clarita, Thaís Valdés, has to stop the action because she cannot find a suitcase that is supposed to be on the set. She yells to the off-screen crew, "Caballeros, the suitcase," and the other two actors, Daysi Granados and Luis Alberto García Jr., join in the complaint. After Granados protests by saying "Caballeros, we cannot work like this," a suitcase is thrown to her hands. She passes it to Valdés, and the dramatic action resumes as if nothing had happened. *Plaff* includes other sequences marked by an "imperfectly cinematic" entertainment, such as the moment when actress Daysi Granados interrupts her performance because she forgets her lines, and the scene in which the reflection of a mirror reveals a group of people observing the shooting of the film. These moments engage audiences in a series of narrative disruptions that ridicule not only the notion of a seamless text magically unfolding in front of the spectators but also the ordeals of the filmmaking process. Furthermore, beyond any possible superficial interpretation of "imperfection" vis-à-vis Cuban cinematic practices, the film's obvious technical flaws could have been prevented or corrected before its release. Thus, the inclusion of these "imperfect" scenes that reveal the Cuban filmmaking experience can be read both as a way of documenting the creative and artistic processes in a nonindustrialized country and as a sarcastic commentary on the somewhat stereotypical, if not overdetermined, assumptions or ideas about films in Latin America.

Concha and the Melodrama of Cuban Female Characters

The construction of the film's plot around a female character and the use of a melodramatic *telenovela* style constitute another example not only of *Plaff*'s "imperfectly cinematic" entertainment but also of how Tabío continues to work with Cuban cinematic traditions while parodying them. Through the conflict between Concha and Clarita, *Plaff* exposes the social and political friction between two different Cuban generations: the revolutionary generation that lived the transition from Batista's government to Fidel's republic, and the younger, post-Revolutionary one that is more critical of the island's economic and political circumstances. The use of these two female characters to comment on Cuba's national affairs provides a line of continuity with earlier ICAIC films. As Marvin D'Lugo explains, "the female figure has emerged in Cuban films as the agency through which a new range of critical discourses about Cuban culture in general and the revolution in particular are enunciated."[42] D'Lugo continues his argument by examining how the use of women as an allegory of the nation has been naturalized almost to the point of transparency. He explains that this tendency, however, "is not as static and unoriginal as it may at first appear," and he refers to *Plaff* as an example in which "the tradition of allegorizing the nation through female characters is intentionally parodied."[43] Since all of the examples mentioned in D'Lugo's essay are dramatic films (e.g., Jesús Díaz's *Lejanía* (1985), Gutiérrez Alea's *Hasta cierto punto* (1984), Solás's *Lucía*, Vega's *El retrato de Teresa*), Tabío's transposition of the woman-as-nation allegory to the comedy genre can be read as an interrogation of the role that gender plays in the island's social formations and in its cultural products. Furthermore, this transposition serves to reflect critically about the implications of the equation woman-as-nation in some contemporary academic studies addressing Latin American cultures.[44] Thus, the incorporation of a hypermelodramatic *telenovela* style in the film becomes not only one of the ways in which Tabío "intentionally" parodies ICAIC's allegorizing tradition but also an avenue for exploring the relationship between gender and melodramatic texts such as *telenovelas*.

In "The Melodrama in Latin America," Ana M. López explores the way in which a dialogical relationship has developed between "telenovelas" and the New Latin American Cinema. When examining the case of Cuba, López explains that "the cinema has looked to television in order to increase the size and composition of its national and international audience."[45] She adds that "the search for popular mass audiences has led Cuban filmmakers to adopt the still popular melodramatic forms and televisual styles and to recirculate and reformulate these discourses in order to facilitate their critical apprehension by a general public."[46] By exploring Cuba's national conflict in the microcosm of the home through the constant confrontations of Concha with Clarita, Tabío's film presents a parodic reformulating of what López has called "the thematic characteristics of the melodramatic 'telenovela'—the emphasis on contemporary women, the family and problems of contemporary society."[47]

Other Cuban films, like Solás's *Lucía* and Vega's *El retrato de Teresa,* also investigate national issues by looking at women and their role in society.[48] Yet two main differences set these films apart from *Plaff:* the home does not constitute the primary metaphorical space for the general conflicts of the nation, and the conflict revolves around a woman and a man, not two women. These earlier films primarily deal with issues related to machismo and use the home as one of the referents for exploring the differences between the articulation of social discourses about gender equality in the domestic sphere and the public sphere (especially, the workplace). For example, in the third segment of *Lucía,* Tomás's exaggerated jealousy forces Lucía to quit her job in the fields and stay home after they get married. For a while, Lucía is literally confined to the house. Yet, her "prison" becomes the place where she finds freedom via education (through the republic's literacy campaign). Although this segment's conclusion might be somewhat ambiguous, by the end Lucía has articulated that she cannot go back to Tomás if he does not change his *machista* attitudes. *El retrato de Teresa* also juxtaposes the domestic and the public realms as a way of commenting on how Cuban women can find themselves caught up between their duties to the republic and their duties to their families and households. Although Teresa takes excellent care of her house and family, Ramón, her husband, keeps complaining about Teresa's dedication to (cultural) activities outside the home. After trying to reconcile with her abusive and adulterous husband, Teresa walks away from him. In fact, the narrative of *El retrato de Teresa* as well as the three different stories that compose *Lucía* begin and end in a space outside the home, whereas *Plaff*'s story opens and closes in the same location: Concha's house (and this order applies to the film with and without the "accidental intervention" of the projectionist).[49]

Rather than serving as a focal point for exploring machismo's double standards, in *Plaff* the home works as a convenient location where two different Cuban generations coexist and collide. After getting married, José Ramón and Clarita move in with Concha because they do not have any other place to live. This situation provokes a number of heated encounters between Clarita and Concha, who thinks that what Clarita ultimately wants to do is to throw her out of the house and keep it for herself. Thus, the house becomes the symbol of Cuba in the late 1980s, and the conflict between these two characters can be translated as the battle over who will determine the island's ideological future.

Although these two women have one argument outside the house (at Concha's workplace), the rest of their encounters happen while they are in the home and revolve around their having to share a living space.[50] In fact, all the scenes in which eggs are thrown at Concha take place while she is at her house. *Plaff*'s circumscription of the main tension within the domestic space of the house can be understood as part of what B. Ruby Rich calls "the current phase" of the New Latin American Cinema that "turn[s] away from the epic toward the chronicle, a record of a time in which no spectacular events occur but in which the extraordinary nature of the everyday is allowed to surface."[51] Furthermore, *Plaff*'s circumscription within the domestic sphere facilitates the incorporation of melodramatic or "tele-novelistic" elements.

Although other Cuban films have also incorporated melodramatic elements to their narratives, *Plaff*'s use of melodrama, especially in the construction of Concha as a character, differs from other "classical" Cuban films.[52] For example, *Lucía* overtly links the personal conflicts of its three main characters, the three different Lucías, to Cuba's history and politics. The betrayal of the first Lucía by her suitor Rafael works as a metaphor of Spain's political treatment of Cuba during the late nineteenth century. This metaphoric correspondence permits audiences to read Lucía's public assassination of Rafael not only as a crime of passion but also as a patriotic act. Lucía's unstable marriage and her ensuing widowhood in the film's second segment symbolically stand for the island's precarious political position during the 1930s and the failed 1933 revolution, respectively.[53] Finally, Lucía's tribulations with her husband's unfair *machista* treatment in the film's last segment suggests that the Cuban republic faces some serious internal social problems that need to be addressed immediately.[54]

In contrast to the three Lucías, Concha's personal conflicts revolve around exaggerated fears of being deceived and abandoned by men, resulting from her late husband's numerous illicit love affairs. Concha is constantly presented as a frightened, paranoid, distrustful woman who cannot fully enjoy life and who consequently makes life difficult for those close to her. Tabío presents Concha's emotions through the use of a melodramatic *telenovela* style. In her analysis of Pastor Vega's *Habanera* (1984), López describes this style as the transformation of "the everyday spaces of the heroine into sites of emotional signification that are explored through the insistent use of closeups."[55] However, *Plaff*'s farfetched accentuation of this style—in terms of acting, music, camera angles, plot twists—works to change Concha's emotional reactions into humorous subtle comments on gender roles in Cuba. The scenes when Concha talks to the *Virgen Santa Bárbara* exemplify these changes, especially the scene in which Concha bitterly remarks to the figure: "For you it's easy, you can be a man or a woman at your leisure, but I'm a woman from the moment that I wake up till I go to bed."[56] Another example is the moment after Concha observes her suitor, Tomás, give a ride to a young woman who had begged him to drive her to a club. Concha starts to doubt Tomás's faithfulness and goes into a depressed state. The action cuts to an extreme close-up of Concha's anguished profile coming in and out of the frame as she swings in a rocking chair. The intermittent visual disruption produced by Concha's swinging destabilizes the familiar style and conventions of a *telenovela* used in this scene—the protagonist's expressions of suffering, the dimly lit atmosphere of the room, and the overdetermined emotionalism of the nondiegetic piano score—to the point of rendering the situation risible, hyperbolic, and absurd. In this manner, *Plaff* sardonically comments on *telenovelas* and their style, while still "taking advantage of some television techniques . . . to make [itself] more accessible to audiences."[57]

The role of *telenovelas* and melodramas in relation to the Cuban social imaginary is further examined in a scene in which Concha and two female friends actually watch a *telenovela*. While a fight between a couple in the *telenovela* can be heard in the background, Concha's friends are shown having an extremely emotional response to the televisual text. The two women sob and express their sadness and disdain for men, with Concha perplexed by their reaction. Although the film presents Concha as a character who does not seem to understand the codes of popular media culture,[58] her unresponsiveness to the *telenovela* is significant because it marks a departure for this otherwise very emotional character. Concha's indifference can be read as a challenge to the myths and misconceptions of *telenovelas* and melodramas in general as texts full of excessively emotional elements that foster political and ideological alienation in their (mainly female) audiences.[59] This scene also provides an intertextual reference to *El retrato de Teresa,* which included two scenes in which three different female characters from different social and racial backgrounds are shown watching a *telenovela* (interestingly, none of them is Teresa).

Although Concha's conflicts arise from her relationships with men (her late husband, Tomás, José Ramón), her emotional outbursts are triggered by Clarita. For Concha, Clarita represents part of an inconsiderate younger generation that does not valorize the advantages brought by the Revolution. As Concha says in one scene in which she had fought with Clarita over certain administrative procedures: "[Clarita] thinks like that all the time. For her everything is absurd and everything is incorrectly done. A humble girl to whom the Revolution has given everything, including a career, and she's always protesting, protesting, protesting." For her part, Clarita condemns her mother-in-law for being antiquated and narrow-minded when it comes to facing Cuban life in the late 1980s. Clarita wants Concha to understand that blind dogmatism is one of the main issues hindering the republic's development. For Clarita, to be critical of what does not work in Cuban society does not constitute an anti-Revolutionary position. The battle between the two women develops until Concha dies of a heart attack because of her paranoia about being tormented through witchcraft. Nevertheless, her death takes on a new meaning when the "first reel" reveals that Concha herself was the first person to throw an egg with an evil spell (in this case, a spell to drive Clarita away from José Ramón). Concha's (self-inflicted) death suggests that part of the survival of Cuban society depends on the negotiation of the different ideological positions that exist in the island. The ideals of the Revolution cannot be dogmatically lived thirty years after the island's independence. However, Concha's death does not represent the triumph of Clarita's generation. Clarita's entrapment in the gargantuan bureaucratic nightmare of the Cuban government shows that having a critical stance toward the Revolution does not necessarily offer any solution out of the problems existing in Cuban society.[60] It might be a start, but there is a lot of work to be done.

Conclusion

Through the everyday lives of Concha and Clarita, *Plaff* succeeds in commenting on the social and political state of Cuba during the late 1980s. The film's comedic effects achieved through parody "clearly function as a way of addressing and engaging the Cuban audience in serious national issues."[61] In addition, the use of parody to interject these comments establishes a fairly safe arena for rethinking and negotiating Cuba's social, political, and cultural positions because "parody's transgressions ultimately remain authorized—authorized by the very norm that seeks to subvert."[62] Thus, Tabío's constant mockery of cinema and its practices makes it acceptable to interrogate problems existing in Cuban society, such as the extreme governmental bureaucratization that still hinders the lives of Cubans. The use of parody to promote critical dialogue points at another challenge that ICAIC filmmakers have been facing since the late 1980s: how to find creative ways to comment on Cuba's contemporary life without being condemned by the government for not adhering to the republic's Revolutionary agenda. Although questions about artistic freedom vis-à-vis Cuba's government are not new,[63] the polemic banning in 1991 of Daniel Díaz Torres's film *Alicia en el pueblo de Maravillas* pointed at the precarious position in which filmmakers could find themselves while attempting to explore the relevant issues affecting their society.[64]

Tabío's post-*Plaff* directing collaborations with Gutiérrez Alea, *Fresa y chocolate* (1993) and *Guantanamera* (1995), present another side of this filmmaker's career.[65] Although these films use a very traditional style of cinematic storytelling, both of them examine pressing issues affecting Cuban society:

homophobia and the question of what constitutes a "true" Revolutionary subject in *Fresa y chocolate,* and the island's material deterioration as well as governmental corruption in *Guantanamera.* Be it through a hilarious parody like *Plaff* or a (melo)dramatic collaborative work like *Fresa y chocolate,* Tabío's films reaffirm the position of a filmmaker who wants to engage audiences in critical dialogues while still providing them with "imperfect" entertainment.

Notes

Earlier versions of this paper were presented in 1994 at the Society for Cinema Studies Conference and at the Fifth Berkeley Film Conference. I thank David Anderson, Jossianna Arroyo, Teshome Gabriel, Bambi Haggins, and Marilyn Manners for their comments and suggestions on earlier versions of this essay. I am extremely grateful to Ana M. López for generously sharing materials on Cuban cinema that I might not have had access to otherwise and for asking key questions that helped me rethink and better contextualize certain parts of my argument. Finally, special thanks to Chon Noriega for his insightful suggestions and, most important, for his constant academic encouragement.

1. For a more detailed explanation of the different historical components that led to the official constitution of the New Latin American Cinema, see Ana M. López, "An 'Other' History: The New Latin American Cinema," in *Resisting Images: Essays on Cinema and History,* ed. Robert Sklar and Charles Musser (Philadelphia: Temple University Press, 1990), 308–30.

2. In "Eurocentrism, Afrocentrism, Polycentrism: Theories of Third Cinema," Robert Stam identifies some of the changes that affected Latin America—as well as the rest of the world order—during the 1980s. As he states: "what was once called the period of 'third world euphoria' has given way to the 'crisis of existing socialisms,' the frustration of the hoped-for 'tricontinental revolution' (with Ho Chi Minh, Frantz Fanon, and Che Guevara as key symbolic figures), the realization that the 'wretched of the earth' are not unanimously revolutionary (nor necessarily allies to one another), and the recognition that the international geo-politics and the global economic system have obliged even socialist regimes to make some kind of peace with transnational capitalism." In *Otherness and the Media: The Ethnography of the Imagined and the Imaged,* ed. Hamid Naficy and Teshome Gabriel (Chur, Switzerland: Harwood Academic Press, 1993), 233.

3. Néstor García Canclini, "Will There Be Latin American Cinema in the Year 2000? Visual Culture in a Postnational Era," in *Framing Latin American Cinema: Contemporary Critical Perspectives,* ed. Ann Marie Stock (Minneapolis: University of Minnesota Press, 1997), 247.

4. Ibid., 248–49.

5. Patricia Aufderheide, "Latin American Cinema and the Rhetoric of Cul-

tural Nationalism: Controversies at Havana in 1987 and 1989," *Quarterly Review of Film and Video* 12.4 (1991): 62.

6. For a detailed examination of the multiple changes that the ICAIC underwent during these years, see Paulo Antonio Paranaguá's "News from Havana: A Restructuring of the Cuban Cinema," *Framework* 35 (1988): 88–103; and Peter B. Shumann, *Historia del cine latinoamericano* (Buenos Aires, Argentina: Legasa, 1987), 176–79.

7. Paranaguá, "News from Havana," 91.

8. Ibid.

9. The title, *Se permuta,* literally means "for exchange." In the context of the film, it refers to the act of exchanging a housing space for another.

10. The title of the film, *Plaff,* is an onomatopoeia for the sound produced when an egg crashes against a surface. The second part of the title means "too afraid of life."

11. Galiano also informs that the film won the best screenplay award as well as the third-place award for fiction film in the 10th International Film Festival of the New Latin American Cinema. In "Plano general," *Cine Cubano* 126 (1989): 94.

12. Ibid.

13. Alex Fleites, "*¡Plaff!* o el sonido del riesgo," *Cine Cubano* 125 (1989): 86.

14. Maryse Condé, "Cinema, Literature, and Freedom," *Ex-Iles: Essays on Caribbean Cinema,* ed. Mbye Cham (Trenton, N.J.: AWP, 1992), 372. Condé's essay explores the different issues affecting the constitution of a Caribbean cinema. She points out that the main problems faced by Caribbean countries are those related to film production and exhibition. Condé presents the example of the Cuban government's involvement in the island's film industry as one of the few viable economic alternatives to emerge in this geocultural area. Yet this involvement is not without problems. As she states: "Since it was a sponsor, the state wanted to get its money's worth, and the official/filmmaker became the *griot* of a system."

15. Ibid.

16. Tabío continues his self-reflexive exploration of cinema in his most contemporary films *El elefante y la bicicleta* (1995) and *Enredando sombras* (1998).

17. Julio García Espinosa, "Por un cine imperfecto," 1969, in *Hojas de cine,* vol. 3 (Mexico City: Cultura Universitaria, 1988), 77. As Michael Chanan puts it "imperfect cinema requires socially and politically functional films . . . [in them] the style and the idiom of the film is subordinate to its purposes, never the other way round." In *The Cuban Image: Cinema and Cultural Politics in Cuba* (London: BFI Publishing, 1985), 284.

18. Julio García Espinosa, "Respuesta de Julio García Espinosa a la revista chilena de cine *Primer Plano,*" 1972, *Hojas de cine,* vol. 3 (México: Cultura Universitaria, 1988), 90–91.

19. Ana M. López, "Parody, Underdevelopment, and the New Latin American Cinema," *Quarterly Review of Film and Video* 12.1/2 (1990): 65.

20. In an interview with Dennis West, film director Daniel Díaz Torres *(Alicia en el pueblo de Maravillas)* explains that Cuba's economic condition constitutes the principal problem that ICAIC filmmakers have been facing since the mid-1980s. As he says, "The economic condition holds us back. Our annual production of features has dropped from six or eight to only two or three. And documentary production has also declined." Díaz Torres indicates that coproductions with other countries have become one of the approaches to solve this financial problem. He states, "The funds that flow in from these projects can be reinvested in our own productions. We've got to move beyond this difficult stage and make a great effort to maintain Cuban film production." Díaz Torres has since directed other films, including *Quiéreme y verás* (1995). In Dennis West, "Alice in a Cuban Wonderland: An Interview with Daniel Díaz Torres," *Cineaste* 20.1 (1993): 27.

21. Linda Hutcheon, *Theory of Parody: The Teachings of Twentieth-Century Art Forms* (New York: Methuen, 1985), 32.

22. In fact, it is also necessary to remember that the audience's context of reception also informs the understanding of a text as parody. For example, my original reading of *Plaff* as a parody was strongly dependent on the folklore and popular sayings of the Caribbean island where I grew up, Puerto Rico. *Plaff*'s plot is constructed around the mystery of who is tormenting Concha by throwing eggs at her with "evil spells" on them. At a cinematic level the film is constructed around narrative and technological errors such as ending the film with the story's first sequence, having images upside down, and having dialogues and images out of sync. Although it might not seem evident, the film's story and its cinematic construction have something in common. In Puerto Rico, one of the popular connotations of the word "egg" is "error" or "mistake." Similarly, if a film, a theater play or a television show has any kind of flaw—in terms of technical elements or performance—when it is presented, these flaws or errors are referred to as "huevos." Thus, *Plaff*'s story and its filmic discourse are constructed around the parodic juxtaposition of the literal and the popular meanings of the word "egg."

23. Julianne Burton, "Revolutionary Cuban Cinema: An Introduction," *Jump Cut* 19 (1978): 19.

24. Octavio Cortázar's documentary short *Por primera vez* (1967) provides an insight to the work of these "cine móvil" units.

25. Tzavi Medin, *Cuba: The Shaping of a Revolutionary Consciousness,* trans. Martha Grenzback (Boulder, Colo.: Lynne Rienner Publishing, 1990), 90.

26. Linda Hutcheon, "An Epilogue: Postmodern Parody: History, Subjectivity, and Ideology," *Quarterly Review of Film and Video* 12.1/2 (1990): 125.

27. Other Cuban comedies like *Las aventuras de Juan Quin Quin* and *La*

muerte de un burócrata also use their opening sequence/credits to set their agendas, either in terms of style or the topics that will be explored. As Anna Marie Taylor argues in her essay "Imperfect Cinema, Brecht, and *The Adventures of Juan Quin Quin*," one of the film's main projects is to deconstruct the conventions and techniques associated with mainstream (Hollywood) cinema. In order to perform this task, *Juan Quin Quin* is constructed as "primarily escapades through different cinematic genres," starting with "the introduction and credits [which come] straight out of cinemascope Westerns" (*Jump Cut* 20 [1979]: 27). *La muerte de un burócrata*'s opening credits are presented as a series of resolutions signed by the film's director, Gutiérrez Alea. These resolutions, which are shown through the unfolding of a roll of paper, include five sections: (1) to name those who have taken part on the film, (2) to disclose the names of those who worked behind the cameras, (3) to disclose the names of the musical pieces used in the film and their authors, (4) to solemnly declare gratitude to different agencies who contributed in the making of the film, and (5) to dedicate this film to a number of artists. (Interestingly, the only Cuban name included in the list of people to whom Gutiérrez Alea dedicates the film—a list that comprises a diverse number of artists ranging form Luis Buñuel, Akira Kurosawa, and Marilyn Monroe, to Jean Vigo and Orson Welles—is *Plaff*'s director and his future collaborator, Juan Carlos Tabío.) The credits-as-a-resolution format announces the director's satirical perspective on the prominence of bureaucracy in Cuba.

28. Tomás Gutiérrez Alea, "La dialéctica del espectador," 1982, *Hojas de cine*, vol. 3 (México: Cultura Universitaria, 1988), 189.

29. Hutcheon, *Theory of Parody*, 11.

30. *Plaff*'s plot also explores this idea of accelerating the creation of things for the wrong reasons through the character of Clarita, who constantly tries to persuade different bureaucrats to produce industrial quantities of an inexpensive polymer she has invented (which will represent a benefit for the island's economy). After Clarita has been turned down by a number of these bureaucrats, one comes to her house and informs her that they will build a factory for the production of the polymer. He also adds that they have only a month to construct it because they need to inaugurate it on the day designated to commemorate the role of the chemist in society. Although Clarita complains about the folly of this idea, the man informs her that it will be done that way.

31. This (intentional) break in the film's chronological order provides a twist to earlier examples of nonlinear storytelling in Cuba. Whereas *Las Aventuras de Juan Quin Quin* did not follow a chronological order as a way of breaking away from the traditional film structure (and presumably enabling audiences to become more critical of the cinematic experience), *Plaff* uses it as a device to keep the audience interested in discovering both who is throwing eggs at Concha and who was the first person to do it.

32. Paranaguá, "News from Havana," 99.

33. John King, *Magical Reels: A History of Cinema in Latin America* (London: Verso, 1990), 165.

34. Quoted in Paranaguá, "News from Havana," 100.

35. This technique that *Plaff* borrows from *Las aventuras de Juan Quin Quin* has also a thematic continuity with *La muerte de un burócrata,* in which the main issue explored was how oppressive bureaucracy can become even in a society that has achieved its main goal, independence. Most recently, Tomás Gutiérrez Alea explored bureaucracy again in *Guantanamera* (1995).

36. Timothy Barnard, "Death Is Not True: Form and History in Cuban Film," *Mediating Two Worlds: Cinematic Encounters in the Americas,* ed. John King, Ana M. López, and Manuel Alvarado (London: BFI Publishing, 1993), 234–35.

37. Susana Velleggia explains that although García Espinosa has attempted to clarify the meaning of the adjective "imperfect" in "imperfect cinema," especially in terms of style, some superficial interpretations of the concept based on ideas of laxity and negligence still exist. In *Cine: Entre el espectáculo y la realidad* (Mexico City: Claves Latinoamericanas, 1986), 126.

38. Marvin D'Lugo, "Transparent Woman: Gender and Nation in Cuban Cinema," in *Mediating Two Worlds,* ed. King, López, and Alvarado, 287.

39. Ronald Gottesman, "Film Parody: An Immodest Proposal," *Quarterly Review of Film and Video* 12.1/2 (1990): 2.

40. Espinosa, "Por un cine imperfecto," 76.

41. It is important to remember that even though Cuba has a particularly strenuous economic situation (mainly, but not exclusively, because of the U.S. embargo), Castro's government has always been generous when it comes to sponsoring ICAIC's filmmaking projects.

42. D'Lugo, "Transparent Woman," 280.

43. Ibid., 287.

44. See, for example, Doris Summer, "Irresistible Romance: The Foundational Fictions of Latin America," in *Nation and Narration,* ed. Homi K. Bhabha (London: Routledge, 1990), 71–98; and Teshome H. Gabriel, "Thoughts on Nomadic Aesthetics and Black Independent Cinema: Traces of a Journey," in *Out There: Marginalization and Contemporary Cultures,* ed. Russell Ferguson, Martha Gever, Trinh T. Minh-ha, and Cornel West (Cambridge: MIT Press, 1990), 395–410.

45. Ana M. López, "The Melodrama in Latin America: Films, Telenovelas, and the Currency of a Popular Form," *Wide Angle* 7.3 (1985): 12.

46. Ibid.

47. Ibid.

48. *Lucía* is divided into three different segments, and each one has a central character called Lucía: the first one takes place in 1895, the second one in 1933, and the last one during the 1960s.

49. *El retrato de Teresa* starts with Teresa and her family on a boardwalk and ends with Teresa walking down a crowded street. "Lucía 1895" starts with Lucía and her friends walking down a street and ends with Lucía's unofficial detention in the same street after stabbing Rafael. "Lucía 1933" begins with an overhead shot of Lucía working in a factory and ends with Lucía in a street. "Lucía 1960–" opens with Lucía running out of her house (the scene shows only the exterior of the house) and into a truck that will take her to the fields where she works, and it closes with Lucía and Tomás on a beach.

50. That Concha has to share her house with José Ramón and Clarita can be understood as Tabío's comment on the continued existence of the problem he explored in *Se permuta,* i.e., the lack of housing facilities for Cuba's population.

51. B. Ruby Rich, "An/Other View of Latin American Cinema," *Iris* 13 (1991): 12.

52. Probably the most obvious case is *Lucía,* especially its first segment. For an analysis of the use of melodrama in this film, see Chanan, *The Cuban Image;* Teshome H. Gabriel, *Third Cinema in the Third World* (Ann Arbor, Mich.: UMI Research Press, 1982); and King, *Magical Reels.*

53. The use of Lucía's relationship as an allegory of the nation is further supported by the segment's ending. Lucía's pregnancy can be understood as a sign of political hope for Cuba.

54. The issue of machismo is also explored in other Cuban films, such as Sara Gómez's *De cierta manera* (1974–77), Vega's *El retrato de Teresa* (1979), and Gutiérrez Alea's *Hasta cierto punto* (1984).

55. López, "The Melodrama in Latin America," 12.

56. In Cuban syncretic tradition, Santa Bárbara is also *Changó,* a Yoruba male deity, the god of thunder.

57. López, "The Melodrama in Latin America," 12.

58. In another scene, Tomás asks Concha if she liked the film that they went to see. She responds: "It was very sad." And he replies: "But, Concha, it was a comedy!" Concha then says: "No wonder I didn't understand it."

59. In "Tears and Desire: Women and Melodrama in the 'Old' Mexican Cinema," Ana M. López explains how certain members of the New Latin American Cinema movement severely criticized and condemned the melodramatic films produced in Latin America in the 1930s–1950s for being vehicles of cultural colonization. In *Mediating Two Worlds,* ed. King, López, and Alvarado, 147–150.

60. Gutiérrez Alea's *La muerte de un burócrata* satirically explores bureaucracy's oppressive effects in Cuba during the 1960s.

61. D'Lugo, "Transparent Woman," 287.

62. Hutcheon, *Theory of Parody,* 75.

63. For example, Fidel Castro's now infamous "words to the intellectuals" in 1961 ("Dentro de la revolución, todo. Fuera de la revolución, nada."/"Within the Revolution, everything. Against the Revolution, nothing.") were triggered

by intellectual and artistic debates that question the place of art and culture as well as the notion of artistic freedom inside the Revolution. For more details, see King, *Magical Reel,* 149–153; and Peter Shumann, *Historia del cine latino-americano* (Buenos Aires, Argentina: Legasa, 1987), 159–62.

64. For more information about this incident, see Kelly Anderson, "ICAIC and the Cuban Movie Crisis," *The Independent* (April 1992): 11–12; and Dennis West, "Alice in a Cuban Wonderland: An Interview with Daniel Díaz Torres," *Cineaste* (July 1993): 24–27.

65. As mentioned earlier, Tabío's most recent projects *El elefante y la bicicleta* (1995) and *Enredando sombras* (1998) continue the director's self-reflexive exploration of cinema and comedy. Unfortunately, these films have not had the same distribution as his coproductions, and it has been impossible for me to see them. Short reviews in film festival catalogues (e.g., the 1995 Puerto Rico International Film Festival) as well as conversations with other scholars and cinephiles confirm this information.

Part III

Local as Global Politics

ALTERNATIVE MEDIA

10

Grassroots Video in Latin America

Patricia Aufderheide

■ ■ ■ ■

Latin American grassroots, or "popular," video is heralded for its possibilities for social mobilization and information equity, long-standing issues in development communication.[1] And it has spread rapidly, with the rise of the video cassette recorder internationally. Its use in the 1980s and 1990s suggests, however, that it played neither the liberating nor the demonic role often assigned to new media technologies. It has, instead, often been a useful strategic tool, both on-air and off-air, when used in conjunction with social organizing. Privatization and the end of welfare-state strategies, however, imperiled many of the video organizations established in the last two decades of the twentieth century.

Growing from the Grassroots

The boom in grassroots video in Latin America shared in a much longer tradition of "alternative," usually oppositional media.[2] Video production accompanied the rapid growth of video cassette recorder ownership, often with loosening of import rules for consumer electronics. By the 1990s, although VCRs were still a luxury item, penetration—the number of VCRs compared with the number of television sets—was as high as a third (Mexico), with Argentina (30.5 percent) and Brazil (26 percent) close behind.[3]

Hundreds of centers of production bloomed, particularly in Brazil, Argentina, Peru, Mexico, Ecuador, Bolivia, Venezuela, Uruguay, Colombia, and Chile, with work ranging from union documentaries to church video newsletters and indigenous documentation of ceremonies.[4] In many countries, video organizations were associated with political or social causes, e.g., feminist organizations such as Cine Mujer in Colombia and Lilith in Brazil.[5] Socially conscious independents often worked in tandem with issue organizations such as the Chilean Women for Life, family members of "disappeared" persons.

The most elaborated single institution for grassroots video in Latin America in the 1980s and early 1990s was the Brazilian TV dos Trabalhadores, or Workers' TV, founded by media activists Luis Fernando Santoro and Regina Festa. Created in 1986 by the powerful autoworkers' union headed by Luis Ignacio da Silva (Lula), Workers' TV produced sometimes broadcast-quality works, training tapes, and documents of speeches and events and also has an archive containing off-air and other stock footage. Its projects were built on member enthusiasm. During a 1986 general strike in Brazil, the union-based Workers' TV project suddenly found videotapes flooding in from union groups nationwide. Members had documented local strike events and hoped to see what was happening in other areas of the country. Initially surprised by the spontaneous outpouring, Workers' TV members edited the tapes into a single video. An interunion confederation then distributed it to members, circumventing commercial TV news.[6]

The first developed network of video producers, the Associação Brasileiro de Video no Movimento Popular, also began in Brazil. Founded in 1984 and including some forty groups, it was born out of the videotaping of the founding of the Central Única dos Trabalhadores (CUT), an interunion confederation opposing the state-run union system.[7] Other formal organizations were founded in Peru, Argentina, Bolivia, Ecuador, and Mexico, as well as informally in Chile and Uruguay. In Peru, video centers grew out of long-standing educational work in video done by nongovernmental agencies in both rural and urban areas;[8] a data bank, Videored, was also established, by the Instituto para America Latina.[9] Uruguayan video centers proliferated, involving members in both production and viewing. Even in countries where audiovisual production of any kind was very limited, such as Paraguay, video festivals showcasing independent video were being held by the beginning of the 1990s.[10]

Film festivals began to incorporate video—at the New Latin American Film Festival in Havana, the Guadalajara Book Fair in Mexico, the Gramado and Bahia festivals in Brazil, the Viña del Mar festival in Chile, and the Cartagena Film Festival in Colombia. Regional conferences and video festivals were held in Santiago in 1988, in Cochabamba in 1989, and in Montevideo in 1990.[11] Producers' networks emerged from these interchanges; indeed, some Latin American producers were incorporated into global video networks. For instance, Vidéazimut, with its head in Montreal, Canada, is a coalition of organizations from Africa, Asia, Latin America, Europe, and North America.

Institutions were crucial to this grassroots video boom. In several countries, including Brazil, Ecuador, Colombia, and Chile, the Catholic Church provided funds, in-kind resources, and spaces to show work.[12] Several nations, including Chile and Brazil, mandated public channels.[13] Universities were also important bases. In Bolivia, for example, some universities ran television channels.[14] Film schools have also been important training sites. Many aspiring videomakers came out of the activist-oriented International School of Film and Television located in San Antonio de los Baños, Cuba, which has drawn students from throughout Latin America, as well as a few from Asia and Africa. Other film schools such as the Mexican Centro de Capacitación Cinematográfica and the Guadalajara University School of Video have trained people who have returned to community and organizing settings with their skills.

International liaisons were also important in this growth.[15] Nongovernmental organizations (NGOs) such as the Canadian Vidéo Tiers-monde and the Italian Centro Internazionale Crocevia shared expertise and resources. Northern NGOs concerned with social issues such as maternal health and the environment have supported video work on their concerns. The Rockefeller Foundation invested in bolstering Latin American video, as did the MacArthur Foundation, throughout the 1980s and 1990s. International aid and development organizations, governmental and nongovernmental, have also invested in grassroots video.

Such video was used for practicing public speaking and other performances and for documentation, documentaries, fiction, and critical viewing. Commercially produced work was used to stimulate analysis of media.[16] Unions and social organizations developed extensive archives of meetings, demonstrations, and other functions. The highly organized poor neighborhood of Villa El Salvador in Lima, Peru, for instance, has a historical archive on video.[17]

Video built on the experience of the politicized "alternative cinema," *nuevo cine* (New Cinema), which had its heyday in the 1960s and early 1970s.[18] In Chile in the late 1970s, for instance, an underground VCR network showed banned works such as the New Cinema epic documentary of the decline and fall of the Allende government; *Battle of Chile,* by Patricio Guzmán; and other works by Latin American New Cinema filmmakers, in community centers, churches, union halls, and social clubs. Gradually news reports, documentaries, and critiques of official news circulated on underground networks, sometimes moving the equipment as well as the tapes.[19] That network evolved into aboveground production groups, including

Teleanálisis and Proceso,[20] and fostered more open communication during and after elections in 1989.[21]

In Brazil, the independent social action video group TV Viva used video for popular education, employing "mobile cinema" strategies pioneered by New Cinema activists. TV Viva made public health documentaries such as *The Condom* and analytical documentaries such as *The Drought*, sharply critical of then-President Collor's handling of social welfare in the drought-afflicted Brazilian northeast. Members of the group, working with other social action groups or agencies, would show the tapes to groups of one hundred to two hundred people in the countryside, holding discussions afterward.[22]

From the mid-1980s to the mid-1990s, local "street TV" like TV Viva became a feature of urban life in poor neighborhoods of several major Brazilian cities.[23] A small team would preproduce some materials and project these segments, along with live discussion and presentations, from trucks in central locations. Often community members were integrated into the production process, either as advisors or as producers. The goal was to stimulate public discussion and through it to strengthen community life. Subjects could range from public health (AIDS, malaria, cholera, nutrition) to electoral issues (the importance of not selling your vote, ballot issues such as creation of a historic district) to cultural performances and recipes. In Rio de Janeiro, TV Maxambomba established a routine of performing several times a month in the Rio suburbs, the notorious Baixada Fluminense. São Paulo's street program, TV Anhembi, was launched in 1990. Almir Almas, who ran the São Paulo street program for four years, recalls audiences that numbered between one hundred and five hundred people.[24] In Santarém, in the Amazon basin, TV Mocorongo, begun in 1989, was not "street TV" but "river TV"; members of a nongovernmental organization that promotes public health coordinate TV into their river circuits, providing a means of audiovisual exchange of information and perspectives among river communities.[25]

Similar in concept was Waiting Room TV, begun in 1994 and produced in Belo Horizonte, Brazil. It was projected in several public health posts with a large turnover, thus reaching thousands of viewers per month. Evolving with local community participation, the show interspersed person-on-the-street interviews (some functioning as advertisements for services) with recipes, public health advice, and short children's programs developed by other independent producers. Community residents began to drop into the clinics just to see the latest monthly installment of Waiting Room TV.[26]

Not Ready for Prime Time?

Independent video has always been rare on mainstream television in Latin America, particularly for art-experimental work. Exceptions included the idiosyncratic and diverse productions of the Brazilian Olhar Electrônico,[27] whose members went on to work in various aspects of commercial television; rural development programs broadcast in indigenous languages in Bolivia and Peru;[28] and occasional experiments on cable television, whose programmers often seek out a local or regional fillip to an often largely international feed.[29]

Grassroots video, meanwhile, was typically excluded, both from nationalized and private mainstream television. Producers have had more luck launching a video on broadcast outside their own country than within it, because international broadcasting organizations such as the International Broadcasting Trust, Channel 4, and other European broadcasters have commissioned work. Such commissions also have sometimes stimulated international coproductions among Latin American videomakers, including the work of Brazilian Cecilio Neto with Chilean Pablo Basulto, and give producers national prestige.[30]

In much rarer cases, low-power or other highly local television has provided some access for grassroots producers. ECO-TV was launched by Brazilian social and environmental activists in 1991, with a prehistory to 1978. In four beach communities near Rio de Janeiro with a broadcast audience of 400,000, stations authorized under a peculiar mixed public-private arrangement—they are basically retransmitters that are allowed to carry local programming—would share programs related to ecological issues produced at a center in Rio de Janeiro. The effort drew primary funding from the nationalized Brazilian oil company Petrobras, which maintained coastal refineries and drew constant criticism from local communities for them. The service produced a daily, half-hour news show, all done with local reporters, and a 90-minute talk show. Video in the Villages, a Brazilian project to foment Indian cultural identity via video use, in 1995–96 produced a monthly, one-hour broadcast program linked with the state university and aired on state educational TV, in the interior state of Mato Grosso. Produced in collaboration with Indians and starring Indians as anchors and subjects, it was called *Programa do Indio*. (Although the translation is "Indians' Program," this is a sly joke, since the term is slang for "a big drag"). The program features snappy graphics, teasers ("Identify this place"), segments that parallel mainstream programming ("Indians Who Get Things Done" takes as its model a popular news segment called "People Who Get

Things Done"), cultural information, and hot debates on topics such as ecological damage to Indian lands done by development projects.[31]

This, however, was highly atypical. One producer drew a generally applicable distinction between "those who make TV [television] and those who make VT [videotape]," [32] a logical distinction, given the norms of the television business. Throughout Latin America, television is still highly centralized, usually private, advertiser-driven, and entertainment oriented. It reaches virtually all sectors of the population, typically extending to 80 percent of urbanites.[33] Its programming is anchored with the immensely popular prime-time *telenovela*, a form that straddles the miniseries and the soap opera. Brazil and Mexico export worldwide, with formats such as variety, music, talk, and comedy shows as well as *novelas*.

Electronic media, one Brazilian scholar says, "has involved the selling of the ideology of consumption for those who can afford it." [34] Owners and advertisers are at least as powerful as governments in setting agendas; political change has not drastically affected distribution structure or corporate goals. Brazil's TV Globo dominated the market throughout political shakeups [35] and has now transformed itself into the leading multichannel television provider as well. Even television with strong government participation, such as in Colombia, has a format whose stability derives from advertiser power.[36] Where public- or government-sponsored television is an ancillary service, it is often hostage to commercial forces, as happened in Uruguay.[37] Having many channels does not necessarily mean increased access. Bolivia has many virtually unregulated commercial channels, featuring low-quality, sometimes pirated international programming.[38]

Latin American television can be rich in wit, social relevance, and national cultural style. Recent Brazilian *novelas* have dealt with bureaucratic corruption, single motherhood, and the environment; class differences are foregrounded in Mexican *novelas*, and Cuba's *novelas* are bitingly topical as well as ideologically correct. Characters, as in U.S. popular culture, are complex cultural artifacts.[39] But there is a great gulf between TV and "VT" producers.

Ideological Ambition

Grassroots video production evolved within ambitious ideological contexts. Its development, like much of the "alternative" media, was seen by many as part of the attack on transnational and elite control of information.[40] It has also been seen optimistically, as it has in the United States,[41] as an example of technology's overcoming social constraints, and often with as blind an affection for technology.[42] Chilean Hernan Dinamarca, for instance, heralds "this process that is democratizing audiovisual communications and recuperating Latin American identity through video," seeing video as "capable of showing the images of a society prohibited from recognizing itself in the electronic circus."[43] This focus on promotion of public life directly involves aesthetic issues, he notes, contrasting popular video with crudely commercial Brazilian TV: "The search for a popular language that is not crude, imbecile or manipulative is a very great challenge."

These perspectives partake of a long tradition, analyzed extensively by Latin American communications scholars, of alternative media's jockeying for a place on the national informational agenda.[44] Among the unexamined assumptions that can creep into these perspectives, they note, are the notions that media messages in themselves have the power to liberate (or dupe) and that media production is by definition empowering.

Videomakers have envisioned video with a mission to construct or reconstruct civic and cultural life. In manifestos, producers described video use as "a major initiative of the democratic and participatory use of audiovisual communication,"[45] so that, as participants at a later meeting declared, "our people appear at last on the screen as the protagonists of the time in which they live and to which they aspire."[46] Videomakers vowed to "oppose ourselves to neocolonialist and culture-deforming practices of transnationals . . . and to make video an arm of struggle in the improvement of the social processes that Latin America and the Caribbean are undergoing."[47]

Claudio Ceccon, executive secretary of the Rio group Centro de Criação de Imagem Popular (Center for the Creation of the Popular Image), describes one of the group's efforts as an attempt to promote civil society:

> The Popular Video Project is an experiment with media usually used to reinforce oppression. Our idea is to use it to respond to questions that commercial mass media seem to be unable to address as they should, such as, Can democratic values be constructed within daily life? Can the experience of popular movements be recognized and become a model for others?[48]

These statements echo the long-standing rhetoric of New Latin American Cinema and speak most directly to the ambitions and mind-set of politically motivated independent producers. New Cinema had upheld the social mission of art, as part of the aesthetic of colonized, neocolonized, or oppressed peoples of the Third World or underdeveloped world.[49]

In a time of collapse of political ideologies and of economic crisis, video became, for some of the old guard of New Cinema, a new hope. Mexican filmmaker Paul Leduc called it "the cinema of the salamanders" succeeding the cinema of the "dinosaurs"—his generation. Brazilian critic Fernão Pessoa Ramos called it "the bastard relative, still not quite of a stature with its cousin," the legatee of "alternative cinema."[50] Indeed, many once and future filmmakers and video artists turned to the medium, simply for its affordability,[51] at the same time that nonprofessionals and activists began experimenting with it.

Some video organizers, using that model, have called for government subsidy and support to independent producers, and for independent producers on behalf of silenced majorities to assume the challenge of confronting mainstream media.[52] Speaking out of a long tradition of oppositional media, they called for video to transcend its local and grassroots objectives and to "[conquer] the space of the mass media."[53]

In contrast (but not necessarily in opposition, in practice), others such as Valdeavellano (1989) and Cardoso (1989) argue that the strength of video is in the process, not the product, and that other measures may be more important than the impact of video on television.[54] Examples might be the effect that training videos or documentaries could have on a land rights movement; the strengthening of group solidarity from documenting group events; the forging of international relationships; the building of civic skills; and decentralized information networks. Some practitioners have begun asking how such dispersed practices can evolve beyond, in the image of one Catholic church organizer, the family-photo-album and holiday-slide-show model.[55]

The product/process argument is ultimately one of emphasis, with both sides agreeing on the importance of popular participation in production and the utility of video to support goals such as social empowerment of the disenfranchised, diversity of information sources to strengthen democracy, and the growth of an autonomous audiovisual culture.

Assessing the Value of Video

The history of committed cinema was cautionary for those who dreamed of making inroads into commercial television. Entertainment cinema has always vastly outsold serious filmic expressions such as those of New Cinema. While the "electronic circus" in Latin America may be as vapid and vulgar as anything on North American television, it is also often an indigenous or regional product. People who may want to be "protagonists of the time in which they live and to which they aspire" may not want to do it in prime time.

But in fact, video activists rarely competed for viewer attention with on-air entertainment programming. When they did occasionally get airtime, producers sometimes played cannily on the difference between grassroots and commercial televisual styles and purposes. The television campaign for Brazilian presidential candidate Lula in 1989, conducted under laws that mandated some broadcast time for each major candidate, exemplified the contrast between its candidate and "glossier" ones. In one ad, a housewife threw candidates into her shopping cart as if they were detergent, then testified from her kitchen sink that Lula worked better than the others. The ad frankly acknowledged the expectations and frameworks of commercial television (and packaged politics) and then manipulated them. Commercials like these were, apparently, an important element in a dramatic increase in voter support for Lula and for other Workers' Party candidates in the 1989 campaign.[56] They were coupled, however, with an elaborately organized face-to-face campaign.[57]

In another Brazilian political campaign, for governor of the state of Acre, small-scale video on air leveraged large-scale political results. Workers' Party candidate Jorge Viana, with almost no public recognition, used government-reserved airtime to challenge a candidate from a right-wing party. The rancher, with impressive support in the polls, had invested heavily in high-gloss television. Viana's low-tech ad ridiculed the rancher's grand development schemes. Piqued, the rancher began attacking Viana in his ads. The tactic boomeranged, giving Viana enough support to knock the rancher out of the election.[58] In both campaigns, low-tech video made it possible to use the available time, but success was defined by the political strategizing that went into the ads' design.

Off-air grassroots video work has had a variety of uses, tied directly to social organizing. For example, during collective bargaining, one Brazilian union used unedited videotapes of the bargaining process to educate tens of thousands of massed rank-and-file workers.[59] *The Triumph*, a videotape made by the Mexican collective Video Servicios and decrying rain forest destruction, was widely shown by regional environmental groups.[60] Similarly, the tapes of Brazilian collective Lilith circulated widely among working women's organizations and unions, with some organizations even creating video lending libraries.[61] Video newsletters have sporadically functioned in several institutional contexts.

Confidence building and community pride were other, self-defined

objectives of grassroots video. In Mexico a group of poor housewives resisting evictions worked with producers from Cine Mujer to create a short
training tape, *Housewives,* in which activists role-play an eviction; they repeatedly used the tape in organizing. Some kinds of event documentation
tapes might have this signal confidence-building utility. Also in Mexico, a
Oaxacan village corporately sponsored purchase of a videocamera, bought
with proceeds from migrant labor in the United States and mastered with
the help of independent Mexican videomakers. One product is *Our Cooperative Work Project,* documenting a day of mutual labor to repair the municipal building. Villagers eventually used in their own community meetings a much longer version than the 10-minute one available in the United
States.[62]

One unusual case, in which the social impact was wide-ranging, was
Pathway of the Souls, made in a Bolivian village with the help of independent producers and national and international nongovernmental organizations. Bolivian villagers reenacted the theft and export of ancient weavings
with ritual significance. By circumstance a human rights lawyer in the
United States saw the video, which was apparently originally made to warn
other villages of the possibility of theft. He alerted other professionals, and
ensuing legal actions resulted in the discovery and return of some textiles,
as well as in tightened U.S. customs procedures.[63]

Lowlands Amazonian Indians have used video for information sharing,
organizing, creating a data bank, and building archives of traditional practices.[64] Anthropologist Faye Ginsburg has noted that, worldwide,

> indigenous media offers a possible means—social, cultural, and political—
> for reproducing and transforming cultural identity among people who have
> experienced massive political, geographic, and economic disruption.[65]

This appears to be the case among at least two groups of Brazilian Indians,
the Nambikwara and the Kayapo.

The Nambikwara became involved with video through Video in the
Villages, run by Vincent Carelli at the Centro de Trabalho Indigenista in
São Paulo. This project is one example of a trend to put media in the hands
of people who have long been the subjects of ethnographic film and video.[66]
Many of the groups Carelli has worked with have seized upon video for its
ability to document in extenso lengthy rituals that mark the group's cultural
uniqueness.[67] For them, the process of videomaking, with immediate view-

ing and archiving, has been the center of attention, rather than creating a product for outside consumption.

Carelli coproduced a project with a Nambikwara leader, documenting a cultural ritual. After taping, Nambikwara viewed the ritual and offered criticisms, finding it tainted with modernisms. They then repeated the ritual in traditional regalia and conducted, for the first time in a generation, a male initiation ceremony—taping it all. (This experience is recounted in a short tape, *Girls' Puberty Ritual,* produced by Carelli with a Nambikwara leader for outsiders.) Using video reinforced traditional values rather than precipitating a Faustian bargain. It did change the terms, however, by reinforcing the emerging concept of "traditional" in contrast to Brazilian culture.

The Kayapo are among the best-known Brazilian Indians internationally, partly because of their video work, promoted as a tool of cultural identification by the anthropologist who works most closely with them. Like other tribes such as the Xavante who had extensive contact with Brazilian authorities and media, the Kayapo seized on modern media technologies early.[68] Besides intimidating authorities with the evidence of recording equipment and therefore accountability,[69] the Kayapo quickly grasped the symbolic expectations of Brazilian mass media for Indians. They cannily played on the contrast between their feathers and body paint and their recording devices to get coverage. Even staging public events for the purpose of attracting television crews, they were able to insert, although not ultimately control, their message on Brazilian news by exploiting that contrast.[70]

Kayapo have also used their video resources for a variety of indigenous and autonomous purposes: to document internal cultural ceremonies in meticulous detail; to communicate internally between villages; to develop an archive; and to produce clips and short documentaries intended for wide audiences. Their video work, asserts anthropologist Terence Turner, has not merely preserved traditional customs but in fact has transformed their understanding of those customs as customs and their culture as a culture.

Turner found that video equipment, expertise, and products often fed into existing factional divisions. Particular Kayapo leaders used the equipment in their own interests, sometimes as a tool to subdue their enemies, sometimes as evidence of personal power. Turner noted:

> The introduction of video and its use for such communal purposes will
> inevitably affect the internal relations and level of social consciousness

among members of the community in direct proportion as it affects the relation between the community as a whole and the enveloping society or state.[71]

The Next Challenge

In the later 1990s, with the reconstruction of relatively open political practices accomplished in many places, economic privatization and a push for internationally open markets followed in Latin America. This happened in tandem with an explosion of new communications technology options. Cable TV, cell phones, MMDS (or "wireless cable"), and other innovations brought new consumer choice and the prospect of decentralizing, democratizing, and diversifying opportunities.

At the same time, however, video activists lost international foundation support and the political and moral high ground of working in "the opposition." Increasingly, their survival strategies needed to include competitive business plans. The marketplace was not forgiving to noncommercial initiatives, and newly open policy processes were also subject to highly organized corporate forces.

The Brazilian case was exemplary. The government of Fernando Henrique Cardoso, which took power in January 1995, articulated and began to implement a trend toward privatization, breakdown of old systems of entitlement, and encouragement of civil society. As an anchor to this process, the government rigidly controlled inflation and created a strong currency. Nonprofit video producers immediately faced financial crisis, since the Plano Real dramatically reduced the buying power of foreign grants by shrinking the difference between the dollar and local currency.

At the same time, the broad coalition of forces that brought forth democracy and a new constitution fell apart. Some of the Workers' Party governments fell from power, resulting in collapse of ambitious popular video programs. A certain skepticism among international funders about the wisdom of funding media projects autonomously became general. With the departure of Santoro, who became a political consultant, Workers' TV became a mere service organization for the union. Street TV operations collapsed in Recife and São Paulo. The breakup of Petrobras imperiled ECO-TV. *Programa do Indio* went into hiatus for lack of funding. The ABVP, once an organization most of whose members were representatives of institutions, became an organization largely made up of struggling individual producers. Its video rental business and production workshops failed to cover costs, and it effectively went into hiatus in 1995.

At the same time that economically the movement was thrown into the marketplace, dramatic changes in communications policy promised new opportunities—for those who could mobilize political pressure. In 1995 the Ministry of Communication introduced, for the first time, nonpolitical criteria for electronic media licensing and regulated cable TV. It began to institute enforcement procedures for license renewal. Popular video producers applied pressure on policymakers regarding the issues of community low-power TV and cable TV.

The optimistic argument that market values can invigorate public life became, by the end of the 1990s, a necessary article of faith even among grassroots, social-action video producers. For instance, after hosting a demonstration event of community TV, Julio Wainer, the organizer of the workshop and a veteran video activist and teacher, argued to the ministry:

> Community TV stations can be of fundamental importance for local development, not just in social but in economic terms. People who see themselves and recognize themselves on TV (not only on the crime news or during special election programs) have more tools with which to know and value themselves. Community TV . . . can intensify local social relationships, deepen the identity and diversity of our people, and give voice to millions of marginalized Brazilians. . . .
>
> The benefits are many, not only to the community served but also to business people who will have a chance to advertise; to the electronic equipment and maintenance industries; to communications professionals and technicians; to the public, which will have another place to meet and converse; and to students, schools and businesses in communication, which will have a permanent laboratory.[72]

Unfortunately, far more powerful interests were also lobbying for the ministry's attention. Commercial broadcasters succeeded, at least in the short run, in stalling out reform.

Many of the same problems afflicted activism around cable TV. Although powerful commercial interests and conflicts of interest among producers and activists resulted in a minimalist approach to access channels, the law ultimately did set aside channels for governmental, cultural, and educational use.[73] Funding problems crippled many initiatives, particularly by universities, but one success story was that of TV PUC—the São Paulo Catholic university's attempt to use the educational channel set-aside. It was not, however, one with much good news for grassroots activists. Gabriel Priolli, the veteran journalist who produces the channel, considered the fact that only Brazil's elite can afford cable TV and that they zap between channels, so he adopted a high-culture talk show format.[74]

The democratizers who turned in the 1980s and 1990s to socially committed video faced, by the turn of the century, a grossly unequal race with corporate and political interests that also seized the opportunities offered by open political process and the open market. They also maintained an embattled but persistent vision of grassroots use of audiovisual media, a vision that is likely to be carried into an era of networked communication.

Notes

The author thanks Patricia Boero, Julianne Burton, Faye Ginsburg, Douglas Gomery, Lawrence Lichty, Stephan Schwartzman, Joseph Straubhaar, and Karen Ranucci for contributions and comments. She thanks the Fulbright Commission in Brazil for funding visits to Rio de Janeiro, São Paulo, and Curitiba in relation to popular video. An earlier version of this essay was published as "Beyond Television: Grassroots Video in Latin America," *Public Culture* 11 (1993): 579–92, and this essay also appears in Patricia Aufderheide, *The Daily Planet: A Critic on the Capitalist Culture Beat,* also published by the University of Minnesota Press.

Sources for video include Karen Ranucci, LAVA, 124 Washington Place, New York, NY 10014, 212-463-0108; Pedro Zurita, Videoteca del Sur, 512 Broadway, New York, NY 10003, 212-334-5257; Women Make Movies, 225 Lafayette Street, #206–7, New York, NY 10012, 212-925-0606; Video Databank, 37 S. Wabash, Chicago, IL 60603, 312-899-5172.

1. Hamelink, *Cultural Autonomy in Global Communications;* Atwood and McAnany, *Communication and Latin American Society;* Mowlana and Frondorf, *The Media as a Forum for Community Building.*

2. Reyes Matta, "Alternative Communication."

3. "Region at a Glance."

4. Ranucci, *Directory of Film and Video Production Resources in Latin America and the Caribbean;* Santoro, *A imagen nas mãos,* 59–94.

5. Burton and Lesage, "Broadcast Feminism in Brazil."

6. Santoro, *A imagen nas mãos,* 74–75.

7. Ibid., 68.

8. Peirano, *Educación y communicación popular en el Perú.*

9. Thede and Ambrosi, *Video the Changing World,* 224.

10. Dinamarca, *El video en America Latina,* 121–36.

11. Santoro, "O video popular no Brasil."

12. Santoro, *A imagen nas mãos,* 83–94.

13. Dinamarca, *El video en America Latina,* 151–53; Aufderheide, "In Search of the Civic Sector."

14. Dinamarca, *El video en America Latina,* 123–24.

15. Thede and Ambrosi, *Video the Changing World.*

16. Santoro, *A imagen nas mãos,* 97–98.

17. Roncagliolo, "The Growth of the Audio-visual Imagescape in Latin America," 27.

18. See Aufderheide, "New Latin American Cinema Reconsidered."

19. Guzmán, "El video, formato o arma."

20. Santoro, *A imagen nas mãos,* 87–88.

21. Dinamarca, *El video en America Latina,* 137–54.

22. Di Tella, "Video in Latin America," 45.

23. LaSpada, "Grassroots Video and the Democratization of Communication."

24. Almas, pers. comm., 20 October 1995.

25. Caetanno Scannavino, general coordinator, ABVP and director, TV Mocorongo, pers. comm., 15 December 1995.

26. Cristina Ferreira, pers. comm., 15 December 1995.

27. Meirelles and Tas, "Produção independente—idéias e propostas."

28. Roncagliolo, "The Growth of the Audio-visual Imagescape in Latin America," 29.

29. Burton and Lesage, "Broadcast Feminism in Brazil," 228.

30. Patricia Boero, pers. comm., 1 September 1992.

31. Bastos, "Vincent Carelli dá voz aos índios brasileiros."

32. Waismann, "Produção independente—idéias e propostas," 190.

33. Straubhaar, "Television and Video in the Transition from Military to Civilian Rule in Brazil."

34. Oliveira, "Mass Media, Culture, and Communication in Brazil," 212.

35. Straubhaar, "Television and Video in the Transition from Military to Civilian Rule in Brazil"; Besas, "Globo Grabs the TV Jackpot in Brazil."

36. Fox and Anzola, "Politics and Regional Television in Colombia."

37. Faraone and Fox, "Communication and Politics in Uruguay."

38. Rivadeneira Prada, "Bolivian Television."

39. Mattelart and Mattelart, *The Carnival of Images,* 82–87.

40. For example, Schwarz and Jaramillo, "Hispanic American Critical Communication Research in Its Historical Context," 68; Simpson Grinberg, "Trends in Alternative Communication Research in Latin America."

41. Paper Tiger Television Collective, *ROAR.*

42. Blau, "The Promise of Public Access."

43. Dinamarca, *El video en America Latina,* 74, 116.

44. Simpson Grinberg, "Trends in Alternative Communication Research in Latin America."

45. *A veinte años de Viña del Mar,* 1.

46. *Manifiesto de Santiago.*

47. *Encuentro de realizadores.*

48. My translation, Ceccon, "Uma semente em solo fértil," 28.
49. Rich, "An/other View of Latin American Cinema"; Aufderheide, "New Latin American Cinema Reconsidered."
50. Ramos, "Una forma histórica de cinema alternativo e seus dilemas na atualidade."
51. Di Tella, "Video in Latin America."
52. Santoro, "O video popular no Brasil"; Festa and Santoro, "New Trends in Latin America"; Roncagliolo, 1992.
53. Roncagliolo, "The Growth of the Audio-visual Imagescape in Latin America," 29.
54. Fontes, "Defining Popular Video."
55. Bruce, "Televisión y video popular," 88.
56. Santoro, pers. comm., 10 December 1989.
57. Straubhaar et al., "The Role of Television in the 1989 Brazilian Presidential Election," 52.
58. S. Schwartzman, pers. comm., 12 August 1992.
59. Fontes, "Defining Popular Video," 11.
60. Ranucci and Burton, "On the Trail of Independent Video," 200.
61. Burton and Lesage, "Broadcast Feminism in Brazil," 229.
62. Ranucci and Burton, "On the Trail of Independent Video."
63. K. Ranucci, pers. comm., 23 July 1992.
64. Aufderheide, "Making Video with Brazilian Indians."
65. Ginsburg, "Indigenous Media," 96.
66. Ruby, "Speaking For, Speaking About, Speaking With, or Speaking Alongside."
67. Carelli, pers. comm., 23 January 1992.
68. Turner, "Visual Media, Cultural Politics, and Anthropological Practice."
69. Smith, "Space Age Shamans."
70. Turner, "The Social Dynamics of Video Media in an Indigenous Society."
71. Turner, "The Social Dynamics of Video Media in an Indigenous Society," 74.
72. Wainer, "A TV comunitária de baixa potência."
73. Aufderheide, "In Search of the Civic Sector."
74. Priolli, pers. comm., 15 December 1995.

References

Atwood, R., and E. G. McAnany. *Communication and Latin American Society: Trends in Critical Research, 1960–1985.* Madison: University of Wisconsin Press, 1986.

Aufderheide, P. "In Search of the Civic Sector: Cable Policymaking in Brazil, 1989–1996." *Communication Law and Policy* 2.4 (autumn 1997): 563–93.

———. "Making Video with Brazilian Indians." In *The Daily Planet: A Critic on the Capitalist Culture Beat.* Minneapolis: University of Minnesota Press, 2000.

———. "New Latin American Cinema Reconsidered." In *The Daily Planet: A Critic on the Capitalist Culture Beat.* Minneapolis: University of Minnesota Press, 2000.

A veinte años de Viña del Mar: Por el video y la televisión latinoamericanos (Twenty Years after Viña de Mar: For a Latin American Video and Television). Havana, Cuba: IX Festival Internacional del Nuevo Cine Latinoamericano (December 1987).

Bastos, G. "Vincent Carelli dá voz aos índios brasileiros" (Vincent Carelli Gives Indians a Voice). *O Estadode São Paulo,* Caderno Dois (7 December 1995): 1.

Besas, P. "Globo Grabs the TV Jackpot in Brazil." *Variety* (23 March 1992): 82.

Blau, A. "The Promise of Public Access." *The Independent* (April 1992): 22–26.

Bruce, I. "Televisión y video popular: Las otras caras del poder" (Television and Popular Video: The Other Faces of Power). *CEPAE* (Dominican Republic; July–December 1991): 80–89.

Burton, J., and J. Lesage. "Broadcast Feminism in Brazil: An Interview with the Lilith Video Collective." In *Global Television,* ed. C. Schneider and B. Wallis (Cambridge: MIT Press, 1990).

Cardoso, R. "Popular Movements in the Context of the Consolidation of Democracy." Working Paper no. 120, CEBRAP, University of São Paulo, Brazil, 1989.

Ceccon, C. "Uma semente em solo fértil" (A Seed in Fertile Soil). *Proposta* 43 (FASE, Rio de Janeiro, n.d.): 26–31.

Dinamarca, H. *El video en America Latina: Actor innovador del espacio audiovisual (Video in Latin America: Innovative Actor in Audiovisual Space).* Santiago, Chile: ArteCien, 1991.

Di Tella, A. "Video in Latin America." *Review: Latin American Literature and Arts* 46 (fall 1992): 42–46.

Encuentro de realizadores (Meeting of Producers). Havana: XI Festival Internacional del Nuevo Cine Latinoamericano, 12–15 December 1989.

Faraone, R., and E. Fox. "Communication and Politics in Uruguay." In *Media and Politics in Latin America,* ed. E. Fox (Newbury Park, Calif.: Sage, 1988), 148–56.

Festa, R., and L. Santoro. "New Trends in Latin America: From Video to Television." In *Video the Changing World,* ed. N. Thede and A. Ambrosi (Montreal: Black Rose, 1992), 84–93.

Fontes, C. "Defining Popular Video: Emerging Strategies in Latin America and the United States." Paper presented at International Association for Mass Communication Research, São Paulo, Brazil, August 1992.

Fox, E., and P. Anzola. "Politics and Regional Television in Colombia." In

Media and Politics in Latin America, ed. E. Fox (Newbury Park, Calif.: Sage, 1988), 82–92.

Ginsburg, F. "Indigenous Media: Faustian Contract or Global Village?" *Cultural Anthropology* 6.1 (1991): 94–114.

Guzmán, P. "El video, formato o arma: Alternativa popular de la información audiovisual en Chile" (Video, Tool or Weapon: People's Alternative for Audiovisual Information in Chile). In *Video, cultura nacional, y subdesarrollo* (Mexico City: Filmoteca de la UNAM, 1985), 55–60.

Hamelink, C. *Cultural Autonomy in Global Communications: Planning National Information Policy.* New York: Longman, 1983.

LaSpada, S. "Grassroots Video and the Democratization of Communication: The Case of Brazil." D.Ed. thesis, Teachers College, Columbia University, 1992.

Manifiesto de Santiago (Manifesto of Santiago). Santiago, Chile: Primer Encuentro Latinoamericano de Video, April 1988.

Mattelart, M., and A. Mattelart. *The Carnival of Images: Brazilian Fiction Television.* New York: Bergin and Garvey, 1990.

Meirelles, F., and M. Tas. "Produção independente—idéias e propostas" (Independent Production—Ideas and Proposals). In *TV ao vivo: Depoimentos* (Live TV: Testimony), ed. C. Macedo, A. Falcão, and C. J. Mendes de Almeida (São Paulo, Brazil: Brasiliense, 1988), 173–89.

Mowlana, H., and M. H. Frondorf. *The Media as a Forum for Community Building.* Washington, D.C.: Paul H. Nitze School of Advanced International Studies, Johns Hopkins University, 1992.

Oliveira, O. S. "Mass Media, Culture, and Communication in Brazil: The Heritage of Dependency." In *Transnational Communications: Wiring the Third World,* ed. J. Lent and G. Sussman (Newbury Park, Calif.: Sage, 1991), 200–214.

Paper Tiger Television Collective. *ROAR: The Paper Tiger Television Guide to Media Activism.* New York: Paper Tiger Television Collective (339 Lafayette St., New York, NY 10012), 1991.

Peirano, L. *Educación y communicación popular en el Perú (Education and Popular Communication in Peru).* Lima, Peru: Centro de Estúdios y Promoción del Desarrollo, Instituto para America Latina, 1985.

Ramos, F. P. "Una forma histórica de cinema alternativo e seus dilemas na atualidade" (A Historical Outline of Alternative Cinema and Its Dilemmas in Practice). In *Vinte anos de resistencia: Alternativas da cultura no regime militar,* ed. M. A. Mello (Rio de Janeiro, Brazil: Espaço e Tempo, 1986).

Ranucci, K. *Directory of Film and Video Production Resources in Latin America and the Caribbean.* New York: Foundation for Independent Video and Film, 1989.

Ranucci, K., and J. Burton. "On the Trail of Independent Video." In *The Social*

Documentary in Latin America, ed. J. Burton. Pittsburgh: University of Pittsburgh Press, 1990.

"The Region at a Glance." *Variety* (23 March 1992): 88.

Reyes Matta, F. "Alternative Communication: Solidarity and Development in the Face of Transnational Expansion." In *Communication and Latin American Society: Trends in Critical Research, 1960–1985,* ed. R. Atwood and E. G. McAnany (Madison: University of Wisconsin Press, 1986), 190–214.

Rich, B. R. "An/other View of New Latin American Cinema." *Iris* 13 (1991): 5–28.

Rivadeneira Prada, R. "Bolivian Television: When Reality Surpasses Fiction." In *Media and Politics in Latin America,* ed. E. Fox (Newbury Park, Calif.: Sage, 1988), 164–70.

Roncagliolo, R. "The Growth of the Audio-visual Imagescape in Latin America." In *Video the Changing World,* ed. N. Thede and A. Ambrosi (Montreal: Black Rose, 1992), 22–30.

Ruby, J. "Speaking For, Speaking About, Speaking With, or Speaking Alongside—An Anthropological and Documentary Dilemma." *Visual Anthropology Review* 7.2 (fall 1991).

Santoro, L. F. *A imagen nas mãos: o video popular no Brasil (An Image in the Hands: People's Video in Brazil).* São Paulo: Summus, 1989.

———. "El video popular en Brasil: El momento es de organización" (People's Video in Brazil: This Is the Moment to Organize). In *Video, Cultura Nacional, y Subdesarrollo* (Mexico City: Filmoteca de la UNAM, 1985).

———. "O video popular no Brasil: A febre e as miragens" (Popular Video in Brazil: The Fever and the Mirages). Unpubl. manuscript, 1991.

Schwarz, C., and S. Jaramillo. "Hispanic American Critical Communication Research in Its Historical Context." In *Communication and Latin American Society: Trends in Critical Research, 1960–1985,* ed. R. Atwood and E. G. McAnany (Madison: University of Wisconsin Press, 1986), 190–214.

Simpson Grinberg, M. "Trends in Alternative Communication Research in Latin America." In *Communication and Latin American Society: Trends in Critical Research, 1960–1985,* ed. R. Atwood and E. G. McAnany (Madison: University of Wisconsin Press, 1986), 190–214.

Smith, G. "Space Age Shamans: The Videotape." *Americas* 41.2 (1989): 28–31.

Straubhaar, J. D. "Radio and Television in Latin America." In *Encyclopedia of Latin American History.* New York: Charles Scribner's Sons, 1996.

———. "Television and Video in the Transition from Military to Civilian Rule in Brazil." *Latin American Research Review* 24 (1989): 140–54.

Straubhaar, J. D., with O. Olsen and M. Cavallari Nunes. "The Role of Television in the 1989 Brazilian Presidential Election." In *Brazil and Mexico: Contrasting Models of Media and Democratization,* ed. I. Adler, E. Mann, J. Straubhaar, and N. Vieira. Occasional Paper 6. Thomas J. Watkins Institute for International Studies, Brown University, 1991.

Thede, N., and A. Ambrosi, eds. *Video the Changing World.* Montreal: Black Rose, 1992.

Turner, T. "The Social Dynamics of Video Media in an Indigenous Society: The Cultural Meaning and the Personal Politics of Video-making in Kayapo Communities." *Visual Anthropology Review* 7.2 (1991): 68–76.

———. "Visual Media, Cultural Politics, and Anthropological Practice." *The Independent* (New York; January–February 1991).

Valdeavellano, P. "América latina está construyendo su propria imagen" (Latin America Is Constructing Its Own Image). In *El video en la educación popular,* ed. P. Valdeavellano (Lima, Peru: IPAL, 1989), 73–130.

Wainer, J. "A TV comunitária de baixa potência: Recado ao Ministério das Comunicações" (Low-Power Community TV: A Message for the Ministry of Communications). Unpubl. manuscript, 1995.

Waismann, S. "Produção independente—idéias e propostas" (Independent Production—Ideas and Proposals). In *TV ao vivo: Depoimentos* (Live TV: Testimony), ed. C. Macedo, A. Falcão, and C. J. Mendes de Almeida (São Paulo: Brasiliense, 1988), 189–93.

11

Latin American Women's Alternative Film and Video

THE CASE OF CINE MUJER, COLOMBIA

Ilene S. Goldman

■ ■ ■ ■

For nearly twenty years Cine Mujer in Colombia has carved out a space for women's alternative media in a country with relatively little film production. Cine Mujer slowly evolved from a feminist media collective to an independent production company, producing more videos and filling a need created by the women's movement and the multitude of women's resource centers throughout Colombia. The group merits a special place in the history of Latin American film and video because it is has survived unsteady economics and ever-changing politics for an uninterrupted period of time. Cine Mujer's history encapsulates the changes that Latin American women filmmakers and feminists have endured. Further, the group's successful transition from a loosely organized collective to a structured production company demonstrates one way in which the political engagement of the New Latin American Cinema has been incorporated into today's less overtly militant films and videos.

The number of Latin American women working in short film and commercial video formats has skyrocketed in the past twenty years, especially documentary filmmakers and videomakers working with groups established in the early years of the Latin American women's movement. Catalyzed by the United Nations Conference on Women held in Mexico City in 1975 and by the inauguration of the United Nations International Decade for Women in 1976, women in developing countries began to participate in an international discussion about women's roles in development, education, health care, population control, and other issues. In Latin America, the UN meetings were followed by the Primer Encuentro Feminista Latinoamericano y del Caribe (The First Meeting of Latin American and Caribbean Feminists, hereafter referred to as the Encuentro) convened in

Bogotá, Colombia, in 1981. Although many of the women's movements began in the cities, led by urban educated women, feminists in developing countries were quick to reach out to their rural sisters, exchanging information and working to train women to help themselves. During the UN Decade for Women, many groups formed especially to use alternative and mainstream media to reach women. In most cases, they also sought to infuse these media with new perspectives. Latin America experienced its own wave of such groups, some lasting for one or two months, others surviving for a number of years.

The most prominent of the Latin American film and video groups were Cine Mujer in Colombia, Cine Mujer–Mexico, Grupo Miércoles in Venezuela, and Lilith Video in Brazil. Except for Cine Mujer in Colombia all of these groups disbanded after a few years. Cine Mujer–Mexico was subsumed by Zafra, Mexico's largest film distribution company, and was later dissolved. Grupo Miércoles, founded in 1978, produced its first film in 1981 and, until it disbanded in 1990, "attempted to represent from a feminist point of view a certain 'reality' of women's oppression within the marginalized sectors."[1] In 1983 Brazil's Lilith Video began to produce videos and television programs about contemporary Brazilian women. Emphasizing how diverse groups of women approach their lives, Lilith strove to use video as a medium to aid feminism as politics.[2] In an interview-based format, Lilith gave women, from prostitutes on the streets of São Paulo to sugarcane fieldworkers, their own voice. Lilith Video broke up in the early 1990s, and some of the original members organized another group, Comunicação Mulher.[3]

Videos made by these groups, currently available for rental in Latin America from Cine Mujer in Colombia and in the United States from Women Make Movies, interrogate similar themes, expressing woman's particular reality within a given national framework. Grupo Miércoles and Lilith Video typically used more interview footage than either Cine Mujer–Mexico or Cine Mujer in Colombia. By allowing the women being documented to speak for themselves, Grupo Miércoles and Lilith Video attempted to perforate the class boundaries between filmmaker and filmed. Class difference itself—the filmmakers in these four groups were all urban, educated middle-class women—aided the survival and success of each group, giving them access to technology, training, production funds, and exhibition networks. Grupo Miércoles, Lilith Video, and Cine Mujer–Mexico folded not because of lack of talent or skill but because they fell victim to shifting government policies on film and video production, national economic and political changes, and internal problems.

While all of these groups comprised urban educated women, the Sistren Collective in Jamaica exemplifies efforts made by rural and poor women on their own behalf. Sistren was founded in 1977 to produce stage plays and street theater "about how we suffer as women": "Working-class women's personal experiences form the base and inspiration for Sistren's many theatrical productions, their collective organization and drama techniques. Their progressive political agenda explores working-class women's daily struggles."[4] Although Sistren concentrated on theater production, the collective has also produced three video documentaries, published two books, and publishes a quarterly journal.[5]

In an article on the Sistren Collective, Ketu Katrak notes that "[in] creating an artistic space, through drama, for women's personal stories, Sistren illustrates how the very naming of personal oppressions is a first step towards a struggle for social change."[6] Oppressed peoples suffer not only from political and economic hardship—they also are victims because they cannot speak themselves, their cultural identity is suppressed by the dominant culture. Alternative communications open a space for these peoples to explore their identity, express their realities, and articulate their concerns. As Mina Ramirez notes, "In contrast to the one-way information flow which is controlled by political and economic powers, alternative communication shifts its focus to the stories being told by marginalized and exploited sectors of society."[7] In Latin America and the Caribbean, women are using alternative communication to tell their stories. These stories, once told, provide a common denominator for organizing, acting, and building alternative institutions like women's resource centers. Both the process of telling and the process of experiencing the telling serve to build a collective identity and a self-awareness that has strengthened the women's movement.

Cine Mujer, Bogotá: A Historical Overview

Cine Mujer experimented with alternative communication and gained a reputation early on for hard-hitting films that represented the reality of Colombian women. When Sara Bright and Eulalia Carrizosa met in 1975, they agreed that they were no longer satisfied with simply commenting on, critiquing, or talking about issues that concerned them as women. As filmmakers trained in Great Britain and Colombia, respectively, Bright and Carrizosa felt a need to disseminate information that might help other women in their struggles.[8] They began with a narrated slide show arguing for freedom of reproductive choice. Although *La realidad del aborto* (*The Reality of Abortion,* 1976) did not convince the Colombian Congress to legalize abortion, the experience did convince Bright and Carrizosa that the way to reach women effectively was through audiovisual media. After trying unsuccessfully to raise funds to make a film of the slide show, Bright and Carrizosa made their first feminist film, *A Primera Vista (At First Glance,* 1978). They registered Cine Mujer as a nonprofit foundation in Bogotá in 1978. Cine Mujer's original membership included Rita Escobar, an established actor; Patricia Restrepo, a filmmaker from Cali; and Dora Ramirez, an architect from Cali. Clara Riascos, another Caleña studying film in Bogotá, joined in 1981. That same year, Cine Mujer hired as a secretary Fanny Tóbon, a former Roman Catholic nun with administrative experience whom they quickly asked to join the collective as an equal member.

These young women founded Cine Mujer with the immediate, short-term goals of creating counterhegemonic representations of women and of serving the women's movement with audiovisual media. Their feminism was informed both by the burgeoning Colombian women's movement and by Anglo-American feminist texts that Bright had brought back from her years of studying film in London in the early seventies. Despite their familiarity with Anglo-American feminist film theory and filmmaking and their awareness of the French New Wave, Italian Neo-Realism, and the New Latin American Cinema through their involvement in various film clubs, they did not realize that they were exploring a mode of alternative communications that women in other developing nations were also beginning to find potent. In the early 1980s, however, they met other Latin American women who were working with alternative media to strengthen women's movements. Cine Mujer immediately joined forces with these media makers, establishing networks for sharing work and ideas and ultimately participating in a pan–Latin American television series on girls' experiences, as well as becoming the region's largest distributor of women's alternative film and video.

Cine Mujer's first short films were funded in part by Focine, Colombia's state film agency that operated from 1978 to 1993. In the late 1970s, Focine sponsored a number of competitions to promote the production of short films under 12 minutes. In addition to receiving production funds, the winning projects were screened in commercial theaters before feature-length fiction films.[9] Thus, the audiences for Cine Mujer's first films were predominantly middle-class people who had leisure time and cash to go to commercial cinemas. In an effort to appeal to this audience, Cine Mujer made films about urban middle-class women. Quickly, however, diverse groups began to request and use their material: working-class women's resource centers, high schools and universities, and political organizations and unions seeking to include women in their movement.[10] As their audience grew and diversified, Cine Mujer responded by attempting to transcend the social boundaries in their early films, addressing an imagined community of women rather than members of a particular class, race, or ethnic affiliation. In this way, Cine Mujer participated in the underlying political and economic challenges faced by the growing feminist and women's movements. As these movements grew in the mid-1980s, Latin American women organized and unionized to protect their rights as workers and as mothers. Women created support systems for each other on a community level, encouraged and enabled each other to pursue entrepreneurial endeavors, and—through the media itself—sought to reimage women within the national imagination. Much of Cine Mujer's work in this period emphasizes, documents, comments upon, and evaluates these concerns.

The increased demand for their work helped Cine Mujer broaden its financial support and increase production. Once identified as a conduit for women's issues, Cine Mujer received support from various government agencies, international nongovernment organizations (NGOs), and community-based groups. Cine Mujer's newly established Videoteca also generated income through the distribution of its own work as well as that of other Latin American women film and videomakers. This expansion in Cine Mujer's audience base and financial support initiated a prolific period characterized by a high degree of autonomy as Cine Mujer acquired its own video editing equipment and expanded the Videoteca. Between 1983 and 1988, Cine Mujer produced sixteen works: twelve video documentaries, one film documentary, two short fiction films, and a narrative fiction video.

But the increased demands also led to a reorganization of the collective. During these five years, Cine Mujer evolved from an informal group to an established production and distribution company with a hierarchical division of labor. Although this appears to be at odds with the Colombian feminist movement, Cine Mujer's reorganization epitomizes what Francesca Miller has called "the constant reinvention of feminism . . . visible in many aspects of the contemporary women's movement in Latin America."[11] The greatest internal problems experienced by these women's groups derive from instability due to inadequate resources and from the total commitment required in collective work.[12] Because everyone is expected to do everything, women's collectives experience a high burnout rate. Cine Mujer's successful procurement of financial and technological resources stabilized the organization, virtually eliminating one major internal obstacle. The members' ability to diagnose the collective's other internal problems allowed them to continue producing, albeit at the expense of the original collective structure. In this case, the "constant reinvention of feminism" deferred the feminist pursuit of nonhierarchical and informal organizational structures but in the process brought the group into direct mediation among community-based groups, the state, and NGOs.[13]

For Cine Mujer, this process was aided by the increased use of video in the mid-1980s by the Colombian government in support of its national development projects. With the introduction of U-matic video technology in 1978, video was quickly adopted in both private and public sectors because of its low cost, speed of production, and relative ease of transport and exhibition. But as Ramiro Arbeláez notes in *El espacio audiovisual en Colombia,* "there exists a parallel activity in video linked to official programs on the part of Ministries, departmental and local governments and decentralized organizations."[14] Two state agencies in particular emphasize video production: Audiovisuales, an office of the Ministry of Communications; and the Colombian Institute of Culture (Colcultura). But as Arbeláez notes, the majority of state-commissioned videos are made by independent producers.[15] This makes independent production and the state's own use of video not so much "parallel activities" as interdependent ones. Cine Mujer is one of the most prolific producers of state-commissioned videos, showing a high degree of crossover between its own activities and those of the ministries. In 1985, for example, Colombia's Department of Agriculture commissioned Cine Mujer to produce a three-part series focusing on rural and peasant women's organizing in the wake of the Primer Encuentro of Campesinos. Since then, Cine Mujer has worked regularly with the Ministry of Communication and the Ministry of Health. In addition, state agencies frequently rent Cine Mujer's videos, and many have purchased copies of *A la salud de la mujer,* Cine Mujer's 1992 series on women's health.

Cine Mujer's location among these local, national, and transnational forces resulted in an emphasis on conventional documentary and broadcast standards, together with a dispersal of authority within the documentary across civil society (from the people concerned to various independent and governmental experts). Since 1981, Cine Mujer has concentrated more and more on documentary, emphasizing the goal of conveying practical information. In order to be aesthetically suitable for television broadcast in a very conservative country, Cine Mujer's ¾-inch video documentaries increasingly resembled mainstream documentary. Indeed, the videos made between 1983 and 1988 have excellent production values and are well researched and informative. They tend, however, to follow a predictable formula, combining personal testimony with experts and dramatization. Each uses interviews with the people directly concerned—the domestic workers, the community mothers, the loan recipients—with images of the community efforts involved in organizing and evaluative comments by experts and by women who benefit from these efforts.[16] I will discuss the implications of this aesthetic conventionality vis-à-vis feminist audiovisual production and feminist politics in the next section.

By 1989, Cine Mujer was an established production company seeking to increase its international visibility, to access more-diverse audiences and mass media, and to explore alternative uses of video. Toward these ends, Cine Mujer initiated projects in serial production, interactive video production, and international cooperation. These projects were all undertaken in collaboration with NGOs and grassroots organizations, signaling the start of a period in which Cine Mujer has built a new kind of partnership with various women's groups—these projects emphasize, at both the textual and metatextual levels, cooperation and bridge building among governmental agencies, grassroots organizations, and NGOs as the most effective way to foment change within any and all of these groups. The first of these projects, *A la salud de la mujer* (*To Women's Health,* 1992) was Cine Mujer's first series and its largest project to date. The second, *Ver estrellitas por los ojos* (*Seeing Little Stars with Your Eyes,* 1992), combined psychodrama with video production to empower young prostitutes and help get them off the streets. Finally, Cine Mujer participated in Women and Communications, an Italian-sponsored project to investigate issues of women and communications in Latin America.

A la salud, Ver estrellitas, and Women and Communications also reflect the new shape and vision Cine Mujer had achieved at the end of its first decade. By the end of the 1980s, Cine Mujer had lost many of its original members and had irreversibly opted for hierarchical organization. By 1989, Sara Bright, Dora Ramirez, Fanny Tobón, and Patricia Restrepo had broken with Cine Mujer. Bright, Restrepo, and Ramirez took leaves of absences to pursue other interests and dedicate more time to their families. Each chose not to return to Cine Mujer, although Bright and Restrepo remain in contact with the group; in 1995 they coproduced Cine Mujer's segment for the international *5 Minute Project,* a series of twenty-one 5-minute videos created by women around the world for international broadcast during the United Nations Conference on Women in Beijing, China, in September 1995. Tóbon's departure from Cine Mujer was much less amicable, the result of personality and power clashes with Clara Riascos and Eulalia Carrizosa. Tóbon continues to be the executive producer of many of Bright's videos and also worked on the *5 Minute Project* video. Riascos and Carrizosa stayed with Cine Mujer until 1995, producing more ambitious projects intended for larger audiences. They were joined in 1989 by Patricia Alvear, a sociologist who is currently running Cine Mujer single-handedly, with the help of a full-time secretary and a messenger/ production assistant, while Carrizosa and Riascos take their own leaves of absence.

When Riascos and Carrizosa decided to leave Cine Mujer temporarily in early 1995, they and Alvear recognized that after eighteen years the organization had arrived at a critical impasse. In July 1995, Alvear, with the help of an independent consulting firm, began investigating options for the future of Cine Mujer. This evaluation, performed with the help and advice of all of the former members, will decide whether Cine Mujer should cease to exist, handing over its distribution to another entity, or whether Cine Mujer can evolve yet again, this time as a communications center that would house a library and Videoteca, publish a newsletter, serve as a facilitator for cooperation among different women's groups, and even produce commissioned videos. Although the discussion of Cine Mujer's options may sound pessimistic and may seem to indicate that Colombia cannot support a feminist film and videomaking endeavor, it is important to emphasize the impact that Cine Mujer has made on the audiovisual community. Largely because of Cine Mujer's pioneering efforts, by the early 1990s other groups had begun producing videos that highlighted women's issues and were gender-conscious; the percentage of women working in audiovisual fields in Colombia has increased noticeably in the past twenty years; and the women's groups that Cine Mujer's members helped to found continue to perform important services in the community. Thus, Cine Mujer does not arrive at this crossroads as a result of dwindling demand or a waning women's movement. Rather, Cine Mujer has created a viable space for women's alternative media production within Colombia. Indeed, as the women who have participated in Cine Mujer decide the group's future, Sara Bright was finally able to make a film about reproductive rights and abortion. Bright feels that the group has come full circle, especially since the elusive dream of producing some version of *El derecho de escoger* has finally been fulfilled.[17]

Political Engagement through Formal Dialectic

A close look at select texts demonstrates that despite its internal upheavals, its abandonment of collective production, and its increasingly conventional aesthetics, Cine Mujer continuously developed work that expressed the particular reality of Colombian women. The group's history emphasizes the contradictions inherent in creating and maintaining a feminist film collective within a constantly changing national and international economic, political, and social environment. Cine Mujer's films and videos demonstrate the group's ability to adapt audiovisual approaches and a feminine language vis-à-vis this sociopolitical and economic context, while remaining independent and autonomous. The following textual analyses focus on Cine Mujer's most innovative and successful pieces. Many of these films and videos were produced at moments of change for the group, and their production contexts greatly informed the works and the direction Cine Mujer took thereafter. These analyses include discussions of the extratextual circumstances and repercussions, arguing that both the textual and the extratextual informed Cine Mujer's development over the years. The close readings highlight the core issues of Cine Mujer's organization and the development of an audiovisual language to express women's "distinct vision," demonstrating the inextricability of aesthetic, formal, and social issues within the group's history.[18]

Cine Mujer's first short film, *A primera vista* (*At First Glance*, 1978), explores the contradictions between an ordinary woman's everyday life and the depiction of women in advertising. The film's content addresses issues that were also of major concern to feminist filmmakers and feminist theorists in Europe and North America. Contrasting the woman who "appears" in advertising images with the real woman who "acts," the film echoes the theories of Laura Mulvey and John Berger, to which Bright had been exposed during her years in London.[19] *A primera vista*'s critique of media representation of women adds a dimension absent from Berger's "men act, women appear" dichotomy and Mulvey's discussion of the woman's "to-be-looked-at-ness." Drawing from Bright's inner strife about her own work in making television commercials, its pointed comparisons problematize the female wage-earner's complicity in advertising images, whether as model, cameraperson, or consumer.

The protagonist wakes up and prepares for work, showering, eating breakfast, dressing, and reading the newspaper. Moments of apparent reverie (in color) interrupt her actions (in black and white). Her quick shower, for instance, is intercut with a romanticized scene of the same woman in a luxurious bubble bath. Juxtaposing black-and-white images with color adds to the perception of the idyllic scenes as fantasies and the "real" scenes as somewhat dull. We discover at the end, however, that the protagonist models in television commercials and that these "fantasies" actually represent work she has done. Emphasizing the contrast by alternating black and white with color points out how mass media intentionally undervalue women's lives, causing them to crave the glamour of their Technicolor dream sisters. The formal contrasts stress the contradictory economic relationship between women's fantasies and their daily realities: women's fantasies are commodified, placed outside the "real," so that they must be purchased as object or performed as wage labor.

A primera vista's intermingling of social act and media fantasy became a consistent element in the work of Cine Mujer. Part of its political approach to making alternative media involves critiquing mainstream or official representations of gender through formal dialectics. The goal was to provoke the audience to recognize their own lives in the films, to discuss the contradictions, and, finally, to agitate for change. In the early films, the contrast between the lives of real women and their relationship to their commodified images was deepened by the screening of Cine Mujer's films in commercial theaters before the feature film. Later, the production and exhibition of Cine Mujer's videos within the framework of governmental agencies fostered discussions that examined the official structures, how they affected women's lives, and how they might be changed.

The ordinary woman's envy of her idealized counterpart leads to discontent, as Cine Mujer illustrated in *Paraíso artificial* (*Artificial Paradise*, dir. Patricia Restrepo, 1980). This 9-minute fiction expresses the dissatisfactions of a middle-aged housewife who feels that life has passed her by. Because *Paraíso artificial* is the one early film that has been lost, we must rely on newspaper accounts and memories for an understanding of the film. A Medellín paper described the film as a woman reflecting on her marriage in a direct address to the camera. Flashback scenes interrupt the monologue, illustrating her dissatisfaction: "She is realizing that she does not have her own life, that her life revolves like an unknown satellite around her husband who has been converted into a star." [20]

The attribution of this film to a single director foreshadowed the division of labor and the assigned roles that would later supplant collective production. Individual expression also became a battleground in Cine Mujer's definition of "collective." For Restrepo, *Paraíso artificial* continued a search for a language with which to express women's experiences: "In *Paraíso artificial*, I intended to juxtapose the monologue with the scenography in order to break the linear narration." [21] Like other feminist filmmakers, she strove to create alternative images by utilizing the medium in a more experimental way. She believed that a reordered narrative would cause viewers to rethink their position both as spectators and as participants in the struggle for social equality. This re-visioning of narrative structure grew from two distinct sources—Restrepo's understanding of the French New

Wave, and 1970s Anglo-American feminist filmmaking and theory. Like Mulvey, Restrepo posited a destruction of visual pleasure in order to make way for a new paradigm for representing women. Restrepo's search also had to do with a position articulated within the New Latin American Cinema, a position with which she was intimately connected via her work with the Cali Group and her marriage to Carlos Mayolo. The Cali Group's films and later Restrepo's own films engaged Julio García Espinosa's definition of a socially and politically charged cinema, an "imperfect cinema" that would "show the process which generates the problems" and would be "the opposite of a cinema principally dedicated to celebrating results, the opposite of a self-sufficient and contemplative cinema, the opposite of a cinema which 'beautifully illustrates' ideas or concepts." [22] Restrepo sought to reconcile these theoretical concerns—of gender and of nation—in her work through a formally experimental language that would elicit, in García Espinosa's words, "the process which generates the problems" and would provoke the viewer to contemplate actions for resolving the problem.

Restrepo was thwarted in her formal and theoretical experimentation by one of the problems Cine Mujer tackled in the first five years—a lack of formally delineated guidelines for the kind of work the group wanted to produce. There was simply an assumption that everyone agreed on the aesthetic approach they would take to signify their politics. But although they agreed generally about feminist issues, each woman had her own ideas and concerns to voice and her own mode of expression. Thus, Restrepo's need for aesthetic experimentation led to Cine Mujer's first internal division when the collective rejected her script for *Por la mañana,* a short narrative based on a poem by Jacques Prévert. [23] The script proposed an experimental narrative following a woman through her daily routine of making coffee, lingering on her sadness. The events would repeat, filmed at various speeds and from various angles. Cine Mujer's executive council reasoned that although they liked the concept, it was not political enough in that it did not agitate or offer solutions. Restrepo, dedicated to producing *Por la mañana,* left Cine Mujer in late 1979 and made the film with her own resources. She eventually returned to the collective and remained for about five years. Her experimental approach to narrative, however, led to her permanent retirement from Cine Mujer in the mid-1980s.

By choosing not to produce *Por la mañana,* Cine Mujer steered away from experimental modes of documentary and narrative that sought to destroy viewing pleasure in order to stir response. The work that follows this juncture questions dominant culture through its content, always including a discernible political viewpoint and always intended to be accessible to the general public. These decisions were not a rejection of Mulvey or of Anglo-American feminist theory. Rather, Cine Mujer negotiated a destruction of convention at the level of subtle formal play by using a dialectical formal approach seen in much of early New Latin American Cinema.[24] Still, internal conflicts such as the *Por la mañana* incident reveal the paradoxes inherent in collective production, particularly where "collective" refers to both a work model and an assumed identification. Formal guidelines about Cine Mujer's politics and aesthetics still do not exist, but because of the disintegration of the ideal of collective production and the development of a particular documentary approach, these kinds of creative disputes have not caused other ruptures.

In the collective's third fiction film, *¿Y su mamá qué hace?* (*And What Does Your Mother Do?*, 1981), as in the previous films, Cine Mujer counterposes "real" and "fantasy" within the conventional narrative format to critique women's daily life. The film demonstrates Cine Mujer's commitment to finding a language with which to express women's particular reality while still appealing to an audience that expected conventional entertainment. In *¿Y su mamá qué hace?* a housewife devotes her hectic morning to getting her husband and children ready for work and school. She wakes them all up, sees that the children are bathed and clothed, runs into the street to buy fresh milk from the vendor, prepares and serves breakfast as well as lunch boxes for the children, and feeds the baby. *¿Y su mamá qué hace?* presents these mundane chores through an inspired use of fast action. As the mother goes about her business, her actions are sped up, shown in triple speed with a frenetic musical track. The children's and husband's actions, filmed in real time and accompanied by romantic music, seem slow and deliberate in comparison. In the film's concluding sequence, a kind of coda, the contrast is ironically punctuated in the schoolyard when, in response to the eponymous question, the son tells his playmate, "She doesn't work. She stays at home" ("Ella no trabaja. Se queda en la casa").

The deep affinities between the collective and women's organizations in Colombia appear in *Llegaron las feministas (Here Come The Feminists)*, Cine Mujer's first video, which documented the first Encuentro, held in Bogotá in 1981. Mixing shots of discussion tables, talking-head interviews, and performances, *Llegaron las feministas* introduces the Latin America women's movement in a way that stresses the variety of issues under consideration and the diversity among the women involved. Most important, women talk about issues that are usually suppressed—abortion rights, sexuality (and especially lesbianism), reproduction, contraception, and forced sterilization. They share experiences of organizing women in rural areas, of fighting for the vote, and of being denied basic human rights by the power of the church. Women tell their own stories, and the viewer witnesses the sense of freedom, knowledge, and community that they gain in doing so.

Most of Cine Mujer's video documentaries after 1981 build on the conventional structure used for *Llegaron las feministas*. The video belongs to a moment in Latin America when the number of independently produced films and videos by women was increasing markedly. The majority of these works were documentaries. As Liz Kotz has noted, "[T]he vagaries of sexism don't sufficiently explain why so many women are producing documentaries, since the majority of work is made without institutional support. . . . Certainly documentary work provides an important point-of-entry for film/videomakers involved in collective and community organizing." [25] Documentaries also served the women's movement on a psychological level—allowing people who are underrepresented in the dominant media an opportunity to represent and record their own reality, their own culture, and their own point of view. Cine Mujer quickly favored documentary over fiction production precisely to fill the needs of community organizers in these ways.

Cine Mujer's films and particularly their film documentaries (*Carmen Carrascal*, 1982 and *La mirada de Myriam* (*Myriam's Gaze*, 1986), however, investigate the limits of categories and conventions. Cine Mujer's first film documentary, *Carmen Carrascal* (dir. Eulalia Carrizosa), is a poetic portrait of a rural Caribbean coast peasant woman who developed a new basket-weaving technique and used the income to send her children to school. The filmmakers spent an extended period of time establishing a relationship with Carmen Carrascal, her family, and her community. The resulting film crosses class barriers subtly and sensitively while continuing to interrogate the effect of socially constructed gender divisions on women's development.

Carmen Carrascal documents the life of a real woman whose experiences resonate for many other rural women. It reenacts Carmen's journey to Bogotá to receive an award from the president and tells how this led to marital problems and caused her to temporarily "lose her mind." A compelling intimacy and concern replaces the universal appeal of fiction that gave the first films their poignancy. The Colombian viewer identifies with Carmen's struggles and learns about a part of the country and a way of life that may be foreign. By documenting an actual Colombian woman (rather than illustrating her plight with a fictionalized character), the film contributes to a tradition of using film and video to allow community members to tell their own history. The extensive preproduction period spent developing a relationship with Carmen reflects an understanding of the mode of anthropological filmmaking pioneered in Colombia by Marta Rodríguez and Jorge Silva, Gabriela Samper, Gloria Triana, and others.

La mirada de Myriam (dir. Clara Riascos, 1986) continues the effort begun in *Carmen Carrascal*—to reclaim and record the lives of ordinary Colombian women whose extraordinary efforts to contribute to their community and to transform their lives demonstrate women's productivity.[26] Filmed in muted colors and accompanied by a gentle music track, *La mirada de Myriam* nonetheless leaves the speaking to Myriam. It is her story, and she tells it eloquently. But like much of Cine Mujer's best work, *La mirada de Myriam*'s brilliance lies in its mingling of elements of documentary and narrative filmmaking. The film begins as a conventional documentary about a single mother of three who must build a life in one of Bogotá's *barrios de invasión,* or squatter settlements.[27] But *La mirada de Myriam* quickly challenges viewer expectations for testimonial authenticity with dramatized flashbacks, narrated in voice-over by the adult Myriam and acted by a child actor. Myriam's flashbacks interrupt the narrative present to provide a glimpse of the narrative past, including her memory of having her "evil eye" cured by a mystical healer. As Myriam's memory (narrated in voice-over), the flashbacks introduce her subjective understanding of how her childhood and subsequent marriage brought her to the moment when this film was made. The flashbacks structure the viewer's understanding of her narrative present in dramatic terms, divulging biographical and psychological information that would not be apparent in a conventional or more sociological documentary account of Myriam as an adult. It is Myriam's subjective truth, as elucidated in her flashbacks, that animates the antithesis between her past and present, and between the personal testimony and social condition and the media narratives. Her visual flashbacks haunt us, not only because of the hardship of Myriam's life but also because they testify to the perpetuation of poverty, to the vicious circle that Myriam strives to break. By narrating these dramatized flashbacks in her own voice, Myriam takes control of her history, which seems to enable her ability to control her present.

In *Lucero* (dir. Sara Bright, 1988), the most powerful of Cine Mujer's fictions, the dialogue between "reality" and "fantasy," or between objective and subjective realities, is at its most complex, elucidating how gender stereotypes affect young girls, especially in the poorer classes. Lucero is a lower-class adolescent girl who feels overwhelmed from all sides. Her mother works as a domestic in an upper-class home. After school, Lucero is left alone to cook, clean, and wash laundry at home or to work in a bar serving coffee and beer. She also earns tips in a manner typical of Bogotá's poor youngsters—standing in parking lots, she guards cars for shoppers for small change. When her mother lectures her about her responsibilities, complaining that Lucero ignores the housework to play with her friends, Lucero responds in a hushed voice that she works too.

For Lucero, "safe" places and "fun" moments with friends frequently take on a menacing feel. The school playground becomes a war zone when a group of boys with pretend guns simulate a paramilitary attack, leaving Lucero's doll lying broken on the asphalt. A man dressed in a black wool jacket with a black leather cap and boots appears in the doorway to Lucero's courtyard, startling her as she plays jump rope. As she walks the streets, Lucero is pursued by this (imaginary?) man whose ogling and comments threaten her. Even the relative safety of her mother's embrace is threatened when Lucero dreams that her mother has been mugged on a bus, stabbed, and left bleeding in the street. Overwhelmed by her violent, demanding world, Lucero escapes only in her fantasies. She imagines a middle-class world where a mother *and* a father take her to the amusement park. Her fantasy life is reminiscent of *A primera vista*'s fantasy sequences, reflecting a dichotomy between Lucero's life and an imaginary childhood that she knows via television and magazines.

Lucero was Cine Mujer's contribution to Visión Latina, a project that originated at the 1986 Havana Film Festival. Visión Latina was designed as an international television series composed of programs from ten participating Latin American and Caribbean countries.[28] Each program developed the theme of a teenage girl whose reality represents in some way the reality of her country.[29] Thus, the series placed women's stories within a national narrative for international broadcast and distribution. In this way, Cine Mujer's distribution of the Visión Latina project forged and strengthened connections with other makers of films for and about Latin American women, while *Lucero* demonstrated that Cine Mujer's feminist agenda included reaching across Colombia's borders to Latin American women of many nationalities.

As members of the feminist community in Colombia, Cine Mujer's producers continually assess how they can best serve Colombian and Latin American women. In the early 1990s, Cine Mujer identified a need for health care education specifically directed toward Colombian women.[30] Their project responded directly to the women's movement by reaffirming the fundamental importance of women's knowledge of their own bodies and of their right to make informed health and reproductive decisions.[31]

With financing from the NGO's UNIFEM (the United Nations Development Fund for Women) and CEBEMO (the Dutch international development program agency), they produced *A la salud de la mujer* (*To Women's Health*, 1992), a thirteen-part video series accompanied by informative pamphlets that covers all facets of women's physical, mental, and social health.

A la salud takes a holistic approach to women's health, emphasizing prevention and personal responsibility for health care. The series consists of an introductory segment and twelve 25-minute programs, each dealing with a specific facet of women's health. It covers various stages of a woman's life cycle, from puberty to old age, with special emphasis on reproduction. The programs are chronological, beginning with a young woman's fear about menstruation and puberty; discussing conception, birth, and postpartum care of mother and child; and culminating with programs about menopause and death. Among other issues, the series touches on hygiene, nutrition, infertility, domestic violence, depression, environmental and job-related health, alternative health care, health legislation, and the medical system. Reflecting Colombian and Latin American women's reality, the series pays special attention to the infamous "double day," the arduous labor of a wife and mother who works outside the home and is also responsible for all the household chores.

Three key concepts organize the project: "what the woman can do for herself," how the woman relates to medical systems, and the relationship between the woman and her community. Hosted by well-known Colombian actress Vicky Hernandez,[32] the series combines dramatization, animation, and direct narration. A dramatic narrative organized around a specific health problem personalizes each episode. The narrator interrupts to add information or to narrate the story, connecting the personal with local and national dimensions of the problem. Throughout, graphics, expert testimony, and interviews with health experts and average women supplement the narrator's comments and the dramatic segments. Although designed for working-class women, *A la salud* was presented successfully to a wide range of audiences because of the intelligent and humorous presentation of the series. Each program in the series functions as a single unit in addition to working integrally as a whole, allowing for more diverse uses for the series.

One of the greatest strengths of the series is the emphasis on helping women to help themselves. *A la salud* tapped into a global move to include women in the development process, offering an example of the growing body of alternative media production contributing to, as Pilar Riano Alcala writes, "participation as a central condition and instrument of transformation."[33] Stylistically, *A la salud* combines narrative and documentary conventions and contrasts "fantasy" with "reality," like most of Cine Mujer's other work. Carrizosa and Riascos each directed half of the episodes, and although the series coheres around a Cine Mujer style, each director's personal aesthetic concerns are evident too. Far from undermining the series' impact, this adds to its richness and heightens the entertainment value.

With another special project, *Ver estrellitas por los ojos* (*Seeing Little Stars with Your Eyes,* 1992), Cine Mujer experimented with finding new ways to use video technology to effect social change. In a weekend workshop, the filmmakers taught basic video skills to a group of teenage prostitutes and guided them through the process of reconstructing their own image. While exhibitions of Cine Mujer's work are frequently used to facilitate discussions in workshops and forums, Cine Mujer had never before attempted to instigate change through the process of imparting video production skills.[34] Although it is fascinating to watch the girls participate in psychodrama scenarios (led by Rita Escobar) and to learn how they perceive themselves, *Ver estrellitas por los ojos* is not one of Cine Mujer's strongest pieces. Cine Mujer's talents lie in polished, finished work, and *Ver estrellitas por los ojos,* being more about process than product, does not deliver on this level. On the other hand, it is an important experiment in finding new ways to use communication technology to empower women.

The last of the projects that define the 1990s, Women and Communications, took place simultaneously in Colombia, Argentina, and the Dominican Republic and was a comprehensive investigation of women's roles and concerns in Latin American communications industries. With Women and Communications, Cine Mujer committed its resources to extensive research rather than to a particular production project. Eventually, in the third phase of this massive project, they hoped to use the results of their research to convince Colombian television of the necessity of broadcasting a weekly series on women, to be produced, of course, by Cine Mujer. By 1995, funding and commitment for broadcast time for the series still had not been secured.

Throughout its seventeen-year history, the members of Cine Mujer have maintained the perspective that women have a distinct vision, that women see and experience life differently from men. They have never lost sight of their original goals—to further the feminist movement through the production of audiovisual materials that specifically address women's issues. By the early 1990s, however, Cine Mujer had relinquished its identity as a feminist film collective, operating instead as a production company and distributor. Nonetheless, Cine Mujer retains strong relationships with the

Bogotá feminist movement. Women's organizations continue to view Cine Mujer as a provider of educational materials, thereby providing the group with economic security. Meanwhile, members and former members of Cine Mujer continue to serve on the executive boards of some of these organizations.

The Bogotá film community respects the niche that Cine Mujer created for itself as the foremost producer of films and videos for and about Colombian women. Until Sara Bright and Patricia Restrepo began producing videos independently of Cine Mujer after 1989, no one had challenged Cine Mujer's role as a producer dedicated to feminist audiovisual media. Other filmmakers incorporate gender questions and a feminist perspective into their work, but none concentrate exclusively on these issues. In fact, for better or worse, many filmmakers state outright that they leave questions of gender to Cine Mujer. Cine Mujer was founded to meet short-term goals of communicating to and for a burgeoning women's movement. It became a twenty-year experiment in women's alternative communications that has proven the importance of women's film and videomaking as well as the symbiosis between Latin American women's movements, Latin American women's audiovisual media, and social change. Although Cine Mujer was able to establish working relationships with NGOs, government agencies, and grassroots' organizations—demonstrating the importance of building coalitions in Latin American feminist political action—the goals of the Colombian women's movements have not all been met. Today Cine Mujer grapples with how it can best evolve to continue serving Colombian and Latin American women.

Notes

This essay derives from my dissertation, "Cine Mujer: Fifteen Years of Feminist Film and Videomaking in Bogotá, Colombia." I would like to thank the members and former members of Cine Mujer for allowing me unlimited access to their archives and for sharing their memories with me. I am grateful to Chuck Kleinhans, Julianne Burton-Carvajal, and Chon Noriega for their constructive criticisms of earlier drafts of this article. Verónica Wilthew helped with translations. Warm gratitude to Margarita de la Vega for introducing me to Cine Mujer and Colombian women's cinema. A special thanks goes to the de la Vega family and to all the filmmakers who opened their homes to me.

1. Karen Schwartzman, "A Descriptive Chronology of Films by Women in Venezuela, 1952–1992," *Journal of Film and Video* 44.3–4 (fall–winter, 1992–93): 36.

2. Julianne Burton and Julia Lesage, "Broadcast Feminism in Brazil: An

Interview with the Lilith Video Collective," in *Global Television* ed. Cynthia Schneider and Brian Wallis (New York: Wedge Press, 1988), 225–29. *Beijo na boca (A Kiss on the Mouth),* Lilith's poignant video about prostitutes, is available for rental through Women Make Movies in New York.

3. Sylvia Mejia, personal interview, New York, August 1992. Mejia is a Colombian filmmaker and cofounder of Imagen Mujer, a women's filmmaking and videomaking group established in Cali, Colombia, in 1991. Further information about the exact dates of the Lilith split has been difficult to attain. Research letters and questionnaires sent to the members of the former Lilith collective remain unanswered.

4. Ketu Katrak, "The Sistren Collective: Women Dramatize Their Lives," *African Commentary* (August 1990): 27.

5. Cine Mujer distributes Sistren's videos in Colombia and Latin America through its catalogue.

6. Katrak, "The Sistren Collective, 27; emphasis in the original.

7. Mina M. Ramirez, "Communication As If People Matter: The Challenge of Alternative Communication," in *The Myth of the Information Revolution: Social and Ethical Implications for Communication Technology,* ed. Michael Traber (London: Sage Publications, 1986), 108.

8. María Elvira Bonilla, "Cine Mujer: Un cine de mujeres para todos, contra viento y marea," *El Pueblo* (Bogotá; 11 June 1981), Women's sec.

9. For a detailed history of Focine, see Paul Lenti, "Colombia: State Role in Film Production," in *Mediating Two Worlds: Cinematic Encounters in the Americas,* ed. John King, Ana M. López, and Manuel Alvarado (London: British Film Institute, 1993), 214–21. See also Guillermo Jaramillo, "Focine: Tiempo de morir," *Kinetescopio* 18 (Medellín; March–April 1993): 19. For the official documents creating Focine and legislating its functions, see "Creación y estructura de Focine," 1978, in *Hojas de cine: Testimonios y documentos del Nuevo Cine Latinoamericano* (México: Fundación Mexicana de Cineastas, 1988), 267–73.

10. Unfortunately, economic constraints and the lack of film and video equipment limited the diffusion of Cine Mujer's work to rural areas until the mid-1980s.

11. Francesca Miller, *Latin American Women and the Search for Social Justice* (Hanover, N.H.: University Press of New England, 1991), 223.

12. Gita Sen and Caren Grown, *Development, Crises, and Alternative Visions: Third World Women's Perspectives* (New York: Monthly Review Press, 1987), 94.

13. Ibid.

14. Ramiro Arbeláez Ramos, *El espacio audiovisual en Colombia: Infraestructura y marco jurídico* (Universidad de Valle, Colombia, Colección de Edición Previa, Serie Investigaciones), 15.

15. Ibid.

16. See Cine Mujer's filmography for a complete listing of these videos.

17. Sara Bright, telephone conversation, August 1995.

18. The term "distinct vision" is Sarah Bright's. In an interview in the late 1980s, Bright and other members of the collective discussed the ways in which women and men perceive and see the world differently. *Cinemateca: Cuadernos de cine colombiano,* no. 21 (special issue devoted to Cine Mujer, exhibition catalogue, n.d.), 12–13.

19. Laura Mulvey, "Visual Pleasure and Narrative Cinema," *Screen* 16.3 (1975): 6–18; John Berger, *Ways of Seeing* (New York: British Broadcasting Co., 1977).

20. Carlos O. Uribe, "Un trabajo para destacar: Los filmes de Cine Mujer," *El Mundo Semanal* (Medellín; 7 August 1982).

21. Patricia Restrepo, interviewed by Agosto Bernal, n.d., Bogotá, Colombia.

22. Julio García Espinosa, "For an Imperfect Cinema," trans. Julianne Burton, *Jump Cut* 20 (1979): 26. Carlos Mayolo and Luis Ospina, key members of the Cali Group, continued to work together throughout the 1970s, and in 1977 they produced *Agarrando pueblo* (*Ripping People Off*), a fiction film about foreign documentary filmmakers who scour Bogotá, looking for misery they can film and staging it when they cannot find sufficiently sordid situations. Filmed in muted colors with a lot of hand-held camerawork, the film at first appears to be a documentary about documentary filmmakers. Slowly, the constructedness of *Agarrando pueblo* and of the film within the film are revealed. The filmmakers enter a shack erected on an empty lot and use it, without the resident's permission, to film a scripted interview with a poor family. (The viewer is aware that the poor family is actually a group of actors made up to look impoverished and dirty.) As the narrator speaks to the camera, the resident of the shack interrupts, cursing the film crew and rejecting their money by wiping his ass with it. The opportunist filmmakers keep the camera rolling as he rants and raves. He finally opens up a can of film and destroys it. Then, suddenly calm, he asks someone off-camera if his performance was OK. This episode is yet another staged moment of Colombian "misery" and "poverty." The film reveals constructed documentary elements and their fictitiousness and satirizes many of the state-sponsored short films for using the nation's poor and downtrodden in order to assure box office returns.

23. The poem in question is Prévert's "Déjeuner du matin."

24. The dialectical formal approach derives from an idea of Marxist dialectics that establishes a relationship between human subjective experience and objective reality. Within the New Latin American Cinema, dialectics were used to examine the relationship between human consciousness and social and historical change. Documentary footage and fictional elements (frequently acted by nonprofessionals) are juxtaposed in order to expose clashes between "subjectivity" and "objectivity" and to expose the limitations of revolution. The interruption of narrative flow draws the audience into a dialogue with the film,

fostering an active (and politicized) viewing experience. Two Cuban films are frequently noted for their dialectical approach—Sara Gómez's *De una manera* (*One Way or Another,* 1974) and Tómas Gutiérrez Alea's *Hasta cierto punto* (*Up to a Point,* 1983). Both films use documentary footage and nonprofessional actors as counterpoints to their fictional narratives, causing the audience to think about the relationships created between fiction and "reality" as the films examine the Cuban Revolutionary process. As Julia Lesage has written, filmmakers use dialectical methods because they "work with the confidence that they can elucidate and contribute to ongoing social process, and their work has a unique historical effectiveness because there is a fruitful, dialectical relation between audience, filmmaker, and film." See Lesage, "*One Way or Another:* Dialectical, Revolutionary, Feminist," *Jump Cut* 20 (May 1979): 20.

25. Liz Kotz, "Unofficial Stories: Documentaries by Latinas and Latin American Women," *The Independent* (May 1989): 24.

26. *Socorro Fajardo* and *Zulia Mena* (both 1993), two videos commissioned by Fedevivienda, continued this project in the early nineties. Stylistically, they follow the pattern of video documentaries that evolved after *Llegaron las feministas.*

27. *"Barrios de invasión"* translates literally as "invasion neighborhoods," or "squatters' settlements." These settlements consist of shacks constructed of corrugated metal, plywood, or any scrap materials that families can find. Situated on the outskirts of the city, *barrios de invasión* are causing Bogotá to grow, stretching the city's limits far into the mountains. Because they are unofficial and impoverished neighborhoods, there generally are no basic services (water, electricity, phones, etc.). This is a phenomenon in most major Latin American cities, each of which has developed its own term for squatter settlements.

28. According to correspondence between Cine Mujer and the organizers in Peru, parts of the series were broadcast in Uruguay, and Spanish and Cuban television stations have expressed interest in the series. Concrete information about the actual broadcast and viewership for Visión Latina is currently unavailable.

29. Visión Latina press kit, comp. Panorama Producciones and the Cuban Television and Radio Institute, n.d. In addition to *Lucero,* Cine Mujer distributes the programs that have been completed to date: *María* (dir. Alfredo Obando, Bolivia, 1988); *Janet* (dir. Daniel Diez, Cuba, 1988); *Isabel* (dir. Helle Toft Jensen and Torben Vosbein, Denmark, 1988); *Aytana* (dir. Lola Besses, Spain, 1988); *Ana* (dir. Jorge Bayarres, Uruguay, 1988).

30. Like the women's movements across the world, Latin American women have been responding to the strategies for women's development outlined at the Nairobi Conference in 1985. Leading these initiatives on a macro-level is the World Health Organization, which in the 1980s launched its special initiative Women, Health, and Development (WHD). WHD responded specifically to the international integration of women into development projects

and continues this focus today. "WHO: Women, Health, and Development," *INSTRAW News* 18: 42–44.

31. Clara Riascos, personal interview, July 1993, Bogotá, Colombia.

32. Hernandez starred in many of Colombia's recently produced feature films: to mention a few, *La estrategia de caracol* (*The Strategy of a Snail,* 1993), *Confesión a Laura* (*Confession to Laura,* 1990), *Técnicas de duelo* (*Dueling Techniques,* 1988), *La mansión de Araucaima* (*The Mansion of Araucaima,* 1986), and *Carne de tu carne* (*Flesh of Your Flesh,* 1983).

33. Pilar Riano Alcala, *Empowering Women through Communication: Women's Experiences with Participatory Communication in Development Processes* (Canada: International Development Resource Center, November 1990), 9.

34. *Ver estrellitas por los ojos* parallels the direction that localized alternative communications has taken throughout Latin America. Several urban video-makers have taken their cameras to the streets and put them in the hands of the children who live there so that those children might create images of themselves. In Rio de Janeiro, Beti Formaggini worked with a group of street children to produce *TV Rappy* (1994). The children used High 8 video to represent themselves, parodying and taking issue with their representation on the Brazilian news media. Brazilian television shows them as police cases—violent, drug-addicted children without humanity. Borrowing from the aesthetics of music videos, complete with a "VJ," or guide to their world, the children recorded their own point of view—their culture, their humanity, their dreams. In Guatemala, Ameri-visión, an independent production company led by Austin Haeberle, worked with a group of street children in Queztaltenango to produce a television program in 1994. For one segment of the program, the children produced a music video of Michael Jackson's "Heal the World." While Jackson sings, the camera follows a poor boy through his day, contrasting his dreams of a nice home and a father who takes him to the fair and to the park with his life in a shack, hunting for work on the streets each day.

Filmography of Cine Mujer, Bogotá, Colombia

Projects that are not available for rental through the Videoteca, because the rights are owned by the funding organizations, are indicated by an asterisk. Films that are available for rental outside Colombia are indicated with an asterisk.

Translations of film titles are mine, with the exception of films that have been subtitled for international distribution or were made with both Spanish and English translations for UNICEF.

1976: *La realidad del aborto* (*The Reality of Abortion,* slide show with narration). Dir. Bright/Carrizosa.

1978: *A primera vista* (*At First Glance,* 35mm film, 10 min.) Dir. Bright/ Carrizosa.

1980: *Paraíso artificial* (*Artificial Paradise*, film, 9 min.). Dir. Restrepo.

1981: *Llegaron las feministas* (*The Feminists Have Arrived*, ¾-inch video, 53 min.). Dir. Cine Mujer.

1981: *¿Y su mamá qué hace?** (*And What Does Your Mother Do?*, film, 9 min.). Dir. Carrizosa. U.S. distributor: Women Make Movies.

1982: *Carmen Carrascal** (film, 27 min.). Dir. Carrizosa. U.S. distributor: Women Make Movies.

1983: *Ni con el pétalo de una rosa* (*Not Even with a Rose Petal*, ¾-inch video, 20 min.). Dir. Cine Mujer.

1983: *No violencia (No Violence*, longer version of *Ni con el pétalo*).

1984: *Buscando caminos* (*Finding Ways*, ¾-inch video, 20 min.). Dir. Bright.

1984: *En qué estamos* (*What We Are In*, ¾-inch video, 48 min.). Dir. Cine Mujer.

1985: *Campesina* (*Peasant Woman*, ¾-inch video, 15 min.). Dir. Bright.

1985: *Desencuentros* (*Disencounters*, film, 15 min.). Dir. Dora Cecilia Ramírez.

1985: *Diez años después* (*Ten Years Later*, ¾-inch video? 45 min.). Dir. Riascos.

1985: *La mujer se organiza* (*Woman Organizes*, ¾-inch video, 13 min.). Dir. Bright.

1985: *Momentos de un domingo* (*Sunday Moments*, 35mm film, 25 min.). Dir. Restrepo.

1985: *Políticas de desarrollo para la mujer campesina* (*Developmental Policies for Peasant Women*, ¾-inch video, 10 min.). Dir. Bright.

1986: *La mirada de Myriam** (*Myriam's Gaze*, 35mm film, 25 min.). Dir. Riascos. U.S. distributor: Women Make Movies.

1987: FUNDAC* (¾-inch video). Dir. Riascos.

1987: *La matriz** (¾-inch video, 10 min.). Dir. Bright.

1987: *La trabajadora invisible* (*The Invisible Worker*, ¾-inch video, 19 min.). Dir. Riascos.

1987: *Un paso con la mujer/Un salto al desarrollo* (*A Step for Women/A Leap for Development*, ¾-inch video, 35 min.). Dir. Riascos.

1988: *Calidad* (*Quality*, ¾-inch video, 25 min.). Dir. Bright.

1988: *Lucero* (*Firefly*, ¾-inch video, 25 min.). Dir. Bright.

1991: *Alimentación familia** (*Family Nutrition*, ¾-inch video, 25 min.). Dir. Nhora Rodriguez.

1991: *¿Ella se lo buscó?* (*Was She Asking For It?*, ¾-inch video, 20 min.). Dir. Carrizosa.

1992: *A la salud de la mujer* (*To Women's Health*, ¾-inch video, 13-part series, 25 min. each). Dir. Cine Mujer (Riascos and Carrizosa).

1992: *El juego de la vida** (*The Game of Life*, ¾-inch video). Dir. Ana María Echeverrí.

1992: Mujer y comunicación (Women and Communication, research project). Dir. Alvear and Cine Mujer. 1992: *Ver estrellitas por los ojos* (*Seeing Little Stars with Your Eyes*, Beta video). Dir. Rita Escobar.

1992: *¡Oiga Doctor!** (*Listen Doctor!*, ¾-inch video, 25 min.). Dir. Riascos.

1992: Public service announcements (2)* (¾-inch video, 30 sec. each). Dir. Riascos.

1993: *Lactancia maternal** (*Maternal Lactation,* ¾-inch video). Dir. Riascos.

1993: *Socorro Fajardo** (¾-inch video). Dir. Carrizosa.

1993: *Zulia Mena** (¾-inch video). Dir. Riascos.

12

Local Television and Community Politics in Brazil

SÃO PAULO'S TV ANHEMBI

Brian Goldfarb

■ ■ ■ ■

In 1992, at the ninth annual Videobrazil International Festival in São Paulo, Brazil, Jon Alpert, veteran U.S. video activist and cofounder of New York City's Downtown Community Television (DCTV), was interviewed by São Paulo's alternative television enterprise, TV Anhembi. Standing in front of the dazzling thirty-six-monitor video wall mounted to TV Anhembi's plush mobile production/exhibition unit, Alpert recalled that DCTV "started just like this, with a truck on the street" (fig. 12.1). He continued: "But instead of a hundred TV sets, we had only one and the power used to break all the time and we used to electrocute ourselves. But this is how we started—on the street."[1] Indeed, formal and strategic similarities do exist between alternative TV enterprises separated by nearly two decades, substantial political and cultural differences, and vast geographical space.

In this respect, DCTV is representative of numerous U.S. and Latin American media groups that were formed in the early 1970s through the 1980s with the goal of using Portapak and new consumer video technology for community organizing.[2] Established in 1989 and disbanded in 1992, TV Anhembi sustained many of the defining agendas and practices initiated by these groups. Like the activities of earlier groups in the United States and Latin America, its advocacy and activist work centered on issues often elided by network and public television. Also like these groups, TV Anhembi produced shows that foregrounded current affairs and politics with the aim of fostering television countercultures or subcultures that would loosen the hold of mainstream television on public culture. Moreover, TV Anhembi employed similar tactics for highlighting community participation and shifting TV viewing out of the private confines of the home.

FIGURE 12.1 *TV Anhembi interviews Downtown Community Television's Jon Alpert at the ninth annual Videobrazil International Festival in São Paulo, 1992.*

But TV Anhembi's upscale technical apparatus and government support set the group apart from the preceding examples of community media. The high-tech mobile unit against which Alpert is framed in the above interview should indicate to viewers that TV Anhembi represents a new and significantly transformed relationship between alternative TV collectives and sources of power and finance. TV Anhembi's state-of-the-art technology, along with the scale and sophistication of its productions, suggests an apparently higher level of support than that received by U.S. alternative media groups. What are the particular cultural and political circumstances that made TV Anhembi and its high-tech enterprise a possibility at precisely that historical place and moment? More than anything, its means of support and the mechanisms that brought about its formation are local products of a crisis of legitimacy within the Latin American cultural and political landscape of the late 1980s. The failure of established parties across the political spectrum to garner popular support was clearly registered in the success of São Paulo's nascent Workers' Party (Partido dos Trabalhadores) in the 1989 election, ushering in the mayoral administration of Luiza Erundina. TV Anhembi was quickly brought into being by this media-savvy left administration with the idea that community media was integral to the success of party politics, and party support was integral to the success of community agendas—a reciprocal situation that has few real parallels in the history of U.S. alternative television. As coordinating producer Almir Almas explains, TV Anhembi's goal was to educate people about the potential for engaging in community politics through television (fig. 12.2). By using alternative television strategies, he suggests, "people will learn to find their own solutions to the grave problems that afflict the city."[3] The situation Almas describes suggests that the São Paulo government aimed to use community media to promote a more direct form of participatory politics rather than to consolidate its authority over the community. This strategy was in line with the broad-ranging attempts of the Partido do Trabalhadores to reorient government toward the inclusion of local representatives on neighborhood and special-interest councils.

What, then, is the significance of this one example among the diverse community media projects currently in operation in Brazil? And what are the implications of this enterprise's short-lived history for media activism in Brazil and other (national and local) contexts? TV Anhembi is an important case to consider because it makes clear the complexity and specificity of relationships that currently exist in various alternative television

FIGURE 12.2 *Almir Almas of TV Anhembi, 1992.*

practices. In São Paulo and elsewhere, we are seeing alternative television ventures emerging out of a sometimes unlikely convergence of disparate community interests and broader institutional and governmental politics. It is crucial that we take note of the specific effects these unlikely media alliances are having on programming, censorship, technology access, funding, and so on. Moreover, it is important to consider how these recent projects and programs are changing the meaning of terms such as "community" and "alternative media"—terms that have become commonplace in U.S. writings on video and television history. In the case of TV Anhembi we see the emergence of a new concept of "community" in which television plays an integral role, and a new concept of "alternative media" aligned with state institutions (at least at the municipal level). The Erundina administration introduced some new ways of bringing together the apparently contradictory techniques and approaches of local video activists, government agencies, and popular television forms. Although TV Anhembi was short-lived, it stands as an example of some potentially viable alliances and strategies, and some of the potential risks, of state-subsidized alternative television production. My analysis below suggests that the confluence of movement strategies and government media initiatives can result in a somewhat contradictory move toward both a more centralized and a more heterogeneously community-based alternative television practice.

TV Anhembi's Local History

The formation and role of TV Anhembi were inextricably linked to the political climate of São Paulo in 1989. The Erundina administration, sensing the popular support it might generate with and through cultural venues, established a dynamic network of city agencies and programs devoted to the production of politically informed popular culture—a kind of culture that spoke to the interests of local constituencies and communities rather than to a broadly constituted mass public. This apparatus was coordinated through a newly established city agency nominally devoted to tourism (Anhembi Turismo e Eventos da Cidade de São Paulo) and servicing a wider range of cultural forms, including TV Anhembi. Thus, TV Anhembi came into being as a government-backed alternative media production group and venue tailored to the political agenda of the Erundina administration and to the local interests of São Paulo communities.

But TV Anhembi's formation signals a development much more far-reaching than a single municipality's support of an agenda of decentralizing media knowledge and fostering atomized participatory democracy. This seeming contradiction—state-run media joined with decentralized media groups—was the by-product of a crisis in party politics throughout Brazil and other areas of Latin America in 1980s. As Orlando Fals Borda has explained, since the late 1970s "the loss of legitimacy by parties and governments has created a power gap, which [social] movements, in their expansive evolution, have been filling locally and regionally in their own way." [4] By the late 1980s the ascendant local movements began to form coalitions that were clear contenders for political power. The Erundina administration in São Paulo was put into office by building a form of party politics around a coalition of local movements. Once in power, the Workers' Party government of Erundina made various attempts to incorporate the diverse interests of its many constituents—through the creation of neighborhood councils and other community-focused city agencies, and the adoption of movement strategies designed specifically for local organizing, such as using local community television to foster political participation. TV Anhembi is the product of a media politics that emerged from this confluence of movement strategies and a nascent (and, as it turns out, short-lived) Workers Party government.

In urban centers an array of established local social movements and organizations had come to pose popular alternatives to the party politics apparatus that had risen up to challenge the military regime. This state of affairs reflected a political crisis that was more broadly felt across the continent. The political and economic upheaval over the past two decades in Latin America generally has led to a situation in which many local movements have been able to thrive while numerous political parties founded during this period were short-lived. Leaders of local social movements gradually developed tactics to leverage their rooted local support against elected officials, enabling them to sway policy decisions over specific issues. In effect, these organizations used this local leverage to negotiate for representatives within a myriad of community and issue-oriented city agencies created by politicians to mitigate their loss of centralized power. [5]

More recently, many urban Latin American grassroots organizations have joined forces. With this move toward coalitions and unification across issues and constituencies, programs for change began to shift from framing initiatives as local concerns to representing them as broader issues—for example, the lack of a neighborhood day-care facility might be cast in terms of the larger issue of child-care policy vis-à-vis the status of women workers, drawing support from other neighborhoods and regions. It is not that politics has become more universalized, but that there has been a shift toward the formation of strategic and delimited alliances across groups in the formation of coalitions that acknowledge, rather than subsume, class, cultural, and regional differences.[6]

This tendency within the Latin American political arena had become particularly strong in São Paulo by 1989. Grassroots organizations had earned strong constituencies based on their effective mobilization around pressing local needs and had begun to see the benefits of alliances with other groups across the municipality. The formation of these alliances required that leaders negotiate unified political programs that went beyond the immediate and local agendas upon which the popular support of each organization was based. São Paulo's newly elected Workers' Party government emerged precisely out of the success of this move toward coalition building and a broadening of agendas:

> [T]he Workers' Party of Brazil (Partido dos Trabalhadores) . . . despite its name, is not, for any practical purposes, a party (at least not like the others are), a fact that its founders and directors admit. It is the outcome of an all-embracing process of organization involving sectors of workers, community and religious leaders, and organic intellectuals (including Paulo Freire, the educator) who drew up a common program of political, economic, social, and cultural action that went beyond the limits of associational or local concerns and now covers the whole of Brazilian society.[7]

The São Paulo Workers' Party, then, was the outcome of this heterogeneous mix of micropolitics and macropolitics. Its success in the 1989 election was a political coup unforeseen by most involved, including active party intellectuals like Paulo Freire, a scholar and writer who served as the administration's secretary of education after playing a formative role in the evolution of the party.[8]

TV Anhembi was conceived as a semiautonomous project funded through the city's Office of Tourism and Events and was implemented almost immediately after Erundina took office. The administration drew staff for the project from alternative video groups that were affiliated with community organizations; from independent producers who worked within local social movements; and from progressive elements within the television industry. The group regimented a range of political and cultural institutions around agendas spanning local community and city-wide concerns in a manner that mirrored the coalition-based formation of the Workers' Party

FIGURE 12.3 *A crowd views a production of TV Anhembi's* Fala São Paulo, *1992.*

itself. However, TV Anhembi's autonomy allowed it to address specific community interests without a program of explicit connection to the Workers' Party agenda. Indeed, the very structure of TV Anhembi reflected the uniquely interdependent but unified alliances that were the administration's trademark.

The same principle is exemplified in TV Anhembi's programming. The group's primary production project was a series of closed-circuit, site-specific live video events entitled *Fala São Paulo (Speak São Paulo)*. The series was uniform in format, yet relied little upon thematic or narrative continuity between programs. It was important that individual programs could stand on their own, because the majority of audience members were unlikely to have attended shows produced in other neighborhoods (fig. 12.3). More important, though, this format enabled TV Anhembi to produce programs that played to specific issues of regional concern. Thus, although the show was centrally backed by the mayor's office and was produced out of a relatively unified political agenda, it was able to take up atomized issues and represent a range of localized, and even competing or nonpartisan, points of view.

Episodes of *Fala São Paulo* were media events that took place four or

FIGURE 12.4 *Almir Almas hosts an episode of* Fala São Paulo, *1992.*

more times a month. Each program was shot and closed-circuit simulcast (or screened with minimal delay to accommodate some mixing and special effects) in one of the squares, parks, or streets of the city. Audiences reflected the demographics of the particular neighborhood and varied in size from two hundred to nearly a thousand people. Although these programs were taped and archived for future screenings in venues ranging from organization meetings to broadcast television, their primary function was to facilitate local and site-specific exchange through this genre of the on-site simulcast "town meeting." Programs were hosted live by media activists and well-known television personalities (fig. 12.4). These hosts took up a particular social or political issue such as poverty and homelessness among urban youth or the changing roles of women in the city, facilitating a dialogue among audience members and invited guests, who included distinguished personalities, musicians, academics, experts in various fields, and government officials (fig. 12.5). Working from inside the mobile production van, TV Anhembi's crew pieced together live feed from cameras trained on the host, guests, and audience members with prerecorded video that included short tapes by community groups, clips from broadcast news, and footage TV Anhembi produced specifically for that show. This footage was juxtaposed with live feed to highlight or comment on the specific discussions taking place. Different parts of the program were then simultaneously screened on the different monitors that made up the van's video wall, resulting in a kind of mobile real-time/time-delay collage (fig. 12.6). Like town meetings, these shows were highly reflexive in the sense that cast and audience were composed of essentially the same people.

Although TV Anhembi's programs drew primarily on the scene at hand, popular media genres such as the variety show and the *telenovela* (a genre akin to the U.S. soap opera) were also appropriated along with news footage and other material in order to tap into popular discourses and concerns that cut across cultural, gendered, and class positions within and across groups. Brazilian alternative media throughout its history has appropriated popular genres for uses such as political parody, but TV Anhembi's link to city government provided professional equipment and technical expertise that allowed a more direct engagement with popular forms. TV Anhembi

FIGURE 12.5 *Participants in* Fala São Paulo *communicate via the mobile video wall, 1992.*

FIGURE 12.6   *TV Anhembi's mobile production and exhibition unit, 1992.*

employed sympathetic talent from within the industry, effectively blurring the boundaries between community television and broadcast television.

The use of a popular television form like the *telenovela* to foster public dialogue on issues of social relations isn't groundbreaking in itself. As Nico Vink has shown, the mainstream *telenovela* already has been an important force in public discourse and social change.[9] What is important is the way in which TV Anhembi reversed familiar forms of viewer identification and combined them with community video forms to elicit a less conventional genre of public discussion and debate.

One successful example of TV Anhembi's use and transformation of popular media genres is an episode of *Fala São Paulo* titled "Women of São Paulo"—an episode that happens to draw on the *telenovela* genre. "Women of São Paulo" begins with a vignette preproduced by TV Anhembi and featuring actress Acorda Raimudo, star of the popular *telenovela Alfredo Alves* (fig. 12.7). Acorda plays a distinctly out-of-character role: lying in bed, she demands of her subservient husband, "Where's the coffee? Is there coffee?" She continues in this *"macha"* vein, complaining loudly that her husband has not laundered and ironed her clothes. In a documentary about this episode of *Fala São Paulo,* we see the TV Anhembi crew projecting this vignette on the video wall of their mobile production unit. Passing pedestrians on the busy São Paulo street stop and watch (fig. 12.8). The crew then turns the camera on the audience, soliciting responses to Acorda's performance. These responses are simulcast on the video wall, allowing the audience members to watch themselves and hear one another's responses on the video display. The audience debates domestic relationships—how they are, how they "should be." As the discussion unfolds, the crew uses specific responses as a springboard to project video segments on related issues produced by other community groups, thereby expanding the critiques of issues of gender roles and family life. Strategically dividing the video wall, the crew combines live discussions of the *telenovela* vignette with tapes like *Black Women of Brazil,* by the Lilith Women's Video Collective (a tape that includes interviews with women of color about how they are represented in the media), or TV dos Trabalhadores's *Todos os dias sao seus (Everyday Is*

FIGURE 12.7 Telenovela *actress Acorda Raimudo in TV Anhembi's "Women of São Paulo," 1992.*

FIGURE 12.8 *Crowd views "Women of São Paulo," 1992.*

Theirs), a documentary about Brazilian women and AIDS. In this manner, TV Anhembi's crew creates a productive intersection of genres, an intersection that exceeds the potential of individual forms used: the *telenovela,* the variety show, or the community documentary.[10]

Cinema Novo, Broadcast Television, and Brazilian Video Activism

TV Anhembi was tailored to its political and viewing context; however, it also emerged from an established tradition of politically engaged film and television culture in Brazil. It was this convergence of an established discourse on film and video activism and the coalition politics of the Workers' Party that informed TV Anhembi's distinctive approach. TV Anhembi directly drew on two interrelated traditions of Brazilian media: Cinema Novo (the work of Glauber Rocha, Nelson Pereira dos Santos, Carlos Diegues, Joaquim Pedro de Andrade, and others) and Brazilian community video (groups including TV Viva, the Lilith Women's Video Collective, TV dos Trabalhadores, Video Memoria, and TV Brixiga).[11] The latter tradition emerged, in part, out of a crisis around Cinema Novo's position of outright resistance to popular media forms, a crisis that took place after the military coup in 1964. The saga of Cinema Novo's relationship to popular cinema, and the strategies these directors developed to confront it, parallels in many ways the relationship between party and social movement politics described previously.

Cinema Novo began as a critical response to the popular cinema of the 1950s and early 1960s. It was part of a broad cultural movement aligned with the rise of leftist political parties and opposing a liberal government. After the unexpected 1964 military coup, the newly established military regime implemented government communications policies that fostered a monopolistic mass-communications system in Brazil. Throughout the subsequent decade, Cinema Novo lost ground through a failure to engage the diverse interests of various constituencies in their battle against mass-entertainment policies and the government-fostered media enterprise, TV Globo (a component of the Globo communications monopoly, which was consolidated by the early 1970s). Cinema Novo directors and leftist intellectuals were forced to rethink their relationship to popular media genres. At the same time, leftist oppositional parties were losing ground to local neighborhood groups and movements.

It was during this period of retrenchment that community video groups began to take over from Cinema Novo as a means of political organizing. Ingrid Sarti, in her study of independent video in Brazil, provides a concise analysis of the ambiguous and complex relationship between television and politics during this period. She explains that whereas "video technologies made possible the centralization of programming and hence the national television networks," these same technologies were also deployed as part of the vanguard challenge to the regime-fostered vertical structure of the television industry.[12] Thus, community video was part of the direct response to the monopolistic private network entities like TV Globo. But it can also be seen more broadly as a historical solution to the crises that came up among Cinema Novo intellectuals around the problem of the popular. The disavowal of popular film genres by early Cinema Novo directors was an aesthetic formulation of a leftist, anti-imperialist political program. As Randal Johnson and Robert Stam point out, Cinema Novo directors and theorists formulated a philosophy and a practice aimed at developing a national culture and identity in the face of foreign (especially U.S.) economic and cultural imperialism. They asserted the political urgency of creating a film aesthetic that engaged with the realities of underdevelopment and its causes—an aesthetic formulated in direct opposition to Hollywood and mainstream auteur cinema that dominated the Brazilian media.[13]

By the late 1960s, Johnson and Stam explain, Cinema Novo's filmmakers "realized that although their cinema was 'popular' in that it attempted to take the point of view of 'the people,' it was not popular in the sense of having a mass audience." [14] Thus, the films of Cinema Novo saw limited Brazilian distribution, in part because of government censorship and repression but also because of the filmmakers' own embrace of an elite avant-garde aesthetic. Critical debate over these issues within the movement caused a radical rethinking of popular cultural forms. In his 1975 "Manifesto for a Popular Cinema," filmmaker Nelson Pereira dos Santos argued that, by engaging with popular culture, film producers would reach a wider audience, address "the legitimate claims of the masses," and "defend popular political ideas." Moreover, he suggested that the use of popular cultural vernaculars would help break down distinctions between audience and producer.[15] Significantly, for Pereira dos Santos, popular vernacular included Afro-Brazilian and indigenous religious and cultural forms. This marked the emergence of a focus on the specificities of identity that had not been central to early Cinema Novo's more totalizing and programmatic left agenda.

Cinema Novo's decline was also linked to the relative decline of film as a popular cultural form with the rise of television. Luiz Fernando Santoro suggests that Cinema Novo's inability to sustain its critique of popular forms and genres as manifestations of imperialist culture was symptomatic of the growing presence of domestically produced television. The productions by entities like TV Tupi, TV Excelsior, and TV Globo increasingly overshadowed Hollywood and Brazilian mainstream cinema, outstripping its mass appeal after 1964.[16] As Carlos Eduardo Lins da Silva points out, "Television . . . experienced extraordinary growth after the military takeover and served as one of the instruments (ideological and instrumental) for the consolidation of monopolistic capitalism which it represented." [17] Thus, Cinema Novo's biggest ideological contender was no longer the cinema— it was television.

But television and the cinema were qualitatively different kinds of ideological forces. Unlike the cinema, which drew on U.S. and European productions, the Brazilian broadcast television industry that had grown up quickly under the wing of the repressive military government of the 1960s and 1970s produced programs that were characteristically "Brazilian" in content.[18] As a popular media form, Brazilian television increasingly drew upon national cultural forms, politics, and social concerns as it sought to compete for the home market against U.S. and other Latin American media entities. This can be seen most clearly in the rise of the *telenovela* as a distinct genre and not merely a reflection of the U.S. soap opera—a develop-

ment that was the key to the ascendance of TV Globo as the leading television producer in Brazil.[19] Networks like TV Globo used two strategies to
create a genre with much broader appeal: they drew upon national cultural
traditions, and they made increasing reference to issues of contemporary
social concern. Michèle Mattelart and Armand Mattelart explain this dual
strategy as having its origins in 1968 with *Beto Rockefeller,* the first popular
Brazilian network *telenovela* to break significantly with U.S. conventions of
melodrama:

> Since "Beto Rockefeller," the *novella* has never ceased to refer to certain
> problems of Brazilian Society: racial prejudice, the condition of women,
> the relations between Catholicism and Afro-Brazilian religions (*Umban-
> dismo*), industrial pollution, corruption, misery, urban violence, neighbor-
> hood struggles, and so forth. It has continued to take up the challenge of
> realism in a genre originally devoted to love triangles and affairs of the
> heart.[20]

It can be said that in its infusion of a melodramatic drama with strategies
of realism, and in its increasing focus on national culture, the television
industry successfully co-opted a central agenda of Cinema Novo directors:
combating cultural imperialism. Despite its cultivation by the military
state, Brazilian television's increasing treatment of national social, political, and cultural concerns throughout the 1970s was symptomatic of a
broader tendency toward liberalization of dominant ideological and political mechanisms of power. Thus, Cesar Guimarães and Roberto Amaral
have argued, the television industry (and the Globo network in particular)
played a crucial role in the eventual unseating of the military regime, realigning itself with the ascendant liberal government.[21] In terms of both
party politics and mass media, left producers were challenged by a powerful
new liberal opposition with a distinctly nationalist appeal.

As the first generation of alternative video producers began to take over
and transform the media politics of Cinema Novo in the middle of the
1970s, they worked within the media landscape shaped by the Brazilian
broadcast television industry. This new generation of media activists recast
media politics by providing a communications venue for myriad local issues
and points of view elided by the liberal broadcast television industry. Video
activism, in effect, paralleled the widespread retreat from national party
politics that marked the multiplication of localized social movements. Like
the later Cinema Novo theorists, they embraced popular modes—but with
a characteristically local rather than national focus. Sarti explains why video

producers were at first more concerned about opposing mainstream media on the level of content rather than aesthetic form:

> Brazilian video producers . . . hung their hopes on the success of an original and decentralized type of production. By the early 1980s a young generation of producers with great creative force had emerged on the electronic media scene.
>
> The young producers knew their work would be seen by a public addicted to the TV Globo model of great technical virtuosity. They therefore tried to show what TV Globo hid from the population.[22]

Video technology allowed producers to achieve a more immediate and local form of media politics than could be achieved with film. Video production was less expensive and distribution was less reliant on government (and commercially) regulated venues—a fact that would seem to make it the ideal medium for carrying out the type of popular engagement and breaking down of distinctions between audience and producer later advocated by Cinema Novo directors such as Pereira dos Santos. But as relatively inexpensive video equipment became available in the middle of the 1970s, it was not, for the most part, the directors of Cinema Novo who initiated political uses of the newly introduced medium but nonprofessionals from within the social movements themselves. As Alberto López, coordinator of the Brazilian Association of Popular Video (ABVP) recounts:

> En Brasil, existe una jerarquización peyorativa entre el cine y el video. Sin duda, hay algunos cineastas que han pasado a producir video; para ellos ese pasaje fue algo natural, porque el video se dio en los movimientos sociales de una manera muy espontánea. Los movimientos sociales se aproprian del medio antes que los profesionales.

> [In Brazil, there exists a pejorative hierarchy between cinema and video. Without doubt, there were some filmmakers who switched to video production; for them the change was natural, because video found its place so spontaneously in the evolving social movements. The social movements appropriated the medium before the professionals.][23]

The Brazilian video movement reflects a broader tendency throughout Latin America toward expanding the uses of the medium to meet the various needs of emerging social movements.[24] It also spans various levels of professional expertise and institutional affiliation. López describes a successive development of three modes of video production in emerging social movements:

> [H]ay TVs comunitarias que trabajan básicamente en tres formas: hay algunas que surgen del proprio Movimiento (por ejemplo en favelas en Río), que aunque son trabajos aún embrionarios, se están haciendo y están tratando inclusive de profesionalizarse también; hay otro tipo que es un relación de interacción y generalmente ocurre con estudientes de comunicación; y otras, como TV Viva, que son ONGs que tienen un trabajo profesional, funcionan con la cooperación internacional, y producen para los movimientos.

> [There are basically three forms of community television at work: one that develops directly out of and remains connected to particular movements (for example, in the *favelas* in Rio)—this work is quite primitive, yet always growing and becoming more professional; there is another type that occurs out of interrelations between independents, usually students of communication, and social movements; and finally there are those like TV Viva that are nongovernmental professional organizations, supported with international cooperation (funding), that produce tapes for various movements.] [25]

López points out that there has been a recent increase in community production aimed at broadcast venues. What is absent from his account is that production of high-quality tapes directed at broadcast has increased incorporation of independent producers from the nonprofit sector into the commercial broadcast sector. This shift also has affected the content of work produced by nonprofit groups, such as TV Viva, that work for social movement groups but are trying to get their programs out to a broader public. Sarti notes that later independent videographers "became more concerned with the search for new languages and the development of the art of video than with their subject-matter." She continues, "The technical experimentation and excellence of their productions had become the calling card for commercial television." [26] But many of these independent videographers, she goes on to explain, were also engaged in community television production, and as a consequence their politics was compromised by privileging aesthetics and technique. But it is also possible to conclude that this situation allowed those producers who were also working with community groups to get a foot in the industry door. This alternative take on Sarti's analysis suggests that higher production values can in some instances function as a means of mainstreaming community video and community politics. Indeed, this is precisely the situation that we find with TV Anhembi. Almas, for example, notes that the tendency toward the professionalization of community video producers bears a direct relationship to the specific politics of TV Anhembi: "The industry is changing and opening its eyes to what community groups are doing. . . . Carlos Freitas, one of the founding members of TV Anhembi and our electrical engineer, went on to do work for MTV. And there are community video groups like TV Viva that are beginning to produce some programs for TV Globo." [27] Almas provides a narrative in which the industry does not simply co-opt independent talent; by incorporating its producers and programs, it learns the lessons of independent video and community politics. The industry's interest in purchasing community programming was a signal that it had become sensitive to the broadening appeal of local movement politics. This is not surprising, since the Brazilian television industry has adapted and rapidly transformed to account for political liberalization throughout a period when independent and community video was coming into its own. This was a matter not only of the networks' increasing appeal to national cultural values mentioned above but also of their active incorporation of popular discourse in their mode of production.

TV Anhembi and the National

The idea of the incorporation of popular discourse into media texts brings us back to my earlier discussion of the Brazilian *telenovela* and allows me to return to my earlier claim that TV Anhembi shows like *Fala São Paulo* incorporated not only the genre of the electronic town meeting but also popular forms like the *telenovela*. As Mattelart and Mattelart explain, *telenovelas* are in a sense coscripted by their audiences: "the production system allows for . . . the participation of the audience in the development of the serial: the daily reactions of the audience influence the evolution of the characters and the outcome of the story." [28] Even more to the point, Mattelart and Mattelart propose that the *telenovela* is, for Brazilian culture, the equivalent of an "echo chamber of public debate." [29] As they explain, *telenovelas* are more than a central theme of everyday discussion, debate and rumor; they are public events widely covered in the mainstream press. The television industry extends the strategic commandeering of popular responses to other forms of programming as well. They cite as evidence of this more participatory mode the fact that talk and variety shows often encourage home-audience telephone participation in the live show.

What distinguishes TV Anhembi from mainstream Brazilian media, as well as antecedent community video organizations like DCTV, is its aggregate aesthetic and structural innovations that linked local movement concerns and popular cultural forms to facilitate broader public debates. "Democratization of the means of communication" was for TV Anhembi more than the technical facilitation of TV production within the idealized public sphere of the urban streets. It was an array of strategies for bringing together community concerns and high-tech aesthetic values of art video and broadcast television. A particularly successful part of TV Anhembi's project was the development of strategies to appropriate and subvert broadcast genres—an aspect of their project that clearly situates TV Anhembi at the cutting edge of postmodern media techniques.

As I suggested earlier, TV Anhembi's form was intimately connected to the particular social and political milieu that swept Erundina's administration into office. The project was discontinued in 1992 when the Erundina administration was succeeded by a less sympathetic city government. The history of TV Anhembi cannot be separated from the local, short-lived, and distinctive political administration that sponsored it. However, it is important to consider the legacy of TV Anhembi after 1992. The array of local social movements active in São Paulo remains a considerable source of alternative media production. In 1993, Almas expressed uncertainty about the possibility of creating another TV Anhembi, but nonetheless he asserted that he would "continue to search for funding to form new groups like TV Anhembi," because "[w]ithout cable access, we need this sort of alternative venue in Brazil."[30]

Although I have used the example of TV Anhembi to stress the particularity of the Brazilian media landscape and its various distinct groups, TV Anhembi does provide a useful comparison or counterpoint to discussions about alternative media projects in other regional and national contexts. Undoubtedly, as U.S. community media organizations face the impending reconfiguration and deregulation of communications networks (including the information superhighway and the cable and telephone conglomerates), the example of TV Anhembi suggests the need to rethink terms such as "community" and "alternative media." TV Anhembi, by bringing together apparently contradictory techniques and approaches of local video activists, government agencies, and popular television forms, demonstrated the viability of some alliances and strategies. But TV Anhembi's short history also warns of some of the potential risks of conceiving community through state-subsidized alternative television production. As Almas notes, "TV Anhembi's heavy reliance upon the mayor for financial support was in the end a big problem. . . . There just weren't adequate alternative means of support in São Paulo to replace the resources that the Erundina administration had provided."[31]

Notes

1. I draw upon two sources for most of the descriptive and historical information on TV Anhembi: video footage from TV Anhembi's series *Fala São Paulo,* and an unpublished interview that I conducted in the fall of 1993 with Almir Almas, who was the coordinating producer of TV Anhembi throughout its existence. All quotations of Almas are drawn from this interview. A sample reel of TV Anhembi's work is available for rental from the International Medial Resource Exchange, 124 Washington Place, New York, NY 10014.

2. Other North American groups include Top Value Television (TVTV), Ant Farm, Paper Tiger, and Deep Dish Television (New York City) and Portable Channel (Rochester, New York). See Deirdre Boyle, "A Brief History of American Documentary Video," *Illuminating Video: An Essential Guide to Video Art,* ed. Doug Hall and Sally Jo Fifer (San Francisco: Aperture/Bay Area Video Coalition, 1990), 51–70.

3. Sandra Ventura, "O último programma da TV Anhembi," *Diário do comércio* (São Paulo, 8 January 1993).

4. Orlando Fals Borda, "Social Movements and Political Power in Latin America," in *The Making of Social Movements in Latin America: Identity, Strategy, and Democracy,* ed. Arturo Escobar and Sonia E. Alvarez (Boulder, Colo.: Westview Press, 1992), 305.

5. Discussing the same situation with a less optimistic slant, Ruth Corrêa Leite Cardoso describes how political administrations have at times been able to play competing community groups off one another and how community groups have had to compromise their goals to form coalitions that "claimed to represent the 'true will' of the entire neighborhood." Ruth Corrêa Leite Cardoso, "Popular Movements and Consolidation of Democracy in Brazil," in Escobar and Alvarez, *The Making of Social Movements,* 295.

6. Fals Borda, "Social Movements," 305.

7. Ibid., 306.

8. Paulo Freire, *Pedagogy of the City* (New York: Continuum, 1993).

9. Nico Vink, *The Telenovela and Emancipation: A Study on Television and Social Change in Brazil* (Amsterdam: Royal Tropical Institute, 1988).

10. On the productive uses of combined genres, see Chon A. Noriega, "Gender Bending, Genre Blurring: Willie Varela's *A Lost Man,*" 1992, unpubl. ms.

11. A detailed description of many of these groups is provided in Luiz Fernando Santoro's comprehensive history of popular video in Brazil, *A imagem*

nas mãos: O video popular no Brasil (São Paulo, Brazil: Sumas Editorial Ltda., 1986). See also Karen Ranucci, *Directory of Film and Video Production Resources in Latin America and the Caribbean* (New York: Foundation for Independent Video and Film, 1989).

12. Ingrid Sarti, "Between Memory and Illusion: Independent Video in Brazil," in *Media and Politics in Latin America: The Struggle for Democracy,* ed. Elizabeth Fox (London: Sage Publications, 1988), 157.

13. Randal Johnson and Robert Stam, "The Shape of Brazilian Film History," in *Brazilian Cinema,* ed. Randal Johnson and Robert Stam (Austin: University of Texas Press, 1982), 30–36. See also Glauber Rocha's 1965 manifesto, "Down with Populism," in *Twenty-five Years of the New Latin American Cinema,* ed. Michael Chanan (London: British Film Institute, 1983), 15–16. Rocha's manifesto is representative of early arguments for an avant-garde aesthetic that refused popular tastes. In it, he described popular culture as a form of illiteracy fostered by the United States and Europe with the aim of fostering underdevelopment in Latin America.

14. Johnson and Stam, "The Shape of Brazilian Film History," 36.

15. Julianne Burton, "Nelson Pereira dos Santos: Toward a Popular Cinema," in *Cinema and Social Change in Latin America: Conversations with Filmmakers,* ed. Julianne Burton (Austin: University of Texas Press, 1986), 135.

16. Fernando Santoro, *A imagem nas mãos,* 62–63, 85.

17. Carlos Eduardo Lins da Silva, "Transnational Communication and Brazilian Culture," in *Communication and Latin American Society,* ed. Rita Atwood and Emile G. McAnany (Madison: University of Wisconsin Press, 1986), 104.

18. Cesar Guimarães and Roberto Amaral, "Brazilian Television: A Rapid Conversion to the New World Order," in *Media and Politics,* ed. Fox, 124–37.

19. Ana M. López, "The Melodrama in Latin America: Films, Telenovelas, and the Currency of a Popular Form," *Wide Angle* 7.3 (1985): 5–13. López notes three differences between Latin American *telenovelas* and U.S. soap operas: "Unlike American soaps, *telenovelas* always have clear cut stories with definite endings that permit narrative closure; they are shown during prime-time viewing hours; and they are designed to attract a wide viewing audience of men, women and children" (p. 8).

20. Michèle Mattelart and Armand Mattelart, *Carnival of Images: Brazilian Television Fiction,* trans. David Buxton (New York: Bergin and Garvey, 1990), 79.

21. Guimarães and Amaral, "Brazilian Television," 125–37.

22. Sarti, "Between Memory and Illusion," 160.

23. Alberto López, interview with *VideoRed,* "Universos diversos y puntos de encuentro en la producción audiovisual brasilera," *VideoRed: Revista del audiovisual latinoamericano* 4.17 (Lima, Peru: IPAL; October–December 1992): 15; my translation.

24. Rafael Roncagliolo, "The Growth of the Audio-visual Imagescape in

Latin America," in *Video: The Changing World,* ed. Nancy Thede and Alain Ambrosi (Montreal, Que.: Black Rose Books, 1991), 22–29. Roncagliolo classifies these uses within five overlapping categories: (1) video records—the use of video to gather the history of a community to support the community's organizing processes, which form both its subject and its object; (2) group video—the use of video for education within groups, as a communication link between villages and generally as a mechanism for obtaining feedback within movements; (3) special events video—the use of video at public events as a mechanism of outreach and mobilization; (4) counter news video—video aimed at a broader public, with the purpose of "confronting the 'official [televised] version' of events" through the establishment of alternative videocassette distribution networks; (5) mass broadcast video—the production of video programming from the perspective of social movements explicitly for broadcast television.

25. Alberto López, interview with *VideoRed,* 15–16; my translation.
26. Sarti, "Between Memory and Illusion," 160.
27. Almir Almas, unpubl. interview with author, New York City, fall 1993.
28. Mattelart and Mattelart, *Carnival of Images,* 131.
29. Ibid., 79.
30. Almir Almas, unpubl. interview with author.
31. Ibid.

13

Steadfast Love and Subversive Acts

THE POLITICS OF *LA OFRENDA: THE DAYS OF THE DEAD*

Kathleen Newman

In this Day of the Dead celebration,
people mock death and gender
and whatever else needs a little push.

—La Ofrenda: The Days of the Dead

■ ■ ■ ■

In the guise of a documentary, a comparative study of Mexican and Chicano celebrations in remembrance of the dead on the first two days of November each year, *La Ofrenda: The Days of the Dead* (1988) is itself both an offering *(ofrenda)* and a subversive communicative act.[1] Whereas the previous documentary collaboration between filmmakers Lourdes Portillo and Susana Muñoz, *Las Madres: The Mothers of the Plaza de Mayo* (1985), had focused on the resistance of a group of women to State terror in Muñoz's native Argentina, *La Ofrenda* explores Portillo's cultural heritage: a Mexico of childhood memory and today's Mission District, the Chicano and latino barrio of San Francisco, California. The script by Portillo, Fenton Johnson, and B. Ruby Rich, however, purposefully denies biography as an organizing principal of the film by creating an anonymous voice-over commentary. The alternation of two nameless narrators, one male and one female, serves to stress historical and cultural continuity, in counterpart to the community events and many interviews presented in the film.[2] Foregrounding its gendered narration, the film specifically "speaks to" the latino community, to all women and men who, like Portillo, have journeyed at some time from Latin America to the United States or who live simultaneously in both cultures. The film also addresses children, the progeny of the patriarchal and matriarchal narrative voices, thus affirming latino culture and history within the contemporary multicultural society of the United States and contemplating a future diverse society in which, hopefully, there would be no racism. Finally, imitating the playful Mexican and Chicano relation to death that the film considers a socially "healthy" intimacy with mortality and humility, *La Ofrenda* playfully mocks its viewers, giving all of us, whatever our heritage, "a little push" toward a radical transformation of social relations, toward a better life for the entire community through a different conceptualization of temporality and subjectivity.

The promotional flyer for the film includes the widely quoted statement by Mexican writer Octavio Paz, the same quotation chosen to close the film: "The word death is not pronounced in New York, Paris or London, because it burns the lips. The Mexican in contrast, is familiar with death, jokes about it, caresses it, sleeps with it, celebrates it, it is one of his favorite toys and most steadfast love." Yet the flyer also describes the film's female narrator as expressing a "Chicana's quest to understand her culture," which "evokes the loving and sometimes humorous nature of Mexican attitudes toward death in a film saturated with color and life." By juxtaposing these two statements, the flyer reveals one of the underlying strategies of the film: death as the Chicana's steadfast love will be revealed in the film to be slightly different from death as the steadfast love of the Mexican (male) citizen.[3] In other words, "death" pronounced by contemporary Chicana lips, in contrast to a nearly silent but omnipresent anglo culture of death, has a different meaning.

In fact, the viewer sees "death" pronounced on Chicana lips quite late in this 50-minute film. The first and greater part of the film is dedicated to the Day of the Dead in Mexico, with seven narrative segments, as opposed to four in the second part of the film, which takes place in San Francisco. These first seven segments include (1) all the preparations by an *abuelita* (grandmother) and her family in Oaxaca for the observance—cleaning the cemetery plots, arranging the orange *cempazúchitl* (marigold) flowers on the grave, preparing a special family meal, praying at the home altar created in memory of the departed grandfather, and, finally, gathering with the rest of the community for the night vigil in the candlelit cemetery; (2) a synthetic history of indigenous concepts of death, in particular, Mitla, the land of the dead; (3) a meditation on the conquest and the fall of the imperial Aztec city of Tenochtitlán; (4) the lineage of the *calavera* (skeleton) as cultural icon, from José Guadalupe Posada's engravings to Diego Rivera's great murals and the contemporary papier-mâché *calaveras* of folk artists such as the Linares family of Mexico City; (5) interviews in front of the Templo Mayor in the center of Mexico City with elderly white tourists from the United States as to what they understand of the Aztec concept of death; (6) a conversation with a creator of *matachines* (here, wooden skeletons with arms and legs manipulated by strings) in his workshop; and (7) an analysis of the "baile de Oaxaca," a street celebration with a mock funeral in which men play women's roles, by means of a lengthy interview with the man who plays the character of the widow in the celebration.

The second part of the film contains footage of the Day of the Dead celebrations in San Francisco and includes shots of the altars in Mission District gallery spaces and the now traditional evening parade. These are interspersed with interviews with psychologist Concha Saucedo and artist Amalia Mesa-Bains, widely known for her altars/installations for women such as Frida Kahlo or Dolores del Río, and three people's descriptions of altars: one woman explaining the meaning of each item on an altar, one man remembering in particular a friend who has died of AIDS, and one woman explaining an altar by children that is dedicated to all the children who are dying in all the countries. The final segment, before the Paz quotation, presents a classroom of children in San Francisco who discuss with their teacher what they would wish for a classmate whose mother has died or for themselves before they die.

This narrative segmentation serves to suggest that Day of the Dead celebration in the Mission is a continuation of the celebrations in Mexico. Clearly intended for use in classrooms, the film reinforces pride in one's culture among Chicano students and deepens the understanding of Chicano and Mexican culture among non-Chicanos. Yet the pace of the narrative also underscores the distance between the Mexican and Chicano cultures; the slower pace of the first part, with its calm appreciation of ritual and of a more rural life, contrasts with the urban, slightly more frenetic celebrations in the briefer second part. By stressing that the celebrations in Mexico are an extension of indigenous cultural practices, the film also necessarily suggests the ways in which the Mission celebrations are distinct: they are an act of will, that is, a conscious, political effort to continue Amerindian and Mexican traditions.[4] Indeed, the first person interviewed in the second part, Concha Saucedo, indicates that the Chicano celebrations express those aspects of a culture that people separated from their homeland wish to keep, observing that even Chicanos born in the United States "are in a foreign culture." She explains that the Day of the Dead celebrations are an "acknowledgement that we all share the same ancestor, whether it is an ancestor who died yesterday or who died a thousand years ago."

This latter understanding of community and history, this affirmative Chicano understanding of subjectivity and temporality, becomes, as the narrative progresses, one of two central subversive gestures of the film with respect to its general multiracial audience. The film will seek to align, albeit briefly, the Chicano and non-Chicano spectators' sense of time and the social relations that constitute self and other. It will do so in conjunction with another subversive gesture, which occurs in the final segment of the first part, the segment featuring a lengthy interview, mentioned above, on the meaning of an *ofrenda* with the man who plays the character of the widow. It is at the beginning of this segment that the male narrator states that during the "Day of the Dead celebration, people mock death and gender and whatever else needs a little push." On screen at the segment's end, the man-as-widow, still in makeup and partially in costume, makes an offering of an apple to the camera, a gesture simultaneously humorous and serious, literal and figural, which redefines momentarily gender, sexual, and class relations of the viewer and the Mexican community as represented in the film. These two highly self-conscious gestures ultimately rework the documentary goals of the film. In order to examine what these two gestures mean and how they are finally linked in the film, we must first consider the impact of the widow's words and gestures on the process of narrative cohesion for the film as a whole.

Eve Crosses Over

The opening images of street celebration in Oaxaca center on the men in masks and costumes dancing through the crowd, though there are visual asides, such as shots of a child in the skeleton costume, a young *calavera,* dancing with an adult. For the first time, the male and female narrators depart from their celebration of their indigenous past and their lament of the horrors of the conquest to critique contemporary Mexican society:

> MALE: In this Day of the Dead celebration, people mock death and gender and whatever else needs a little push. We remember the dead by celebrating life. In the general disorder of the fiesta, everyone forgets himself but enters otherwise into forbidden situations and places. Music and mere noise are united, not to re-create or recognize themselves, but to swallow each other up.
>
> FEMALE: In the rigidity of Mexican society, where rules of behavior have been prescribed for thousands of years, it's in the fiesta and the *comparsa* where we can allow ourselves to be free momentarily, to expose our inner selves to the rest of the community.

In that the "general disorder of the fiesta" is very brief, the viewer is given to understand, from the street theater images, that two of the most rigid

STEADFAST LOVE AND SUBVERSIVE ACTS ■ **289**

systems in Mexican society are class and gender. Yet this is not the European carnivalesque, where the sovereign is brought low for a day only to be confirmed more solidly and centrally powerful in the process. Rather, the symbolic exchange of the roles of power in the fiesta confirm the mortality of all and the return of power to none. Granted, on the surface, men playing women's roles in the *comparsa* parodies the patriarchal gender system in which men are inscribed in the positions of power. The men play the women as flighty creatures: the daughter with the sick husband is ineffectual; the widow is pitied for loving a man who abused her or mocked for trying to find a new husband at the funeral of the last one. But when the fictional doctor places a banana as phallus between the legs of the dying man already in his coffin, that which is considered male sexuality and virility, not to mention patrilineality itself, is shown to be farce. Farce with both feet in the grave, however, neutralizes all the inequality of class as well. Here it is important to remember that widowhood signals, in many narratives, not merely a civil status but a new economic identity. The widow of the *comparsa,* although beneficiary of the male's now lost wealth, will one day be a *calavera,* like everyone at the celebration. As the designer of *matachines* said in the previous segment about the symbol of the *calavera:* that is how we have to see ourselves. Though both in the *comparsa* and in the scene in the film the economic meaning of widowhood is displaced onto themes of sexuality, death-as-equalizer nonetheless eradicates all class divisions.

The forbidden situations and momentary exposure stressed by the male and female narrators seemingly locate sexuality in a timeless abandon beyond procreation and the responsibilities of childrearing. The filmmakers have the narrators underline the symbolic, celebratory suspension of the rules of behavior that discipline the populace and therefore constitute its specific social organization, so that the narrators' commentary can anticipate the interview with the man-as-widow, he/she who subsequently undermines the social divisions of class, gender, and sexual orientation represented on film and integral to the film as a communicative act. The man-as-widow explains the customs of the Day of the Dead while seated next to an altar filled with fruits and flowers and other offerings. Intercut with his/her explanation are shots of the widow in the celebration, until the point at which the man-as-widow takes off his/her veil, wig, and feather boa. In terms of gender, his/her image shifts; he/she becomes a man in a black dress with smudged, theatrical face paint. The blended gender of the fully costumed widow becomes an indeterminate gender halfway between the separate gender identities of male and female. Significantly, it is in this state of indeterminacy that the man's voice defines the *ofrenda.* Over shots of the *abuela as she chooses* fruit from her altar to give to a neighbor, he narrates:

> Even the poor feel an obligation to make an offering. Like when they offer you an apple, they do it with a smile. They expect nothing in return. They share with you. That is the tradition. That is the legend.
>
> The word offering has a very special meaning in our Indian culture and in all cultures. The offering means love and love has no price. I believe that this tradition, that the Mexican people have deep inside, will never end. The offering continues.[5]

In his black dress and white makeup, he is a revealed *calavera,* a *calavera* who then offers the camera an apple. What sort of temptation is this offering from Eve, as widow, as *calavera,* as death? How is the man-as-widow, now the man-as-*calavera,* now the man-as-Eve, linked to the appearances of the *abuela,* herself a widow, in the opening segment and in the seventh segment?

First, in terms of visuals, Eve is a transvestite *calavera,* offering the spectator the unrestricted sexuality of the celebration.[6] Because this sexuality is unrestricted, it is also socially undefined. It is a sexuality not categorized; neither heterosexuality nor homosexuality as currently constructed in the United States or Mexico, it is merely sexuality. Second, in terms of visuals and sound, this Eve also incorporates all the meanings ascribed to the *abuela.* Far exceeding patriarchal notions of the widow activated and neutralized in the *comparsa,* in the film the *abuela*-as-widow is one who "expects nothing in return," who loves unconditionally, who loves everyone, all generations, living and dead. Her love is different from the steadfast love Paz describes as defining a (male) Mexican's relation to death. In Paz's equation of love and death, one relates to death for how ultimately it will define one; Paz's love is one of closure and definition. As spoken on the lips of the widow, the *abuela*'s love always "continues": it is without end and without restriction. As defined by Paz, a Mexican's loving relationship with death is equivalent to a fatalism determinant of a Mexican national identity. As defined by the merged figures of the transvestite *calavera* and the grandmother, spoken in indeterminacy, the film's steadfast love, rather, is the liminality of life and death, the very liminality celebrated in the Day of the Dead. This film's political project is to redeploy, lovingly, the liminality of life and death to the liminality of Mexican and U.S. cultures. Eve-as-*abuela* crosses over the cultural divisions between latino and anglo cultures, bringing with her a commitment to equality. Class, gender, and sexual orientation are celebrated as identities while simultaneously subverted as social divisions. Eve-as-*abuela* incarnates a community solidarity that is inclusive of everyone.

The film's momentary actualization of sexual, gender, and class neutrality and indeterminacy makes possible the symbolic transformation of border as dividing line into border as potentiality. In the final moments of the first part, the film's steadfast acceptance of liminality enacts the subversion of the unjust social systems whose complete transformation the film advocates. Addressing its spectators as fellow celebrants who would accept the offering of the apple, who would enter into knowledge of difference and diversity, who themselves would also make an offering expecting nothing in return, the film transports its spectators across various social borders. This allows the viewers to reevaluate previous passages and then to turn their attention to "whatever else needs a little push."

Fading to black after shots of *comparsa* celebrants, including the widow, leaving the open and public space of the street, this segment's ending also is not closure but continuation. The establishing shots of the second part— the Golden Gate Bridge, the streets of the Mission District—linger on a Galería de la Raza mural of the Calavera Catrina, Posada's famous *calavera* of a "fashionable lady,"[7] therefore linking the widow-as-*calavera* and the Calavera Catrina. In the fourth narrative segment, a shot of Posada's engraving is followed by one of Diego Rivera's mural for the Hotel Prado, *Sueño de una tarde dominical en la Alameda Central,* which shows Frida Kahlo, a young Rivera, José Martí, and other historical figures surrounding Posada's Calavera Catrina, to which Rivera has added an elegant dress and feather boa. Thus, in the film, Rivera's Calavera Catrina anticipates the widow, feather boa very much in display, of the "baile de Oaxaca." By association with the San Francisco Calavera Catrina, the widow-as-*calavera* is immediately back on the street, restricted by no border, ready to become a Chicana *calavera*. Within a few shots she will be a young woman whose face is being painted as a *calavera* for the Mission District's celebration of the Day of the Dead.

Coatlique, Children, and Anglos: Death Crosses Over

In language, the factor of cohesion, that is, "the means whereby [linguistic] elements that are structurally unrelated to one another are linked together, through dependence of one on the other for its interpretation,"[8] is a matter of continual reappraisal by the interlocutor, while listening or reading, of that which has been stated before in light of that which has just been communicated. Likewise, the film spectator's continuous reevaluation, in the process of viewing, of previous formal elements, powerfully engages the viewer in the constitution of a film's always multiple meanings. As will be shown below, in the case of *La Ofrenda,* the creation of indeterminacy and liminality in the film's narrative at the very moment the film switches location from Mexico to the United States (shifting from first to second part) requires the viewer to assume momentarily the viewpoint of the Chicana-as-*calavera* if the previous seven segments are to maintain their cohesion. Interestingly, in the transitional moment, the viewer—as the female narrator said of the family awaiting the return of their dead on the night of the celebration—"lives not in anticipation, but in memory."

The female narrator's opening line of the film is this: "What seemed unimportant then has now possessed my memory. How we treated one another, how we lived, takes on great significance." At this point in the film's narrative, the objective of the first part is revealed in retrospect: that is, beyond documenting the Day of the Dead in Mexico and capturing those cultural elements that will be preserved in Chicano celebrations, the film argues that the Mexican culture of the *ofrenda* is better, for one and for all, than the anglo culture of death found in the United States. The crucial phrase in the opening line is "how we treated one another." The treatment, shown in the film to be equitable, is the measure of community or a society. The film argues that this treatment derives from subjectivities whose basis is the collective capacity to offer always, without fail, that which needs to be offered to one another. The film also argues that such subjectivities require the specific temporality celebrated in the Day of the Dead.

Two narrative elements, carefully introduced in the first part, become crucial to the argument about temporality: the imagery of children, deployed as a trope of cyclical time, and the representation of anglo cruelty, both individual and societal. While childhood and childhood memories (such as the child's eye-level shot of the *abuela*'s feet during the walk to the cemetery in the film's opening sequence) are evoked in the first narrative segment, the importance of the imagery of children does not become fully evident until the second and sixth segments—in other words, between the presentations of the grandmother and the widow. Segments two and three are responses to questions raised by the female narrator: "What is there in me of my Indian past?" and "What is in me of that conqueror of yesterday?" Predominantly montages of pre-Columbian and colonial art and architecture, with increasingly dramatic voice-over (including readings of translations of Cortez's letters to the king), the two segments suggest that indigenous culture will outlive the culture of the oppressors: "Under the veneer of westernization, the cultures of the Indian world, that have existed for thirty thousand years, continue to live, sometimes in a magical way, sometimes in the shadows." The "magical" connection is dramatized in an interview in the second segment, at the ruins of Mitla ("the land of the dead") next to the Church of San Pablo, between the unit director or cinematographer (male voice in off) and a group of campesinos, three adults and two children. Pressed by the ("Western") questioner, the elder campesino explains, smiling, that the camera should allow the questioner to see the spirits about which the latter is inquiring. As the group laughs at the questioner, the shot pulls tight on the face of one of the young boys, who shyly hides his gap-toothed smile behind his hand. In quick succession, shots of still photos of pre-Columbian statues of smiling boys, with a sound bridge of laughter, encompass the boy in cyclical time. This cyclical time is the film's version of indigenous concepts of temporality, a version in which repetition and renewal are an affirmation of history.

This latter designation of cultural continuity, of community identified always diachronically as well as synchronically, is associated with the life cycle in a second juxtaposition of a child's face and artwork in the sixth segment. During the interview in the *matachines* workshop, there is a close-up shot composed of a young girl's face and part of a *matachines* box display, in which can be seen a small flower and a white-haired wooden *calavera* whose legs and arms the girl is manipulating (fig. 13.1). The girl's luminous smile, half in shadow of the box, affirms all that is joyous about the sense of temporality that the Day of the Dead celebrate. She is a *calavera* full of life, and there can be nothing macabre in the foreknowledge of her death. The "magical" laughter and smiles of these children will serve as a counterpoint to Paz's designation of death as the favorite toy of a Mexican (presumably adult) male. While both children's faces express the deference of children before adults, the editing, not in the least deferential, reveals the ways in which the children thoroughly exceed any explanations the adult female narrator can offer in her investigation of her cultural heritage. The young girl who will be a *calavera* and the boy whose face affirms thousands of years of Amerindian history subvert the linear lament of the two narrators. The children's freedom in the film's version of cyclical time, that is, the indeterminacy of their individual future and their steadfast promise of collective renewal, argues for a better temporality than the one in which the film's narrators and spectators currently exist.

In the transition between the second and third narrative segments, the imagery of children is metonymically associated with another temporal

FIGURE 13.1. *A scene from* La Ofrenda: The Days of the Dead. *A young girl beside a* matachines *box display. Courtesy of Direct Cinema.*

cycle, the often violent cycles of politics, broadly defined. After the sequence of the boy's smiling face, a montage of images of nature (moon reflected in the water, etc.) and Aztec sculptures, the narrators present in synthesis the history of the conquest. It is here that the female narrator, questioning what Indian past informs her present, answers in affirmation: "Even greater than the stone sculptures, I carry inside of me the strength and weight of a brilliant and terrible past," as the camera tracks, at low angle, the famous statue of Coatlique, the female earth deity (now housed in the Museum of Anthropology in Mexico City) with dual serpent heads, a necklace of skulls, and a skirt of serpents. Interestingly, the narrator's affirmation elides the violent history of the Aztec empire with the violence of the Spanish conquest, rendering pre-Columbian history as monolithic as the statue itself. This is, however, the second shot of the maternal deity Coatlique. Coatlique first appeared earlier in the sequence, just after a shot of the massive Coyolxauhqui Stone, the great horizontal disk on which is represented the dismembered body of the goddess Coyolxauhqui, defeated in battle by her brother Huitzilopochtli (uncovered in 1978, the stone is part of the Templo Mayor excavation in central Mexico City). These two female deities, complexly linked in Aztec symbology (the latter often as the daughter of the former) though not in the film, become the visual referent for the subsequent statement read from Cortez's letters that he tore down the Aztec's "principal idols," modifying therefore "the ancestral memory" of the narrators. If the principal idols are suggested to be female—indeed, not only female but female operating within violent social orders—then the memory that the female narrator is investigating becomes maternal, connecting over time to the situation of women within our own violent political order. The film affirms Coatlique's and the female narrator's maternal responsibilities in time, that is, reproduction as the creation of life and as the creation of the present time, while Coyolxauhqui's dismembered body is, in the film, the briefest reminder of the political structures and violence that might undermine community and divest death of its joy.

The "brilliant and terrible past" that the female narrator "carries inside" her is next associated with the anglo culture of death in the fifth segment. Returning to the Templo Mayor, first seen in the pan that opened the fourth segment, which moved the spectator in time and space from the ruins of the Templo Mayor to the streets of modern Mexico City, the fifth segment consists of three interviews on the street with anglos identified as "Americans Touring Mexico." The responses of the tourists are striking for what they reveal about anglo xenophobia and ignorance, while the sequence is striking for the gentleness with which it treats these white *abuelos* for whom in the future, however they are remembered by kith and kin, no one will scatter cempazúchitl petals on the Day of the Dead. The tourists are asked (female voice in off) what they think about the Aztec concept of death. Every answer reveals a complete inability to conceptualize history and culture, let alone another culture's concept of death. The tourists answer the question from the perspective of how death affects them. The first man jocularly says that maybe it (Aztec culture in general?) was a good idea because he and the other members of the tourist group are getting to the age "where we have to start worrying about death." The second person interviewed, a woman, superimposes Christian theology onto the Aztecs, explaining that the promise of an afterlife made poverty in the present life bearable and death something to which to look forward: "We fear death, but the Indians didn't." The final woman interviewed is a tall white widow, with soft white hair, who wears a white dress and hat. She is the image of ghostliness and, given the soft white hair, possibly anticipates the *calavera* in the little girl's *matachines* box in the next segment. Her anecdotal narrative, which ends with the words "It's just heartbreaking," is heartbreaking. Arms crossed, she asserts that in general people don't want to talk about death, giving as an example her relatives who didn't want to listen to her talk about her husband's death or share her grief. Her narrative suggests that which will be made explicit in the second part: the anglo culture of death is unhealthy for individual and community.

This segment, with its anglo ghosts lost at the Templo Mayor, is key in the construction of the Chicana narrative point of view that organizes the film. While the male and female narrators construct a linear history by mediating on cyclical time, the organizing perspective created by all elements in the first half of the film finally is revealed to be specifically Chicana. The children and the anglos in the narrative segments between the presentation of the *abuela* and the man-as-widow are viewed by one who belongs to both Mexico and the United States, and one who is younger than a grandparent but caring, even parental, toward the children. The narrative cohesion of the seven segments of the first half, in which the Chicana perspective is unfolding, prepares the explicit, full embrace of the knowledge of a Chicana-as-*calavera* in the second half. At this structural midpoint, the journey in memory of the Chicana narrator now has brought her home to San Francisco to meet her other self: the Chicana-as-*calavera*. The liminality and indeterminacy introduced in the seventh segment, and its reworking of the prior film narrative, have made possible that she crosses back to her home with her subjective duality and nonlinear temporality assured: death as affirmation crosses with her. The Chicana-as-*calavera* on screen at the beginning of the second part momentarily incarnates the film's overarching narrative authority. The Chicana-as-*calavera* in the Mission District in San Francisco is one who recognizes the meaning of and historical connections among Coatlique, children's smiles, and anglo ignorance. The Chicana-as-*calavera* is the community and the nation as located in history.

Chicano Arts: "La Cultura Cura"

On the surface, the second part of *La Ofrenda* might appear to be a less layered narrative. The two narrators are less prominent in the second part because the interviews with Concha Saucedo and Amalia Mesa-Bains serve as principal commentary on the Mission District celebrations and the three altars that are shown in detail. Saucedo, a psychologist, speaks directly of the ways in which "culture heals," as does Mesa-Bains, who at several different points discusses why Day of the Dead celebrations have attracted so many non-Chicanos:

> MESA-BAINS: Death is almost an obscenity in this culture and among latinos and Chicanos, particularly in the Mission District community around

the time of Día de los Muertos, death is made to be lovable, life-giving, joyful, ironic . . . all the things other people can't have. I believe that is why it [the celebration] has grown, the highly proportionate number of people outside the community joining in.

MESA-BAINS: Life and death are truly the core experiences that will, in fact, bind people together, and that to me, there is a kind of space between life and death and that space is healing. Art is about healing. When people participate in art, when they make it, when they see it, it is the same thing as making yourself well.

While Mesa-Bains identifies the liminality between life and death as a space of healing for both latino and anglo cultures, the interview with Saucedo reminds the spectator of divisions internal to Chicano subjectivity: by maintaining cultural traditions, Chicanos will heal wounds inflicted by a surrounding anglo culture. Health, then, is individual and political.

In fact, the emphasis on health raises the question of the nature of the threats to health that Chicanos face, and allows the Chicana-as-*calavera* to subvert any temporal stasis that might be thought inherent in documentation, filmic or otherwise. The nature of the threats are revealed in the three altars discussed in depth. The explanation of the first altar, presented in Spanish, focuses on the meaning of each of the requisite items, such as the special bread, candles with ribbons, flowers, water, or incense, and emphasizes, as in the Mexican celebrations, the temporal connection between the living and the dead: the dead "appreciate our efforts on this day" and they will return "even if we are far from our country." One threat, then, is an anglo concept of time that severs present from past, the living from the dead, and, significantly, separates one nation from another. The artist who designed the second altar explains that it commemorates friends and relatives who died of AIDS or who died young in accidents. These loved ones died tragically, but their spirits are embraced and they are not forgotten. The skull at the top that bears the name SIDA (the Spanish acronym for AIDS) is familiar, like a candy sugar skull with the name of a loved one. This second altar suggests that another threat is the political climate in the United States, where there is insufficient funding for AIDS research and for medical care and support services for those who are HIV positive. These politics are part of an anglo culture of death that foments tragedy and permits social divisions. The third altar is dedicated to "all the children dying in all the countries" in the numerous wars and conditions of poverty and is filled with offerings by other children, such as a toy a child had been given by her mother before the mother died. The daughter wished to share the toy with the spirits of children who would return on the Day of the Dead. The violence of war and economic violence threaten the Mission community from the outside, for like the plague of AIDS, this violence is allowed to spread by an inhumane politics of exclusion. The U.S. governmental politics of exclusion and that of other nations, threatens the health of the Chicano community. Against this death threat, this threat of eradication, is arrayed the community solidarity created by dancing *calaveras* and joyous offerings.

In its appreciation of the ways in which "people mock death and gender and whatever else needs a little push," the film itself pushes its spectators more than a little bit. When death crosses over with the Chicana-as-*calavera* from Mexico to the United States, from memory to the present, the spectator must cross too. In this crossing, which reveals the ways in which subjectivities complexly activate historical knowledge, the spectator, whatever his or her various subjectivities, must view from within the Chicana-as-*calavera*'s temporality. Within her time, "whatever else needs a little push," though it may be systemic in nature, cannot be static. Indeed, everything in the category "whatever else needs a little push" seriously threatens the community by undermining the appreciation of liminality and indeterminacy that makes community possible in the first place. Community is possible only when difference is appreciated as potentiality. This appreciation is the film's *ofrenda* to the various spectator positions it addresses.

In another context, Amalia Mesa-Bains has argued convincingly that Chicana artists have played a determinant role and provided a "new aesthetic vocabulary" in furthering the cultural transformations that will allow the populace of United States as a whole to realize the potential of its multiculturalism.[9]

> Narration, the circumscription of domestic space and spirit, indictment, and ceremony are often fissured in a constantly shifting language. These artists move freely within broad sensibilities and intentions, breaking pre-existing categories and enlarging the feminine. Reclaiming our past and marking our experiences through our culture and lives have been the real contributions of Chicana artists. Their work continually recasts an open identity where tradition and innovation must live together.[10]

La Ofrenda: The Days of the Dead is one such work that "recasts an open identity" at the same time as it is an indictment of the politics of exclusion that may well undermine the United States as a collectivity in some near future. The Chicana-as-*calavera,* constructed in the film as its principal narrator, on whose lips the word "death" does not burn, addresses the film's spectators with exactly the "broad sensibilities and intentions" described above. So broad are they, in fact, that she crosses thirty centuries of time and two nations of space to reach her audience. Having arrived home, however, she creates a new *comparsa* in which her viewers are invited to dance. The final segment of the film takes place in a multiracial classroom in San Francisco. The teacher has asked his students to think either of what they would wish for themselves before they die or what they would wish for their classmate whose mother has died just recently. One child wishes that their friend will feel better when he comes back to school, others that their children would stay healthy, a brother would take care of a mother, no one else would die, they would see their best friend, or a friend would be already married. The last wish in the film is that of a young girl for a reunion of all her friends before she died. When the teacher asks, smiling, if she would invite him, she, smiling, silently shrugs and everyone in the room laughs together. Will the adults (male) be invited? The Chicana-as-*calavera* would definitely invite one and all, but will the children invite the generations to which the spectators belong? What are the future conditions that will bring everyone to the *comparsa?*

Between the final quotation by Paz and the credits, there is a montage of shots from the cemetery in Oaxaca and the classroom in San Francisco. The familiar brass band music, local and localizable, which has accompanied the Day of the Dead celebration sequences plays once again. The brief image of the female celebrant who incarnates the Chicana-as-*calavera,* first introduced at the beginning of the second part, reappears: her face now fully painted, she breaks into a radiant smile much like those of the children in prior sequences. As physical incarnation of the film's principal narrative perspective, this Chicana-as-*calavera,* intentionally or not, wears the filmmakers' rather mischievous final smile(s). By participating in the Chicana temporality that the film has enacted as an *ofrenda* to its audience, the viewer engages with the filmmakers' joyfully subversive politics of community.

Postscript

In the 1990s, Lourdes Portillo has worked in documentary film as well as video and video installation. Her short video *Columbus on Trial* (1993),

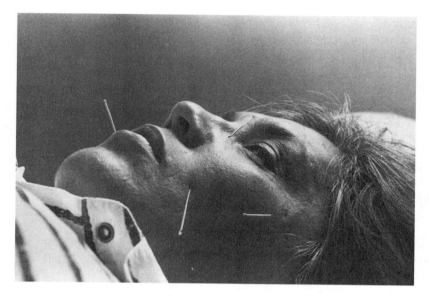

FIGURE 13.2. *A scene from the documentary* El diablo nunca duerme (The Devil Never Sleeps, *1995*). *Courtesy of Lourdes Portillo.*

made with the comedy troupe Culture Clash, presented a notably decisive solution from the perspective of a *chola* character to the "encounter" between Europe and the Americas. Her feature-length documentary *El diablo nunca duerme* (*The Devil Never Sleeps,* 1995),[11] shown in a shorter version on PBS, examines the layers of familial and public narrative surrounding the death of the filmmaker's uncle in Mexico and the filmmaker's own relation to film as a critical medium for the public discussion of history and politics, gender and sexual orientation, and the struggle for justice (fig. 13.2). Portillo's next video, set to premier in Chicago in late 1998, is a study of the young female fans of the late Tejana singer Selena.

Notes
Preliminary ideas for this paper were presented at the conference "Cruzando fronteras: Primer encuentro de cineastas y videastas latinas, México–Estados Unidos," Colegio de la Frontera Norte, Tijuana, Mexico, 29 November–2 December 1990. This article first appeared in *Spectator* 13.1 (fall 1992): 98–109.

1. Distributed by Xochitl Films, 981 Esmeralda Street, San Francisco, CA 94110. For a comprehensive discussion of the issues raised by the film, see Rosa Linda Fregoso, *The Bronze Screen: Chicano and Chicana Film Culture* (Minneapolis: University of Minnesota Press, 1993).

2. The credits acknowledge use of excerpts from Octavio Paz's *Labyrinth of Solitude,* Carlos Fuentes's "On the Run," *Mother Jones* (1988), and an Aztec poem; however, the narrators only twice distinguish between excerpts and original text in their voice-over.

3. Published in 1950, *The Labyrinth of Solitude,* by Octavio Paz, predates current standards of gender-neutral language. In the Spanish of the period, "el mexicano" could have been meant to be inclusive of all Mexicans, men and women, but given the patriarchal inferences in the text (i.e., that a Mexican treats death the way a man treats a woman in what Paz must have considered a normative heterosexual relationship), this statement indicates that Paz views citizenship to be an exclusively male identity.

4. Tomás Ybarra-Frausto discusses the celebrations as an act of volition in "*Recuerdo, descubrimiento, voluntad:* Mexican/Chicano Customs for the Day of the Dead" in the *Día de los Muertos* exhibition catalogue of the Mexican Fine Arts Center Museum, Chicago, 1987–1990.

5. Spoken in Spanish with English subtitles.

6. See Marjorie Garber's *Vested Interests: Cross-Dressing and Cultural Anxiety* (New York: Routledge, 1992) for a discussion of the ways in which transvestism is culturally constitutive.

7. See José Guadalupe Posada's *Popular Mexican Prints,* ed. Roberto Berdecio and Stanley Applebaum (New York: Dover, 1972), 15.

8. M. A. K. Halliday and Ruquiaya Hasan, *Cohesion in English* (London: Longman Group, 1976), 27.

9. Amalia Mesa-Bains, "*El mundo femenino:* Chicana Artists of the Movement—A Commentary On Development and Production" in *Chicano Art: Resistance and Affirmation, 1965–1985,* ed. Richard Griswold del Castillo, Teresa McKenna, and Yvonne Yarbro-Bejarano (Los Angeles: UCLA Wight Art Gallery, 1991), 131–40. See also her essay "The Real Multiculturalism: A Struggle for Authority and Power," in *Different Voices: A Social, Cultural, and Historical Framework for Change in the American Art Museum* (New York: Association of American Art Museum Directors, 1992), 86–100.

10. Mesa-Bains, "*El mundo femenino,*" 140.

11. A collection of essays on this film will be edited by Rosa Linda Fregoso for the University of Texas Press.

Contributors

■ ■ ■ ■

PATRICIA AUFDERHEIDE is associate professor of visual media in the School of Communication, American University. She is the cultural and senior editor of *In These Times,* and serves on the editorial board of the *Journal of Communication Law and Policy.* She is the author of *The Daily Planet: A Critic on the Capitalist Culture Beat* (Minnesota, 2000), *Communications Policy and the Public Interest: The Telecommunications Act of 1996,* and *Media Literacy,* and is the editor of *Beyond PC: Toward a Politics of Understanding* and *Conglomerates and the Media.*

CHARLES RAMÍREZ BERG is University Distinguished Teaching Professor in the Department of Radio-TV-Film at the University of Texas at Austin. He is the author of *Poster Art from the Golden Age of Mexican Cinema* and *Cinema of Solitude: A Critical Study of Mexican Film, 1967–1983.* He is currently working on two books on Latino images in Hollywood cinema.

GILBERTO MOISÉS BLASINI is a doctoral candidate in the Critical Studies Program in Film and Television at the University of California at Los Angeles. He is currently writing his dissertation, "Fasten Your Seat Belts, It's Going to Be a Bumpy Ride! Road Movies and American Culture after 1967."

JULIANNE BURTON-CARVAJAL is professor of literature and Latin American and Latino studies at the University of California, Santa Cruz. She is the editor of *Cinema and Social Change in Latin America: Conversations with Filmmakers* and *The Social Documentary in Latin America,* and is coeditor of *Horizontes del segundo siglo: Investigación y pedagogía del cine mexicano, latinoamericano, y latino. Three Lives in Film,* life histories of three pioneering women filmmakers from Latin America, is forthcoming.

SETH FEIN is assistant professor of history at Georgia State University, where he is a member of the Center for Latin American Studies. He has published and lectured widely in the United States and Mexico about U.S.-Mexican relations, international history, cinema, and mass culture. His works include chapters in *Close Encounters of Empire: Writing the Cultural History of U.S.–Latin American Relations, México–Estados Unidos: encuentros y desencuentros en el cine,* and *Through the Mexican Lens: Perspectives on the Cinema of Mexico,* as well as articles in *Studies in Latin American Popular Culture, Nuevo texto crítico, Secuencia,* and *Historia y grafía.*

CLAIRE F. FOX is assistant professor of Spanish and Portuguese at Stanford University. She is the author of *The Fence and the River: Culture and Politics on the U.S.-Mexico Border* (Minnesota, 1999), and her essays have been published in *Iris, Social Text,* and *Discourse.*

BRIAN GOLDFARB is assistant professor of art and art history at the University of Rochester, where he teaches theory and production of digital media. As curator of education at the New Museum of Contemporary Art in New York, he organized the exhibition *alt.youth.media.* He is currently working on a book about media, pedagogy, and electronic culture.

ILENE S. GOLDMAN teaches film studies in the Chicago area and is a former member of the board of directors of the Chicago Latino Cinema. Her writing has appeared in *JumpCut, The Independent,* and *Film Quarterly,* as well as in the anthologies *The Ethnic Eye: Latino Media Arts* and *Framing Latin American Cinema: Contemporary Critical Perspectives,* both published by the University of Minnesota Press.

MONICA HULSBUS is a doctoral candidate in critical studies at the School of Cinema-Television at the University of Southern California. Her dissertation focuses on new technologies and popular culture, and she has published articles addressing issues of national, sexual, and racial identity in film and television.

ANA M. LÓPEZ is associate professor of communications at Tulane University. She is coeditor of *Mediating Two Worlds: Cinematic Encounters in the*

Americas and *The Ethnic Eye: Latino Media Arts* (Minnesota, 1996). Her forthcoming book, *Third and Imperfect: A History of New Latin American Cinema,* will be published by Minnesota.

KATHLEEN NEWMAN is associate professor of Spanish and Portuguese and Latin American studies at the University of Iowa. She is author of *La violencia del discurso: estado autoritario y la novela política argentina* and coeditor of *Critical Passions: Selected Essays by Jean Franco.*

CHON A. NORIEGA is associate professor of film and television at the University of California, Los Angeles. He is the author of *Shot in America: Television, the State, and the Rise of Chicano Cinema* and has edited *Chicanos and Film: Representation and Resistance* and *Urban Exile: Collected Writings of Harry Gamboa Jr.* and coedited *The Ethnic Eye: Latino Media Arts,* all published by the University of Minnesota Press.

LAURA PODALSKY is assistant professor of Spanish at Bowling Green State University. Her writing has been published in *Framing Latin American Cinema: Contemporary Critical Perspectives* (Minnesota, 1997), *Foro Hispánico, Velvet Light Trap,* and *Mediating Two Worlds: Cinematic Encounters in the Americas.* She is currently completing a book, *Urban Negotiations: Transforming Culture, Consumption, and Space in Buenos Aires, 1955–1973.*

HARMONY H. WU is pursuing her doctorate in critical studies at the School of Cinema-Television at the University of Southern California. She is writing her dissertation on horror hybridity, with feminist and cross-cultural perspectives. Her work has appeared in *The Spectator, International Gay and Lesbian Review,* and film anthologies.

692289

DH

791.
430
98
VIS